Swearing and Cursing

Language and Social Life

Editors
David Britain
Crispin Thurlow

Volume 22

Swearing and Cursing

Contexts and Practices in a Critical Linguistic Perspective

Edited by
Nico Nassenstein
Anne Storch

DE GRUYTER
MOUTON

ISBN 978-1-5015-2681-7
e-ISBN (PDF) 978-1-5015-1120-2
e-ISBN (EPUB) 978-1-5015-1108-0
ISSN 2364-4303

Library of Congress Control Number: 2020930323

Bibliographic information published by the Deutsche Nationalbibliothek
The Deutsche Nationalbibliothek lists this publication in the Deutsche Nationalbibliografie; detailed bibliographic data are available on the Internet at http://dnb.dnb.de

© 2021 Walter de Gruyter, Inc., Berlin/Boston
This volume is text- and page-identical with the hardback published in 2020.
Typesetting: Integra Software Services Pvt. Ltd.
Printing and Binding: CPI books, GmbH, Leck

www.degruyter.com

Contents

Thomas Stodulka
Foreword —— VII

Part I: Othering and abjection as deep practice

Anne Storch and Nico Nassenstein
1 "I will kill you today" – Reading "bad language" and swearing through Otherness, mimesis, abjection and camp —— 3

Timothy Jay
2 Ten issues facing taboo word scholars —— 37

Alexandra Y. Aikhenvald
3 "Damn your eyes!" (Not really): Imperative imprecatives, and curses as commands —— 53

Alice Mitchell
4 "Oh, bald father!": Kinship and swearing among Datooga of Tanzania —— 79

Anne Storch
5 Aesthetics of the obscure: Swearing as horrible play —— 103

Felix K. Ameka
6 "I sh.t in your mouth": Areal invectives in the Lower Volta Basin (West Africa) —— 121

Part II: Cultural mobility as context of transgression

Joseph T. Farquharson, Clive Forrester and Andrea Hollington
7 The linguistics of Jamaican swearing: Forms, background and adaptations —— 147

Muhammad Muhsin Ibrahim and Aliyu Yakubu Yusuf
8 'Don't say it in public': Contestations and negotiations in northern Nigerian Muslim cyberspace —— 165

Nico Nassenstein
9 Mock Chinese in Kinshasa: On Lingala speakers' offensive language use and verbal hostility —— 185

Ricardo Roque
10 The name of the wild man: Colonial *arbiru* in East Timor —— 209

Part III: Disruptive and trashy performance

Angelika Mietzner
11 Found and lost paradise: Bad language at a beach in Diani, Kenya —— 239

Janine Traber
12 The *sexy banana* – artifacts of gendered language in tourism —— 259

Anna-Brita Stenström
13 English- and Spanish-speaking teenagers' use of rude vocatives —— 281

Elisabeth Steinbach-Eicke and Sven Eicke
14 "He shall not be buried in the West" – Cursing in Ancient Egypt —— 303

Neal R. Norrick
Afterword —— 327

Index —— 333

Foreword

Of fat white buffalos, dirty dogs, and sleazy machos – A tender hoo-ha on swearing, mocking and belonging

> Well he's not very handsome to look at
> Oh he's shaggy and he eats like a hog
> And he's always killin' my chickens
> That dirty old egg-suckin' dog
>
> (*Dirty Old Egg Sucking Dog*, by Jack Clement/John R. Cash, 1966)

"Wow. You are big now! Big Thomas! Who would have thought? Biiiiig!", Habib greeted me, a few months ago at a street intersection in the center of the Javanese court city of Yogyakarta, Indonesia, where we had spent so many nights, days and significant parts of our lives between 2001 and 2015. Habib was an outspoken young man that I had befriended over the last decade through my research on the coming of age on the streets of Java. The now 35-year old had spent over twenty years as a 'street kid', wandering elegantly back and forth between local ostracism or neglect and transnational NGO attention. "You are fat now, bro! Crazy!", he assured me, with a big grin on his face, pinching my belly, raising his eyebrows, taking a puff at his thick clove cigarette, before bursting into laughter with a loud (and rather "un-Javanese") "huhuuuuuiiiiiiiiiiiii!" Passing motorbike drivers, bus conductors, customers at a mobile chicken skewers stall, and a few pedestrians, many of them dressed in senior high-school uniforms, had "inconspicuously" turned their gaze and attention towards the odd spectacle at the street corner.

I had learned over the years that public cursing, swearing, joking, mocking and insulting was an essential part of collective identification with street-related communities and a bold performance of communicating one's desire for belonging. Such "rituals of obscenity" could at times resemble staged cursing competitions, where two or more young men insulted each other with obscenities until one of them ran out of words, idioms, or modified proverbs. By means of such rhetorical contests, hierarchies could be subtly questioned and newcomers socialized into (sub)culturally valued speech and interaction practices. The otherwise sanctioned raising of one's voice in public, or the penalized public articulation of swear words and other made-up vulgar expressions, was particularly celebrated during the nightly sit ins at crowded street corners. Since public swearing was considered inappropriate in a local context in which refined speech and reserve, deference and devotion were the dominant and appreciated way of interacting and communicating in public, the young men created their own "happy language" based on a subverted form of the Javanese alphabet, in order to camouflage their mocking of cultural elites and political authorities. Furthermore, the Indonesian language's abundance of everchanging acronyms was adapted to new meanings. For example, *SH*, originally the academic title for *Sarjana Hukum* (Bachelors of Law) became *Susah Hidup* (hard life); when the protagonists spoke of *SMP* (*Sekolah Menengah Pertama* 'Junior High School'), they were actually referring to those NGOs that provided food and other supplies without any restrictions or further demands for reciprocation (*Sudah Makan Pergi* 'leave after you eat'). When they said they attended *UGM* or *Universitas Gajah Mada* (one of Indonesia's leading universities), they actually meant *Universitas Gelandangan Malioboro* ('University of the Malioboro Homeless'), referring to their "home" in the public spaces.

"Like a big fat white buffalo! I wonder how your meat tastes – huhuuuuiiiii!", Habib continued to challenge me. I felt that he was not only waiting for my counterattack; he was testing my loyalties to the community that I had once so proudly embodied through style and speech during the heydays of my previous fieldworks. I had not returned either to Yogyakarta or the street corner in a couple of years. That morning, I had bumped into Habib as I made my motorized way through the crowded streets to one of the city's many campuses. He knew that I had become a lecturer at a German university, and I had heard that he became a carpenter in a renowned wood carving workshop, as well as creating extra income by busking at street junctions and in restaurants. Back at the formerly familiar street corner, I felt observed by the passersby in the immediate surroundings. Habib had publicly and raucously called me a "big fat white buffalo", after all. Probably adding to the spectacle was the fact that I wore clean shoes, long pants, and a rather formal shirt. My hair was neatly combed. This style was not only different from the days we had spent years together on the city's streets, but my "fashion" was also different from Habib's sandals, his muscle shirt covering only parts of his tattoos, and worn-out jeans. I felt embarrassed in quite a few ways, yet I was hesitant to respond adequately in his terms. I felt that swearing back at him, as I used to do, might have been perceived as highly disruptive to my own appearance towards the surrounding public and their assumed normative social, cultural and linguistic expectations regarding the well-dressed foreigner. How would swearing and cursing affect Habib? For better or for worse? I remembered this feeling of "being torn" from my previous fieldwork in the city. Whereas I had initially quietly withdrawn from such awkward situations, I had learned through the years that they could tip me off into subversive and affective forms of communicating my solidarity with street-related communities, who were socially and morally positioned at the city's margins. Habib's grinning face kept testing me as to whether I was willing to testify to my ongoing desire to belong to the "street community", or not. I had translated his emotive ways of addressing me in public into a challenge: "Whose side are you on?"

"You dirty dog, you criminal, where did you steal this filthy cigarette?" it burst out of me. "I am sure you tricked some poor old lady, huhuuuuiiiiiiii!", I continued and started laughing loudly. Habib threw his arms in the air and made obscene dancing moves with his hips and upper body. He burst into laughter. "You ..., you dirty German tank, you bulldozer! You, ... you ..., you sleazy macho ... You funny-faced fish, who I love more than my egg-sucking dog!" – and so forth. After a few more exchanges of laughing, shouting and swearing at each other we hugged and wandered off to the nearest food stall, where we ordered iced tea and cigarettes. None of the onlookers asked any questions or addressed us. We were inconspicuously ignored by the public, its ears and eyes. They looked through us. After catching up at the crowded food stall in the center of Yogyakarta for an hour, Habib and I parted. Once back on the streets again, already making our ways in different directions, we turned around one last time with grinning smiles. "Criminal," he hissed. "Coward," I replied, and I made my way to the air-conditioned library at the other end of town.

Thomas Stodulka

Part I: **Othering and abjection as deep practice**

Anne Storch and Nico Nassenstein

1 "I will kill you today" – Reading "bad language" and swearing through Otherness, mimesis, abjection and camp

Abstract: This chapter approaches swearing and cursing practices from a more holistic perspective, and critically questions the narrow view on swearing as demarcated and extracted "swear words". By exploring the many faces of swearing, this contribution aims at opening up new perspectives and intends to challenge the established understanding of "bad language" by presenting examples from different African contexts. The focus lies on labels and naming practices of the Self and the Other, on a bitter form of laughter, as well as on bodily substances that function as dangerous matter; all circling around swearing/cursing as a form of Otherness, mimetic practice, abject substance, camp and generally, as an expression of power. Introducing to the study of swearing and cursing, this chapter includes speakers' creativity, agency, the fluidity of language(s) and the importance of context and embodiment, aiming to open the floor for the multifaceted and transdisciplinary strands found in the different subsequent chapters.

1.1 Setting the scene: The many faces of swearing

In *Aguirre: The Wrath of God*, Werner Herzog's (1972) famous journey into the abyss of the colonial nightmare, several boundaries are crossed – the boundaries between the known and the unknown, order and chaos, and sanity and madness. The film's main character, played by Klaus Kinski, ventures into the dark night of the soul in such an unsettling way that another boundary is crossed, and this time again and again, namely the boundary between fiction and reality. In a way similar to that of Aguirre, the 16th century conquistador he impersonated, Kinski raged, cursed and swore, plunging the people around him into varying stages of irritation, consternation and despair. His fits of raving madness, as his behavior was often described, had a very special quality, however, as his diction and choice of words were usually immaculate: not so much yelling at people, Kinski rather addressed them with carefully selected swear words, clad in well-constructed sentences and delivered with enormous aplomb. Later, after Kinski's death, director Werner Herzog (1999) would tell the story of their collaboration in several films, and how they would often go through Kinski's tantrums together, meticulously analyzing a performance of the rage and madness of a true genius.

With Kinski's scripted albeit compelling and challenging performance, both artists tie in with the powerful performances of border crossers of indigenous societies in Amazonia (where the film was largely shot), but also across the globe: shamans in many American and Asian societies, as well as the blacksmiths of West Africa, tricksters, members of spirit possession cults and healers are all divine fools, holy masters of disorder and transgressors of norms and certainties alike. They may say what otherwise is unspeakable, attack with words and put into question anything that may otherwise seem safe and granted.

What is so interesting about these boundary crossers and executors of rage is that the use of bad language and offensive gestures is so obviously performed according to a cultural script. Swearing and cursing never does just "happen", is never an outburst resulting from the loss of control, but on the contrary, is controlled and based in context. This aspect of swearing, not as something linked to violence, or to the pathological side of language (like, for example, Tourette's syndrome), but as something merely *performed* as being marginal, and yet of central importance to societal order, is the focus of the present book. The contributions brought together in this volume aim at a sociolinguistic, ethnographic and sociological discussion of swearing and cursing practices. Moreover, these practices are explored by paying special attention to the possibility of using a more emic perspective on both language and culture.

This includes developing a broader approach: away from the well-established study of construction mechanisms of swear words (e.g., comparisons of swear terms based on animal names, body part terminology, etc.), and towards a study of linguistic creativity and speaker agency. Furthermore, this also involves the discussion of gesture, the use of objects, laughter, body effluvia (e.g. spit), and other aspects of communication that are often considered as not being part of language itself – such as placement and movements, but also censorship and avoidance, for example.[1] Yet they are part of the setting where the theatrical performance of the divine fools who seem to be the true experts of transgressive language takes

---

[1] This chapter has greatly benefitted from inspiring discussions with numerous colleagues. We are grateful to all contributors to this volume for their ideas, creativity and also critical comments. Moreover, we thank all interlocutors during various research visits in Africa and beyond, who have helped us to broaden our understanding of swearing and cursing. The series editors are warmly thanked for their support and help. We are indebted to Mary Chambers for proofreading all texts and providing numerous valuable comments. All shortcomings are our own responsibility.

place. To look at swearing and cursing in such a holistic way helps us to uncover the tremendous power inherent in linguistic border-crossing: these norm-violating actions are irrevocably associated with the ability to restore order. In order to escape the threatening chaos, it is necessary to realize that in language there is the potential of liminality. And liminality requires agents who are able to cross boundaries, to shuffle to and fro. In this situation of performing transgression, it is of existential relevance to overthrow previously established order, challenge the sacred and deal with violent power.

Swearing, in its potential to violate norms, is linked closely to performances of excess and transgression, and presenting the performer as a liminal person, acting in a liminal context. Such performances may be lifetime performances, in front of huge audiences (as in Kinski's case), or short and involving only a small group of addressees. The point is that being offensive, by swearing and cursing as well as through these other language practices, is *in principle* achieved through transgression, through border-crossing. And both professional swearing performers and "average" speakers alike use the power of words and linguistic performance to defend order, to enhance social norms through language. Hence, while the notion of a linguistic taboo is to articulate and implement a set of rules on what cannot, or rather must not, be said, "propositional" or "inter-individual" swearing (see Jay and Janschewitz 2008: 269) systematically violates these rules, resulting in what Pinker (2007) labels as "abusive language", which, in an amusing twist, has the power to restore order.

The frequency of swearing in discourse, therefore, is an interesting feature of tabooed language, having social regulatory functions, but at the same time violating social regulations. While inter-individual swearing practices are usually understood as markers of rudeness, impoliteness or abuse, they can equally incorporate emphatic and face-building notions (as in *This is fucking awesome*), and thus respond to very diverging social needs within a community. In contrast, cathartic swearing as the expression of the speaker's emotional state is channeled in ways that make anger manageable. It often consists of formulaic language and ritual speech, upon which morphological and syntactic restrictions can be imposed, as well as restrictions of context and applicability.

Both inter-individual as well as cathartic swearing and cursing have been dealt with in the body of literature available on the topic, such as Jay (2000, 2009a, 2009b), Jay and Janschewitz (2008), Ljung (2010), Mohr (2013) and Vingerhoets, Bylsma and de Vlam (2013), to mention just a few that constitute the current state of the art. Hereby, major themes of swearing usually correlate to cross-linguistically pervasive taboos – bodies and their effluvia, organs and acts of sex and excretion, disease and death, naming, touching and seeing persons, and preparing and consuming food: this makes swearing rich in anthropological implications. Preferences for particular strategies in swearing (e.g., based on words for excretion organs, products of metabolism, food, plants, etc.) shed considerable light on how specific strategies of transgressive language serve as emblematic markers for membership of a community or group, and on how they are therefore used as inclusive and identity building strategies, rather than as strategies to exclude in discourse.

Sociolinguistically, this is a rather challenging aspect of agentive language, especially when taking a fresh look at non-hegemonic sociolinguistic settings, where diverse linguistic repertoires are shared and norming is achieved by making reference to diverse cultural concepts and identity constructions. Such settings are often seen as typically non-metropolitan ones (Blommaert 2013), multilingual and multicultural, and individuals' complex swearing biographies, which change through processes of socialization and contextualized language acquisition are only now gaining attention from linguists, as the relevance of alternative practices becomes more clear. Therefore, apart from the above-mentioned insights, this volume aims to take another perspective on the study of swearing, also in terms of theory-making. While most accounts analyze swearing practices according to northern paradigms by taking a closer look at discourse structures and the lexical dimension of swearing, the chapters of the present volume also include metalinguistic reflections on swearing based on local ideas about language, and consider different language concepts from the Global South. These approaches to swearing are based on swearing as a holistic concept, understanding silence, laughter, gestures and the body as meaningful forms of swearing, as well. This also entails options of *not* using swear words in order to swear; there are also other boundaries that can be crossed, such as those erected, for example, by patriarchy and coloniality. Therefore, the alleged subaltern can turn swearing patterns around and reposition sender and receiver in a specific post-colonial situation; this is done through powerful forms of Othering that play with the pejorative names that usually index authoritative hierarchies. Noise, vomit, disgusting language, abjection and camp can also be interpreted as forms of swearing, as will be shown in Sections 1.2–1.4.

Hence, instead of simply referring to swearing as transgressive language, we aim to unveil how swearing can teach us about speakers' language concepts and how an alternative perspective can classify swearing as a form of secrecy and a way of silencing. Swearing can here be understood as pointing at secret practice, secret knowledge and unspeakable concealments. The inclusion of Southern Theory, Queer Theory, and a post-colonial angle can thereby help to broaden our understanding of bad language, building upon the rich semiotic encodings of swearing practices that we find all over the world. Another aspect of swearing practices that exceeds the framework of transgression is that of performativity: Who is part of the audience of these outbursts, and who is an addressee? How much do divine madness and secrecy challenge or restore roles and order?

1.2 Naming the self, constructing the Other's Other

One of the most rewarding questions to ask, it seems, is the question about the reasons why people might direct swearing at themselves. Why Kinski constructed himself as a divine madman is rather clear: as a tremendously intelligent publicity concept, he kept his audience interested in him, as did other artists by means of personality exploitation (Staiger 1991). But there are also less obvious indexicalities of referring to oneself in pejorative or transgressive ways. What seems to characterize them is that, in principle, many such swearing practices are not so much patterned as turns that are coupled into interchanges between two participants, but are performed as speech acts by singles. Like response cries, which in Erving Goffman's (1978) sense are exclamatory words that are uttered "in the hope that this half-license it gives to hearers to strike up a conversation will be exercised", swear words are often uttered without a clear indication of the addressee. A public utterance such as *fuck!*, for example, is not expected to yield a turn such as *oh yes, and shit also!*, and even swear terms more clearly directed at a specific audience, like mother-based abusive utterances and pejorative names, belong to rather ritualized speech styles, where turn-taking works differently than in non-insulting language. The public utterance of such response cries, Goffman observes, "constitutes a special variety of impulsive, blurted actions – namely, vocalised ones. [...] [These are] violating in some way the self-control and self-possession we are expected to maintain in the presence of others, providing witnesses with a momentary glimpse behind our masks" (1978: 120).

This is one of the reasons why swear terms are frequently accompanied by imperatives and commands (*die already, bastard!*, *clean this up, bitch!*), and why they trigger considerable emotional investment. Swear terms not only consist of words that express notions that are otherwise forbidden, they are also used in a way that makes the hidden and controlled emotions of the speaker-performer discernible. And this is crucial: the emotional investment in and reaction to swearing is precisely what makes it a highly effective social tool. Emotions such as hatred, anger, fear, and so on are here part of every-day routine operations (Barbalet 2001) that help to organize and negotiate communality and social norming.

One thing that makes swearing so powerful is the way swear words are created: they refer to what is not supposed to be referred to, making the recipient of the obscene, profane, and blasphemous vulnerable to being Othered, being discarded. And the systematic and often excessive ascription of negative attitudes, derogatory names and subaltern identities to marginalized, oppressed or liminal groups are frequent phenomena in settings of inequality, imperialistic or colonial power constellations. In these contexts, swear terms and emotionally highly agentive transgressive language continuously breach boundaries between exclamative blurtings and directed proper names: a highly derogatory Othering term would turn into someone's name – as an individual and as a name for an entire group.

But pejorative labels and abusive terminology can be filled with new meaning, agency and identity, removing them from epistemic dependencies in terms of a "relocation of the thinking" (Mignolo 2002); prominent examples of socio-political terminology are ambiguous terms such as *nigger/nigga*, which has turned into "a badge of identity and solidarity" (Allan and Burridge 2006: 84) among groups of people of color. There is, however, more to that twist: it is a powerful means to turn the gaze from the center to the margins, and to look at what has been discarded. Communities and individuals who adopt, as an act of post-colonial mimesis and reflexivity, ascribed negative labels, derogatory identities and abusive terminology and use them in fresh contexts as forms of self-ironic emblems, remodel ascribed roles and construct the Other's Other. This is, again, an emotionally significant process, often associated with humor and linked to new contextualizations, according to Taussig's (1993: 52) mimetic paradox that "the copy […] is not a copy" or mere image of the former. But even though the creation of in-group identities in settings of unequal power relations often translates into ironic self-reflective discursive strategies, the mimetic interpretation of the Other as swearing practice is different and needs to be seen as embedded in coloniality (Chow 2014). And like the disgusting flea in Donne's poem *The flea* (1595), the bad word in shared communicative practice can thus be filled with the essence of two persons, who are, irrevocably, tied together through this experience:

> Mark but this flea, and mark in this,
> How little that which thou deny'st me is;
> Me it suck'd first, and now sucks thee,
> And in this flea our two bloods mingled be.

The flea, in our case the Othering swear word, thus "bites" both the addressee and the swearer himself, filled with new meaning and with mingled reflexivity as a powerful symbol of discursive garbage.

Swearing here is a highly reflexive and deconstructing genre. Reflexivity, however, is not a power controlled by those who may claim ownership of language and knowledge (over history, ideas, and so on): Congolese street children who are confronted with witchcraft accusations and, being described as cannibals, *baphaseur* 'sleepers' and *bandoki* 'witches', turn these "negative signifiers to a social group" (Heinonen 2011) into prestigious labels, deliberately manipulating semiotics and practices. Young Rwandans, too, in the streets of Kigali, name themselves *abaníga* 'niggers', transforming a strategy of Othering adopted from US-American Hip Hop discourse into a new in-group terminology with a covert prestige, to the outrage of more traditional elders. Women living in polygynous units in communities of the Nigerian Middle Belt perform Otherness by turning colonial tribalistic terminologies and discourse into ambiguous and ironic epithets (Storch 2011), such as 'man-eater' and 'heathen'. The imitation of performances of gendered Otherness and mimicking practices of witchcraft and magic results in mimetic excess (Taussig 1993): the mimesis of Southerness and alterity is an oscillating, violent play with words and metaphors, where swearing is suddenly both mimesis of the Other, and mimesis of the Other's Other.

Accusing the Other as a practitioner of witchcraft and as belonging to a second world, a *deuxième monde*, which is located at the intersection between the real world and a spiritual fictitious world, is a common practice in many settings worldwide. However, witchcraft is often ascribed to an allegedly superstitious Global South, as opposed to ideas of 'rational and realistic thinking' in the Global North. Local and regional witchcraft beliefs have been modified and instrumentalized in the 1980s by charismatic American preachers of Pentecostal and evangelical churches, who founded branches of their churches first in Nigeria, then later also in the DR Congo and other African countries. Socio-economic and political problems led to an increasing marginalization of children as the societal scapegoats for misery and family problems, and to an increase in witchcraft accusations against them. In most cases, child witches are expelled from their homes and adopt the offensive labels of Othering as semiotic self-reflexive identities in unequal power constellations. The anthropologist Filip de Boeck (2004: 162) observes that "the demonization of the witch in church discourse makes the witch itself more omnipresent in the social field" in the Congo, as an ironic twist in society's attempt to marginalize the bewitched; this also relates to the frequent occurrence of witchcraft terminology.

The importance of sorcery-related terminology used as a strategy for marking one's marginalization in Congolese society becomes obvious when taking a look at the elaborated register that includes numerous terms for 'witch, sorcerer' and equivalents for 'to bewitch, to hex, to jinx'. Nassenstein (2014) lists 22 out of 636 lexical items of youth language that are related to the semantic field of witchcraft, while nowadays even more such terms have emerged, as stated by Lingala speakers from the Congolese capital. It seems that once child witches have adopted the derogatory labels that they are confronted with in society, new lexemes have to be coined that have not yet been reconquered as decentered and self-ironic emblems by the alleged witches. A former child witch from Kinshasa emphasized the mimetic character of swear words, and the semiotic power of the discarded, explaining how accused children engage in the self-reflexive appropriation of marginalizing labels (held in Congolese French and Lingala):

> Quand on leurs insulte [sic], exemple *ozá ntshor!, ozá ndoki, boyé boyé*, eux aussi prennent ce truc-là, ne pas qu'ils vont le coller pour eux-mêmes que "accepté, que oui", il est sorcier. Il ne va jamais le dire par lui-même que oui, il est sorcier. Peut-être qu'il est sans conscience ou avec conscience, là ça dépend. Mais la seule chose que je peux dire en cela, les enfants de là rue le collent ce nom par eux-mêmes pour montrer un peu une capacité de superiorité et ne pas parce qu'il dit il accepte "oui je suis sorcier", non. Ils utilisent ça "yes, *nga nazá ntshor, nga nazá vrai mumpongo* [mumpɔŋɔ]", *mumpongo* c'est surtout le terme qu'ils utilisent. *Nazá vrai mumpongo, nazá vrai tshor. Nakobaré yó leló, leló vraiment nakobaré yó, nakolakisa yó que nazá vampire*. C'est le mot qu'ils utilisent beaucoup, c'est quand ils sont énervés pour montrer à l'autre qu'il est superieur que lui, et il a beaucoup des esprits (...), c'est pourquoi il utilise ce mot-la: *Nga nazá vampa. Vampa*, donc ça signifie 'vampire'. *Nga nazá tshoroma, nga nazá vrai vrai vrai mumpongo* – ça maintenant, il est en train de confirmer qu'il est un vrai sorcier par rapport au temps qu'il a commis dans la rue par rapport à l'autre. Et puis, il a beaucoup plus des esprits de se battre ou bien de faire quelque chose de mauvais que l'autre. C'est pour prouver à l'autre qu'il est un peu superieur ou il est plus grand que lui. (...) *Y'ozá elóko ya moké, ozá sósó, ozá sósó*. Bon, il est en train de lui dire cela, pas vraiment qu'il va le transformer mais pour lui montrer sa superiorité pendant sa duration ou bien le temps qu'il a passé dans la rue.

> [When they are insulted, for example *ozá ntshor!, ozá ndoki, boyé boyé* [you are a witch! you are a sorcerer, like this and that], they also take that thing, not that they will adopt it themselves as "accepted, yes", [that] (s)he's a witch. (S)he will never say it him/herself that yes, (s)he is a witch. Maybe unconsciously, [but not] consciously, there it depends. But the only thing I can say is that street children make use of that name by themselves to show a capacity of superiority but not due to the fact that they have accepted "yes I am a witch", no. They use this "yes, *nga nazá ntshor, nga nazá vrai mumpongo* [mumpɔŋɔ]" [I'm a witch, I'm a real sorcerer], *mumpongo* [sorcerer]. *Nazá vrai mumpongo, nazá vrai tshor. Nakobaré yó leló, leló vraiment nakobaré yó, nakolakisa yó que nazá vampire* [I am a real sorcerer, I am a real witch. I will kill you today, today I will really kill you, I will show you that I am a vampire]. That's often the term they use, that's when they are annoyed to show to the other one that (s)he himself is superior to him/her, and that (s)he has many spirits (...) that's why (s)he uses that word: *Nga nazá vampa* [I am a vampire]. *Vampa* therefore means 'vampire'. *Nga nazá tshoroma, nga nazá vrai vrai vrai mumpongo* [I am a warlock, I am a real real real sorcerer] – there (s)he confirms that (s)he is a real witch considering the time (s)he has spent in the street compared to the other. And also,

(s)he has many spirits for fighting or to do something worse than the other. (...) *Y'ozá elóko ya moké, ozá sósó, ozá sósó* [you are a small thing, you are a chicken, a chicken]. So, (s)he is saying that, not really in order to transform (/and curse) him/her but to show him/her his or her superiority during the time spent in the streets.]
(Carter Omende, May 2016, authors' translation)

It becomes obvious that the rich repertoire of witchcraft labels in Lingala has an indexical iconic value: the more offensive terms are recaptured by the possessed children, the more power they incorporate. The more terms are coined by society to denounce them, and are then self-reflexively possessed, the more powerful the witches become. They thus collect derogatory names and labels ascribed by society as an onomastic evidence of subversive critique and ownership. When analyzing the witchcraft register in the Lingala spoken by street children, the 'witches' thus developed an apparent eagerness to list, discuss and count all terms that they could possibly think of as derogatory labels with which they were shouted at in the streets.

Interestingly, the self-designation as 'vampires' (as in the text example above) is bound to common tropes in witchcraft discourse: the fact of sucking out someone's blood and life is an emblematic metaphor of turning spiritual power into Othered physical power, stealing lifeblood and constituting bodily danger. Disdained witches turn into vampires, which enables them to interfere with their accusers, relocating not only derogatory labels but also redirecting witchcraft accusations from an epistemological and metaphorical level to the dimension of real life and the messy streets.

Performance plays an important role here. The alleged witches perform transgressive rituals of intoxication, prostitution and *shado*, playful boxing, in the streets of Kinshasa where garbage becomes a symbol of the playground for the discarded, for the messy. In this arena, so-called witches perform witchcraft in a *deuxième monde*, as also described by de Boeck (2004: 158), quoting a child witch who reports that "at night we fly to the houses of our victims with our aeroplane that we make from the bark of a mango-tree. When we fly out at night I transform myself into a cockroach"; this child also narrates cannibalistic practices. This shows that not only are derogatory labels adopted in the mimetic construction process of the Other's Other, but that the epistemological act of Mignolo's (2002) *relocation* is not only thought but also performed, as a form of spatial incorporation of the environment. The discarded live, bewitch and perform in a surrounding of messy garbage in Kinshasa's cemeteries, gutters and swamps – representative of abandoned places, using abandoned language (i.e. decentered and recaptured swear words). Over the past decades, Congolese citizens have colloquially renamed the city Kinshasa, formerly known as *Kinshasa la Belle* 'Kinshasa the beautiful' and now labeled *Kinshasa la Poubelle* 'Kinshasa the dustbin' (see Figure 1.1):

Figure 1.1: Changing names, changing power relations – *Kin la (pou)belle*.
Note: Images like this one are frequently shared via social media.

The extrinsic label of serving as a "dustbin" here becomes the witches' messy and mimetic space of transformation, and a symbol of the subaltern soiling, or contamination, within allegedly established hegemonies of naming and being named, showing the appropriation of labels by the Other(ed), and the power of self-reflexive language use.

The unpleasant and the outcast in culture have been explored, perhaps most influentially, by Julia Kristeva in her work on *Pouvoirs de l'horreur* (1980), which also provides a theoretical framework for the work that language does when it refers to horror. Kristeva calls the disgusting and horrible "abject", which is defined as anything that represents endangerment of the cultural Self and that transcends the boundary between subject and object, between pure and impure, proper and improper etc.: the corpse is abject, and so is milk skin, stickiness, and incest. What is of particular interest for our analysis of swearing practices is Kristeva's observation that revulsion as a reaction to the abject is not removal from one's body (e.g., by vomiting), but takes place in language and in laughter, as discursive vomit that helps to dissociate the Self from the abject. Abject theory hereby provides some very interesting and helpful approaches to language and to the subjectivity in language practices; these approaches were made use of in work on the abject and outcast that followed Kristeva's book (Bernstein 1992).

What precisely makes tropes and motifs that trigger discursive vomit attractive in communication? Cultural scripts can also be read from the perspective of what or whom they discriminate. The Other, whom these scripts cannot integrate (or do not want to), is abject – subjugated people, homosexual people, ethnic minorities, sick people, but also more generally women, for example. Abject theory here has considerably helped marginalized people to speak back: the concept of affirmative abjection – contesting societal norms – provides access to exteriority and helps to negotiate social relations. Menninghaus (1999) has called this the recapture of the discarded. And precisely the reconstruction of the suppressed, where the abject can undergo a positive inversion through the performance of a legitimate critique on injustice and inequality, is not only a highly creative moment in communication, but also reveals how the center and the margins are always only temporary constructs; the recapture of the discarded is also a way of de-centering.

Constructing the Other's Other does several things: it removes part of the context that helps to construct marginality and recaptures low class styles – the noisy and messy. Inversion in swearing is therefore not only a form of mimesis, but also a form of mobility across conceptional spaces. Guy Schaffer, in his text on 'Queering waste through camp' (2015), identifies as a consequence of these forms of recapture the emergence of camp:

> Like queer theory, discard studies is interested in uneven remainders, things that don't fit neatly into categories. Both concern themselves with the strange and imperfect construction of divisions (in discard studies, that between waste and not-waste; in queer theory, those between hetero/homosexual, between male and female) that do violence to humans, cultures, and environments, while still attending to the fact that these divisions have meaning for people, that they are strategic, and that they structure our thought in ways that are almost impossible to escape.
>
> As a mode of thinking through and beyond and before binaries, or perhaps of thinking binaries promiscuously, queer theory is indispensable to the study of disposal. In particular, the merits of camp as a queer mode of reading trash can blur and transgress and cover in glitter those boundaries between waste and not-waste that are central analytics in discard studies. While camp is a useful mode of reading for any field of study marked by questionable binaries, it is particularly relevant with regards to waste because camp is all about the reevaluation of a culture's trash. Camp offers a mode of celebrating, reappropriating, and rendering waste visible, without pretending that waste has stopped being waste.

The mimesis of abusive language performed by the colonial Other, in other words, results not just in profitable abjection, in the sense of decentering and the recapture of the discarded. It produces altered images, as the copy is not a copy – it is still messy and noisy, it is trash reified as something that might be of value, such as camp. Violent words used in mimetic ways, as inverted abjection, tend to trigger – as discursive vomit – a kind of bitter laughter; they are funny in a weird way, like camp objects, but also disruptive of the former order: words are seen as cheap – as camp; the ones denoted by them are seen as waste. When the trashy labels are productively turned around and filled with new meaning, the Other's Other speaks back, laughs back, and stains the arena in which the Other was formerly ostracized and discarded. The stains, camp or waste mark the re-appropriation and the new constellations of ownership as a self-reflexive act of fouling one's nest, onomastically rearranging hegemonies.

There is one space where such nest-fouling inversion has no limitations any more, namely the space of the ultimate Other. The Jukun-speaking inhabitants of Kona, a village in northeastern Nigeria, call neighboring groups with whom no marriage bonds or joking relationships exist, zòm-`mp`èr 'cannibal'. This term might be somewhat similar to xenophobic terms worldwide, but what is important here is the verb that is used in the construction: zòm means 'bite', not 'eat', and it is the terminology of consumption that indicates that humans here do not eat people, but that there is something worse out there that bites off the flesh from the body as animals do. The dehumanized cannibal does not remain in this removed space, however. The following sequences from folktales presented by the female storyteller Ayaujiri Tijam in Kona in early 1996 illustrate how closely cannibalistic consumption is associated with forms and distances of Othering. Example (1) is a song from a story about two co-wives who go to the bush together in order to cut wood for potash – already a metaphor for what will follow, as the potash is used to make meat tender. One woman puts her infant child under a shrub and then cuts the wood. Meanwhile, the other woman, called áfù 'co-wife/envious one', takes the child back home and cooks it in a broth. After the work in the bush is done, the mother cannot find her child, but then continues to cook the soup which has been prepared, and eats it with her co-wife. Eventually, she becomes very worried about her child, and this is when her co-wife sings a song to her:

(1) Dàsó a-jìŋ   báyì! a-yàgyàgyàg ǹ-jìŋ   báyì,
    Daso 2SG-be.foolish badly 2SG-lick:REP CONS-be.foolish badly
    ás ṹŋ   kpárú ǹ-kad-mì   ŋwù na   né?   ŋwù jèn
    dish   all   CONS-ask-O:1SG child sleep where child lose
    à-jèn   rá?
    part-lose INTER
    'Daso, you are foolish enough! You licked and licked, being so stupid, all the dishes, and then you ask me "where is the child?" The child is lost, right?'

Here, the envious co-wife quite bluntly accuses the mother of having been greedy, eating up a thick soup, a stew too delicious to be just food. Such stories are told frequently, and the songs in them resemble those that co-wives and neighbors sing at each other, expressing envy, hatred and disgust. These songs are ways of swearing, whereby they frame women as cannibals – as the ultimate Other, who is located outside communality. At the same time, these songs are largely performed by the women themselves, and in their swearing battles they ironically perform ultimate Otherness, mimetically interpreting the hegemonic practice of putting women in a space so marginalized, and in conditions so vulnerable, that they are easily Othered and cannibalized. A strategy to de-marginalize themselves is to inverse the derogation and the concept of the cannibal, which in these stories and songs turns into humorous entertainment, and a form of camp – better stories, the hegemonic discourse suggests, are told by the men anyway.

What is so unsettling about constructing the Self as cannibal, in the Jukun case, is that the mimetic performance of such derogatory ways of constructing the Other resulted, during the course of the colonial history, in irony-free, persisting labels: today, several Jukun-speaking groups are represented as 'man-biters', a term now well established as a language name for Kuteb (Shimizu 1980; Lewis et al. 2016; WorldBible, etc.). Besides such abstract, classificatory notions, 'cannibal' now also refers to one's own past; there is an abundance of historical narratives on how the elders – then – considered Europeans particularly pleasant to eat, as they looked as if they had already been skinned. Comments on a visitor's bare and pinkish neck were met with exclamations of appetite and gluttony: a carnevalesque performance of the disgusting flea and its own meal had emerged.

The decentering and demarginalization of swear words as a form of postcolonial mimesis by the colonialized Other, referring to itself with extrinsic derogatory terms, has a strong emblematic character, and is a recurrent pattern that can be found in far more than the above described settings. Naming in a colonial world was addressed quite early in post-colonial theory. Frantz Fanon (1967), as one of the first to analyze the relationship between exteriority (making a person available to his or her environment to be objectified, identified and seized), naming, and racism, observed that while the white colonizer claims the right to have a personal name (without the need to share it with others) and to name others, the black colonized person does not possess the same power. The name of the colonized characterizes its bearer as a generalizable member of a uniform group, a person about whom all is already known, and who may be called by any name given to him or her.

While the one who coins names and uses established labels is generally seen as the one who bears power, and has the possibility to alter the one that is being named, the subversive use of swear words has a tendency to construct the Other's

Other. As has been shown, it is therefore often the Congolese child witch, the Nigerian cannibal and the numerous representations of self-directed, reflexive swearing that we encounter in popular culture and social media reflecting the overturned hegemonies in a post-colonial world. The decentering of pejorative labels that are turned into positive self-referential designations serves as affirmative abjection, and causes a powerful confrontation: the one doing the naming has to face the sticky, messy and stained outcomes of his own unequal swearing and labeling, which he encounters in discarded performance. The garbage of Kinshasa's streets, with roaming street witches and the Jukuns' meaty soup, trigger an intellectual confrontation with the disruptive powers inherent in the camp of one's own alienating ostracism: self-reflexive swear words have the power of returning some of the suffering and misery to the seemingly dominant name giver.

1.3 The bitter laugh

While the Other's Other rather shows the somber side of chaos and order, humor demonstrates a more cheerful and brighter side of the same process. However, as will be shown in the following, swearing can also occur in the form of bitter laughter, which is related to a so-called *Shit Happens* genre of jokes (see Figure 1.2). *Shit Happens* is a simple tongue-in-cheek comment on misfortune and unpleasant in life. The phrase first assumed its popular distribution as a sticker on cars in the early 1980s, and a quick search with the Google Ngram tool reveals a rapid increase of usage in the 1990s, before it becomes less easily searchable as it undergoes all kinds of semantic narrowing and semiotic appropriation. One particular variety of the phrase, which illustrates this process quite well, has gone viral as a meme in the social media: the joke *Shit happens when you party naked* (see Figure 1.3), usually used as an ironic comment on unwanted pregnancies after drunken partying.

However, its increasing popularity is already triggering new connotations, which develop through a creative play with words, images and contextualization. Anything related to transgression and the violation of norms and taboos seems to make a good joke here.

Some of the posts, however, are not as easy to laugh at. The composition of a picture of a corpse and a dog with the phrase is rather unsettling: even though there are sufficient ambiguous and contradictory elements in this post to make it somewhat funny at a first glimpse (naked vs. skeletonized, intact feet vs. destroyed legs, cute little dog vs. scavenger, party vs. war, etc.), there is something here that makes our laughter sound different than before – more "bitter".

Figure 1.2: *Party naked* meme.
Note: http://www.someecards.com/usercards/viewcard/MjAxMi1jYzQ2NjZhYWU4ODc2ZDM1 (accessed 30 November 2018).

Various attempts have been made to explain such bitter laughter: Norrick and Bubel (2009: 37) state that "[c]onversational humor does not always take the form of light hearted banter, it may have a serious, even bitter edge: Boxer and Cortés-Conde (1997) write in this regard of humor as a 'double-edged sword'". But the bitter laughter that we aim to focus on is more than the biting humor described by Boxer and Cortés-Conde. It is rather a "bitter laugh" at misfortune, threat and horror, and the subversive laughter at power and conquest, that we are interested in here: jokes that are based on experiences of utter violence and injustice and that call for laughter that doesn't so much help to solve tensions and disruptions, but rather draws the gaze right to them. This perspective aims at understanding what purpose bitter laughter serves in critical and abusive communicative events, and how it differs from ironic (Wilson & Sperber 1992) or sarcastic laughter, which are based on different speaker-hearer relationships than those in the case studies presented. Bitter laughter equally has to be treated differently from humorous slurs (see Jay 2000) with a targeted immanent funniness. Bitter laughter does not have to be forcefully funny.

Figure 1.3: Inversion of the *Party naked* joke.
Note: http://www.funnyjunk.com/channel/morbid-channel/3824020/MzyYGZm/ (accessed 30 April 2018). Here, a photograph of a victim of the 1984 Delhi riots against Sikhs is used. The poor reproduction of the image is part of the deliberately trashy performance.

This also becomes evident in various other studies, focusing on "improper laughter" (Goldstein 2013; Norrick and Chiaro 2009; Billig 2005; Rowe 1995) and laughter in emotionally demanding contexts (e.g., Attardo 2014). An important theoretical framework for such "tasteless" forms of humor and laughter has more recently been brought forward by Ana Deumert in her monograph on mobile communication (2014). She uses a distinction first suggested by Roland Barthes (1973) between *plaisir* and *jouissance* to explore the notion of sociability. The former concept is glossed as referring to the comforting, cheering pleasure that strengthens social bonds, and the latter to a quite different, unsettling enjoyment which derives from facts known to be inappropriate and offensive, but which nonetheless elicit laughter and mirth. The "bitter" laughter in African narratives of murder and atrocity also addresses a carnevalesque form of excess and abundance of violence, which is reminiscent of Tennessee Williams' "theater of excess" (Saddik 2015), based on the interdependence of laughter, horror and perverse ugliness. It stands as a form of ludicrous laughter (Barasch 1985) at the "brink of unbearable pain and horror, where the only place to go, the only way of dealing with such intense experience, [is] laughter", all in all "sicker than necessary" (Saddik 2015: 7). We aim to show that the "bitter" laugh can also be seen, in this vein, as post-colonial critique, as a reaction to previously experienced violence that is still felt, and as an agentive strategy that emphasizes the fact that the subaltern might laugh if not speak. In 2014, there was a story that went viral in Kampala, Uganda. In a remote village, a mother had apparently failed to watch over her newborn baby, only a few weeks old. While the mother was away, one of the local pigs started to "eat its face", as many Ugandans said. The animal had indeed in a short time completely mutilated the baby's face. A short video that showed the incident was spread via WhatsApp and many people laughed about this story, repeating over and over again "Imagine, the child lost its face, how hilarious … ", followed by a bitter laugh. In the following weeks, we tried to inquire how it could possibly happen that people felt apparent excitement and hilarity about such a tragic incident.

> Okay, the pig and the baby story. It's kind of funny because you know not the fact that the baby was eaten by the pig. What happens is, that the mother goes out to the garden and leaves the baby home, alone. So the pigs were being starved, one pig enters into the house, and eats the baby's face because it's very hungry. So the pig was hungry, eats the baby's face, and that is kind of funny to people because … You know, they imagine the pig starving, and really hungry, and decides to eat a person. So that's what's funny. So people listening to the story end up laughing. But in actual sense they are not laughing because the baby was eaten, they are laughing because the pig was hungry and ends up eating a person. So that's how the story is. (Vivianne Lindah Lamunu, February 2016)

The statement above shows that bitter laughter highlights the role reversal in the story (the pig starving, the child being eaten), and the depersonalization of the real incident, but also fulfills a certain function of narrativity (laughter accompanies the story and is part of it). In similar stories, such as, for instance, an incident where a domestic help was filmed mistreating and abusing a child of the family whom she was supposed to watch over, the same kind of bitterness occurred. Here again, laughter was not a sign of "frightening funniness" as in horror movies, but helped to redirect the horror displayed in the video clip from an interpersonal perspective into nowhere, neither relating it to subject nor object, and playing with ascribed roles of Other and Self, here characterized by the pig and the child. This strategy of depersonalizing a horrible incident increases its abstract character, and makes it less tangible in the concrete world. Laughing deposes something from its context, and makes it unreal, especially when a story contains allegedly inadequate forms of transgression, and an inappropriate reversal of roles and contexts.

Another narrative with a "bitter" form of laughter in its story stems from a corpus of stories collected in Eastern DR Congo, in the middle of a long-lasting and ongoing armed conflict scenario.

> Le jour que la M23 avait pris la ville de Goma, c'était vraiment quelque chose de marrant, parce que même dans les hôpitaux, il y avait tous les infirmes marchaient normalement alors qu'ils boitaient avant la guerre. Et les militaires et tout le monde se cachait à l'hôpital, et se faisaient malade alors que c'était faux. Donc les gens se cachaient dans les hôpitaux. Les militaires parfois disaient aux médecins de les mettre sous sérum. Les gens sont partis dans les hôpitaux, les infirmes marchaient, c'était vraiment quelque chose d'étonnant, et ça fait rire tout le monde! (laughter)
>
> [The day the M23 rebels took the city of Goma, it was really something hilarious, because even in the hospitals, there were the weak and crippled walking normally even though they limped before the war. And the soldiers and everybody was hiding in hospital, and declared themselves sick even though it was faked. Thus, people were hiding in the hospitals. The soldiers sometimes told the doctors to treat them with serum/inject them with something. People went to the hospitals, the crippled ones walked (normally), that was something really astonishing, and that makes everybody laugh!]
>
> (Paulin Baraka Bose, February 2016, authors' translation)

The story narrated above shows how a hospital, as the setting where war-wounded refugees, soldiers and civilians look for treatment, refuge and peace, turns into a tragicomic scene where *les malades imaginaires* perform sickness, which turns out to be a perfect copy of reality due to everyone's past war experience. The former hospital is therefore no longer a hospital, nor a sane place, since it turns into the scenery of a theater play, where boundaries between disease and pseudo-disease become fluid, and where healthy individuals now perform the fate of mass rape victims, wounded militia, and survivors of atrocities.

This type of discursive framing of atrocities and fear has been very common in the narratives we have recorded, as well as in the discussions on them. They all had in common that they were about real, everyday experiences of the messiness and frequent disruptions of life in the post-colony. These horrible jokes and stories are not so much typical of some kind of "African humor" but of a world where "sometimes the only way to deal with the horror [...] is to laugh" (Kerr 2002: 103).

Understanding why laughter would be such an ultimate, or perhaps desperate, option, we argue, in line with Swart (2009: 890), requires us to take into account that "looking at laughter requires an understanding of the historiography of emotions". Providing an analysis of bitter laughter as an expression of particular emotions rather than a comment on their context is intended here to demonstrate that these emotions – horror, hate, fear, disgust and shame – are not marginal or destructive emotions but rather central components of normal social interactions and simple routine operations (Barbalet 2001). Hereby, the unpleasant and the outcast in culture are referred to in highly symbolic form (Menninghaus 1999: 516–517), with laughter – and a particular form of bringing the notion of humor into a relationship with horror – that is utterly meaningful and points to this symbolism.

And, referring once more to Kristeva, the bitter laugh at horror and atrocity is not an uninvolved laughter and does not signify aloofness, but the contrary: it is a reaction to the felt merging of abject and Self. There is something else going on here other than having fun with the transgression of norms: the ubiquity and salience of the bitter laugh (and the jokes invoking it) in the cases dealt with here have something to do with experiences of the post-colony as a place of disruption, injustice, violence and marginalization.

The bitter laugh emitted by individuals of different backgrounds who were involved in liminal and often traumatic events not only had in common that prior "shit had happened", which was then laughed off, but also that all of these case studies were based in post-colonial settings. The bitter laughing protagonists in the shared narratives make use, in fear of cultural endangerment, of affirmative abjection as a critical voice from the post-colony. Western standards of appropriateness in humor, over-generalizations by missionaries, colonial agents and others that "Africans don't do irony" (or allegedly have an over-simplistic sense of humor [Mohlich 1977], as often heard in expatriates' circles still today), and the predefinition of what can trigger hilarity and what should not, has contributed to the dissociation of the African laughing subject.

Constant dissociation from the colonial through subversive laughter, which strictly contrasts with perceptions of "good taste", may trigger a harsh imaginary exclamation "This is not funny!" by the listener. The bitter laughter does not only intend to laugh off the abject, but uses the abject and its inappropriate and to some extent disgusting symbolism as a subaltern critical voice from the South. This correlates with feminist and post-structuralist ideas, as expressed by Irigaray (1985: 163) with the question "Isn't laughter the first form of liberation from a secular oppression?" While in Irigaray's works it is the phallic that is contested, resisted, and constantly rejected by laughing, here it is the colonial and Northern hegemony that is contested in bitter laughs of affirmative abjection. The steady dissociation from predefined forms of laughing, storytelling, and dealing with daily horror, turns the abject into something useful, into a form of disgusting and powerful aesthetics, which can be used to question inequality, and feeds on the shocked facial expressions of the listener. "My horror – my decision how to talk, or laugh, about it" could be summarized as a potential agentive and subaltern justification for verbal (and humorous) excess. Bitter laughter as the closing ritual of a violent, disturbing, inappropriate narrative uses the abject no longer as an endangerment of the cultural Self but as a liminal strategy of critique. What Tuhiwai Smith (1999: 73) writes about language also relates to forms of laughter, which "[i]n the colonised world, however, [...] are not necessarily employed in the same way that First World academics may have used them". African humor and Africans' laughter have often been reduced to a form of harmonic and naive foolishness, according to colonial accounts, and are deconstructed by the bitter laugh which leaves goose bumps and cold shivers down the spine.

The bitter laugh, as found in different African settings, is not a laughter of funniness, hilarity, or cathartic relief, but is rather seen as a way of dealing with horror, and as a kind of swearing practice. It has become evident that laughter in this form diverges from irony, sarcasm and "black humor", and can rather be associated with the iconic representations of *Shit happens*-humor, that equally relate to a broadened understanding of swearing. This broader view of swearing as an inter-individual contending activity that can also be encoded as laughing, is by no means less transgressive or insulting than simply using swear words, but contributes to the complexity of swearing as a multifaceted discursive phenomenon. When swearing is understood as laughing about daily horror, laughter appears as discursive vomit, as a sticky inappropriate mess and as an afterlaugh that leaves a bitter taste, which is to some extent liberation, to some extent abject.

1.4 Bad language and other substances: How words can kill

Swearing, cursing and other forms of transgressive language presented as word lists and analyzed in their metaphorical depth and polysemic width, like, for example, a drastic image or performance, hardly ever come across as particularly appalling, violent or powerful. Vocabularies are, in the typically isolated forms in which they tend to be presented by linguists, often rather amusing to behold and seem to tell eloquently of linguistic creativity and playful ways of using words. Language, other than linguistic data, is by nature communal, a public game that does not unfold its entire meaning and power without context, audience, placement and embodiment. The bitter laugh, mimetic performances of Otherness, the disruptive power of camp and the abject in many ways need to be seen as part of vituperative language, which alone, as a mere list, remains slightly blank. The important thing to be learned from the performances surrounding swear words and curses is that they need embeddedness in context, interpersonal and relational settings to really work; to some extent, we have seen, occasionally the words themselves can even remain unsaid: an image, a bitter laugh or a mimicking performance of gesture, movement and expression will do even without words – a mere hint of a curse is already sufficient to do its work. This is, we argue, in line with an entire way of thinking about language, based on Wittgenstein's *Philosophical Investigations* (1953), a manifestation not of the insignificance of words in certain settings, but of their extraordinary power. The omission of words whilst context and performance persist creates a particular kind of noisy, powerful silence: a sudden gap in the midst of much. Audiences might easily guess what has been left out[2] – words whose sound is powerful even when it is not heard; language in the speechless performances of discursive vomit is dangerous: isolating, damaging and repulsive.

These are the other, more ritualized dimensions of bad language: words – and the signs for them – may have the power to change reality, to actually inflict disease and misery upon an addressee. Cursing, often subsumed under "intra-individual swearing", tends to be considered as entirely equivalent to a form of cathartic swearing that is not directed at a second person but rather helps to make frustration and anger manageable when one trips at the front porch, forgets the door keys or drops a coin. Timothy Jay's (2000) monograph *Why we Curse* understands the act of cursing as seemingly synonymous with swearing. Despite his initial explanation that "[t]echnically speaking, cursing is wishing harm on a person (e.g. eat shit and die)" (2000: 9), he then broadens his understanding of the term, stating that "[c]ursing is the utterance of emotionally powerful, offensive words (e.g., *fuck, shit*) or emotionally harmful expressions (e.g., *kiss my ass, piss off, up yours*) that are understood as insults" (Jay 2000: 9). However, an alternative approach to cursing that takes into account words, context and performance as substantial means to transform reality, might rather focus on the actual meaning of using words along with witchcraft substances, saliva, gifts and bodily substances as powers of transformation and trance in order to drive the addressee into misery, sickness, agony or death. Bodily substance as part of abusive language is harmful, too, and addresses a more spiritual dimension of bad language, often including ritualized communication.

Transgressive and non-conformist speech have moreover often been declared as potentially dangerous language, for instance in Puritan New England, as analyzed by Kamensky (2001: 287) with regard to the speech of so-called witches,

---

2 Incomplete sounds or unheard hints at bad language can occur in manifold ways, such as the emblematic sound of vomiting without making use of verbal utterances, which is perceived as a strong sign of disgust and rejection by the hearer, or for instance a hissing sound when passing someone, or a cursory gesture with one's hand toward the head while driving a car as a way of criticizing other motorists. These "unheard" or unfinished ways of swearing are still perceived as powerful since they often cannot be legally sanctioned or penalized, but clearly deprive someone of power. Despite not using words or finishing a gesture, the semiotic encoding is clear, and sometimes even more destructive due to the hearer's powerlessness against it.

women who did not use careful language, due to the fact that "a suspect's verbal style was one ingredient of a persona that made her a likely witch". New England's numerous witch trials in the late 17th century were often explained as necessary due to the fact that women could be bewitched by another woman's ill words. These examples of disorderly speech associated with witchcraft spread the fear of being similarly bewitched through the power of words.

Numerous African languages reveal cursing registers, through which elderly speakers express status in relation to younger speakers, or through which threats and criticism are uttered. For example, Banyabwisha communities in Eastern DR Congo (near the Rwandan border) reveal clear distinctions between the cursing of elderly people in contrast to younger people's swear words. While old men and women are free to use severe curses in any given situation, younger speakers have a different limited range of bad language that will never reach the severity of elderly speakers' vocabulary. The inventory of this register mostly relates to topics like fertility, social support and community. These swear words are taboo for a majority of speakers, and can only be used by elders, since only they have the power and authority to foresee and put curses on people's childbirth. Among these severe spells are *uzapfa udahétse!* 'you are going to die without ever carrying a child on your back', directed toward women, *uzapfa utabyaye* 'you will die without begetting children' directed to men, or *kamóbwe* 'may you be all alone and an orphan', directed to both.

These severe instances of verbal spells are mainly used when an elderly person sees values, norms and traditions endangered by a younger individual of the same community. It was explained by speakers that a register like this would most likely be used when an older man visits his grandson or nephew and suddenly finds out that he has got married, without letting the older one know about the event and change of marital status. Moreover, spells like the ones listed above are uttered when men's and women's traditional roles are no longer respected in Bwisha, and men take over women's duties such as sweeping the house or washing the dishes, which, according to older people's view, threatens the social order of the community. Casting spells then serves as an attempt to prevent further harm, or to correct the abnormal role reversal through threatening the perpetrators with unknown and unpredictable consequences.

The use and elaboration of old men's cursing register – as is also the case in other African scenarios – usually goes along with ritual spitting, which can either be interpreted as sign of approval or disapproval of a younger Munyabwisha, depending upon the intensity, as explained by one speaker, who differentiated between "good" and "bad" spitting.

Normalement, un vieux, tous les très grandes injures, quand il est énervé, il est libre de les dire, ça passe, comme mon père me disait ça, pour un vieux c'est vraiment libre... d'ailleurs pour nous dans la culture, quand un vieux est énervé il crache sur toi d'une façon bizarre! Mais quand un vieux est content, il t'appelle maintenant et il crache sur ta main. Quand il prend ta main, et il est un peu joyeux et ça le plait, il ne crache pas dessus très fort, mais il va faire quelque chose comme trois fois pf-pf-pf..., quelque chose comme ça. Il va dire que tu sois béni, que tu aies des bons amis, de la réussite... et il prend tes mains et il crache la en disant des mots. Ça c'est dans le bon sens! Maintenant dans le mauvais sens, un vieux peut te voir, il te dit tuuuuhh, maintenant il dit 'kamóbwe!' Des grandes injures pour les vieux c'est toujours en crachant, si tu es là c'est sûr il crache sur toi. C'est comme un code, quand je t'amène chez un Munyabwisha, ou chez un Munyarwanda, Hutu ou Tutsi, s'il est énervé, les gens partent, bon, il va d'abord cracher sur toi et il ajoute une insulte. Ça va ensemble, il crache d'abord et puis il ajoute l'insulte.

[Usually, an elder, when annoyed, he is free to use all very severe insults, it's okay, like my father telling me, for an old man it's really free... moreover, for us in our culture when an old man is upset he spits at you in a weird way! But when he an old man is happy, he calls you and he spits on your hand (palm). When he takes your hand, and he's a bit joyful and that appeals to him, he does not spit onto it very much, but he will do something three times like 'pf-pf-pf' [sound of light spitting]... something like that. He will tell you that you may be blessed, that you may have good friends, and [talk of] success... and he takes your hands and spits there by saying some words. That's in a good sense! Now in a bad sense, an old man can see you, and he tells you 'tuuuuhh' [sound of spitting], now he says 'you may stay all alone and be an orphan'! The severe insults, for old people, it's always by spitting, when you are there it's sure he will spit at you. It's like a code, when I take you to a Munyabwisha, or Rwandan, Hutu or Tutsi, when he gets upset, people leave, okay, he will first spit at you then add an insult. That goes together, he spits first and then adds the insult.]

(Paulin Baraka Bose, September 2015, authors' translation)

Spitting constitutes a meaningful paraverbal act that is frequently found cross-culturally and can stand for a range of semiotic encodings, listed by Poyatos (2002: 130–134) either as a form of "social spitting", as "rejection, anger and aggression", as a "rejection ritual" (such as in parts of India), as a "healing" practice (as found among Native American cultures), or as "playing" (as found in spitting contests among school children). Spitting as a form of inter-individual rejection touches upon the taboo of body fluids (cf. Allan and Burridge 2006), and the transfer of one's own saliva (and thus, anger and aggression) onto the person spat upon can be seen as "intimidating behavior" (Alan and Burridge 2006: 133). This intimidation through body fluid has a strong symbolic meaning and is here used as an emphasis of sacred curses, as also found in Charles Dickens' *Bleak House* (1853: 523), where Mr. Bucket and 'Mademoiselle' interact, and she replies by spitting, and therefore by "infecting" the ground, name and personality of Sir Leicester Dedlock.

Upon my soul I wonder at you!" Mr. Bucket remonstrates. "I thought the French were a polite nation, I did, really. Yet to hear a female going on like that, before Sir Leicester Dedlock, Baronet!" "He is a poor abused!" cries Mademoiselle. "I spit upon his house, upon his name, upon his imbecility," all of which she makes the carpet represent. "Oh, that he is a great man! O yes, superb! O heaven! Bah!

In the case of elderly Banyabwisha, spitting has in both cases (affirmation and rejection) a symbolic function of controlling the younger speakers' hands (and deeds), while the positive hinted spitting serves as a symbol of intimacy, bond, and also healing of the soul. A young speaker is never allowed to make use of the older speakers' register since this is considered a clear taboo, and thus a "swearing mistake", which is immediately sanctioned within the young speaker's community, since she or he is making use of "taboo language" which potentially loses value and inherent power when it is overused. Swear words, which are often curses and maledictions in this sense, belong to the spiritual world, and cannot be accessed by young speakers.

The use of the cursing register that incorporates authority occurs not only when disciplining younger community members. As Alliance, a 25-year old Kinyabwisha-speaking woman from Goma (DR Congo) could tell, corner bars that are frequented by old men become "swearing parlors" (with plenty of *mots grossiers ou injures*, 'heavy words or insults') where the exchange of severe swear words is excessively triggered as soon as drunk customers get into heated arguments over drinks of *umutóbe* 'banana beer', *kasiksi* 'a stronger mixed brew', or after having taken a considerable amount of *kapita mbele* 'banana-based spirit'. The authority and spiritual power of the swearing registers embodied by old Kinyabwisha speakers would lead to less reluctance in the overuse of curses and cases of serious offense. As the young woman told us, younger community members would not usually enter these bars or frequent these places of heated arguments due to their powerlessness against the overstrained use of heavy words. The amount of heavy and powerful words in the air, and the associated uncertainty about their potential negative effect on the addressee who finds himself accidentally in the same room, would usually keep non-initiated people out.

However, curses do not necessarily have to be communicated through language, or through the magic of words paired with spitting, but can equally be transported with gifts, or other bodily substances such as effluvia. Among Nigerian sex workers in Europe (e.g. operating in Italy, France etc.), beliefs are nourished by narratives about former colleagues, who tried to escape prostitution and had to die due to the fact that local experts in witchcraft still kept some of their bodily substances at home in Nigeria, such as curls of hair, cut fingernails,

Figure 1.4: Remains from a conflict between Nigerian sex workers in El Arenal, Spain (photo AS).

pubic hair, or even worn clothes (see Figure 1.4).³ The spell that is believed to be put on these sex workers over an enormous distance, by manipulating substances that are withheld by human traffickers or so-called madams (i.e. their procurers), has an immense psychosomatic impact, and can lead to severe psychological problems or even death.

Similar fear is spread in urban Kampala (Uganda) at local hairdressers' shops, where tufts of hair are often neatly gathered up and taken home by customers for disposal due to the belief that other customers could use them for witchcraft practices. The same applies to sanitary pads: employees in larger

---

3 This was explained by a former Nigerian sex worker, now based in Germany, who had successfully escaped the business.

offices commonly prefer taking them home in order to dispose of them discreetly instead of leaving them behind. The power of hair, menstrual blood and the curse that comes back to the person from whom these substances originate, is expressed by one interlocutor as being based on the fact that biological material can still affect its former owner:

> It doesn't really have to be hair, nails or sanitary towels, it can also be – you know – clothes, something that belongs to you, it says that they can take it to witchdoctors, or voodoo even, they can use these things to link a chain to you. So, they can do anything evil that they want to you. People try to throw these things away... back in the day, many people used to go to the hairdresser, scared about leaving their hair behind because they were not sure where the hair might go. Sanitary towels, too. You believe it's better to throw it where nobody can find it – because it's linked to you. Witch doctors ask for anything that was linked to you. It has your DNA, that's probably what they are looking for.
>
> (Vivianne Lindah Lamunu, May 2016)

Spells cast on bodily substance and curses that are linked to effluvia can equally be seen as swearing practices. They clearly stand for inter-individual imbalances in communication, exerting power onto the addressee not by Othering him/her, nor by using a bitter form of laughter or voice. Instead, these spells and curses imprecate the hearer and cause harm through the power of words, as well as through the power of doing evil via body parts and substances.

1.5 Perspectives: About this book

In their correlation with context and placement, swearing strategies, terminologies and practices, like the performative ways of cursing, are fluid and dynamic. A given language thus does not simply feature a specific "vocabulary of swear terms", but language practices that circle around acts of swearing and cursing. These tend to lose their transgressive and substantial character through frequent use, and are therefore constantly intensified and remade. For example, the German swear term *Arsch*, as in Klaus Kinski's eloquent performances of the 1970s which we elaborated upon above, today does not seem to irritate a great number of speakers. His outbursts now feel slightly dated, while other swear terms, though also excretion-organ-oriented, have gained currency. For a while, quick attacks featuring utterly sexist and deliberately old-fashioned terms such as *Fotze* 'cunt', or even *vertrocknete Fotze* 'dried-up cunt' became popular – first as serious insults, and then as mocking performances of "inadequate speech" among male immigrant youths. The misogynic message encoded in these terms (and the gestures that often go with them) thus quickly became inverted, eventually resulting in an amusing performance of imperfect acquisition of sociocultural knowledge. Meanwhile, a different type of swearing practice is spreading: when asked which swear word would be most offensive in 2016, German adolescent girls replied that this should presently be *Hausfrau* 'housewife' – a term reflecting a gender concept and lifestyle no longer considered desirable and adequate by them.[4] *Arsch*, they added, is now often used as a term that signals familiarity and endearment, with a dash of irony. While swearing research is commonly associated with the study of "bad words" and their implications in the pragmatic foundations of language use, psycholinguistic perspectives, in discourse analysis or humor studies, we aim to open up new perspectives with the present volume. Apart from methodological issues and attempts at challenging the established understanding of "swearing", this also includes the consideration of creativity, fluidity, context, placement, embodiment, power relations and agency.

As has been mentioned above, swearing is often "not what it seems", due to the fact that limited views on swearing in interaction often lack multi-faceted and multimodal forms of encoding. Cursing, witchcraft and transformation as swearing broaden the concept by turning toward the spiritual, and toward secrecy and sacrilege. The various contributions presented in this volume aim to turn the gaze to precisely this powerful creativity in language, and to the ideologemes and concepts that aim at rationalizing this.

In a preamble to this volume, Thomas Stodulka introduces notions of participation, entanglement and empathy to the field of swearing. Referring to his work in Java, Indonesia, where street youths turn a swearing register into a ritualized expression of a marginalized community of practice, he reminds us that what seems to differ quickly resonates with what is considered common practice.

The contributions that follow are grouped in three parts: (I) Othering and abjection as deep practice, (II) Cultural mobility as context of transgression, (III) Disruptive and trashy performance. The power of language to construct Otherness and to elicit the abject, to discard and dissolve, is deep practice that requires work and knowledge on all sides – on the side of the swearer and curser, the side of the audience and the cursed, and the side of the linguist, who turns into some kind of ambivalent player. This field is opened up in Timothy Jay's chapter, which not only presents a current state of the art of

---

4 In German, similar social and gender concepts are expressed with the term *Opi* 'grandad' when used with older men, or *Mutti* 'mommy' with women in their 40s and 50s. Among coeval youths, disrespectful address terms can also refer conservatively to socially undesired appearance and behavior: young men are abusively addressed as *Model* 'fashion model', while young women may simply be called *Schlampe* 'slut' or *Hure* 'whore'. It therefore seems to be a general trend to use these apparently milder abusive terms, which actually constitute powerful insults.

swearing research, but discusses how taboo word research has revealed a number of challenges that researchers have to face and deal with. By discussing ten major issues, he touches upon the difficulty of defining taboo speech, speaker and hearer roles, and the importance of clarifying the context in which swear words are used and also their evolution. He stresses that research on swearing also requires the study of emotion and needs broader and multidisciplinary approaches. Research on "bad language", in other words, is one of the most challenging tasks for linguists. This becomes conceivable in Alexandra Y. Aikhenvald's masterly work on imperative imprecatives, where she expands the established focus on curses and examines the grammatical means of using imperatives in curses and maledictions by looking at constructions and contexts in two languages, Manambu from New Guinea and Tariana from the Amazon. While some languages, such as Manambu, allow for the use of a third person imperative or the irrealis for specific curses, in others, such as Tariana, the use of imperatives may be too strong; speakers therefore tend to employ malefactives. This cross-linguistic contribution combines a pragmatic analysis with a discussion of different grammatical forms and adds new perspectives to common approaches to curses. Alice Mitchell, in her chapter on Datooga swear words, offers a deep gaze at the intertwined relationship between taboo language and kinship terminology, a core field of linguistic anthropology. The kin-based insults studied by Mitchell contribute to a better understanding of offensive language in its social context; due to the specific hierarchy of family members and the role of fathers in Datooga society, they can easily sworn by. She therefore expands the focus of "mother" swear words and curses to a broader look at "kinship". Anne Storch focuses on the intricate meanings of swearing and noisy performances, predominantly in regard to the practices and roles of women in different contexts. By pursuing a more holistic approach to swearing – understanding it as "horrible play" – she looks at shrill voices, incomprehensible yells and other communicative forms such as crying and spitting. Storch thus intends to provide alternative ways of discussing (bad) "language" beyond the mainstream categories. While her specific regional focus is on a migration context in the Mediterranean, she offers various spatio-temporal references to other field sites and contexts. Felix Ameka's chapter focuses on areal invectives in different Kwa languages from the Lower Volta Basin. Comparing shared interactional routines – maledicta and taboo expressions – he takes the multimodal use of emblematic gestures (such as the widespread phenomenon of "suckteeth") with spoken taboo words into account. Ameka claims in his contribution that the facial expressions paired with swear words have not yet been treated in studies on swearing and therefore require further attention. Based on his analysis of selected invectives, he suggests a focus on Southern and indigenous ways of understanding swearing strategies instead of relying only on English labels and terms when approaching swear words and curses.

Although this volume is based on practices of narration and case-studying, its aim is to resist essentialist and exoticizing approaches to a marginalized linguistic field. In other words, there simply is no "African swear language" or "English linguistic taboo", but dynamic and semantically complex practices that betray the fixing effects of linguistic terminologies. Part II explores this in more depth by focusing on cultural mobility as a context of transgression. The joint chapter contributed by Joseph T. Farquharson, Clive Forrester and Andrea Hollington analyzes the etymological background as well as semantic and syntactic aspects of swearing in Jamaican. The authors then include an important example of an adaptation of Jamaican swear words (and their implications) outside of Jamaica and show how swearing practices can be recontextualized. The strength and innovative character of this chapter lies in the non-normative and non-Northern focus on swear words within their local and cultural contexts. Cultural mobility – the constant work of motion – also resonates in practices of censorship. Muhammad Muhsin Ibrahim and Aliyu Yakubu Yusuf deal with the sanctioning of bad language, here discussed against a background of the northern Nigerian movie industry. The authors carefully analyze how censoring in a predominantly Muslim area determines what is permitted and what is not, and how this affects the "Kannywood" industry. Furthermore, this chapter focuses not only on the sanctioning apparatus of state or religious censorship but also on how individuals respond to this when browsing content online, including formerly tabooed content relating to sex and intimacy. In popular culture, but also in daily encounters, mock language as a practice of exclusion and Othering can be understood as a sort of hostile speech act often not included in established approaches to swearing; yet these practices can be easily related to swearing. Building on the body of literature dealing with "Mock Chinese" or "Mock Asian", Nico Nassenstein analyzes language practices in DR Congo that are used in order to ostracize and exclude Chinese migrants. Based on mimicry of Chinese-sounding terms, metalinguistic discourse among Lingala speakers includes the use of a broad repertoire of derogatory names and labels when speaking about Chinese, or even Asian, traders, construction workers and shopkeepers. Nassenstein comes to the conclusion that various forms of mock language, considered from a more holistic perspective, also need to be taken into consideration when looking at swearing and cursing in the Global South.

Turning the gaze to the continuities of transgressive speech, and taking historicity into account, swearing and cursing becomes conceivable not only as deep practice, but as disruptive and trashy performance that is based on scripted roles that seem almost unavoidable. Ricardo Roque's chapter offers a view on (nick)naming practices from East Timor. Critically following the cross-cultural history of the term *arbiru*, he pictures the mimetic use of a label assigned to a colonial officer and then understood by the colonial authorities as a symbol of recognition, failing to grasp the inherent anti-colonial criticism, a response to colonial excess. The multi-facetted development of this term reveals vividly that cursing is not a simple unidirectional act but may involve various actors across a longer time-span, and that the mimetic value of specific words, names and labels may re-interpreted and recontextualized over time. More familiar contexts bear strikingly similar connotations: Angelika Mietzner's chapter looks at a touristic setting on the Kenyan coast, where European tourists and Kenyan "beach boys" interact and bargain. The postcolonial setting of the Kenyan coastline, characterized by specific expectations on both sides, also includes unpleasant and at times bizarre encounters, and the use of swear words and ethnopaulisms created by Kenyans for different groups of tourists marks their agency in a context of strong interdependencies. The analysis of the use of "bad language" in a diverse touristic transgressive setting is the innovative focus of this contribution. Likewise, Janine Traber analyzes a touristic hotspot, the Spanish island Majorca in the Mediterranean Sea, which has turned into a "party island" in its touristic centers, with immense inflows of German and British tourists. Traber focuses on the semiosis of the "sexy banana", a touristic accessory and a phallic symbol that is ubiquitous in the Majorcan tourism sector. Starting off from this, she analyzes the context of transgressive and offensive language with a critical focus on gender. Eventually, she also includes patterns of interaction between tourists and migrants – how transgressive tourist language contributes to "desexualized" images of the latter. In the following contribution by Anna-Brita Stenström, we move back into daily life routines. Her careful analysis of English- and Spanish-speaking teenagers' use of rude vocatives includes data from several Latin American and European countries and comes to the conclusion that rude vocatives may actually serve in-group bonding purposes and function as intimacy markers, while specific swear terms analyzed by her can be understood as intensifiers in interaction but no longer as purely "bad language". This innovative and cross-continental chapter challenges established views on teenagers' "rude" or "vulgar" language. Elisabeth Steinbach-Eicke and Sven Eicke's contribution on Ancient Egyptian swearing and cursing, finally, demonstrates that the communication with the nether world, the gods and the dead were as much shaped by transgression and trashy performance as communication in daily-life encounters. Their analysis of antique curses provides insights into historical vulgarity and its ritual frameworks.

We have started with reflections on the construction of the trickster-like Other's Other, the role swearing plays in it, the meanings of the bitter laugh and powerful curses, as well as the semiotics of substance and performance.

This book offers a meandering walk through the sites of transgression, inversion, mimesis and ruination. In the last chapter, we return to the Other's Other, as a performative concept of youthful resistance. From there, we are safely picked up by Neal Norrick, whose conclusion and outlook provides – as a sweeping blow – a brief yet exhaustive afterword to the present volume. From a pragmaticist's perspective, Norrick summarizes the most salient statements and findings of the studies and discusses them with regard to current trends and theory in swearing research within the field of (socio)pragmatics. This outlook on further research in the field of swearing and cursing marks this book's aspiring intention to inspire colleagues to further pursue a holistic and transdisciplinary pathway in the study of swear words and their context.

References

Allan, Keith and Kate Burridge. 2006. *Forbidden Words. Taboo and the Censoring of Language*. Cambridge: Cambridge University Press.
Attardo, Salvatore (ed.). 2014. *Encyclopaedia of Humor Studies*. Los Angeles: Sage.
Barasch, Frances K. 1985. The grotesque as a comic genre. *Modern Language Studies* 15 (1): 3–11.
Barbalet, Jack M. 2001. *Emotion, Social Theory, and Social Structure*. Cambridge: Cambridge University Press.
Barthes, Roland. 1973. *Le plaisir du texte*. Paris: Éditions du Seuil.
Bernstein, Michael A. 1992. *Bitter Carnival*. Princeton: Princeton University Press.
Billig, Michael. 2005. *Laughter and Ridicule*. London: Sage.
Blommaert, Jan. 2013. *Ethnography, Superdiversity and Linguistic Landscapes*. Bristol: Multilingual Matters.
de Boeck, Filip. 2004 On being Shege in Kinshasa: Children, the occult and the street. In Theodore Trefon (ed.), *Reinventing Order in the Congo: How People Respond to State Failure in Kinshasa: How People Respond to State Failure in the Kinshasa*, 155–173. London: Zed Books.
Boxer, Diana and Florencia Cortés-Conde. 1997. From bonding to biting: Conversational joking and identity display. *Journal of Pragmatics* 27: 275–294.
Chow, Rey. 2014. *Not like a Native Speaker. On Languaging as a Postcolonial Experience*. New York: Columbia University Press.
Deumert, Ana. 2014. *Sociolinguistics and Mobile Communication*. Edinburgh: Edinburgh University Press.
Dickens, Charles. 1853. *Bleak House*. London: Bradbury & Evans.
Donne, John. 1996 [1595]. The flea. In Margaret Ferguson, Mary Jo Salter and Jon Stallworthy (eds.), *The Norton Anthology of Poetry*, 309. London/New York: Norton.
Fanon, Frantz. 1967 [1952]. *Black Skin, White Masks*. London: Pluto.
Goffman, Erving 1978. Response cries. *Language* 54 (4): 787–815.
Goldstein, Donna. 2013. *Laughter out of Place*. Berkeley: University of California Press.

Heinonen, Paula. 2011. *Youth Gangs and Street Children. Culture, Nurture and Masculinity in Ethiopia*. New York/Oxford: Berghahn.
Herzog, Werner. 2003 [1972]. *Aguirre: Der Zorn Gottes*. Berlin: Studiocanal.
Herzog, Werner. 2012 [1999]. *Mein liebster Feind*. Berlin: Studiocanal.
Irigaray, Luce. 1985. *This Sex which is not One*. Ithaca, NY: Cornell University Press.
Jay, Timothy B. 2000. *Why we Curse. A Neuro-Psycho-Social Theory of Speech*. Amsterdam/Philadelphia: Benjamins.
Jay, Timothy B. 2009a. The utility and ubiquity of taboo words. *Perspectives on Psychological Science* 4: 153–161.
Jay, Timothy B. 2009b. Do offensive words harm people? *Psychology, Public Policy, and Law* 15: 81–101.
Jay, Timothy B. and Kristin Janschewitz. 2008. The pragmatics of swearing. *Journal of Politeness Research: Language, Behavior, Culture* 4: 267–288.
Kamensky, Jane. 2001. Words, witches, and women trouble: Witchcraft, disorderly speech, and gender boundaries in Puritan New England. In Brian P. Levack (ed.), *New Perspectives on Witchcraft, Magic and Demonology, Vol. 4, Gender and Witchcraft*, 196–217. New York/London: Routledge.
Kerr, Michael. 2002. *You Can't Be Serious: Putting Humor to Work*. Toronto: Hushion House.
Kristeva, Julia. 1980. *Pouvoirs de l'horreur*. Paris: Seuil.
Lewis, M. Paul, Gary F. Simons and Charles D. Fennig (eds.). 2016. *Ethnologue: Languages of the World, Nineteenth Edition*. Dallas: SIL. http://www.ethnologue.com (accessed 15 November 2016).
Ljung, Magnus. 2010. *Swearing: A Cross-cultural Linguistic Study*. Basingstoke: Palgrave Macmillan.
Menninghaus, Winfried. 1999. *Ekel*. Frankfurt/Main: Suhrkamp.
Mignolo, Walter D. 2002. The geopolitics of knowledge and the colonial difference. *The South Atlantic Quarterly* 101 (1): 57–96.
Mohlich, Helmut W. 1977. Offensive language among adolescent girls at the Kenyan coast. *Paraphernalia* 3: 21–55.
Mohr, Melissa. 2013. *Holy Sh*t: A Brief History of Swearing*. New York: Oxford University Press.
Nassenstein, Nico. 2014. *A Grammatical Study of the Youth Language Yanké*. Munich: LINCOM.
Norrick, Neal R. and Claudia Bubel. 2009. Direct addresses as a resource for humor. In Neal R. Norrick and Claudia Bubel (eds.), *Humor in Interaction*, 29–48. Amsterdam/Philadelphia: Benjamins.
Norrick, Neal R. and Delia Chiaro (eds.). 2009. *Humor in Interaction*. Amsterdam/Philadelphia: Benjamins.
Pinker, Steven A. 2007. *The Stuff of Thought*. New York: Viking.
Poyatos, Fernando. 2002. *Nonverbal Communication across Disciplines, Vol. 2. Paralanguage, Kinesics, Silence, Personal and Environmental Interaction*. Amsterdam/Philadelphia: Benjamins.
Rowe, Kathleen. 1995. *The Unruly Woman*. Austin: University of Texas Press.
Saddik, Annette J. 2015. *Tennessee Williams and the Theatre of Excess. The Strange, the Crazed, the Queer*. Cambridge: Cambridge University Press.
Schaffer, Guy. 2015. Queering waste through camp. *Discard Studies*. https://discardstudies.com/2015/02/27/queering-waste-through-camp/.
Shimizu, Kiyoshi. 1980. *Comparative Jukunoid*. Vienna: Afro-Pub.

Staiger, Janet. 1991. Seeing stars. In Christine Gledhill (ed.), *Stardom. Industry of Desire*, 3–16. London/New York: Routledge.
Storch, Anne. 2011. *Secret Manipulations*. New York: Oxford University Press.
Swart, Sandra. 2009. "The terrible laughter of the Afrikaner" – Towards a social history of humor. *Journal of Social History* 2009: 889–917.
Taussig, Michael. 1993. *Mimesis and Alterity. A Particular History of the Senses*. New York/London: Routledge.
Tuhiwai Smith, Linda. 2012. *Decolonizing Methodologies*. London: Zed.
Vingerhoets, Ad, Lauren M. Bylsma and Cornelis de Vlam. 2013. Swearing: A biopsychosocial perspective. *Psychological Topics* 22 (2): 287–304.
Wilson, Deirdre and Dan Sperber. 1992. *Meaning and Relevance*. Cambridge: Cambridge University Press.

Timothy Jay
2 Ten issues facing taboo word scholars

Abstract: This reflection addresses ten methodological issues language scholars face when conducting research on *taboo words* (defined in Section 1). Finding ways of conducting meaningful research involving taboo words has been my primary scholarly endeavor since 1972 and is rooted in my training in psychological science methods. The major question for me is what methods are appropriate for conducting and reporting research on taboo words?

Years ago (Jay 1977) I addressed methodological problems with research on taboo words, such as how to define the category of taboo words or to obtain accurate word frequency and word offensiveness data. At that time I noted that some standard procedures needed to be established. Unfortunately, in 1970s there was scant research on the topic of how to do such research. Since then a significant body of scholarly research has accumulated (e.g. Bergen 2016; Beers Fägersten and Stapleton 2017; Jay 2009). However, some of the methodological problems that were identified years ago remain with us (e.g. defining the category of taboo words) and a set of new problems have arisen (e.g. describing the brain mechanisms underlying swearing and accounting for cross-cultural differences in swearing).

My goal is to capture the major issues that we face in order to improve the ways we conduct our research, making our efforts more meaningful. These are issues involved in taboo word research that we scholars need to address at some point in our research programs, including those associated with publishing our work. My reflection draws on the lessons learned from doing research with taboo words.

2.1 Defining the category of taboo words

Once the subject matter has been properly defined, a research plan can be built. The first goal of research is *to describe* the phenomenon of interest. The term *taboo* refers to a prohibited or restricted social custom; thus, taboo words are those with restrictions on their usage. Here the term *taboo words* is used collectively to refer to several semantic categories that comprise the corpus of words in many languages that are restricted in usage. We should recognize taboo words as a category of words that includes the following subcategories of offensive words and references: profanity/blasphemy, obscenity/indecency, slang, sex words (for body parts and behaviors), name calling, scatology, racist/gender/ethnic slurs, and vulgarity. Each of these subcategories contains different but overlapping sets of words. Problems in the past have arisen when scholars were not clear in defining what they were studying, for example, using too broadly a specific term such as *profanity* (religious word taboos) or *obscenity* (legally defined sexual and excretory word taboos). The goal for scholars is to be as clear and accurate as possible when defining what they are studying, the topic of their concerns. For a detailed discussion of definitional problems, see Adams (2016), Croom (2014), or Jay (1992, 2000, 2003, 2009, 2017).

Taboo words can be single words but also phrases and conventionalized, insulting emotional expressions and idioms, for example, *you think your shit don't stink, you don't know your ass from your elbow*, or as translated literally from Farsi, *what did you do, eat donkey brain*? We can see what kinds of word taboos exist in a culture by looking at the use of non-taboo euphemisms, which are acceptable words used to replace taboo words. Examples in American English are saying *sugar* instead of *shit*, *darn* instead of *damn*, or *jeezum crow* instead of *Jesus Christ!* The euphemistic expressions stand in as place markers for their more taboo counterparts, which some speakers are reluctant to utter publicly.

Along with knowing why people use taboo words, it is necessary to understand the shades of meaning of taboo words. The categories and sub-categories of taboo words are complex and one has to have a thorough knowledge of the language in question to appreciate the shades of meaning and level of offensiveness of any single word or phrase within a category. Consider the work of Leo Rosten (1968), who examined the different shades of Yiddish insults, such as different ways to refer to a person who is inept: *shlemiel, shlepper, shlimazl, shmegegge*, or *shmo*. If you do not understand Yiddish, you do not appreciate the different shades of meaning implied by these insults. The point is that when we study the meaning of taboo words in a native or non-native language, we need knowledge of what we are trying to analyze in the first place. Without a native speaker's knowledge we might only understand that a word is a taboo word *but* not understand the finer nuances of its uses and offensiveness or recognize the contexts where its use is inappropriate. Native speakers know how to employ pragmatic strategies involving slurs and insults that non-natives or language learners, due to lack of exposure, have not yet acquired.

We must be clear about the taboo words we are studying. Are they sexual terms, insults, religious terms, or slang? In describing the category or sub-category of taboo words, we must not intimate that taboo words are separate from our general semantic lexicon, because taboo and non-taboo words coexist. Consider that sexuality can be described in clinical terms (*intercourse*) as well as in vulgar terms (*fucking*). The referent is the same but the expression used is quite different. Taboo words have a direct semantic connection to clinical terms for the same referent; these terms are not isolated from each other. Taboo words, although studied separately in many cases by those researching taboo words, are part of our general lexicon and cannot wholly be divorced from the general lexicon.

Structure versus function: Describing the subject of taboo word research by delineating the semantic categories involved, that is, the semantic basis for taboo words, is what is called the *structural* approach to taboo words. A good example of the structural approach to language can be found in any of Noam Chomsky's early works on linguistics (e.g. Chomsky 1957), which outlined the grammatical structure of language (and, to a much lesser extent, semantics) with little attention to *why* people speak to each other. The structuralist wants to know if sentence X is a well-formed sentence or what the relationship is between sentence X and sentence Y.

In contrast, the *functionalist* wants to know *why* the speaker said sentence X. As appealing as the structural approach is for many language scholars, it is insufficient to capture all of the interpersonal dynamics involved in the use of taboo words, for example, through humor, self-deprecation, anger, retaliation, or social bonding. What is needed for a complete picture of taboo word use is the elaboration of various uses or functions that taboo words provide for their speakers (and listeners). Functionalism requires research on the behavior behind taboo word use.

2.2 Specifying the behaviors that constitute swearing

The question of categories addresses the nature of the words under study but does not address the question of how and why people use taboo words in public, that is, why they are swearing. To answer questions about behaviors associated with taboo word use we have to look at what people are doing with these words. In other words, we must examine the nature of human interactions, such as what the speaker is trying to achieve with taboo words and how the listener is reacting to them. What are the pragmatics of swear words? What is it that people are doing with them?

Swearing is the use of offensive emotional speech to express our feelings and convey them to others. The primary purpose for using taboo words is emotional expression; venting anger and frustration are good examples of this. Another purpose is to communicate our emotions to others so that they know what we are feeling and will perhaps be affected by the words we use. This might achieve a social goal for us, such as receiving an apology, starting an argument, or gaining some compassion from others. To address the personal and social goals of swearing, we need to know why or how people are using words, or their pragmatic function. Understanding the function of swearing requires knowledge of what we think people are trying to do. These functions are based on our (biased) cultural models of anger, frustration, self-deprecation and humor. The functional approach determines what people are doing with words, the kinds of issues and analysis addressed by Herb Clark (1996) in his book, *Using Language*.

In order to avoid breaking conventions or laws, native speakers carry with them a cultural knowledge of when and how to use taboo words. We also use this sociopragmatic knowledge when we comprehend what others are saying. The notion that there are normative functions for taboo word use implies that there are cultural practices that native speakers learn in order to help them decide what the proper and improper uses of taboo words are; for example, when to tell an offensive joke. If native speakers learn how to use taboo words through experience this means that young children and non-native speakers will be deficient or naïve with respect to adult taboo word competency.

The notion of variable speaker expertise with taboo words raises the *problem of subjectivity*. How do we decide what a child or non-native speaker might intend to do with taboo words? Naïve speakers might understand the meaning of a given taboo word but use the term differently from competent native speakers. Non-native speakers and children, because of their upbringing and education, just may not have had access to learning the pragmatics of swear words, and are thus naïve toward them. We observers (subjectively) might misinterpret what others are doing with taboo words when we listen to children or non-native speakers: did they intend to be insulting or not? Consider complex social problems involving sexual harassment or hate speech; these concepts require a cultural knowledge and a sociopragmatic knowledge of the "who, what, where and when" regarding offensive speech. Changing the context of the speech, any of the cultural elements (who and where) may place the incident outside the definition of harassment. Saying "I'd like to fuck you" to a colleague at work is quite different from saying the same thing to your spouse in your bedroom. Some sociopragmatic experience is necessary to understand this.

My 47 years of research have driven home the point that swearing is a normal, predictable part of human communication. It is a normal human behavior, not a deviant form of communication. Native speakers know that the use of taboo words occurs in a context of general communication between people where one person is usually (but not always) expressing some form of emotion. This is not an oddity;

it's how people communicate emotionally. It is also normal for both children and non-native speakers to be eager to learn the meanings of the offensive words they encounter, whether they will ultimately use them or not.

Dewaele (2004) demonstrated that the emotional strength of swearwords and taboo words is perceived by native speakers to be higher than by non-native speakers. Further, the emotional strength of words is higher for non-natives who learned offensive words in natural contexts than for those those who learned them in a classroom setting. This raises a more general question regarding the relationship between emotion and speech. One of the more mysterious and unpredictable qualities of human communicative behavior is understanding how emotion is expressed through speech: How does anger or depression affect the way we talk and what we say? Can we control these kinds of problematic emotions that offend people? At what point do deep emotions affect speech production? Answering these questions leads to a paradox: we language scholars use *rational*, analytical tools of science in order to understand our involuntary and somewhat *irrational* emotional expressions (see Jay 2003). The pre-verbal or pre-linguistic stages prior to an act of swearing would seem to be impenetrable to linguistic analysis (semantics or grammar) – because the emotional stage and the language stage exist in different codes or formats. Swearing is in language but emotion is not: emotion is pre-verbal; it is not in language, yet.

2.3 Employing appropriate research methods

A good working knowledge of what kinds of research methods were employed in past research is necessary in order that we do not study questions that have already been answered, questions that may be irrelevant, and that we avoid questions that cannot be answered or may be irrelevant in their nature (e.g. What was the first swearword?). Knowledge of past research tells us which research methods should or should not be considered. More importantly, researchers need to address the question of what they are trying to achieve, i.e. what they are trying to find out with our research.

Due to differences in practices across language disciplines, not all research methods are of equal value to scholars. At present, a form of disciplinary isolation exists in language studies, as each discipline has its own preferred methods. Neuroscience, sociolinguistics, anthropology, philosophy, law, medicine, and psychology have different approaches and methods. Each field has its tried and tested methods. Ultimately a scholar has to make decisions based on where research is to be published, such as what journal and readers are the target audience. Each journal has its own scope, purpose, or aim. Find one that suits your needs.

Some suggestions to the novices: Be open minded, inclusive, and multidisciplinary in scope when you are able to do so. Recognize that our unique disciplines usually force upon us a form of adherence to the conventions of our discipline which dictate where and how we publish our research. Each of us, because of these cross-disciplinary differences in training, studies swearing differently. A communication studies scholar would construct imaginary scenarios that use taboo words but these scenarios would not include the actual utterances that a psychologist's field study would report. We venture into troubled waters when we attempt to use methods that are outside of our training. When starting research, we need to stick with the methods we trust the most and not use methods that are outside of our expertise. Our expertise will expand with experience.

Before collecting new data, be aware of what data have already been collected in the form of databases of speech, dialogues or corpus linguistics data. Decide whether previous work is appropriate for your purposes. Some data might be too old or too restricted; it might sample people who are older/younger, more/less religious, or more/less educated than your target population. Researchers who study the frequency or the offensiveness of language samples will have to collect normative data from their own participants because using data from a different population will not coincide with these participants' perceptions and attitudes.

As for publishing research on taboo words, realize that there are many scholarly journals dedicated to the study of language; choose one that fits your outlook and intended audience in terms of methodology and theory. Be careful when framing the scope and meaning of your work. Swearing is a spoken behavior that occurs when people become emotional. It would not be accurate to describe constructed texts from motion pictures, the Bible or Shakespeare's work as natural (real world) acts of swearing, although they do involve the use of taboo words.

2.4 Accounting for how context affects taboo words

The comprehension and production of taboo word expressions is entirely context-dependent. Change the location, social function, or relationship between the speaker and listener and we change the meaning of what is said. The contextual nature of swearing will be obvious to the experienced researcher. The task at hand is to account for the contextual variables that affect how taboo words are used, how they are produced and understood, as well as, in pragmatic terms, what is presupposed or implied.

I have demonstrated people's sensitivity to contextual variables by asking participants to rate the offensiveness or likelihood of different combinations of speakers, words, and locations, for example, *The janitor said "hell" in the parking lot* versus *The student said "shit" in the dean's office* (Jay 1992). We (Jay and Janschewitz 2008) have also demonstrated that native speakers of English are more sensitive to contextual changes in swearing than non-natives and that it takes some time to become familiar to the socio-contextual variables that affect swearing.[1] For example, a non-native speaker might know that *shit* is a taboo word but not be sensitive to where it can (locker room) or cannot be used (dinner with grandparents). Dewaele (2010) has published extensively on L1 versus LX language differences with respect to swearing and the use of taboo words. He has demonstrated, for instance, that non-natives acquire the nuances of swearing better through direct experience in the new language community than through classroom-only exercises.

We can expect to find differences based on age, gender, race and occupation as a function of a language community's values: some communities will be more liberal than others and we will hear swearing there. Swearing is a function of community values. Swearing is also part of masculinity or ritual performances of power associated not so much with liberality but with aspects of gender roles. Different dialects of the same language will also differ according to geographic location and socio-economic status. For those interested in geographical differences in spoken English, there is a valuable resource in the publication of *DARE: Dictionary of American Regional English* (Cassidy 1985). As a native of the state of Ohio, I found that insults I had heard growing up, such as *pus gut* (fat person) or *briar hopper* (similar to *hillbilly*, referring to a rural mountain dweller) were only used and known in southwestern Ohio and not elsewhere in the USA. DARE documents these kinds of regional differences in English language word use: location makes a difference. One of the important lessons in relation to context is that these geographical and intrapersonal

---

[1] The concept of "native speakers" here is based on monolingual speakers or speakers whose mother tongue is English and who at maximum have acquired some knowledge of other languages in school or in their professional careers. Thus, it is a Euro-American perspective, not necessarily one that focuses on a multilingual Nigerian or Singaporean, who may also be considered a "native" speaker of English elsewhere.

differences are critical to understanding how and why people say taboo words (with friends) or do not say taboo words (with strangers) in other contexts. I would not call someone a *briar hopper* where I live now in Massachusetts because no one would understand what it meant.

The main point here is to be sensitive to and to report contextual nuances that affect swearing. Scholars should not reduce or gloss over these important contextual differences in order to report "averages". Answering questions such as "What does the average person say?" glosses over the importance of contextual and personal differences.

2.5 Accounting for how the taboo lexicon evolves from childhood to adulthood

Although language scholars understand that vocabulary changes dramatically from infancy to adulthood, little research has been dedicated to how the swearing lexicon develops with age in the context of a child's evolving social, emotional, and psychological awareness. Our research (Jay and Jay 2013) has examined gender, age, and historical differences in taboo word use, outlining how boys' and girls' lexica changed as they matured.

Children start swearing as soon as they can speak. The extent of the taboo lexicon of three- to four-year olds is impressive; children at these ages are learning name-calling and psychosocial insults, abusive language, common profanities, scatological language, and gender-related insults. The growth in the taboo lexicon starts to level off at about the time children enter elementary school in the United States. Our analysis of child swearing data by age indicated that, with age, the child swearing lexicon changed to become more adultlike. The youngest age groups tended to share few taboo words with adults and did not show significant correlations with adults based on word frequency.

Overall, children showed gender differences in word frequency similar to those found with adults (men swear more than women in public), but the lexica of boys and girls were more different than those of adult men and women, as evidenced by the many points of divergence over time in boys' and girls' vocabularies. The gender difference in word frequency became most obvious at older ages (generally over 5 years), suggesting that the time of transition to school is when adultlike gendered habits underlying emotional expression start to become salient.

Historically speaking, the most frequent words used by adults and children have remained fairly stable, with some minor changes emerging over the last 40 years. Our 2013 study reported similarities and differences in data that we collected during the 1980s compared to our data on taboo word usage recorded 30 years later. There was some differentiation over time in the content of children's taboo lexica. For taboo words that were recorded during both time periods, the frequency relationship can be described by as a significant positive correlation: $r(57) = .67$, $p < .001$. This correlation indicated that children's high-frequency taboo utterances (e.g. *shit*) in the 1980s also tend to be high-frequency taboo utterances in the 2013 sample. Although non-scholars imagine that taboo vocabularies shift dramatically over time, stability is more the rule according to these data.

There are very few if any developmental studies like this one. Obviously, more work needs to be done to show how children acquire and expand the taboo lexicon, especially in non-English societies and between different income/education groups. I should offer a final suggestion: if you are working with non-English participants/speakers, you need to address the differences between boys' and girls' taboo word use and address how children's taboo word use changes as they mature.

2.6 Documenting how the taboo lexicon has evolved historically

The words in our taboo lexica change over time. The potency of some offensive words also declines over time. Profane epithets such as *Jesus Christ!* and *Goddamn!*, once forbidden, are now common. The epithet *sucks*, once referring to oral sex in the 1960s, has now lost that taboo association. The spoken lexicon is organic; it changes and evolves over time. Some words become obsolete and are dropped from usage; other words, especially slang terms, slurs, and insults are coined anew and enter the spoken lexicon. By the time we reach adulthood, it becomes obvious to us that some words have changed their meaning or emotional potency over time. Older insults can lose their power to offend. This means that scholars have to be aware of the evolution of the taboo lexicon over time – the birth and death of taboo words. Some frequent words (*fuck, shit*) have appeared fairly consistently over centuries; others (*lickspittle, milksop*) have not.

Some taboo language changes reflect general cultural value trends, such as cultural shifts from liberal to more conservative values or vice versa. Cultural shifts occurred amidst repressive trends during the Victorian Era in Europe and during the 1920s "prohibition era" in the USA. Language restrictions aligned with these cultural shifts also reflected liberal to conservative values, such that words that were once acceptable become tabooed. I have outlined these kinds of offensive and inappropriate behavior shifts in American history and how they affect our emotional expressions (Jay 2017).

As a consequence of changes in a culture's sociopolitical atmosphere and media standards, our sensitivity to and use of taboo words and insults aligns with whether we grew up during more conservative or liberal trends(e.g. 1960s in the USA). For example, we (Jay 2000) have recorded how men and women in nursing homes will bring to that setting the offensive speech learned during their childhood and adolescent years. We reported 90-year-olds using words like, *hell, damn* or *Jesus Christ!* However, these are not the words that millennials will use when they turn 90. Millennials are more likely to say *fuck* and *motherfucker* than their grandparents. The millennials in their old age will use words that were offensive (but frequent) in the 21st century. We can see shifts in speech etiquette like these over time by looking at media standards, for example, by looking at what offensive words were acceptable in motion pictures or television over time. Obscene, indecent, and insulting epithets that were banned in the early 1900s are now commonplace in our media (Jay 1992, 2017).

2.7 Addressing intra-cultural and cross-cultural differences in taboo word use

One of the primary aims of this book (and the conference which gave rise to it) was to document and discuss current research on swearing in different social situations and geographic locations. Such an effort is bound to offer new insights into similarities and differences in how people use taboo words. The emergence of cross-cultural similarities reveals commonalities in the ways humans express their emotions with taboo words. However, cross-cultural *differences* have emphasized the need to document the unique ways in which different people express themselves. As a consequence, I emphasize that it is not informative for scholars to refer to an "average" speaker cross-culturally and that we should not gloss over cross-cultural differences.

Cultural research on swearing and cursing also needs to address the language practices of marginalized and understudied communities on a global basis; otherwise we will only develop an understanding of swearing that is limited in application. As an example, studies of offensive words in American English are generally restricted in focus to information derived from college students or obtained though surveys conducted over the internet. As a result, we have little information from English speakers in marginalized communities who do not attend colleges or who do not own or use internet communication architecture (see Jay and Jay 2013). Until scholars address these sampling limitations we will continue to perpetuate an inaccurate account of how speakers from all social strata understand and use swearwords.

Another problem for those who study non-native language is that we tend to interpret taboo words in another language through the filter of our native languages (the subjectivity problem). We native English speakers assess what foreign speakers mean when using sexual terminology by using what we know about English terms for sex. As an example of the interpretation problem, I have reported research on the coprolalic words (uncontrollable swearing) that non-English-speaking Tourette's syndrome patients say in their native tongues. Where a English speaking Touretter would utter offensive words such as *shit* or *pussy* or *fuck*, Brazilian researchers (Cardoso, Veado and de Oliveira 1996) translated Touretters' outbursts such as *merda* and *buceta* as *faeces* and *vagina* rather than *shit* and *pussy*. Touretters do not utter clinical terms when they experience their tics; they say the most socially unacceptable words in their lexicon. These translations misinterpret what speakers really said.

Translations from other languages can become more accurate when we have more experience with the culture (not just the words) we are studying, as Dewaele (2004, 2010) has shown. In this case, knowledge from a subdiscipline such as anthropological linguistics may help overcome the translation challenge. This subjectivity problem is not unlike the problem of using our adult lexicon to interpret children's swearing – words that we adults hear as inoffensive (*nerd* or *baby*) are deemed to be very offensive by young children. Here again, we have little research to guide us on what children know about taboo words (Jay and Jay 2013). The point here is to be aware of historical, developmental, and cross-cultural differences that lead to misinterpretations regarding what other speakers mean when they swear. The problem calls for us to develop our understanding of the people we are studying, as well as using informants and translators who can accurately transcribe/interpret what we are hearing.

Here's a final example of how interpretations can go amiss. I once enrolled in a graduate level course on the topic of "metaphors for love" at the University of Massachusetts. Most of the graduate students, and the instructor himself, were non-native English speakers. The instructor was collecting love metaphors in English for a book on the topic which was published several months later. As I studied his metaphor book, I noticed that the analysis did not cover what I would call the more "lusty" aspects of how native English speakers talk about love, sex and interpersonal relationships – the kind of expressions that in the wrong context might constitute sexual harassment, or unwanted sexual comments such as: *you like to sleep around, you are a tramp, we had a quickie, we humped each other* or *s/he's a nice piece of ass* (see Jay 2000). The author of the metaphor book analyzed the affectionate and inoffensive metaphors for love without digging down into how native American English speakers talk about sexual relationships through the use of offensive figurative language.

2.8 Accounting for physiological and emotional correlates of swearing

How the brain is involved in swearing is of primary interest to psychologists and neuroscientists like me. Neuroscience issues have been of lesser concern for those conducting research in the humanities, but even so, accounting for the biological genesis of taboo speech is important for us to understand the whole person. Emotional expressions, to be completely addressed, require knowledge of the physiological correlates underlying emotion: how does a person generate an expression using taboo words from a preverbal feeling (usually anger or frustration?). This kind of knowledge is also important for understanding neurological disorders – people who swear compulsively or cannot swear at all.

Whether you can use neuroscience in your scholarship or not, many scholars of taboo language will be enlightened by a study of the subcortical brain areas involved in swearing (the limbic system, amygdala, and basal ganglia) in order to understand how swearing is affected by brain damage, stroke, Tourette's syndrome or prescription medications. Neuroscience literature can also provide a better understanding of personality differences in swearing that are the product of factors such as religiosity, sexual anxiety/guilt, Type A personality, extroversion, and agreeableness. These are significant psychological aspects of personality. When looking at taboo language in public or in written accounts it is always important to ask, what emotion is being expressed? We can witness emotion at work in public and private places because we have learned how to perceive emotion in others from an early age. However, we do not accurately perceive emotion very well in online or written samples, and this difficulty often leads to misunderstandings in online discourse (Jay 2018).

One final issue involves how multilingual speakers experience emotions in different languages. As a native English speaker, I feel something when I say "shit!" but I do not feel the same when I say *"merde"* or *"scheiße."* Dewaele's research (2004, 2010) has addressed these kinds of multilingual issues, indicating that native speakers feel more emotion in their native languages than they do in non-native languages. If you speak more than one language, you will know what I mean.

2.9 Addressing cross-disciplinary approaches to taboo word research

One of the major outcomes of reading a book like this one, or attending the conference that gave rise to it, is a better appreciation of cross-disciplinary approaches to the topic of offensive speech. Although we will gain a better understanding of how our diverse colleagues conduct their scholarship and what they have found, a grand theory tying together all of these diverse findings is not possible as a result. I have speculated on the nature of a unified theory in psychology (Jay 2000, 2003, 2009), but I am waiting to see what will evolve from these kinds of efforts. Taboo word scholars should not expect in the future to hear of a satisfactory, unified, multidisciplinary theory of swearing. A unified theory will not accrue because our cross-disciplinary research goals and scholarship standards differ greatly across the many disciplines studying swearing.

What we can expect to hear about future swearing research is more in line with the recent book by Beers Fägersten and Stapleton (2017), which exposes new research on non-English languages, employing a variety of different research methods. These kinds of wide-ranging topics will give rise to more interest and research in our various disciplines. This broad interest was not present 50 years ago. When I started studying the literature on taboo words in the 1960s, I had to scour research in several disciplines: psychology, sociology, criminal justice, communication studies, mass media, religion, law, medicine, linguistics, neurology, etc. Now, because there is much more research and scholarship in any single discipline, scholars can comfortably nestle within their own discipline without venturing to read what is published outside; but to do so would be a mistake. Even though it is difficult to understand the methods and jargon emerging from another area of study, do not be reluctant to read the research arising in other disciplines.

2.10 Facing the broader political issues surrounding swearing

Each of us lives in a community and we work in a community of scholars and administrators. I work in a psychology department with a handful of colleagues who are aware of my studies, but I doubt any of them actually read what I publish in psychology and related journals. Outside of my department, I will claim that most of my colleagues have very little idea of what I study or publish. Most of you are probably in a similar situation. In addition to this kind of misunderstanding, we who study taboo words are all subject to the scrutiny and evaluation (for advancement and tenure decisions) of administrators, who, similar to our teaching colleagues, may have little understanding or appreciation of what is takes to be a scholar of taboo words. Do not expect colleagues and administrators to understand what you do or to admire what you study. Some people just will not accept taboo word research as the legitimate field of study that it is, one which merits departmental advancement and tenure (I faced this attitude directly by one of my deans). We study the language that many religious community members explicitly want to prohibit; yet those kinds of attitudes should not restrict our work on campus.

Consider how we study taboo topics, but not the deepest, darkest of psychological secrets (incest, suicide, depression, drug abuse) that lead people to seek the help of mental health workers. Psychiatrists work with patients who have experienced traumas that are difficult to put into words; the patients' problems are in a sense *unspeakable*, maybe even too dark to bring into consciousness. We swearing scholars in this volume study the *speakable taboos*: words that are not supposed to be said in public but *are* said in public. These words are not unspeakable, they are spoken publically, whether our religious colleagues or those with a different moral perspective like it or not. With this apparent social dilemma, studying what shouldn't be said, come obvious social and political consequences. Studying taboos will always be controversial because the subject of the research is inherently taboo too. In a sense, we become contaminated by the words we study. Having faced these issues for four decades, I urge all scholars to persist despite negative reactions from some of our colleagues, administrators, and editors.

It is also our responsibility to debunk myths and misrepresentations of taboo speech and swearing behaviors – that *fuck* is an old acronym, that swearing is abnormal, the sign of an impoverished vocabulary, or mainly a problem for children and teenagers. Whether we like it or not, taboo word research involves political issues (see Jay 2000).

What we study is important and it is associated with social and political problems of our times, such as sexual harassment, discrimination, hate speech, workplace standards, obscenity and more. These are topics that bother a lot of people – our colleagues included. Our research can provide, for all who read it, a better understanding of how humans communicate their emotions in different cultures and situations. We cannot escape the fact that what we study is somewhat dangerous, or at least offensive to others, based on personality factors such as others' religiosity or sexual anxiety. In the end, what we are studying is now a legitimate area of scholarly interest in the context of the important social problems just mentioned. Swearing is a damned interesting and damned persistent behavior, but we scholars need not be damned for studying swearing!

References

Adams, Michael. 2016. *In Praise of Profanity*. New York: Oxford University Press.
Beers Fägersten, Kristy and Karyn Stapleton (eds.). 2017. *Advances in Swearing Research: New Contexts and New Languages*. Amsterdam/Philadelphia: John Benjamins.
Bergen, Benjamin. 2016. *What the F: What Swearing Reveals About Our Language, Our Brains, and Ourselves*. New York: Basic Books.
Cardoso, Francisco, Claudio Veado and Jose Teotonio de Oliveira. 1996. A Brazilian Cohort of Patients with Tourette's Syndrome. *Journal of Neurology, Neurosurgery, and Psychiatry* 60: 209–212.
Cassidy, Frederic G. (ed.). 1985. *Dictionary of American Regional English. Vol. 1, A–C.* Cambridge, MA: The Belknap Press of Harvard University Press.
Chomsky, Noam. 1957. *Syntactic Structures*. The Hague, Netherlands: Mouton & Co.
Clark, Herbert. 1996. *Using Language*. Cambridge: Cambridge University Press.
Croom, Adam. 2014. The Semantics of Slurs: A Refutation of Pure Expressivism. *Language Sciences* 41: 227–242.
Dewaele, Jean-Marc. 2004. The Emotional Force of Swearwords and Taboo Words in the Speech of Multilinguals. *Journal of Multilingual and Multicultural Development* 25: 204–222
Dewaele, Jean-Marc. 2010. *Emotions in Multiple Languages*. London: Palgrave.
Jay, Kristin and Timothy B. Jay. 2013. A Child's Garden of Curses: A Gender, Historical, and Age-Related Evaluation of the Taboo Lexicon. *American Journal of Psychology* 126: 459–475.
Jay, Timothy B. 1977. Doing Research with Dirty Words. *Maledicta: The International Journal of Verbal Aggression* 1 (2): 234–256.
Jay, Timothy B. 1992. *Cursing in America*. Philadelphia, PA: John Benjamins.
Jay, Timothy B. 2000. *Why We Curse: A Neuro-Psycho-Social Theory of Speech*. Amsterdam/Philadelphia: John Benjamins.
Jay, Timothy B. 2003. *The Psychology of Language*. Upper Saddle River, NJ: Pearson.
Jay, Timothy B. 2009. The Utility and Ubiquity of Taboo Words. *Perspectives in Psychological Science* 4: 153–161.
Jay, Timothy B. 2017. *We Did What? Offensive and Inappropriate Behavior in American History*. Santa Barbara, CA: ABC-Clio.
Jay, Timothy B. 2018. Swearing, Moral Order, and Online Communication. *Journal of Language Aggression and Conflict* 6 (1): 107–126. https://doi.org/10.1075/jlac.00005.jay
Jay, Timothy B. and Kristin Janschewitz. 2008. The pragmatics of swearing. *Journal of Politeness Research: Language, Behavior, Culture* 4 (2): 267–288.
Rosten, Leo. 1968. *The Joys of Yiddish*. New York: McGraw-Hill.

Alexandra Y. Aikhenvald

3 "Damn your eyes!" (Not really): Imperative imprecatives, and curses as commands

Abstract: Curses, bad wishes, and maledictions – collectively referred to as imprecations, or imperatives – often appear in an imperative form, as if telling the addressee what to do and where to go, to their detriment. Despite their imperative disguise, they stand apart from true commands in their syntactic properties. Imperative forms have a multitude of uses: they often occur in greeting and farewell formulae, expressions of thanks, and other contexts, without any overtones of a command or a request. Imperative forms in imprecatives, curses and maledictions can be looked at on a par with such speech formulae. However, the "imperative disguise" of imprecations is not universal. An imperative form may be too strong to use in an imprecation or in a curse. This is the case in Manambu, a Papuan language from East Sepik Province (PNG). Tariana, an Arawak language from the multilingual Vaupés River Basin area in northwest Amazonia (Brazil), has a special "malefactive" imperative whose main meaning is to express bad wishes. The form itself was developed as a result of extensive contact with Tucano, the major lingua franca of the area. The discussion is based on immersion fieldwork by the author – the only way of experiencing and documenting the language in its spontaneous use.

3.1 Imperative imprecations: Setting the scene

Curses, bad wishes, and maledictions – collectively referred to as imprecations, or imperatives – are often phrased as if they were commands. They appear in an imperative form, as if telling the addressee what to do and where to go, to their detriment. Despite their imperative disguise, they stand apart from true commands.

Imperatives – whose prototypical function is to tell someone what to do – are versatile in their actual usage (see Aikhenvald 2017, and references there, for a cross-linguistic approach to imperatives and commands, and their functions and meanings). The meanings of positive and negative imperatives in English range from orders, commands, and demands to requests, pleas, advice, recommendations, warnings, instructions, invitations, and permissions. Add to this good wishes, as in *Have a good time*! and curses and imprecations – the expressions of swearing of all sorts, as in *Go to hell!*, *Damn it!*, *Bugger off!* or *Damn your eyes!* (see also Huddleston 2002: 929–931, Quirk et al. 1985: 831–832).

Using imperatives in curses and maledictions extends beyond familiar European languages. Thai boasts a number of abusive expressions with imperative forms, accompanied by terms for diseases to be inflicted upon the person being sworn at. The expression *ta:y hàa* (die + cholera-spirit), lit. 'die of cholera!', is frequently used in Thai "as a rude curse", "directed at a person, but more often used merely as an untargeted exclamation when things suddenly go wrong, for instance, while driving on a highway, one rounds a curve and sees large rocks on the road, or one is pounding nails and accidentally pounds one's own finger" (Tony Diller and Phichit Roinil, p.c.).[1]

Blessings and curses, a familiar feature of colourful interactions in Yiddish discourse, are often cast in imperatives, as in *Zol er lign in drerd* 'May he rot (lit. lie) in hell!' or *Zolstu geyn mit a klog iber di hayzer!* 'May you go with a lament from door to door' (that is, begging) (more examples are in Matisoff 2000: 69–78). So are curses in numerous Ethiopian languages, including Amharic and Gurage (Ethio-Semitic), Oromo (Cushitic), Wolayitta (Omotic), Nuer (Western Nilotic) (Baye Yimam 2013; Fekede Menuta and Fjeld 2016), and Dhasanaac (Cushitic: Tosco 2001: 280–281). Imperative forms feature prominently in curses and swearing expressions in Russian, e.g. *chert vozjmi* (devil take.IMPV) 'damn!' (lit. devil take) or *idi k chertu* (go.IMPV to devil) 'go to hell' (Xrakovskij and Volodin 2001: 236; see also Fjeld 2014: 213, on curses in Norwegian).

An insult or a curse in its imperative disguise may not share all the syntactic properties with imperatives in their prototypical use as directives. An utterance *Fuck you!* contains an imperative form. As shown by McCawley (1971: 3–4), this expression is very much unlike an imperative with a directive function, such as *Close the door!*

Firstly, it cannot be embedded: while it is possible to say *I said to close the door* one can hardly say **?I said to fuck you*. Secondly, it cannot be negated: **don't fuck you* is unacceptable. Thirdly, it cannot be accompanied by a marker of politeness *please*, a tag *won't you*, or rephrased as an emphatic using *do* support: none of **please fuck you*, **fuck you, won't you*, or **do fuck you* appear to

---

[1] The expression *dàek hàa* (eat [vulgar] + cholera.spirit), literally, 'may cholera eat (you)', can also be used as a curse, but is less common. This would be used, for instance, to address the driver of a car which suddenly cuts in front, nearly causing a crash. The curse will be addressed to the offending driver (who does not have to hear it). This can also be used when Thai friends are watching TV together and a populist politician comes on, making impossible promises (this phenomenon in Thai was signalled by Allan and Burridge 2006: 82, given in an incomplete form as *Tai hàa* 'Die of cholera') (Tony Diller and Phichit Roinil, p.c.).

be felicitous. In terms of its meanings and functions, a sentence like *Fuck Lyndon Johnson* is not an 'admonition to copulate with Lyndon Johnson'. Rather, this is a way of 'indicating disapproval' (McCawley 1971: 4).

An imprecation, or a curse, may share their form with an imperative. However, their illocutionary force remains fundamentally different: imprecations express emotional states rather than directive speech acts. This could be a reason why they tend to lack the many grammatical options available to imperatives in their directive functions.[2]

Imperative forms have a multitude of uses – they often appear in greeting and farewell formulae, expressions of thanks, marks of surprise, and turn-taking in discourse, without any overtones of a command or request. Imperative forms in imprecatives, curses, and maledictions, can be analysed on a par with such speech formulae. But is their imperative disguise universal? My own fieldwork on minority languages from two different parts of the world points towards a negative answer.

An imperative may be too strong to be used in imprecations. A brief illustration of this is in Section 2, based on my fieldwork on Manambu, from the Sepik region of New Guinea. Alternatively, a language may have a special "maledictive" form, exclusively for expressing bad wishes. The use and the origin of this form in Tariana, from north-west Amazonia in Brazil, is the topic of Section 3. The final section contains a brief summary.

3.2 Why not an imperative? The case of Manambu

An imperative form – used to direct people what to do – may be judged too strong to be used in curses and maledictions. The Manambu language of the East Sepik Province in New Guinea is a case in point.[3]

---

[2] In Bolinger's (1967: 346) words, expressions like *Go to hell* are "sentences to which no traditional grammarian will deny the status of commands, but would recognise as figures of speech". This captures the special status of imprecations cast as imperatives in English. A cross-linguistic investigation of how the grammatical possibilities of imperative forms in imprecations compare to imperatives in their directive functions (along the lines of McCawley 1971) is a matter for further research.

[3] Manambu is a member of the Ndu language family (together with Iatmul, Yalaku, and a number of other languages: see Aikhenvald 2008a, 2016a). My corpus of Manambu contains

Manambu is highly synthetic, predominantly suffixing, with just two prefixes – the second person imperative *a-* and the causative *kay-*. The imperative has its own paradigm which distinguishes three numbers (singular, dual, and plural) and three persons (first, second, and third). The third person imperative distinguishes feminine and masculine forms. The number distinction is neutralised in the second person: *a-* covers all of the singular, dual, and plural addressees (which can be disambiguated by using a personal pronoun). Manambu shares the property of having a full three-person imperative paradigm with other members of the Ndu family, and a few other Papuan languages, including Kombai-Korowai (de Vries 2017), Nungon (Sarvasy 2017), and Mauwake (Berghäll 2010).

The second person imperative is used in commands which presuppose immediate compliance (see Aikhenvald 2016a: 643–647). A typical example is in (1).

(1) a-wuk! *Manambu*
 IMPV-hear/listen/obey
 'Listen!' (said to a child who was not paying attention)

As in many other languages, a second person imperative can be used in greeting and farewell formulae, and also as an attention-getting device (see a summary in Aikhenvald 2016a: 248–9; 2017, for a general perspective). Third person imperatives can express a command to a third person, or an obligation. Third person imperatives are also used in instructions and descriptions of prescriptive ritual behaviour – what one has to do to avoid the negative consequences of a breach of a ritual. These meanings of the third person imperative are shown in (2).

(2) wuke-kwa *Manambu*
 hear/listen/obey-3person.IMPV.fem.sg
 (a) 'May she listen!'[4] (said to a mother about a little girl who was supposed to listen to a story told in her presence), or
 (b) 'She ought to obey' (lest she breaches a taboo)

---

over 30 hours of transcribed stories of various genres and conversations, and fieldnotes (from participant-observation-based work). I started working on Manambu in 1995. The bulk of the corpus was collected during four lengthy periods of fieldwork in Avatip and surrounding villages in 2001–2014. This corpus is being constantly expanded by on-going interaction with speakers of Manambu. Aikhenvald (2008a) is a comprehensive grammar of the language. Following the proper principles of fieldwork (see Dixon 2010: 309–330; Aikhenvald 2015: 20–29), I have carefully avoided elicitation from the lingua franca.

4 Note that third person imperatives are notoriously hard to translate into English. A translation using 'let' will inevitably involve additional overtones of 'someone letting something happen'.

Third person imperatives in Manambu do not presuppose immediate compliance; they may have overtones of indirect commands and wishes (similar to commands and wishes cast as subjunctive in Luwo: Storch 2014: 143–144, and to third person imperatives cross-linguistically: Aikhenvald 2010: 75).

In many languages across the world, an imperative is not the only means of expressing a directive. Other non-imperative forms can be co-opted to express wishes, suggestions, invitations, or requests. Cross-linguistically, these mechanisms – known as "command strategies" (Aikhenvald 2010: 256–295, 2017: 25–30) – include questions, statements, non-indicative modalities, and irrealis forms. Manambu employs the irrealis to express wishes and refer to events which have not been realised.

As we were attempting to go across a lake off the Sepik River, leading to the village of Yalaku, the water was quite low, and our overloaded canoe got stuck in the mud. Our driver exclaimed:

(3) War-ke-na!   *Manambu*
     go.up-IRREALIS-ACTION.FOCUS+3fem.sg
     'May she (canoe) go up!'

During my stays in the Manambu village of Avatip and in other Manambu-speaking communities and households, I witnessed numerous emotional outbursts – expressions of annoyance and anger in the form of maledictions and bad wishes, all cast either in third person imperatives or in irrealis. Imprecations and curses include the verb *kiya-* 'die' or *pusa-* 'rot', but not the euphemisms with the meaning of 'die, pass away' (e.g. *kuse-* 'finish').

A mother was exasperated by her five-year old daughter's constantly taking things that were not hers and consistently shouting at the top of her voice. The mother exclaimed:

(4) kiya-kwa   kwam te-na   *Manambu*
     die-IMPV.3p+fem.sg   mad   be-ACT.FOC+3fem.sg.SUBJ.NONPAST
     ñan
     child
     'May she die, crazy girl!'

A translation with 'may' adds an extra overtone of epistemic possibility or desire. Translations have to be taken as approximations to the actual meaning they have in the language discussed.

On another occasion, a speaker was annoyed at the reckless behaviour of a herd of ducks in her charge and said (5):

(5) kiya-kwa-di kiya-reb *Manambu*
 die-IMPV.3person-pl die-FULLY
 'May they die, fully!'

I was intrigued by the use of third person imperatives in these expressions, and asked my main teacher if it would be possible to replace *kiya-kwa* in (4) with the second person imperative of the verb 'die', *a-ki*! The answer was negative: I was told that the speaker did not really want her daughter to die, and so the second person imperative would be out of the question. Similarly, the speaker who said (5) did not want her ducks to die – she was simply fed up with their unruly behaviour.

The second person imperative *aki!* was indeed used in the context when the addressee was ordered to die. A speaker had captured a heron-type bird *wu-demali* which was believed to have been eating vegetables in her garden, struck it, and brought it home to die. As the bird lay in agony on the floor of the house, the speaker turned to it and said: *aki ya* (IMPV + die EMPHATIC) 'do die!' (see Aikhenvald 2008a: 367–368, for the description of that incident). She well and truly wanted the bird to die.

A second person imperative is a command par excellence, and it is meant to be realised and complied with. Hence the restriction on second person direct imperatives in imprecations and bad wishes: they are not true directives (in line with McCawley 1971).

Third person imperatives as curses and imprecations can be uttered in the presence of the addressee if the addressee is a child, or an animal. If they are directed at an adult, the person is typically absent. An irrealis command cast in second person is usually directed to a child, in their presence. A naughty girl of about three was paying no attention whatsoever to her mother warning her not to stand too close to the house entrance, for fear she might fall down. Houses in Avatip are high on stilts, and the danger was imminent. The mother shouted:

(6) Kiya-ke-na-ñen! *Manambu*
 die-IRR-ACT.FOC-2fem.sgSUBJ.NONPAST
 'May you die!' (to a naughty girl; meaning I am fed up with you)

Third person irrealis forms have not – so far – been attested in the context of imprecations and curses – perhaps, due to their optative meaning, expressing something one really wishes to happen. Imprecations cast as third person imperatives and as second person irrealis forms are described as 'someone talking when they are fed up' (*sep jina* 'body/skin is tired'), and occasionally with the verb *jike-* 'curse, swear'.[5]

The illocutionary force of a direct second person imperative determines its avoidance in Manambu imprecations and curses. Third person imperative and irrealis, with their meanings of indirect commands and wishes which may not be realised, are a more appropriate choice in such contexts.

3.3 Maledictive imperative in Tariana

A special form for maledictions and imprecations is a feature of Tariana, an endangered Arawak language spoken by no more that 100 people in three villages in the remote areas of north-west Amazonia, Brazil (at the border with Colombia), the basin of the Vaupés River.[6]

Tariana is the only Arawak language spoken in the Vaupés River Basin linguistic area (see a comprehensive analysis in Aikhenvald 2002, 2015: 75–83, and references there). It is surrounded by speakers of unrelated East Tucanoan languages, with whom the Tariana are in constant contact. The main principle of organization is "linguistic exogamy": one absolutely has to marry a spouse who speaks a different language (those who do not do this are "like dogs"). As a consequence, the area is highly multilingual. Every Tariana would know a few East Tucanoan languages, plus Portuguese and Spanish. The major language of the region is Tucano. Most younger speakers of Tariana are using Tucano on a daily basis. As a result, the language spoken by younger generation (aged between 35 and 60) is in many ways different from that of the elders

---

[5] The inventory of Manambu swear words is a matter for further investigation. The verb *jike-* 'swear, curse' is transitive; its object can be either a person cursed, or a swear-word (*sapes*). Swear words include body parts (e.g. *jupwi* 'buttocks'). During my fieldwork, I witnessed Manambu speakers swearing *sotto voce*. I could not always make out the nature of the curse; the curses were said to be so strong that people refused to repeat them to me. These include the curse *wagreb*, typically uttered in a low voice, and intended to inflict serious damage onto someone.

[6] I started working with the Tariana in 1991. The corpus consists of over 35 hours of recordings, including narratives of varied genres and conversations, in addition to fieldnotes. The corpus is being consistently augmented through on-going interactions with the speakers. No elicitation from the lingua franca has ever been used (a grammar, a study of contact induced change, and other materials on Tariana are detailed in Aikhenvald 2002, 2003, 2015). Examples are given in the practical orthography currently in use in the Tariana secondary school in Iauaretê, Amazonas, Brazil (developed jointly with the speakers).

(documented in the 1990s and the early 2000s), and bears a tangible influence from Tucano.

The long-term interaction based on institutionalized societal multilingualism between East Tucanoan languages and Tariana has resulted in rampant diffusion of grammatical and semantic patterns (though not so much of forms[7]) and calquing of categories. Comparison of Tariana with closely related Arawak languages (such as Baniwa/Kurripako, Piapoco and Guarequena) helps identify which features have diffused into Tariana from Tucanoan languages and which are inherited from the proto-language. These include single-word serial verb constructions, evidentials, various classifier contexts, and imperatives (a summary is in Aikhenvald 2002, 2008b).

In terms of its structure, Tariana is highly synthetic, with few prefixes and numerous suffixes and enclitics. Active verbs take person-number-gender prefixes. Stative verbs do not take any person marking. Unlike any other Arawak language, Tariana employs cases for marking grammatical relations; this is another instance of areal diffusion from East Tucanoan languages. We now turn to the Tariana imperatives, and the special position of the malefactive imperative, in Section 3.3.1. The use of the malefactive imperative is the topic of Section 3.3.2. We look at the etymology of the form in Tariana in Section 3.3.3, and offer a few thoughts on the rarity of malefactive forms world-wide in Section 3.3.4.

3.3.1 Imperatives in Tariana

Tariana has nine established imperative forms: (a) formally unmarked simple imperative; (b) secondhand imperative *-pida* 'do on someone else's order'; (c) proximate imperative *-si* 'do here close to the speaker'; (d) distal imperative *-kada* 'do there, away from the speaker'; (e) delayed imperative *-wa* 'do later'; (f) conative imperative *-thara* 'try and do'; (g) polite imperative *-nha* 'please do'; (h) first person hortative imperative *-ra/-da* 'let's do', and (i) malefactive imperative *-tupe* 'do to the detriment of the addressee'.

All imperative sentences are characterised by higher pitch and stronger intensity on the stress syllable of the verb and tend to have falling intonation (which they share with interrogative and declarative sentences: Aikhenvald 2003: 64, 502). An imperative sentence is typically short. If the addressee is

---

[7] A feature of the Vaupés linguistic Area is a strong cultural inhibition against "language mixing", viewed in terms of borrowing forms, or inserting bits of other languages. Speakers who use non-native forms are subject to ridicule, which may affect their status in the community (see further discussion with regard to example 26).

overtly stated, it is postposed to the verb, in contrast to declarative and interrogative clauses where the subject tends to appear before the verb (see Aikhenvald 2010: 92). The full set of imperatives with the verb *-hña* 'eat' is illustrated in (7).

(7a) pi-hña   *Tariana: simple imperative*
      2sg-eat
      'Eat!'

(7b) pi-hña-pida   *Tariana: secondhand imperative*
      2sg-eat-SECONDHAND.IMPV
      'Eat (on someone else's order)!' (that is, eat – you were told to)

(7c) pi-hña-si   *Tariana: proximate imperative*
      2SG-eat-PROXIMATE.IMPV
      'Eat here!' (close to the speaker)

(7d) pi-hña-kada   *Tariana: distal imperative*
      2sg-eat-DISTAL.IMPERATIVE
      'Eat there!' (away from the speaker)

(7e) pi-hña-wa   *Tariana: delayed imperative*
      2sg-eat-DELAYED.IMPV
      'Eat later!'

(7f) pi-hña-thara   *Tariana: conative imperative*
      2sg-eat-CONATIVE.IMPV
      'Try and eat!'

(7g) pi-hña-nha   *Tariana: polite imperative*
      2sg-eat-POLITE.IMPV
      'Please eat!'

(7h) pi-hña-da   *Tariana: first person hortative imperative*
      2sg-eat-1pl.IMPV
      'Let's eat!'

(7i) pi-hña-tupe   *Tariana: malefactive imperative*
      2sg-eat-MALEF.IMPV
      'Eat to your detriment!'

The formally unmarked imperative is the most archaic and the only one Tariana shares with closely related languages, Baniwa of Içana/Kurripako and Piapoco. All other imperatives can be traced to calques from East Tucanoan languages (full analysis of their etymology is in Aikhenvald 2008b: 199). Two additional imperative forms, the immediate imperative *-ya* and the simple imperative *-ri* result from a very recent influence from Tucano. These are restricted to innovative speakers of the language and are considered "wrong" by those who speak the traditional variety.

In addition to the established imperatives, the future suffix *-mhade* can be used with a deontic meaning of obligation as an exponent of a strong command. An example is in (8). This was said by a spirit woman to a man she had captured (in a Tariana story).

(8) nu-ine   pi-dia-mhade   phia   *Tariana: deontic future*
     1sg-with   2sg-stay-FUT   you.sg
     'You will stay with me (meaning: you will have to stay with me, you are obliged to stay with me)'

A deontic meaning for a future form is similar to that of its English equivalent, as in *You will go to school today, young man!* (see Aikhenvald 2014 on future forms in commands and their meanings across the world's languages, including Tariana).

The nine imperatives differ in terms of the following grammatical features: (I) person choice, (II) use with stative verbs, (III) co-occurrence with other imperative markers, (IV) co-occurrence with evidentials (markers of information source), (V) negation, and (VI) co-occurrence with the future marker in its deontic meaning. This is where the malefactive imperative stands apart from all the rest.

I. Person value. Imperatives (a)–(g) occur just with second person (singular and plural). The imperative (h) occurs just with first person plural. The malefactive imperative (i) occurs with any person.

II. Use with stative verbs. Imperatives (a)–(h) cannot be used with stative verbs. In contrast, the malefactive imperative (i) can do so (see examples 15, 17 and 18).

III. Co-occurrence with other imperative markers. Imperative markers in (a)–(h) cannot co-occur with each other in the same word. In contrast, the malefactive imperative (i) can occur together with the secondhand imperative *-pida* (7b) (see 19).

IV. Co-occurrence with evidentials (markers of information source). Imperatives (a)–(h) cannot occur together with markers of information source, or evidentials, obligatory in declarative and interrogative clauses (in agreement with Aikhenvald 2010: 131–141). The malefactive imperative (i) can (see 12).
V. Negation. Imperatives (a)–(h) are negated using the prohibitive *mhãida*. In contrast, the malefactive imperative is negated similarly to a declarative verb, using the prefix *ma-* and the suffix *-kade*, e.g. (9).

(9) ma-nu-kade-tupe   diha   *Tariana: malefactive imperative*
    NEG-come-NEG-MALEF.IMPV he
    'May he not come (to the meeting) to his own detriment!'[8]

VI. The future marker. Imperatives (a)–(h) cannot co-occur with the future marker, in contrast to the malefactive imperative (i). In (10), from a narrative, an exasperated man rejected by a woman expresses his annoyance, by using the malefactive imperative followed by the future marker in its deontic sense of obligation. The woman herself is out of ear-shot.

(10) pipa-tupe-mhade   phia   *Tariana: malefactive imperative*
     2sg+rot-MALEF.IMPV-FUT you.sg
     'You absolutely must rot to your detriment!'

The malefactive imperative stands apart from other imperatives, and resembles declarative clauses in terms of features IV–V – its co-occurrence with evidentials and with the deontic future marker, and the ways in which it is negated. The reason for this may lie in the origin of the form – more on this in Section 3.3.3. Malefactive imperatives differ from exclamations, which, in Tariana, have rising intonation and cannot contain any verbal morphological markers, including those of evidentiality (Aikhenvald 2003: 487, 506).

3.3.2 How to use the malefactive imperative

The meaning of the malefactive imperative is 'do something or let something happen to the detriment of the addressee'. It is used in curses and maledictions,

---

[8] Another option for negating the malefactive imperative involves the prohibitive *mhãida* and the secondhand imperative marker *-pida* (see Aikhenvald 2003: 376); however, these forms do not carry a strong malefactive overtone.

oftentimes as an expression of annoyance and despair in the face of adverse circumstances. A malefactive imperative reflects an emotional attitude (along the lines of Jay, this volume, and Storch and Nassenstein, this volume) and general malevolence. If the addressee is overtly stated, it tends to be accompanied by the nominal pejorative marker -*yana* 'bad one, naughty one' (see Aikhenvald 2003: 97, on its properties).

A malediction may express *Schadenfreude* – gloating over something negative that happened to someone who had done something wrong (reminiscent of the "evil laughter" described in the Introduction to this volume). In (11), a man shunned by a woman (a typical character in Tariana narratives) sees the decomposing body of the woman – who had previously rejected him – floating in the water. He comments using the malefactive imperative in third person and the marker -*yana* twice. The malefactive imperative is in bold throughout the rest of Section 3.3.

(11) ne-nuku   dhumeta-**tupe**   duha-yana   *Tariana*
      then-TOP.NON.A/S 3sgf+feel-MALEF.IMPV   she-PEJ
      nu-na   ma:-na-kade-karu-yana   di-a-pidana   diha nawiki-ne
      1sg-OBJ NEG-want-REL.FEM.SG-PEJ   3sgnf-say-REM.P.REP   he   man-FOC.A/S
      'Then may she, a bad one, feel (like that) to her detriment, the bad one who didn't want me, said the man'

A similar example is in (12). It comes from a similar story about a man not loved by a woman. The man has just found the remains of the woman and assumes that she had been devoured by a snake. His malediction involves an assumption based on general knowledge, which is why the assumed evidential -*sika* appears here (see V in Section 3.3.1).

(12) duhmeta-sika-**tupe**   duha-yana nu-na   *Tariana*
      3sgf+feel-ASSUM.REC.P-MALEF.IMPV   she-PEJ   1sg-OBJ
      du-duiha-ka-kapua
      3sgf-not.love-SEQ-BECAUSE
      'May she-the bad one feel (like that) to her detriment, because she did not love me'

Alternatively, a malediction can contain a wish that something negative should befall the addressee in the future. A man who had seen a scary evil spirit in the jungle said (13), running off to the village to warn others:

(13) di-yami-**tupe**   diha-yana   *Tariana*
    3sgnf-die-MALEF.IMPV he-PEJ
    'May he-the bad one (i.e. the evil spirit) die to his detriment'

A malefactive imperative can be addressed to a second person, as in (10) and (14), provided the addressee is absent or cannot hear them. A speaker told a story about how he almost managed to hunt down a tapir who had been eating the crops in his garden; the tapir managed to escape at the last minute. The speaker quoted himself as saying:

(14) ne-a-ya   pi-pa-**tupe**   phia-yana   *Tariana*
    then/there-EMPH-EMPH 2sg-rot-MALEF.IMPV you.sg-PEJ
    'May you-the bad one die there'

In 90 percent of the narratives collected by the author (see note 6), the malefactive imperative is used with three verbs referring to death – -*yami*/-*ñami* 'die, lose consciousness', -*ñale* 'die, disappear', and -*pa* 'rot, perish, die (mostly of animals)'. The latter verb sounds very rude if applied to humans or spirits (comparable to English *croak* or French *crever*). Other verbs are used more rarely. In a cautionary tale, a woman who happened to catch a glimpse of the magic Yurupary flutes and thus breach a major taboo in the Vaupés culture had to die: her husband was told by his mates to poison her. Her daughters wanted to die with their mother, but the father refused to poison them, as that would have gone against the traditional practice. Before taking the poison and dying, the woman exclaimed:

(15) tarada-**tupe**   *Tariana*
    be.alive-MALEF.IMPV
    'May (they) be alive!' (to their detriment because they will have lost their mother)

In conversations and spontaneous interactions, any verb can be used in short maledictions. After having waited for a long time for her brothers to come and have the lunch she had prepared, Olívia exclaimed in annoyance:

(16) na-siwa na-yeka-**tupe**   *Tariana*
    3pl-self 3pl-know-MALEF.IMPV
    'May they know for themselves to their detriment (where to eat)'

An angry reaction to a teenager leaving the house when it was obviously going to rain was phrased as (17). Examples (15), (17), and (18) contain stative verbs (which do not take a personal prefix) (we can recall, from II in §3.3.1, that stative verbs cannot be used with any other imperative markers).

(17) iya   putsa-**tupe**   di-na   *Tariana*
     rain   be/make.wet-MALEF.IMPV   3sg-OBJ
     'May rain make him wet (to his detriment)'

A typical example of annoyed reaction to someone doing something wrong and suffering for it is (18). This is cast in third person, and was translated to me using the Portuguese expression *bem feito para ele* (literally, well done for him) 'serves him right'.

(18) matsa-**tupe**   di-na   *Tariana*
     be.good-MALEF.IMPV   3sg-OBJ
     'Serves him right' (lit. may it be good to his detriment)

Unlike any other imperative, the malefactive imperative can occur with the marker of the secondhand imperative *-pida* (see III, and 7b). This is illustrated in (19). The first Tariana language workshop was run in June 2000, by the working group consisting of the speakers and myself as a linguistic advisor.[9] The Tariana consist of hierarchically organized clans, most of whom have now lost their language in favour of Tucano, which is the numerically dominant group. The extant speakers of Tariana belong to a lower-ranking clan (the discussion is in Aikhenvald 2003: 11–16). As a consequence, some representatives of high-ranking clans (who no longer spoke the language) were not happy at those with a lower status being in the centre of the workshop and the language maintenance project. There was a feeling, among the speakers of Tariana, that a lot of nasty gossip was going around. The gossip was attributed to an anthropologist who was doing some work with representatives of higher ranking clans. Olivia Brito was visibly annoyed at those who were spreading unfounded rumours about how much money the Tariana speakers were allegedly getting for this, because that anthropologist "told them to" (gossip), and said (19):

---

9 The workshop was generously funded by external grants by the Wenner Gren Foundation and the Australian Research Council, and by the Instituto Socioambiental in Brazil.

(19) na-sape-**tupe**-pida *Tariana*
     3pl-talk-MALEF.IMPV-SECONDHAND.IMPV
     'Let them talk to their detriment following (her) verbal order'

The use of the malefactive imperative forms is described by the speakers as *pa-kwisa-li* (IMPERS-scold/curse/bark-NOM) 'scolding, cursing' or *pa-kwisa-li yaphini* (IMPERS-scold/curse/bark-NOM like) '(something) like scolding or cursing'.[10] Overtly 'scolding' or 'cursing' someone, especially in their presence, tends to be avoided, for fear of negative consequences.

Many Amazonian societies, including the Tariana, share the common belief that there is an explicit cause – most often, sorcery – for every misadventure that happens. The Tariana typically attribute adverse events to the effects of sorcery and evil actions of shamans (a classification of shamans in terms of their powers is summarised in Aikhenvald 2003: 13). In order not to anger a shaman or an evil spirit, one avoids explicit outbursts of negative emotions and anger and also overt argument and criticism of others. The main reason for onset of *adaki* 'serious disease' is believed to be shamanic intervention, often superficially realised as 'anger', and 'scolding'. Avoidance of direct verbal attacks, so as to thwart shamanic vengeance, is tantamount to a face-saving strategy in the European context (in the sense of Brown and Levinson 1987). The verb *-kwisa* 'scold, quarrel' has negative and dangerous connotations (in agreement with Wyss' 1984: 17 categorization of curses as a "magical" speech act).

Someone who dares scold another person in public may have hidden powers, and be an evil-minded shaman in disguise. The corpus of Tariana stories includes a number of cautionary tales to this effect. One such example is (20): a desperate woman dares confront a shaman, scolding him for killing her children (20a).

(20a) matsi-peri-pidana   du-kwisa   di-na   *Tariana*
      be.bad-COLL-REM.P.REP   3sgf-scold 3sgnf-OBJ
      'She scolded him badly'

The shaman reacts, saying (20b). There is no malefactive imperative here, just the shaman's reaction and an almost open threat.

---

10 The root *-kwisa* means 'bark (of a dog)'; the polysemy of 'scold' (of a human) and 'bark' (of a dog) is shared with Tucano *tu'ú*, which has the same meanings (Ramirez 1997: 200), and is, in all likelihood, the result of diffusion from Tucano.

(20b) haw   phia-yana   inaru-yana-mha   nu-na   *Tariana*
      OK   2sg-PEJ   woman-PEJ-PRES.NONVIS   1sg-OBJ
      pi-kwisa   kwe   pi-a-ka   pi-a-mhade
      2sg-scold   2sg-go-FUT 3sgnf-say-REM.P.REP 3sgnf+respond
      di-a-pidana   dhepa   du-na
      3sgf-OBJ   how   2sg-go-SEQ
      'OK, you-bad one, bad woman, you are scolding me, you just see what happens (lit. whichever way you go, you will go), he replied to her'

The pejorative marker -*yana* on the second person pronoun and on the noun 'woman' indicates the shaman's annoyance. The expression which literally translates 'whichever way you go, you will go' has a threatening meaning, similar to English *you just see what happens!* and does not bode well. The following day the woman goes to her garden, falls over, and dies.

The avoidance of cursing someone in their presence is the reason for the rarity of examples of its use with second person addressee. We can recall that both (10) and (14), ostensibly addressed at someone cursed, were uttered in their absence. Even in stories, one adult can rarely address another one with a "scolding" malefactive imperative. An example in (21) is from a story composed by Rafael Brito, the youngest speaker of Tariana, as part of a story-writing workshop in 2000. A man invited his marriageable cousin to join him in an expedition to catch edible leafcutter ants. She didn't want to go (21a). He then got angry and scolded her, using the pejorative enclitic and the malefactive imperative (21b).

(21a) Duha-ne   ma-kasu   nuha phia   paita-ya   pi-a   *Tariana*
      she-FOC.A/S   NEG+go-INT   I   you.sg alone-EMPH   2sg-go
      du-a-pidana   duha
      3sgf-say-REM.P.REP   she
      'She (said): "I won't go, you go alone," she said'

(21b) kai   du-a-ka   keru   di-yena   di-a-pidana
      thus   3sgf-say-SEQ   angry   3sgnf-excede   3sgnf-say-REM.P.REP
      ma:tsite   piha-yana, ne   pi-na   kehuri   ma-kasu
      bad+NCL.ANIM   you.sg-PEJ NEG   2sg-OBJ   leafcutter.ant NEG+go-INT
      inaru   menanite-yana   pi-hña-botha   mesiki   pi-ñami-**tupe**
      woman   not.love+NCL.ANIM-PEJ   2sg-eat-POT   hunger   2sg-die-MALEF.IMPV
      di-a-pidana
      3sgnf-say-REM.P.REP

'After she said this, he got exceedingly angry, "you bad one, as you won't go after leafcutter ants, the bad one who does not love women could eat you, may you die of hunger to your detriment," he said'

The freedom with which the main character scolded his marrigeable cousin – displaying his frustration at her not wanting to go out with him – may have to do with the slightly suspicious relationships between marriageable relatives. The story itself was an invention on the spot, and not a traditional narrative.

A malefactive imperative can be addressed to a naughty child. (22a) was said to a little girl who was trying to go outside the house. (22b) is an explanation, to me, why this was said to her.

(22a) pi-a-**tupe**　　　　　　　　　　　　　　　　　　　　　　*Tariana*
　　　 2sg-go-MALEF.IMPV
　　　 'Go to your detriment!'

(22b) ne　mhema-kade-ka　　　　emite
　　　 NEG　NEG+listen-NEG-REC.P.VIS　child
　　　 'The child is not listening'

On another occasion, the same child was repeatedly trying to bite a rubber ball. An exasperated relative said (23):

(23)　pi-hña-**tupe**　　　ma-hña-karu-peri-nuku　　　　*Tariana*
　　　 2sg-eat-MALEF.IMPV　NEG-eat-PURP-COLL-TOP.NON.A/S
　　　 'Eat to your detriment what is not edible!'

The malefactive imperative hardly ever occurs with first person (see Aikhenvald 2003: 375). This gap correlates with the absence of the practice of "self-cursing" (prominent among other peoples, such as the Gurage of Ethiopia: Fekede Menuta and Fjeld 2016: 365). Sentences with first person object can contain the malefactive imperative, implying detriment to the object. In a story, a man rejected by women has lost all his hopes and decides to jump into a dangerous lake where a snake lives. Before doing so, he says (24).

(24)　mawari　nu-na　　di-hña-**tupe**　　　　　　　　　　*Tariana*
　　　 snake　　1sg-OBJ　3sgnf-eat-MALEF.IMPV
　　　 'May the snake eat me (to my detriment)!'

Malefactive imperative can be used with first person just in the context of laments, regretting an adverse happening and anticipating a negative consequence for the speaker. In (25), the speaker blames himself for inadvertently having breached a taboo. Similar to (10), this sentence contains a malefactive imperative accompanied by the future marker in the sense of obligation.

(25) nuhua ma-nihta-kade-kapua nu-ñami-**tupe**-mhade *Tariana*
 I NEG-think/reason-neg-because 1sg-die-MALEF.IMPV-FUT
 'Because I haven't been thinking, I must die to my detriment'

None of the other eight imperatives can be used in curses or maledictions. Only the unmarked imperative (7a) can be occasionally used as a mock command, that is, a warning disguised as an order to do the opposite of what is commanded. Spontaneous mock commands often reflect speaker's annoyance, e.g. *Go there at your own risk!* or *Tell him, if you like, I don't care* (see Bolinger 1967: 346–347, Ascoli 1978: 406, examples in Börsjars and Burridge 2001: 130, and discussion in Aikhenvald 2010: 244–246).

Mock commands in Tariana are a mark of exasperation and contained anger. In the 1990s and the early 2000s, the rivalry between the two Tariana-speaking villages, Santa Rosa and Periquitos, was rife. There are very minor differences between the two (comparable to those between British and American English). The Tariana of Periquitos tended to insert Tucanoan forms into the Tariana, to the annoyance of those from Santa Rosa, especially Olivia Brito and her brothers. In Olivia's opinion, I was paying far too much attention to the variety of Periquitos, whom she was consistently mocking for using occasional Tucanoan forms – such as *ba* 'evidently'. On one occasion, she told me off for wanting to spoil my Tariana with the Periquitos forms, using a mock command, in (26).

(26) ba **pi-a** *Tariana*
 ba 2sg-say
 'Say *ba*!' (as if you were a speaker of the Tariana of Periquitos who can't speak the language properly, and you still want to be like them) (meaning: do not be like them!)

A malefactive imperative would not be possible in such a context: I was told that Olivia was not really "scolding" me and did not wish that any evil might befall me. The unmarked imperative has a strong illocutionary force, but it lacks the powers of a curse associated with a malefactive form.

Malefactive imperatives share a number of features with declarative clauses. The reason for this may well lie in their origin – the topic of the next section.

3.3.3 Where does the Tariana malefactive imperative come from?

Tariana is the only language in the Vaupés River Basin Linguistic Area to have a special malefactive imperative, used for curses. The origins of the malefactive imperative marker *-tupe* lie in reinterpretation and reanalysis of a single word serial verb construction attested in Tucano, the main East Tucanoan language with which Tariana is in constant contact. The verb *batá* 'break' can be used as a second component in serial verb constructions in the form *bataa'* with an imprecative meaning 'do something to the subject's detriment' (Ramirez 1997: 17). The serial verb construction can be used in a declarative and an imperative sentence, as in (27) and (28). Example (28) contains a simple imperative marked with the suffix *-ya*.

(27) boka-tí   bataa'mi   *Tucano*
     find-NEG   break=MALEF+REC.P.VIS.3masc.sg
     'He hasn't found it to his detriment'

(28) wa'â-bataa'-ya   *Tucano*
     go-break=MALEF-IMPV
     'Go to hell (lit. your detriment)'

The Tariana malefactive marker *-tupe* originates in the verb **-tupa* plus the transitiviser *-i* (Aikhenvald 2003: 48, 2008b: 213, on the phonological process of vowel contraction a+i > e in Tariana). The root **-tupa* has a cognate in Piapoco, a closely related Arawak language. Piapoco *s* is a regular correspondent of Tariana *t* and a regular reflex of Proto-Arawak **t*. The Piapoco root *-supa* is attested in the verb *nu-supá-ida-ca* (1sg-break-CAUSATIVE-DECLARATIVE) 'I break (something) into little pieces' (Klumpp 1995: 80; 1990: 88–89).

The malefactive construction in Tariana is likely to have arisen as a result of a morpheme-per-morpheme translation of a serial verb construction in Tucano. Numerous aspect, manner, and aktionsart markers in Tariana developed in a similar way, by calquing the Tucano serial verbs and translating them morpheme-by-morpheme (see Aikhenvald 2002, and also 2016b, on such loan translations as a continuous source for developing new morphological markers in

Tariana). That the malefactive imperatives in Tariana share features with declarative clauses may be due to their origin in non-imperative constructions.

3.3.4 What is special about Tariana malefactive imperatives?

A special form for a curse with a malefactive meaning appears to be a cross-linguistic rarity. A few languages have special "benedictive" forms used for blessings and good wishes. Such a benedictive form was described for Classical Sanskrit (MacDonnell 1927: 126–127). The benedictive (rarely used in its active voice form and never used in the 'middle' form) shared markers with the optative of the second verbal conjugation (with -s- inserted between the suffix -yā- and the personal inflection shared with the optative), e.g. *budh-yā-t* 'may he awaken'. Ladakhi, a Tibero Burman language from India, has a special benedictive mood, with a special marker *-šik* added to the verb stem (Koshal 1979: 226–227), e.g.

(29) khyorəŋŋi   tshe-riŋ-šik   Ladakhi
     2sg.non.honorific.GEN long-INTR.VERB-BEND
     'May you have a long life' (lit. may your life be long-benedictive)

Kambaata, a Cushitic language from Ethiopia, has a special benedictive form employed just in blessings (Treis 2008a: 406; 2008b: §2.7). The benedictive form is used in third person only, and can be considered a shortened form of a third person imperative (or "jussive"): the third person imperative form *-un* 'masculine singular' corresponds to the benedictive *-u* 'benedictive masculine singular', and *-t-un* 'feminine singular' to *-tu* 'benedictive feminine singular'. An example is in (30) (the form *maassá'-o-he* 'may it bless' comes from the underlying *maassá-u + -he*):

(30) Aan-aakk-á   ayyán-u   maassá'-o-he   Kambaata
     father-PL2-F.GEN spirit-NOM.MASC   bless-3masc.sgBEND-2sg.OBJ
     'May the spirit of your forefathers bless you!'

Special benedictive forms are a cross-linguistic rarity.[11] A special maledictive form appears to be even more rare. Tariana and Tucano are the only languages described so far with a special grammatical mechanism reserved just

---

[11] This statement is based on an investigation of 700 languages (the foundation of Aikhenvald 2010 and then 2017).

for curses and maledictions. Tariana is the only one with a maledictive imperative – a form just for curses and maledictions, covered by the speech act of scolding (Tariana *pa-kwisa-li*).

Why are maledictive grammatical forms so rare? One reason could lie in a cross-linguistic tendency to express fewer grammatical distinctions in negative than in positive contexts (outlined in Aikhenvald and Dixon 1998, as one of the dependencies between grammatical systems). Another, and perhaps a more powerful reason, may stem from cultural attitudes towards curses and maledictions and their inherent powers. Curses and imprecations of all sorts are part of transgressive language (Storch and Nassenstein, this volume), endowed with magical powers and potential spells – words that can kill. We hypothesise that the extreme rarity of grammatical maledictive forms may well be rooted in a general tendency to avoid highly charged negative expressions. Whether or not this is the case remains an open question.

3.4 The imperative disguise: A summary

In many languages, curses, imprecations, maledictions, and benedictions are couched in imperative form. However, the similarity between these and the imperatives in their directive functions is superficial. Curses, imprecations, and maledictions stand apart from commands in their illocutionary force: they do not really imply commanding anyone what to do; rather, they express an emotional reaction (as outlined by Storch and Nassenstein, this volume). In some languages, including English, curses and maledictions cast as imperatives lack the syntactic options of real commands (as aptly outlined by McCawley 1971).

Imperative forms in curses and imprecations are far from universal. An imperative may be too strong for a curse. In Manambu, a Papuan language from the Sepik region of New Guinea, it is inappropriate to use second person imperatives as imprecatives: a second person imperative implies a strong command to the addressee. Using it in a curse or a malediction would imply that the speaker well and truly wishes to inflict damage upon the person cursed. The acceptable alternative is to use third person commands and irrealis forms, also employed to express wishes and indirect orders.

Tariana, the only Arawak language spoken in the multilingual Vaupés River Basin Linguistic Area, takes a different route. The language has a special "malefactive" imperative, whose main function is to express bad wishes and imprecations. Cursing or scolding someone in their face may have negative implications for the addressee and the speaker: a curse can inflict serious damage, and someone who dares utter it may be endowed with hidden magical powers. In their daily life, the speakers are careful not to use malefactive imperative to an addressee within their hearing (unless it is a small child). Other imperatives are not used in curses or maledictions: their illocutionary force is directive only.

The malefactive imperative is the result of contact with Tucano, the main language of the region. The cross-linguistic rarity of malefactive imperatives and grammatical malefactives in general may be rooted in a tendency to avoid strong "transgressive" language which may endanger all the parties.

And last but not least: Collecting materials on curses and maledictions is notoriously difficult, and requires the researcher's immersion into the community and participant-observation of day-to-day life (Jay, this volume, addresses the difficulties which arise for researchers working with taboos, swearing, and curses in the context of European languages). My long-term involvement with the Manambu of north-east New Guinea and the Tariana of the north-west Amazonia in Brazil has allowed me to document various genres of narratives, dialogues, and interactions, including spontaneous outbursts of emotion – which is where curses and maledictions come in. Ideally, linguistic fieldwork should involve observing the language as it is used, on a day-to-day basis, becoming a member of the language community and being treated like a family member. Only through such "immersion fieldwork" can the researcher experience the language in its spontaneous use and document it to a much fuller extent than if one were to concentrate just on recording and transcribing carefully planned narratives, let alone eliciting paradigms or translating examples from a lingua franca. This is a lesson to be learnt by all aspiring fieldworkers, who endeavour to uncover the ways in which a language is used opening up a path to serendipitous discoveries and insights into how people really speak.

Acknowledgements: I am grateful to R. M. W. Dixon, for extensive comments and criticisms, and for suggesting part of the title. Thanks go to Tony Diller and Phichit Roinil, for the extensive information on swearing in Thai, to Firew Girma Worku, for sharing the literature on cursing in the languages of Ethiopia, and to Brigitta Flick, for checking the text.

Abbreviations

1	first person
2	second person
3	third person

ACT.FOC	action focus
ASSUM.REC.P	assumed evidential recent past
BEND	benedictive
COLL	collective
EMPH	emphatic
F.GEN	feminine genitive
fem	feminine
FOC.A/S	focused subject
FUT	future
GEN	genitive
IMPERS	impersonal
IMPV	imperative
INT	intentional
INTR.VERB	intransitive verb
IRR	irrealis
MALEF	malefactive
MALEF.IMPV	malefactive imperative
masc	masculine
NCL.ANIM	noun class for animate beings
NEG	negative
NOM	nominalization
NOM.MASC	masculine nominative
OBJ	object
PEJ	pejorative
pl	plural
POT	potential
PRES.NONVIS	non-visual evidential present
REC.P.VIS	visual evidential recent past
REL.FEM.SG	relative clause feminine singular
REM.P.REP	reported evidential remote past
SEQ	sequential marker
sg	singular
sgf	singular feminine
sgnf	singular nonfeminine
SUBJ	subject
TOP.NON.A/S	topical non-subject

References

Aikhenvald, Alexandra Y. 2002. *Language contact in Amazonia*. Oxford: Oxford University Press.

Aikhenvald, Alexandra Y. 2003. *A grammar of Tariana, from northwest Amazonia*. Cambridge: Cambridge University Press

Aikhenvald, Alexandra Y. 2008a. *The Manambu language from East Sepik, Papua New Guinea*. Oxford: Oxford University Press.

Aikhenvald, Alexandra Y. 2008b. Multilingual imperatives: the elaboration of a category in north-west Amazonia. *International Journal of American Linguistics* 74: 189–225.
Aikhenvald, Alexandra Y. 2010. *Imperatives and commands*. Oxford: Oxford University Press.
Aikhenvald, Alexandra Y. 2014. On future in commands. In Mikhail Kissin et al. (eds), *Future tenses, future times*, 205–18. Oxford: Oxford University Press.
Aikhenvald, Alexandra Y. 2015. *The languages of the Amazon*. Oxford: Oxford University Press.
Aikhenvald, Alexandra Y. 2016a. Imperatives and commands in Manambu. *Oceanic Linguistics* 55: 639–73.
Aikhenvald, Alexandra Y. 2016b. Language contact and word structure: a case study from north-west Amazonia. In Andrea L. Berez-Kroeker, Diane M. Hintz and Carmen Jany (eds.), *Language contact and change in the Americas. Studies in honor of Marianne Mithun*, 297–313. Amsterdam: John Benjamins.
Aikhenvald, Alexandra Y. 2017. Imperatives and commands: a cross-linguistic view. In Alexandra Y. Aikhenvald and R. M. W. Dixon (eds.), *Commands: a cross-linguistic typology*, 1–45. Oxford: Oxford University Press.
Aikhenvald, Alexandra Y. and R. M. W. Dixon. 1998. Dependencies between grammatical Systems. *Language* 74: 56–80.
Allan, Keith and Kate Burridge. 2006. *Forbidden words. Taboo and the censoring of language*. Cambridge: Cambridge University Press.
Ascoli, C. 1978. Some pseudo-imperatives and their communicative function in English. *Folia Linguistica* XII: 405–416.
Baye Imam. 2013. The imagery of cursing in four Ethiopian languages. In L. Berge and I. Taddea (eds.), *Themes in modern African history and culture*, 395–419. Bologna: Libreria universitaria.
Berghäll, Liisa. 2010. *Mauwake reference grammar*. University of Helsinki: Faculty of Arts.
Bolinger, Dwight. 1967. The imperative in English. In *To Honor Roman Jakobson. Essays on the occasion on his seventieth birthday*, 335–362. The Hague: Mouton.
Brown, Penelope and Stephen C. Levinson. 1987. *Politeness. Some universals in language usage*. Cambridge: Cambridge University Press.
Börjars, Kersti and Kate Burridge 2001. *Introducing English grammar*. London: Arnold.
Dixon, R. M. W. 2010. *Basic linguistic theory*. Volume 1. *Methodology*. Oxford: Oxford University Press.
Fekede Menuta and Ruth Vatvedt Fjeld. 2016. Social and pragmatic rules of cursing and other routine formulas in Gurage and Norwegian culture. In Binyam Sisay Mendisu and Janna Bondi Johannessen (eds.), *Multilingual Ethiopia: Linguistic challenges and capacity building effforts. Oslo Studies in Language* 8 (1): 359–386.
Fjeld, Ruth Vatvedt. 2014. The vocabulary of Norwegian cursing and swearing. Some of its history, meaning and function. In Marianne Rathje (ed.), *Swearing in the Nordic countries. Copenhagen 6 December 2012*. Sprognævnets Konferencenserie. Copenhagen: Dansk Sprognavn, 199–215.
Huddleston, R. D. 2002. Clause type and illocutionary force. In Rodney Huddleston and Geoffrey K. Pullum (main authors), *The Cambridge grammar of the English language*, 851–945. Cambridge: Cambridge University Press.
Klumpp, Deloris. 1990. *Piapoco grammar*. Colombia: SIL.
Klumpp, Deloris. 1995. *Vocabulario Piapoco-Español*. Santafé de Bogotá: Associación Instituto Lingüístico de Verano.
Koshal, Sanyukta. 1979. *Ladakhi grammar*. Delhi: Motilal Banarsidass.

McCawley, James D. (Quang Phuc Dong). 1971. English sentences without overt grammatical subject. In Arnold M. Zwicky, Peter H. Salus, Robert I. Binnck and Anthony L. Vanek (eds.), *Studies out in left field. Defamatory essays presented to James D. McCawley*, 3–10. Edmonton, Champaign: Linguistic Research Inc.

MacDonnell, Arthur A. 1927. *A Sanskrit grammar for students*. Third edition. London: Oxford University Press.

Matisoff, James A. 2000. *Blessings, curses, hopes and fears. Psycho-ostensive expressions in Yiddish*. Stanford: Stanford University Press.

Quirk, R., S. Greenbaum, G. Leech and J. Svartvik. 1985. *A comprehensive grammar of the English language*. London: Longman.

Ramirez, Henri. 1997. *A fala Tukano dos Yepa-Masa. Tomo II. Dicionário*. Manaus: Inspetoria Salesiana Missionária da Amazônia CEDEM.

Sarvasy, Hannah S. 2017. Imperatives and commands in Nungon. In Alexandra Y. Aikhenvald and R. M. W. Dixon (eds.), *Commands: a cross-linguistic typology*, 224–49. Oxford: Oxford University Press.

Storch, Anne. 2014. *A grammar of Luwo. An anthropological approach*. Amsterdam: John Benjamins.

Tosco, Mauro. 2001. *The Dhaasanac language*. Cologne: Rüdiger Köppe Verlag.

Treis, Yvonne. 2008a. Zur Grammatik des Befehlens, Wünschens, Segnens und Verfluchens im Kambaata (Kuschitisch). Paper presented at the Asien-Afrika Institut, Universität Hamburg.

Treis, Yvonne. 2008b. *A grammar of Kambaata*. Cologne: Rüdiger Köppe Verlag.

de Vries, Lourens. 2017. The imperative paradigm of Korowai, a Greater Awyu language of West Papua. In Alexandra Y. Aikhenvald and R. M. W. Dixon (eds.), *Commands: a cross-linguistic typology*, 250–65. Oxford: Oxford University Press.

Wyss, Stephan. 1984. *Fluchen. Ohnmächtige und mächtige Rede der Ohnmacht. Ein philosophisch-theologischer Essay zu einer Blütenlese*. Freiburg/Schweiz: Exodus Contacts.

Xrakovskij, V. S. and A. P. Volodin. 2001. *Semantika russkogo imperativa*. Moscow: URSS.

Alice Mitchell
4 "Oh, bald father!": Kinship and swearing among Datooga of Tanzania

Abstract: In the Datooga language of Tanzania, to say 'your mother' or 'your father' to someone can cause offence. Using data from a video corpus of conversational Datooga, this chapter explores these kin-based insults, as well as other affect-laden linguistic practices that invoke kinship relations. Datooga speakers can attest to the truth of something by referring to their opposite-sex parent. Speakers also invoke kin in everyday interjectional phrases, as well as during ritual hunts – a type of speech act known as *gíishíimda*. Though these speech practices do not all constitute "swearing" in the narrow sense of using "bad" language, they resemble swear words in the way they link speakers' evaluations of objects in the world with abstract moral values. In the Datooga case, kinship provides the relevant moral framework; the cultural and moral significance of fathers, in particular, makes them good to swear by. From a cross-cultural perspective on swearing, I suggest that Ljung's (2011) "mother" theme be subsumed under a more general "kinship" theme.

4.1 Introduction

This chapter takes a somewhat lateral approach to the topic of swearing. Rather than exploring what counts as offensive language use in Datooga, it proceeds from the observation that the words 'mother' and 'father' can be used as terms of abuse (Section 4.2) to consider other types of formulaic, expressive utterances that refer to kin. This includes "oaths", or attestations of truthfulness (Section 4.3), and a linguistic practice called *gíishíimda*, in which speakers invoke kin during ritual hunts (Section 4.4.1) or in everyday expressions of surprise (Section 4.4.2). Although the bulk of this chapter does not address "swearing" in the narrow sense of offensive linguistic behaviour, the phenomena under study are related to swearing behaviour by the way they link speakers' evaluations of objects in the world to abstract moral values. Tracing the links between morality, swearing, and the domain of kinship in Section 4.5, I show that these various linguistic practices in Datooga all bear on the question of what swearing is and does in human interaction.

https://doi.org/10.1515/9781501511202-004

In English, the metapragmatic term "swearing" describes (at least) two different linguistic behaviours, as captured in the following definitions from the OED:[1]

i. "To make a solemn declaration or statement with an appeal to God or a superhuman being, or to some sacred object, in confirmation of what is said; to take an oath."
ii. "To utter a form of oath lightly or irreverently, as a mere intensive, or an expression of anger, vexation, or other strong feeling; [...] to use bad language."

Ljung (2011: 1) points out that, unlike English, many languages differentiate these two concepts of "oath taking" and "profane swearing", e.g., German *schwören* vs *fluchen*. Datooga similarly distinguishes between oath-taking and using "bad language" and has a third metapragmatic category which I gloss as 'invocation'. Solemn oath-taking is described in the Datooga bible translation as *qwaak habeawooda*, literally meaning 's/he ate an oath/curse'. This metapragmatic label does not include informal oaths involving kin terms (Section 4.3), which are also distinct from instances of *ng'eaw* 'swear; use bad language'. The verb *ng'eaw* denotes the use of offensive or abusive language, which, as elsewhere in the world, frequently involves taboo concepts relating to, e.g., genitalia and bodily effluvia. As we will see in Section 4.2, the communicative effect denoted by *ng'eaw* can also be achieved by uttering certain kin terms. When Datooga refer to kin in non-abusive exclamations, this is labelled neither bad language, nor oath-taking, but *gíishíimda* 'invocation'. The word *gíishíimda* refers to both "solemn" and "irreverent" (or everyday) acts of invocation. In Datooga, then, everyday acts of oath-taking, insulting, and exclaiming do not constitute a single metapragmatic category but they are connected by the way in which all practices draw on the conceptual domain of kinship to communicate expressive, evaluative meanings.

In professing the truth, trying to offend, and performing surprise or other evaluative stances, kinship terms and names of kin allow speakers to tie their verbal actions to a moral framework that affords these actions a performative strength. The final section discusses the moral nature of kinship relations, suggesting that in certain communities, such as Datooga, the significance of the moral ties between particular individuals make kin terms good to swear with. I also suggest that Ljung's (2011) "mother theme" in his cross-cultural survey of swearing can be subsumed under a more general "kinship" theme.

---

[1] See http://www.oed.com (accessed 23 October 2018).

Datooga people are semi-nomadic cattle herders who inhabit many different areas of northern and central Tanzania. The name *Datooga* also refers to the language, or more accurately a cluster of dialects belonging to the Southern Nilotic language family. The data on which this paper is based was collected from speakers of the Gisamjanga and Barabaiga dialects in several villages of Mbulu District, Manyara Region. Although I use the label "Datooga" for convenience, the linguistic practices described may not be representative of other dialects of the language. Linguistic data presented in this paper come from elicitation, interviews, and a 135,000-word video corpus of spontaneous conversation recorded in everyday settings.

4.2 The kin terms 'mother' and 'father' in insults

In certain linguistic and situational contexts, the kin terms *gwêanu* 'your father' and *géamádu* 'your mother' can be interpreted as insults. When used abusively, these terms occur on their own; they constitute a complete turn. These possessed kin terms also occur in ordinary utterances with no insulting communicative effect and therefore cannot be called 'taboo' expressions – the performative effect is context-dependent (cf. Fleming and Lempert 2011). Nonetheless, these words carry an ambiguous potential, such that after asking an ordinary question like 'Where's your mother?', someone could add the metapragmatic joke, 'I'm not swearing at you'.[2] No other kin terms are known to have this indexical potential.

There are in fact two forms of the second singular possessive of the nouns 'mother' and 'father' in Barabaiga and Gisamjanga Datooga, as shown in Table 4.1. Nominal possession in Datooga involves the secondary form of the noun receiving a possessive suffix, e.g., *ùhùuda* 'head' becomes *ùhùudáang'ú* 'your (sg) head' (see Kießling 2000 on primary and secondary noun forms).[3] For 'your (sg) mother' and 'your (sg) father', this construction gives us *qáamáttáang'ú* and *qwáandáang'ú*, respectively. These terms co-exist with *géamádu* and *gwêanu*; they are used in ordinary conversation but they do not function as insults. The alternative forms *géamádu* and *gwêanu* are formally atypical: the nominal stems *qáamád* 'mother' and *qwáan* 'father' appear to have undergone a morphophonological alternation common to verbs, in which *q* becomes *g*, as well as an alternation found across

---

2 One of my consultants mentioned this in an elicitation session. Another consultant was somewhat reluctant to provide these terms as translations of 'your mother' and 'your father' because of their potentially offensive construal.
3 Note also vowel lengthening in the secondary suffix -*da*.

word classes in which *a:* becomes *ɛ:* (<ea>).⁴ These altered stems also bear an otherwise unattested possessive suffix *-u*. (We also find two forms for 'mother' and 'father' with a third person singular possessor, though the non-prototypical forms are less deviant than *géamádu* and *gwêanu*; see Table 4.1.)

Table 4.1: Possessive paradigm for singular nouns *qéamátta* 'mother' and *qwéanda* 'father'.

possessor	'mother'	'father'
1sg	qéamáttéanyu	qwéandéanyú
2sg	qáamáttáang'u	qwáandáang'u
	géamádu	gwêanu
3sg	qáamáttáanyi	qwáandáanyi
	qáamàtti	qwáan
1pl	qéamàttéanya	qwéandéanyá
2pl	qéamàttéang'wa	qwéandéang'wa
3pl	qáamáttányàawa	qwáandányàawa

Kin term paradigms are known to be sites of "deviant grammatical behaviour" across languages (Dahl and Koptjevskaja-Tamm 2001: 222; Baerman 2014). However, unlike the kin term doublets that Dahl and Koptjevskaja-Tamm (2001) discuss, or the suppletive kin terms in Baerman's (2014) survey, in Datooga the two alternatives for 'your mother' and 'your father' derive from the same lexical item. The origins of this variation are uncertain, but it is possible that the pragmatic ambiguities of *géamádu* and *gwêanu* have motivated the retention of two alternative forms.

Why can the forms *géamádu* 'your mother' and *gwêanu* 'your father' have an abusive interpretation? We know that across a wide range of languages people insult each other by referring to their addressee's mother, as per Ljung's (2011: 41) cross-cultural "mother theme", e.g., Italian *tua madre*; Hungarian *anyád*; Swahili *mamako*. Such forms are usually understood to be abbreviations of explicit sexual references to a person's mother, e.g. Hungarian *kurva anyád* 'your whore mother' (Péter Rácz, p.c.). Offensive references to a person's father are less common cross-culturally, but we can assume a similar logic to explain their offensiveness; both *géamádu* and *gwêanu* may imply a taboo sexual act

---

4 In the typical possessive paradigm, this alternation happens in certain person/number combinations but not in the second person singular (see relevant examples in Table 4.1).

involving the addressee's close kin. While this is a plausible account of why these Datooga expressions can cause offence, I have never heard an elaboration of these single-word phrases to suggest that they are abbreviations of more sexually explicit expressions. And referential semantics only gets us so far: the lexical meanings 'your mother' and 'your father' are not sufficient to cause offence, since, as mentioned above, the alternative forms *qáamáttáang'u* and *qwáandáang'u* do not have this communicative effect. The abusive potential of *géamádu* and *gwêanu* is obviously pragmatically conventionalized, but these expressions do attest to the importance of the semantic domain of kinship for swearing in Datooga. I return to the relevance of mothers and fathers to swearing in Section 4.5.

Documenting abusive language can be challenging. My corpus of everyday Datooga speech contains no tokens of *géamádu* or *gwêanu* being used seriously as terms of abuse in adult speech. However, I did observe the occasional use of *géamádu* in child-directed speech when mothers were scolding their children. For example, in Extract 1, a mother becomes exasperated with her young son after repeatedly asking him to hand her a calabash bowl with which to tend to her cooking pot, which is boiling over[5]:

Extract 1

1 Mother   *góonà gwèaríid òo* (.) *hàbéa Gáagà*
    góonà *gwèar-íi-d* *òo* (.) *hàbéa* *Gáagà*
    give.IMP.SG calabash-PS-UR male.VOC oath PSN
    'give me the calabash (.) good grief'
(Two lines skipped as mother addresses someone else)
2   (1.1)

---

[5] To transcribe Datooga, I use the orthography developed by the Datooga Bible Translation Project, with two differences: I transcribe the uvular stop as <q> rather than <gh> and I indicate surface tone (é = high; è = low; ê = falling). Tone marking is often omitted on vowels before a pause as these vowels tend to be whispered. Characters that differ from the IPA are as follows: <ch> [c]; <ea> [ɛː]; <j> [ɟ]; <ng'> [ŋ], <ny> [ɲ]; <oa> [ɔː]; <r> [ɾ]; <sh> [ʃ]; <y> [j]. Double vowel letters represent long vowels. Other transcription conventions loosely follow those of Conversation Analysis: (.) indicates a pause of less than 200 milliseconds, otherwise the pause length in milliseconds is indicated in brackets; ? indicates rising intonation; ↑ indicates a steep rising intonation; text between > < indicates speech that was uttered faster than usual; = indicates no gap between turns; [and] indicate the start and end of overlapping speech, respectively; .h(h) indicates inbreath.

3 Mother	géayíi góon èaréa gwèaríin bêa gwèanu gíl òo	
	g-éa-yíi góon èaréa gwèar-íin-i	
	AFF-1SG-say give.IMP.SG even calabash-PS-DEM.PROX	
	bêa gwêanu gíl òo	
	ASSOC father.2SG.POSS thing male.VOC	
	'I said give me even this calabash of your father'	
4	(0.55)	
5 Mother	jé	
	[interjection indexing frustration]	
6 Mother	[child's name]	
7	(0.75)	
8 Mother	[child's name]	
9	(0.3)	
10 Child	óoo	
	[response token]	
11 Mother	géamád	
	mother.2SG.POSS	
	lit. 'your mother'	

In line 1, the mother makes her third request for the calabash, repeating and expanding on this request a fourth time in line 3. Receiving no response from her son, in line 5 she utters an interjection indexing frustration; she then produces two summonses (lines 6 and 8) using her child's name, and when he finally answers (line 10), she replies with the form *géamád* (the final -*u* is inaudible here). The position of this utterance is significant: she has finally secured her son's attention (line 10) and chooses to react to her son's first turn at talk with this insulting expression. While "insult" is perhaps too strong for what she achieves in line 11, the utterance places her son's behaviour in an evaluative frame; it expresses her displeasure with his earlier non-participation.

Child-directed uses of *géamádu* suggest that sexual connotations are not necessarily at play in the abusive use of these kinship terms. To say that the utterance in line 11 performs offence by referring to incest would be rather bizarre, since the referent of the kin term 'your mother' is the speaker herself. Rather, the communicative effect – taking a highly negative stance towards the addressee – seems to be what is important here, perhaps working as a trope on the adult insult (Agha 2007). Semantically, the "mother" theme is relevant to the extent that it invokes a moral framework of social conduct within which the child's behaviour can be evaluated. In Section 4.5, I discuss the use of kinship-related insults in other languages, but I note here a remarkably similar usage of *uwaka/ki* 'your mother' and *ubanka/ki* 'your father' in Hausa, which Yalwa (1992: 75) explains can serve "regulative/corrective purposes" in child-directed speech.

4.3 The kin terms 'mother' and 'father' in informal oaths

The same parental kin terms 'mother' and 'father' that may be used to perform abuse also occur in expressions that attest to the truth of a proposition, i.e., these forms can function as oaths. The deictic anchoring of these terms in oaths is different from that of insults, however: in oaths they are anchored to the speaker (i.e. 'my mother', 'my father'), rather than to the addressee:

Extract 2

1	Majirjir	*áníini míi dàw íiyà*
		áníini qáy míi dà-w íiyà
		1SG.PRO PST NEG.COP 1SG.SBJV-go mother
		'I hadn't been, dear' [to the market]
2		(0.7)
3	Majirjir	*ání géawíi néa gêadèenù*
		ání g-éa-wíi néa g-êa-dèenù
		1SG.PRO AFF-1SG-go CONJ AFF-1SG-be.size.of.CP
		'I went when I was like I am now' [an adult]
4		(0.3)
5	Udeaweeda	*àh-áh↑*
		'no!'
6		(0.2)
7	Majirjir	*qwéandéanyú*
		qwéan-déa-nyú
		father-UR-1SG.POSS
		'I swear'

This extract of speech is taken from a conversation between a married woman, Majirjir, and a sixteen-year-old girl who lives nearby and who often visits on her way to the well. They are talking about adolescent girls attending the large, fortnightly markets in nearby towns, and Majirjir states that she didn't go to the market as a girl, but only as a married woman (line 3). Her interlocutor, Udeaweeda, expresses disbelief at this claim by uttering the interjection *àh-áh* 'no' with sharp rising intonation on the second syllable. In response, Majirjir says *qwéandéanyú*, literally 'my father', meaning 'I swear', or 'it's true'. This phrase, and others that perform the same discourse function, points back to an earlier discursive object, in this case the proposition that the speaker only went to the market as a married woman. The utterance in line 7 takes an epistemic stance on the truth value of that earlier proposition, emphasizing that it is true. I label this as an "oath" in English in the sense of a "solemn or formal declaration invoking God (or a god, or other object of reverence) as witness to the truth of a statement" (OED), though these are "everyday" oaths, not especially solemn or formal.[6]

The forms of everyday oaths vary according to the gender of the speaker: women and girls swear by their father; men and boys by their mother.[7] A phrase such as *qwéandéanyú* thus not only indexes a stance towards the truth value of some proposition in the discourse, it projects the speaker's gender as a second-order index (Silverstein 2003). In addition to the form 'my father', female speakers use the expression *jèedá qwâan* for the same function, which translates literally as 'father's stomach'. In male speech, the single word form 'my mother' for oath-taking is not attested in my corpus, but only in combination with *jèeda* 'stomach', e.g. *jèedá qéamátta, jèedíiyá, jèedá qéamátteânyu*. (Datooga has two words for 'mother', *íiyá* and *qéamátta* – see Mitchell 2017 for discussion.) An analysis of the semantic significance of *jèeda* 'stomach' in these expressions would require an excursus into the figurative meanings of this word for Datooga speakers; here I just note that metonymic processes are common in oaths cross-linguistically (e.g., Early Modern English *by God's bones, by God's foot, by God's guts* [cited in Ljung 2011: 100]).

Similarly gendered patterns of oath-taking are attested in other African languages. Kirundi speakers swear oaths by opposite-sex kin: for men, preferably first-born daughters, nieces, and mothers; for women, fathers (Masagara 1997). In Zulu, according to Callaway (1868), men attest to the truth of something by swearing by female relatives and women by male relatives. Kratz (1989: 644) reports that in Okiek, "conversational oaths" take the form *yu* ('like') followed by the name or kin term of specific kin of the opposite sex to speaker (either an avoided senior in-law or a classificatory child of the speaker). Carstens (1983) cites two older sources that claim that the most serious oath a Nama (Khoekhoe) man could take was the name of his sister, with whom he stood in an avoidance

---

6 See http://www.oed.com (accessed 1 November 2018).
7 Even young children are sensitive to this gendered aspect of language use. Before I had noticed the gendered pattern, I swore by my mother and was immediately corrected by a six-year-old boy.

relationship. These gender oppositions in oath-taking practices have been explained in terms of incest, e.g., Callaway (1868) and Kratz (1989), who relates Okiek oaths to curses in which one wishes incestuous relationships upon the cursed.[8] In the case of Kirundi oaths, speakers make literal reference to incestuous relations; see Masagara (1997: 389). The idea here is that speakers show their commitment to the truth by referring to some taboo act – in this case incestuous relations with close kin – that would occur were they found to be wrong. That everyday Datooga oaths involve this same logic is a valid interpretation of why male speakers invoke 'mother' and female speakers invoke 'father', although of course these phrases are now formulaic, with conventionalized performative effects. But these oaths do not relate solely to the incest taboo; they also involve ideas about deference relationships. All of these examples invoke someone to whom you normatively defer, or who normatively defers to you; parental kin meet this criterion in Datooga.[9] I return to concepts of deference and honour in the concluding section.

4.4 *Gíishíimda*: Ritualized interjectional phrases referring to kin

Kin terms also occur in a form of speech called *gíishíimda*. *Gíishíimda* is a metapragmatic label for a category of speech acts which is difficult to translate into English; here I gloss it as 'invocation'. The form *gíishíimda* is a nominalization of the transitive verb *shiim*, e.g., *góoshíim qwàan* 's/he invokes her/his father'. In metapragmatic discussions about this word, several consultants distinguished two types of *gíishíimda*: the act of uttering names upon spearing an animal during a ritual hunt; and referring to one's father or other kin in moments of anger, pain, or surprise. I discuss these two kinds of speech acts in Sections 4.4.1 and 4.4.2, respectively.

Translating *shiim* and *gíishíimda* is not straightforward. What connects the two types of speech act just described is ritualized reference to persons of special significance to speaker, usually close kin. In both cases, *gíishíimda* denotes the calling out of a name or noun phrase as a complete turn at talk. This calling out has a formulaic and figurative quality; a literal summons such as 'my father',

---

8 Callaway (1868: 59) suggests that Zulu oaths can be paraphrased "what I say is true, otherwise I could be guilty of incest with my mother".
9 Note that in English, people also swear to the truth of something by their mothers and fathers, as in phrases like "on my mother's/father's life".

directly addressed to the appropriate referent, would not constitute a case of *gíishíimda*. I have glossed the verb *shiim* as 'invoke', using this English term in its loose sense of uttering, or citing, a name or other referring expression in a ritualized context. However, according to the OED, to 'invoke' properly means to "call on (God, a deity, etc.) in prayer or as a witness".[10] Translating *shiim* as 'invoke' thus implies that *gíishíimda* is a vocative act, when in fact the addressivity of these speech acts is opaque. In the case of ritual hunts, we might argue that young men invoke their fathers as witnesses to their hunting successes – an idea I discuss below. In the case of everyday interjections, though, speakers are not in any meaningful sense "calling on" non-present kin in these performances of emotion. Nonetheless, further investigation of the ideologies associated with *gíishíimda* might reveal connections between invoking and interjecting. We know that in other sociohistorical contexts, expletive interjections have developed diachronically from invocations in prayer, e.g. *Jesus* in English (Gehweiler 2008).

In Datooga, *gíishíimda* is by no means an offensive act. Neither type of speech act would be labelled with the Datooga concept *ng'eaw* 'swear', in the sense of using language abusively. Yet these speech acts bear some likeness to swearing: they are strongly performative; they are formulaic; and they draw on a morally charged domain of meaning – in this case, kinship. The lexicalized interjections discussed in Section 4.4.2 also have much in common with "expletives" in other languages (such as the similarly mild *Oh my God!* in English), as we will see. First we look at the phenomenon of *gíishíimda* in ritual hunts.

4.4.1 *Gíishíimda* during a ritual hunt

Gíishíimda refers to an act of invocation that occurs in the context of youth culture (*qéaréemànéandúuméeda*) among Datooga, specifically, during a ritual hunting expedition. The ritual hunt is a highly significant and indeed life-threatening part of youth cultural practices, in which a group of young Datooga men travels into the bush under conditions of secrecy to hunt large animals such as lions and elephants (Blystad 2000). When a young man successfully spears an animal during a ritual hunt, he calls out the name of his clan, and/or his father's name, as well as the name of his *ng'wàsánéeda*, the young woman he loves and mentors. This behaviour is labelled *gíishíimda*.[11] (See Blystad

---
10 See http://www.oed.com (accessed 30 October 2018).
11 Blystad (2000) describes the *lilichta* ritual hunt in some detail; see 88–94. Although she does not refer to *gíishíimda* specifically, she writes, "[a]t the moment the spear hits the target, the man calls out the names of his spear, his father, his spirit guardian and the name of the

2000, Ch.3, for details on youth culture among Datooga, including the concept of *ng'wàsánéeda*.) From a functional perspective, by naming his clan and/or his father, a young man identifies himself to others present and claims the success of the spearing as his own. From a more symbolic perspective, we should consider *gíishíimda* in the context of a heightened emotional and experiential state: the spearing of an animal is a source of great honour to the spearer and is followed by a period of status transformation (again, see Blystad 2000 for elaboration on this point). This ritual act of naming one's clan or one's father has a religious or sacred quality, then, linking the honour and glory of the spearing with one's kinsmen and ancestors. When a young man invokes his *ng'wàsánéeda*, we might interpret this as an act of dedication that indexically ties the hunter to the object of his love. This tie materially manifests itself on the hunter's return, when his *ng'wàsánéeda* presents him with gifts.[12]

Although this type of *gíishíimda* does not obviously relate to the concept of swearing, I would emphasize that in ritual hunts, the names of kin are invoked at a symbolically transformative, perhaps even transcendental, moment – not when one releases the spear, but as the spear hits its target.[13] Blystad (2000: 101) underlines the "sacred grounding" and even "divine" nature of the ritual hunt. This association of *gíishíimda* with concepts of the sacred is perhaps what motivates its permutation into more mundane acts of emotional exclamation – as in the "curious convergence of the high and the low, the sacred and the profane" that Hughes (1991: 4) observes with respect to swearing. I address these more mundane acts in the following subsection.

4.4.2 *Gíishíimda* in exclamations

The second, more mundane type of *gíishíimda* is when someone calls out the name of a relative or a kin term upon getting hurt, or dropping something, or being surprised. These utterances function like interjections: "a class of words which can stand on their own as utterances and which refer to mental acts" (Ameka 1992: 111). Since these utterances have semantic value, some are more

---

girl he has carried along on the journey" (2000: 89). (My consultants did not mention the spear name, nor the spirit guardian.)
12 Alternatively, a young man might call out the name of a young woman he is in conflict with, who has rejected him. In this case, this young woman will also have to present him with gifts.
13 Evans-Pritchard (1951) reports that Nuer call out their own ox-names as they release their spear. He interprets this as a kind of projection of the self onto the spear.

accurately classified as secondary interjections, and others are not interjections at all, but multi-word "interjectional phrases" in Ameka's (1992: 111) terminology. Ameka reserves the term 'interjection' for the word class, not the utterance type. I will follow this usage, since Datooga has a class of interjections, and these kinship-oriented interjectional phrases can also contain interjections.[14] While I will only discuss interjectional phrases relating to kinship concepts here, Datooga speakers make use of a range of interjectional phrases that do not involve kinship. Among the most common are the (secondary) interjections '*Dàtóo!*', meaning 'Datooga people' and '*sàséeda!*' 'body', both of which get incorporated into interjectional phrases with expressions referring to kin (see below). The semantic domain of the spirit world also provides interjectional material, e.g., '*ng'éanyíidá bádàw!*' 'the underworld'.

Everyday instances of *gíishíimda* can take numerous forms. In metapragmatic discussions of this practice, consultants noted that speakers can say the names of the following kinship categories or units:

(i) *qwêanda* 'father' (and classificatory fathers, e.g., *qwêandá mánàng*' 'father's younger brother');
(ii) *qéambábàaba* 'father's father';
(iii) *húdíiya* 'sister' (noted by one consultant);
(iv) clan name.

These names may occur alone or may be preceded by one of two nouns in their primary form: *hàbéa* or *fáqáya*, e.g., *hàbéa Gáaga* (see Extract 1, line 1), where *Gáaga* is the speaker's paternal uncle, or *fáqáy Àséechéekka*, where *Àséechéekka* is a clan name. The literal meaning of *fáqáya* is unknown, while *hàbéawòoda* means 'oath' or 'curse'. Another noun that combines with names in interjectional phrases is *sáséeda* 'body'; see Table 4.2 for examples. In addition to names, speakers can use kin terms to refer to these individuals, either alone or in combination with the nouns just mentioned, e.g., *hàbéa qwêanda* 'oath of father'. In actual use, I have observed a wide range of exclamatory expressions involving kinship concepts. I extracted 92 exclamation tokens from transcripts of conversation; these are sorted into general types, with examples, in Table 4.2.[15]

---

14 Datooga interjections include items like *sey*, *heaq*, and *ja*, which (to generalize) express disapproval, disgust, and irritation, respectively.

15 An additional form that is attested only once in my corpus and not mentioned by any consultant is *ng'úttòodá qáhêanya*, which literally means 'the spearing of our house' (where 'house' refers to the kinship unit). I wonder if this example of interjectional *gíishíimda* makes explicit reference to the other type of *gíishíimda*, where a man utters the names of kin upon

4 "Oh, bald father!": Kinship and swearing among Datooga of Tanzania — 91

Table 4.2: Exclamations relating to kinship.

Interjectional phrase type	Example(s)	Notes
Dàtóogá 'people' + 'father'	Dàtóogá bàabà	only occurs with bàabà
fáqáya + name / kin term	fáqáy Àséechéekka	'faqay of Aseecheeka!'
	fáqáyá qwêanda	'faqay of father!'
hàbéa 'oath; curse' + name /	hàbéa Gáaga	'oath of Gaaga!'
kin term (+ modifier)	hàbéa qwêanda	'oath of father!'
	hàbéa òorjéedá Gídáhútta	'oath of Gidahutta's son!'
	hàbéa qwêandá wáas	'oath of old father!'
sáséedá 'body' + name /	sáséedá òorjéedá	'body of the son of a Bajuuta
kin term (+ modifier)	Bájúuchêanda	person!'
	sáséedá bàabà	'father's body!'
	sáséedá húdá Gáaga	'body of the daughter of Gaaga!'
	sáséedá Máhèetùun	'body of Maheetuun!'
kin term (+ modifier)	qéambábbàabà	'father's father!'
	qwéandéanyu	'my father!'
	bàabéedéanyu	'my father!'
interjection + kin term	óo qwêandá síqùs	'oh the father alone!'
(+ modifier)	óo bàabwée	'oh father!'
	óo qéambábbàabà	'oh father's father!'
	óo qwéandá mêara	'oh bald father!'

From the examples in Table 4.2, we observe that only certain types of kin seem to feature in these interjectional phrases, as also noted by consultants. The most prominent kinship concepts in exclamations are 'father' and 'father's father'. One cannot help but note that this should be so in a strongly patrilineal society in which a person's father determines their clan identity and is an object of honour and deference. Similarly, one can *shiim* the name of one's clan – a unit organized around, and thus a symbol of, patrilineal kinship. When asked if one could invoke *qéamátta* 'mother' in an exclamatory context, a female consultant immediately rejected this as a possibility, with the explanation *qéamátta éa shéagi* 'mother is distant'. However, the semantic content of these exclamations does not exclusively denote male kin: speakers can make reference to daughters and sisters (as in *sáséedá húdá Gáaga* in Table 4.2). The same consultant explained why one could invoke *húdíiyá* 'sister' (literally 'daughter of mother') in this context as follows:

---

spearing a wild animal. This exclamation may derive its affective force, in that case, partly through reference to the sacred act of spearing.

(1) gídá   májéekì   àbà   héedá   búunèe-   àbà   héedá   héadígà
    thing   strong   PREP place   people   PREP place   men
    '[sister] is an important/powerful thing for peop- for men'

According to this metapragmatic account, *gíishíimda* has to do with the closeness of the kinship bond, and with strength or potency. Closeness here seems to imply membership of the same clan: a person's mother belongs to a different clan and is not an object of *shiim*, while a sister holds the same clan membership. I have no good explanation for why 'sister' should be a potent or 'strong' kinship category, but it may relate to the special economic and social relations that hold between brothers and sisters.[16] The point that only certain types of kin are invoked in *gíishíimda*, and that these only partially overlap with those invoked in insults and oaths, suggests the overarching significance of 'father' as a moral concept for Datooga (see Section 4.5).

In the last part of this section, I want to consider the interactional functions of these interjectional phrases. At the outset I impressionistically claimed that these utterances have "expressive" functions: they express anger, surprise, pain, or other emotional states, much like expletive interjections in other languages. Speakers mentioned 'surprise' and 'anger' in discussions of these phrases. Wilkinson and Kitzinger (2006: 152), in their study of English surprise tokens, show that emotional displays in language are "not involuntary spontaneous emotional eruptions", but rather interactional tools that achieve a variety of social actions. In Kockelman's (2003) analysis of the meanings of interjections in Q'eqchi' Maya, he emphasizes that interjections do more than index emotional states by distinguishing four classes of indexical objects: situational objects (things in the immediate environment); discursive objects (other linguistic signs); expressive objects ("internal" states); and social objects (aspects of status and relationships). While I do not have space to determine the indexical meanings of each form, these categories are useful for thinking more precisely about what interjectional phrases achieve in context. For instance, in Extract 1, line 1, we saw how the mother uttered the interjectional phrase *hàbéa Gáagà* after asking her son to pass her a calabash for the third time (the two earlier requests are not included in the transcript). This utterance indexes an object in the situational context, namely, the child's lack of action. More precisely, it indexes an evaluative stance towards that object – that it is undesirable. As such, *hàbéa Gáagà*

---

[16] When a woman is married, the bridewealth transferred to her natal family belongs to her eldest full brother, and he also owns the dowry cattle that accompany his sister to her marital home, until she gives birth to a son. If a woman gets divorced, she can return to her brother's house (Klima 1970).

simultaneously indexes an expressive object, i.e. how the speaker feels about this state of affairs. But the expressive object (let's call it irritation) is not a communicative end in itself: the mother is coercing her son into action by framing his inertia as a cause for her emotional distress. Through the indexicality of this act of *gíishíimda* (followed later by a term of abuse), she positions the child's behaviour in a moral, evaluative framework that ultimately propels him to fulfil her request – he goes to get the calabash bowl.

However, the speaker's "internal state" is not always relevant to the interpretation of these interjectional phrases, as Extract 3 shows. Just prior to the start of this extract, a woman is sitting inside her house and sees a child approaching with a pile of sugarcane.

Extract 3

1 Woman   *(h)àbéa >qwêand<=míshéarjéega gíyèadú súuhú?*
            hàbéa qwêan-d mishear-jée-ga   g-í-yèadú   súuhú
            oath   father-UR sugar.cane-PS-MR AFF-2SG-convey.CP DEM.PROX.PL
            'good grief=is this the sugarcane you brought?'
2   (0.9)
3   *gwáchà géegásà géa méangùrèey húdèany(u)*
            gwáchà g-ée-gásà   géa   méangùrèey
            earlier AFF-1PL-want.IS REL.PRO.PL sorghum
            húdèa-ny(u)
            daughter.UR-1SG.POSS
            'we wanted sorghum ones, my daughter'

In line 1, the woman responds to a specific situational object – the pile of sugarcane in the girl's arms. The interjectional phrase *hàbéa qwêanda* indexes this object as undesirable, as in our previous example, or at least as problematic in some way. The speaker then carefully informs the child that she has brought the wrong item (her polar question raises the possibility that there is an alternative kind of sugarcane she might have brought; the utterance in line 3 then states what was wanted, using a distancing past time modifier and plural subject). The interjectional phrase indexes an evaluative stance towards a situational object: it reveals a "discrepancy" in participants' understandings of the unfolding of events (Wilkinson and Kitzinger 2006: 173). As such, *hàbéa qwêanda* serves to pre-empt the explanation to the girl that she had brought the wrong kind of produce. To the extent that the interjectional phrase indexes an expressive object in line 1, the communicative effect is to publicly evaluate an object in the world as problematic rather than to express the speaker's psychological experience.

In Extract 3, the exclamation occurs as the initial reaction to something, but not all interjectional phrases invoking kin have this spontaneous quality; they can also be delayed (see also Wilkinson and Kitzinger 2006):

Extract 4

1 Woman (inaudible) *qúuttá síida hêedá máanálí héet Tàl ès Sálá(h)am (hh)*=
                qúud-dá   *síi-da*   *hêe-dá*   *m-áa-nálí*   *hêe-dá*
                mouth-UR   person-UR   place-UR   NEG-1SG-know.IS   place-UR
                Tàl ès Sáláam
                Dar es S.
                '[they'll take] a person's voice I don't know where, to Dar es Salaam'
2   =[hehehehehe
3 Sister   [hehehehehehehehe
4 Woman .hhh ooo(h)oo. [hehehehe
5 Sister   [he he .hhh=
6 Woman =*óo qwéandá mêara*
                oo   *qwéan-dá* *mêara*
                oh   father-UR bald.SG
                'goodness me'

In Extract 4, a woman refers to my recording equipment (just after a newcomer has joined the interaction and greeted me), commenting that people's voices will be taken somewhere like Dar es Salaam. She begins to laugh as she completes the utterance and she and her sister both continue to laugh for approximately five seconds. The woman then utters the interjectional phrase *óo qwéandá mêara*. The indexical object of this utterance is ambiguous: it might be her proposition about the recording going to Dar es Salaam (a discursive object) or it might refer to the camera or general recording event (situational objects). As in the previous examples, the phrase indexes a situational discrepancy – in this case, something out of the ordinary – but the evaluative tone is one of humour rather than undesirability, hence the laughter. Importantly, this interjectional phrase is not an initial response; it's not performing some "as-if visceral" emotional reaction (Wilkinson and Kitzinger 2006: 155). Rather, *óo qwéandá mêara* seems to function in the opposite way, as a summarizing or closing move (cf. the use of Arabic *inshallah*, also an invocation, in topic closure, as discussed in Clift and Helani 2010). After this utterance, the conversation moves on to other topics. The interactional effect of invoking one's father here, then, differs from our other cases, although all three examples index an evaluative stance.

To make claims about the default and secondary functions of these interjectional phrases in Datooga would require more in-depth interactional analysis of all tokens in the corpus. However, with this brief analytical investigation we have moved beyond the idea that these interjections straightforwardly express bodily experiences such as "surprise" or "pain". Rather, these phrases index some object in the situational or discursive environment and evaluate that object as discrepant, i.e. undesirable and/or unexpected. The evaluative stances that speakers communicate by uttering these forms of exclamation can have different interactional functions, including mobilizing a response to a request; pre-empting repair of a mistake; or closing a sequence.

4.5 The sociolinguistics of *gíishíimda*

In addition to the situational and interactional meanings that arise from the use of interjectional phrases, utterances like *hàbéa Gáagà* also index social relations. Kockelman (2003) includes "social" objects among his four classes of indexical objects of interjections (see Section 4.4.2). By "social objects" he means the social roles and relationships of speech participants that an interjection points to; for instance, a particular interjection might stereotypically index female speakers. In our case, *gíishíimda* practices, particularly those involving names, index kinship relationships between the speaker and specific individuals. A speaker can exclaim '*hàbéa Gáagà*' because she is the (classificatory) daughter of a man named Gaaga. The referential content of this phrase denotes a particular individual, and by using the phrase in the context of *gíishíimda*, the speaker indexes her own genealogical relatedness to them. By analogy, a speaker who exclaims '*óo qwéandá mêara*' can be understood to be indexing the relationship between herself and her own father (as opposed to referring to the general category of 'father'). The creative aspect of these utterances, evidenced by the way speakers modify kin terms with adjectives such as 'bald' or 'black' or 'old', supports this interpretation.

This social indexing has two interesting implications. First, it means that interjectional practices are, to some extent, variable across speakers. The use of interjections such as *Dàtóo!* are not speaker-anchored and do not demonstrate much inter-speaker variation. Kinship-based interjectional phrases such as *qwéandéanyu* 'my father' are similarly uniform across speakers, even though they may denote distinct individuals. But *gíishíimda* phrases containing names index the specific social identity of the speaker. This leads to the second and related point, which is that a speaker's use of interjectional phrases indexes membership of a particular kinship unit. The linguistic practice of *gíishíimda* constructs categories of speaker on the basis of kinship ties and thus reinforces concepts of relatedness and belonging. A good illustration of this social meaning of *gíishíimda* can be seen in the utterance transcribed in (2). Just prior to this utterance, a young woman has met her mother-in-law's sister for the first time and hears her utter the expression *sáséedá Máhéetùun* 'Maheetuun's body'. She responds to this with the metalinguistic comment in (2):

(2) Máhéetúun g-óo-shíim-ày qáh-êa-ng'wà séaní
 PSN AFF-2PL-name-PLUR house-PS-2PL.POSS all
 'All of you at your house invoke Maheetùun!'

Although the speaker probably doesn't know this, Maheetuun is the name of these women's father's father. In observing that this name is a shared point of reference in different peoples' *gíishíimda* practices, the daughter-in-law categorizes those individuals as belonging to a kinship unit, namely *qáhêang'wa* 'your house'. As such, she explicitly reflects on the links between behavioural practices and concepts of kinship – the topic of the final section.

4.6 Conclusions: Morality, honour, kinship, and swearing

This chapter has examined a range of kinship-related linguistic practices in Datooga: the use of the kin terms 'your mother' and 'your father' in insults; the use of the kin terms 'my mother' and 'my father' in informal oaths attesting to truthfulness; and the use of kin terms and names of kin at the moment of spearing an animal during ritual hunts, as well as in more mundane contexts of communicating unexpectedness. In all these cases, except for the ritual hunt, kinship is invoked in acts of evaluation. Insults constitute negative evaluations of the addressee; oaths constitute evaluations of the epistemic status of a proposition; and in interjectional phrases, kin terms index evaluations of a situational or discursive object as unexpected or discrepant. This final section considers explanations for why kin are invoked in this range of speech contexts.

First, though, I want to emphasize the relevance of the general theme of kinship for swearing practices across cultures. We know that kinship often figures in insults, and we also find kinship references in the interjectional expressions of languages other than Datooga. As mentioned above, Ljung (2011) identifies a "mother theme" in his cross-cultural survey of swearing. Drange et al. (2014) explore this theme further in adolescent speech in Norwegian, English, and Spanish, showing that swearing by mother is present in all three languages (though significantly more common in Spanish). As we've seen, 'mother' is only one kinship category invoked in Datooga swearing and oath-taking, and different categories are found in other languages, too: Drange et al. (2014) cite examples of British teenagers using the form *your dad* and even *gran* as insults. In Hausa, the utterances 'your mother' and 'your father' can both be harsh insults, as well as in the Nigerian language Tarok (Blench 2012). The expression 'your father's head' is an insult in the Thai language Kam Muang (Howard 2007), as well as in Malaysian.[17] The very same expression can also be used as a curse in Dominican Patwa (Paugh 2005). As for interjectional phrases, the concept of 'mother' figures in Italian *mamma mia* and in Kannada (*amma*) is "a cry of surprise or distress" (Bean 1975: 315), while American English has *oh brother*. Datooga is perhaps more unusual in invoking fathers and grandfathers in interjectional contexts. Nonetheless I propose that Ljung's (2011) mother theme is a subtype of a broader theme of "kinship" in cross-cultural swearing practices.

Why do speakers of different languages invoke kin in contexts of swearing, insulting, oath-taking, and expressing surprise and other evaluative stances? On one level, the kinship theme doesn't actually matter: for individuals, these expressions produce their interactional effects regardless of their referential meaning. But from a socio-historical and cross-cultural perspective, the semantic thread of "kinship" that runs through these practices invites explanation. One argument might be that kin terms easily acquire affective indexical meanings (Besnier 1990) and "emotion-laden" words are good candidates for swear words (Pavlenko 2008: 148). An alternative, though related, argument is that in many if not most communities, kinship relations are of abiding moral significance, and "people swear by what is most potent to them" (Hughes 1991: 249). Relations between kin are moral in the sense that they involve long-term rights, obligations, and commitments, whether economic, political, and/or social in nature (Bloch 1973). The notion of honour is important here: an individual's honour is often linked to that of their kin; and ethical codes stipulate that one

---

17 This phrase was recently used in the Malaysian House of Representatives: https://www.malaymail.com/s/1659614/furore-in-parliament-as-kepala-bapak-insults-fly (accessed 8 November 2018).

should honour certain kinship relations (cf. one of the Ten Commandments in the Bible). Abusive swearing targets this concept of honour with respect to the addressee's kin, offending by dishonouring, sometimes through an explicit combination of kinship terms and taboo concepts, e.g. *motherfucker*, and sometimes more implicitly. Oaths of truth-telling rely on an understanding of familial honour to support a speaker's claim: in Section 3, we saw how truth is placed in an inverse relationship with the most dishonourable possibility of incest. For Datooga, invocations of kin in ritual hunts also seem to relate to both personal and familial honour at a spiritually charged moment. The mundane or "profane" uses of kin terms in exclamatory contexts function as tropes of these more solemn invocations, a dynamic they share with expressions like *oh my God* in English.

I have brought together the concepts of kinship relations and morality in a general way here; the huge literature on kinship, ethics, and morality in social anthropology could help refine these ideas. Nonetheless, the link between kinship relations and moral sensibilities emphasizes something important about swearing and related practices: by swearing, speakers stake claims and make evaluations on the basis of things that matter to them, and things that matter are defined by shared moral frameworks. Ljung's (2011) work on swearing does not mention morality, although it would be difficult to explore "religion", one of his major swearing themes, without reference to morality. Drange et al. (2014) approach the topic when they offer a cultural explanation for the prevalence of swearing by mother in Spanish, arguing that it relates to the sacred status of 'mother' in Catholic countries. For the patrilineal Datooga, 'father' is a key symbolic figure who links an individual to their clan and their ancestral kin. Fathers are objects of honour, and as we have seen, are invoked in all the linguistic contexts discussed in this chapter. We might go so far as to say that fathers (and fathers' fathers) are 'sacred' – they occupy a high position in the moral order, and so are good to swear by. The position of mothers is more complex – they figure in insults and oaths but not in *gíishíimda*. An important next step for ethnographic work on the kinship theme in swearing practices is to account for such differences by teasing out the social and ethical associations of different types of kin.

In closing, I would also like to suggest that the kinds of practices discussed in this chapter can help substantiate anthropological claims about communities being "kinship-oriented" or "organized by kinship". These everyday speech habits draw on notions of kinship because kinship relations loom so large in Datooga understandings of the moral order. Even as that order might shift and change, highly conventionalized linguistic practices relating to swearing, oath-taking, and evaluating reflect – and re-constitute – a communal preoccupation with kinship.

Abbreviations

1	first person
2	second person
3	third person
AFF	affirmative
ASSOC	associative
CONJ	conjunction
COP	copular
CP	centripetal
DEM	demonstrative
IMP	imperative
IS	inflectional suffix
MR	multiple reference
NEG	negative
PL	plural
PLUR	pluractional
POSS	possessive
PREP	preposition
PRO	pronoun
PROX	proximate
PS	primary suffix
PSN	personal name
PST	past
REL	relative
SBJV	subjunctive
SG	singular
UR	unit reference
VOC	vocative

References

Agha, Asif. 2007. *Language and social relations*. Cambridge: Cambridge University Press.

Ameka, Felix. 1992. Interjections: The universal yet neglected part of speech. *Journal of Pragmatics* 18 (2): 101–118.

Baerman, Matthew. 2014. Suppletive kin term paradigms in the languages of New Guinea. *Linguistic Typology* 18 (3): 413–448.

Bean, Susan S. 1975. Referential and indexical meanings of *amma* in Kannada: Mother, woman, goddess, pox, and help! *Journal of Anthropological Research* 31 (4): 313–330.

Besnier, Niko. 1990. Language and affect. *Annual Review of Anthropology* 19 (1): 419–451.

Blench, Roger. 2012. Tarok exclamations and interjections. Unpublished manuscript. http://www.rogerblench.info/Language/Niger-Congo/BC/Plateau/Tarokoid/Tarok/Grammar/Tarok%20exclamations.pdf (accessed 9 November 2018).

Bloch, Maurice. 1973. The long term and the short term: The economic and political significance of the morality of kinship. In: Jack Goody (ed.), *The character of kinship*, 75–88. Cambridge: Cambridge University Press.

Blystad, Astrid. 2000. *Precarious procreation: Datoga pastoralists at the late 20th century*. Bergen: University of Bergen PhD dissertation.

Callaway, Henry. 1868. *Nursery tales: Traditions and histories of the Zulus in their own words*. Natal: Springvale Mission Station.

Carstens, Peter. 1983. The inheritance of private property among the Nama of southern Africa reconsidered. *Africa: Journal of the International African Institute* 53 (2): 58–70.

Clift, Rebecca and Fadi Helani. 2010. Inshallah: Religious invocations in Arabic topic transition. *Language in Society* 39 (3): 357–382.

Dahl, Östen and Maria Koptjevskaja-Tamm. 2001. Kinship in grammar. In Irène Baron, Michael Herslund and Finn Sørensen (eds.), *Dimensions of possession*, 201–225. Amsterdam: Benjamins.

Drange, Eli-Marie Danbolt, Ingrid Kristine Hasund and Anna-Brita Stenström. 2014. "Your mum!": Teenagers' swearing by mother in English, Spanish and Norwegian. *International Journal of Corpus Linguistics* 19 (1): 29–59.

Evans-Pritchard, E. E. 1951. Some features and forms of Nuer sacrifices. *Africa: Journal of the International African Institute* 21 (2): 112–121.

Fleming, Luke and Michael Lempert. 2011. Introduction: Beyond bad words. *Anthropological Quarterly* 84 (1): 5–13.

Gehweiler, Elke. 2008. From proper name to primary interjection: The case of gee! *Journal of Historical Pragmatics* 9 (1): 71–88.

Howard, Kathryn. 2007. Kinterm usage and hierarchy in Thai children's peer groups. *Journal of Linguistic Anthropology* 17 (2): 204–230.

Hughes, Geoffrey. 1991. *Swearing: A social history of foul language, oaths and profanity in English*. Oxford: Blackwell.

Kießling, Roland. 2000. Number marking in Datooga nouns. In Rainer Vossen, Angelika Mietzner and Antje Meissner (eds.), *Mehr als nur Worte. Afrikanistische Beiträge zum 65. Geburtstag von Franz Rottland*, 349–366. Cologne: Rüdiger Köppe.

Klima, George J. 1970. *The Barabaig: East African cattle-herders*. New York: Holt, Rinehart and Winston.

Kockelman, Paul. 2003. The meanings of interjections in Q'eqchi' Maya: From emotive reaction to social and discursive action. *Current Anthropology* 44 (4): 467–490.

Kratz, Corinne A. 1989. Genres of power: A comparative analysis of Okiek blessings, curses and oaths. *Man* 24 (4): 636–656.

Ljung, Magnus. 2011. *Swearing: A cross-cultural linguistic study*. Basingstoke: Palgrave Macmillan.

Masagara, Ndinzi. 1997. Negotiating the truth through oath forms. *Journal of Multilingual and Multicultural Development* 18 (5): 385–401.

Mitchell, Alice. 2017. The pragmatics of a kinship term: The meaning and use of *íiyá* 'mother' in Datooga (Nilotic). In Raija Kramer and Roland Kießling (eds.), *Mechthildian Approaches to Afrikanistik: Advances in language based research on Africa. Festschrift für Mechthild Reh*, 287–301. Cologne: Rüdiger Köppe.

Paugh, Amy L. 2005. Multilingual play: Children's code-switching, role play, and agency in Dominica, West Indies. *Language in Society* 34 (1): 63–86.

Pavlenko, Aneta. 2008. Emotion and emotion-laden words in the bilingual lexicon. *Bilingualism: Language and Cognition* 11 (2): 147–164.

Silverstein, Michael. 2003. Indexical order and the dialectics of sociolinguistic life. *Language & Communication* 23 (3–4): 193–229.

Wilkinson, Sue and Celia Kitzinger. 2006. Surprise as an interactional achievement: Reaction tokens in conversation. *Social Psychology Quarterly* 69 (2): 150–182.

Yalwa, Lawan Danladi. 1992. Socio-cultural and linguistic implications of abusive expressions in Hausa. *Ufahamu: A Journal of African Studies* 20 (1): 68–84.

Anne Storch
5 Aesthetics of the obscure: Swearing as horrible play

Abstract: This chapter is concerned with swearing and performances of affect. It discusses transgressive language in the form of yelling and screaming, and conflict that translates into accusations of magic and witchcraft. Swearing here is seen as doing things with words (Austin 1962), in the sense of speaking as doing, when words obtain the power to change reality (Grehan 2004). This perspective on swearing highlights the ways in which transgressive, reality-changing speech is performed: the shrill voice, the words turned into incomprehensible yells, the difficulties in finding words at all, and the use of other communicative means instead: spitting, crying, embodying. Uttered swear words that only faintly resemble "words", and whose meaning can only be guessed through their embeddedness in context, are, to the linguist, a semiotically very complex aspect of language practice: this is language and yet it isn't. Noisy performance and embodiment are aspects of swearing practices that are decidedly opaque and even unintelligible. Violent outbursts of offensive speech often involve language that is pure agency but not, by itself, immediately intelligible to others. Linguistic opacity in swearing may signify emotions such as pain, fear, anger and wrath (Jay and Janschewitz 2008), but in ritual settings – as reflected in witchcraft and trance discourses – also has the power and agency to transform the other. Noisy performance and lack of words negate cooperative strategies and behavior, and swearing here is not fun and play, but rather sheer violence and transgression (Williams 2011). While other forms of swearing violate social norms, these forms of transgression threaten existences (Madadzhe 2012; Grehan 2004). Loud, unintelligible, out-of-key communicative performance therefore creates fear – there is a secret dimension here that is frightening (Taussig 1999) – and signifies an inescapable relation with those who have provoked it, and who are exposed to it. I argue that precisely this aspect of swearing as horrible play invites us to grasp language as reaching far beyond words, and, from an emic perspective, to consider the multiplicity of the speaker.

The chapter focuses on swearing and noisy performance and is especially interested in the practices of and perspectives on women. Moreover, the chapter addresses the intercultural semiotics of hostile communicative practices by including a discussion and analysis of performances and practices in migration settings, such as in a Mediterranean tourism context. As such a take on swearing involves listening to what should not have been said, and writing what should not be written, at least from the perspective of the players concerned, I aim at finding alternative ways of discussing "language": besides referring to more common types of "data" (my own field data), I discuss notes from my personal field diaries, poetic texts, art, and music.

5.1 At night

Walking down a narrow lane, hardly visible where it begins, where it branches off the main street, down which a late-night bus passes, with just a handful passengers on board. People park their scooters there and dump garbage at where one moves in, enters this lane, becomes almost invisible in its unlit messiness. No street lights here. The billboards of the bars around suffice. As we move on, walking carefully along this short street and trying to figure out what these heaps of thrown-away things might be (might have been), we already see the sea in front of us, moonlit water that begins right after the paseo, which lies between the end of the lane and all this salty water. In a dark corner in front of us there is something that moves. A sudden realization of the possibility of the existence of other life than ours in this dead zone. We get closer, and at once we understand that it is too late to go back. We have moved too far already for a return, which by now would resemble a flight rather than decency and concern. In front of us there is a man who leans on a gate, his face turned to us: white, a bit old, tired, his hair grey. A red sports shirt, blueish Bermuda pants. He tries not to return our stubborn gaze. A women stands close to him, her back turned to us. She bends down, towards the side, elegantly (like Garbo in *Camille* of 1937, when she is forced by the Baron to pick up her fan). She bends down to the side and does not bow her head and does not kneel. She gets up again and spits to her left. Again she bends, elegantly. And then she shrieks, very loud and very sudden. Comes up, moves away from him, with a loud and shrill yell. His pants are unzipped and his hands come up, as if in defense. *Ich hab dich nicht angefasst! Ich hab sie nicht angefasst!* – 'I didn't touch you! I have not touched her!' he says, obviously confused and helpless in his sudden state of being all alone in front of that shabby gate. She looks as if she wanted to scold him, slap him, and she shouts at him, hurls words at him that I do not understand clearly enough to make sense of her anger. Perhaps she wants to tell him that he should have warned her that there were people, that they were seen. But her yelling has a high-pitched quality that sounds staged, like a performance of chastity and upbringing: this blow-job was merely a misunderstanding, nothing that she normally does, not she, not here. She turns to us, round open eyes and a mouth full of yells, and I think that she looks as if there is a complicit smile hidden somewhere. Perhaps, I think, she was angry that he didn't warn her about being quick in his response to her actions. I ask whether she is ok, and she nods, yes, yes. The lane falls silent again, and I move on and step onto the paseo, where people floating out of the bars and night clubs walk towards their hotels, heated bodies under the bright streetlights.

There is yelling on the paseo, too (I will come to that later). Men walk in groups, wearing their group t-shirts or group party hats, and yell their favorite party songs as groups. Deep male voices, laughter that sounds like shouting; there is some hostility in it as well, because boundaries, even those around cheerful partying groups, are always exclusive and somewhat hostile. Others therefore pass quickly by, without making any attempt to join in. The paseo for several kilometers parallels a sandy beach, providing a link between the warm and shallow Mediterranean waters and hundreds of souvenir shops, cafés, bars, party locations and strip clubs. El Arenal is not a large town, just very close to the airport, which makes it ideal for tourists coming over to Mallorca from Germany or elsewhere in order to spend a long weekend. It has been the place for party tourists since the eighties, but now seems to be fading. Where there were thousands of partying men and women (more men than women), now only a few hundred spend money on beer, extra-large sausages and cheap sex in back rows. As soon as the shows they have come for – aged crooners, topless table dancers, male strippers – are over, the paseo and the beach are cleaned by huge machines, tractors pulling and pushing brushes and hosepipes and other tools. And while the last drinks are served to a few tired clients, the paseo is ready for yet another round of manipulated consumption and scripted transgression.

All the more reason to go back the next day and really explore the back lane. What would it look like? Will there be any traces of the night? So we went once more. The haunting thing we saw there was not the many condoms and torn condom wrappings, the catheter someone seems to have pulled out there, the scruffy socks and moist underwear all over the place, the patches of bodily fluid slowly drying up under the morning sun, and the feces in between all that. It was the bamboo mat that covered the iron gate against which the man was leaning last night – in front of which stood a woman, bent to the side, who spat, bent once more, and shrieked and yelled. The mat bore the silhouette of men: hundreds of them, thousands maybe, all leaning there and rubbing off bit after bit of the bamboo straw. Even if they had cleaned that back row like they cleaned the paseo, sanitizing it so that the next night's clients could come, this spot was actually a hole which could not be sanitized away – a mark that resulted not from leaving something there but from taking something away: tiny pieces of straw, and maybe other almost invisible things, too.

Figure 5.1: Door with impression of men (photo AS).

As we stood there, this impression of men reminded me of the photo of the shadow of an erased person which Eiichi Matsumoto had taken on a hot August day in 1945 in Nagasaki (Figure 5.1). A sight of horror, not because of the unabashed dispersal of sperm and contraceptives, which one expects anyway, but because of this strong presence of erasure. The bodies of those men, the voice of that woman, they had both become non-presences at this particular place, resonating and uncanny. The shrieking voice of last night had something to do with the erased surface I was staring at now. Not a surface any longer, but an inscription. The shrill yell suddenly took control of the surface: not as a shriek of horror; more powerful than this. It felt like a curse, like a yell that *made horror*, that told us go away, into the light of the paseo and of this new day. Similarly, it forced us to move on before we could even see that the man was already lost, was almost swallowed by that man-like looking hole behind him. All that would remain of him was a bit of substance spat to her left. Resonances of the uncanny, shrill yelling in the darknesses of other nights. And as if sound and darkness working together remade lost time: absences (of words, of men) as a means of the recovery of time are magical because they concern that which we deem unconscious, or which we once considered insignificant, or both.

5.2 Much earlier

A bit earlier, I had been interested in multilingual practices among West African migrants in El Arenal. Mallorca, like other destinations of mass tourism in Spain and Italy, was not only reachable for Nigerians, Senegalese and others, but was also considered profitable: One could always start a small business or find a job as a maid. Tourism promised a steady demand for workers and good networking opportunities. At least that was what people said they were told before they left. After a difficult, often traumatic journey, many found themselves earning meagre incomes as street vendors, lavatory attendants and sex workers. The West African women I had spoken to about their linguistic journeys talked about the languages they had learned since leaving home, the ways in which they communicated with customers and clients, and the nicknames with which they addressed each other. Names were important, as something it is better not to reveal easily, and as words that could categorize the other, put him firmly into his place. There was no transgressive talk though, not here, not for them. Then there was waste in front of a door in Son Gotleu, a quarter of Palma where many African and Spanish immigrants lived in an often violent neighborhood. Fingers zipping her lips together told of a woman's fear of the consequences of telling too much. Or perhaps of her fear of letting what had happened take control.

What power lay in that gesture! As we sat there, in a shabby shop that sold suitcases as well as tickets home, to Nigeria, a woman who had been asked about how *she* had arrived here, whether on a plane or a boat, did nothing more than move the tip of her index finger and thumb from the left to the right of her closed lips. Silence. No story to pass out of this mouth. In the gigantic corpora built and used today by linguists, would that count? I assume it would not.

"These are stories licensed by that disconcerting halo of innocence granted the guest, visitor to an unknown land with his stumbling gait of perception", Michael Taussig (2015: 116) writes on storytelling in Palestine. Violence and transgression in language are perhaps not about swear words but about the compulsion to scream while a story is told, even if it is told merely by a moving fingertip. It must also be in the scream itself, the shrill yell. There are different possibilities to make sense of this. We photographed (documented) that silent woman's shop, and merely by accident recorded (documented) that nocturnal back lane scream. We could digitally analyze it, I assume, measure it, also measure the size and humidity of that back lane, and of the shop as well, maybe. But I prefer to trust in the power of the narrative and continue to tell my stories. Stories whose horror is banal. Still referring to Palestine, Taussig makes an important point about this:

> And if that's not enough, we must not be so naïve as to think that the visitor, like myself, however shocked and filled with rage, is not also fascinated by this horror and, to that extent, in a complex way, complicit with it. This alone makes such storytelling and retelling a treacherous activity. Joseph Conrad called it "the fascination of the abomination," an accurate if ponderous rendering of the stock in trade of war journalists and war photographers, especially the latter, wild men and wild women to the core, too much in love with their work which soon settles into banality. But that is as nothing compared with the conceit of the reader of their work, secure at one remove from the action, yet no less likely to be buoyed up by the tempestuous currents of attraction and repulsion inflaming it before succumbing to indifference and turning the page or clicking the mouse.
> (Taussig 2015: 117)

And because I think Taussig is right about this dynamic in storytelling, I want to continue my story, there where the uncanniness of the yell left me with the faint feeling that this was, ultimately, about another yell in another place, much earlier.

Much earlier, I had spent much time in the northeastern part of Nigeria for linguistic fieldwork. It didn't feel like fieldwork, then. Even though I had been trained in African linguistics and anthropology, the concept of the "field" had been difficult throughout. Equipped with wordlists and exercise books for grammar samples, I was supposed to participate in the peoples' daily lives in order to study – what? Language: an unusual construction of a verb, Arabic loan words, compound nouns. But I only really learned about what language might be when I digressed from the daily routines of my discipline. Going out to the fields, climbing an ancient settlement hill, hunting for rodents in the bush and for bats in a cave, watching the quick movements of bugs and moths near the generator-fueled lights at night was what everybody else did.[1] Children mostly, who, like me, lacked the knowledge of an initiated adult, would do this, and people who went to the fields in order to check that things were in order. No expert knowledge was required, just curiosity and nobody around to ask me to get back to my

---

[1] Some of this was not as undisciplined as it now might seem. During many research trips, I collected rodents and bats on behalf of my father, whose field was zoology. I believe some of them still form part of the Senckenberg Institute's collection at Frankfurt. At the same time, this activity helped me to achieve the naivety needed to really participate. In any case, I remain grateful for that.

linguistic data. While sharing daily-life practices that were often what I would today consider playful, I came across all those things which were formerly told to inexperienced youngsters. That one does not tell words in "the language" (they meant Hone, a Jukun language only spoken by people in the village, and not Hausa that everybody else spoke) to a child or a foreign person just "like that". This language needed to be treated with care, because its phrases consisted not only of morphemes but also – even more so – of spiritually agentive substance. Language in this particular case, the case I was supposed to study, was pure agency, secret and powerful. It was kept hidden throughout, so that many of the children who went along with me, whom I went around with, grew up speaking Hausa and English, perhaps Bolanci as well, but not Hone. People who had settled in the village wouldn't learn its language either, for the same reason: too dangerous to be given to those who would deal with it carelessly. One morning I walked down a guinea corn field that was close to harvesting. Corn stalks of almost two meters, birds fluttering atop. There was a small platform in front of me with a little shade made of some piles of wood and some leaves. I expected a guard to sit under this shady roof, a young boy perhaps, who was supposed to drive away the birds from the crops. Not expecting anything unusual I went on. As I reached the platform, which was very close to the footpath I took, the air was suddenly filled with shrill, loud yelling that fell on me in a single explosion of motion, light, and sound. It rattled on a chain, tried to get me and take me with it, threw itself at me with all its might. It was unlike anything I had ever seen or heard before – there was the sheer power of what was hidden underneath the veil, the energy of all that had to be kept secret. And now it had come out, and I, standing there, would escape only because its rattling chains were too short to reach me on that edge of the footpath.

Shrill yelling, and all I managed to say was *gafara dai*, 'excuse me'. Excuse me for having stepped into your hell. On the platform, or rather its edge, was an old woman. She was tied to one of the wooden posts with a chain. She wore a ragged wrapper, nothing more. No headscarf, no underwear. No words, just a voice. The expression of her face I do not remember. I remember the little bowl of water and some food wrapped into a sheet of paper somewhere on her platform. I remember I thought that at least somebody feeds her. And as she continued to scream, now in a hoarse voice between shrill shrieks, I went back. Later, when I had the chance to talk to Malam Mohammad Dada, who by then had taught me The Language, I asked about the platform. She had been put out there by her family, he said. A witch, and, no, she did not yell. She talked, but in a particular language that was only used by those who were under the spell of witchcraft. To me, it sounded like yelling, but actually, he said, it was cursing. Dangerous to some but not to all. She was safer out there, no need to worry.

Cursing, I had believed before that day, was a practice that decidedly relied on words. Giving names and hurling phrases, language-as-action that potentially affected one's social standing in hostile encounters. What if I had spent time there with the old woman? What would the outrageous noise have done to me? Would it have affected me also? James Grehan (2004) discusses such possibilities in a study on the power of words and of body expressions in Ottoman Damascus. Here, too, we rely on storytelling, for obvious reasons: "We cannot, after all, hear people from the distant past speak; they have left us only written records which contain little more than traces of conversations, expressions, and mannerisms" (Grehan 2004: 992). What has been told by those who wrote about remarkable communicative acts, Grehan points out, was, on the one hand, the ideal of speech as controlled and dignified behavior:

> During sexual intercourse, for instance, it was forbidden to talk or make any other sounds "for good or evil". Silence should also accompany the excretory functions, which produced their own prim anxieties. [...] The ulama were extremely attentive to ceremony and distinction, and actively engaged in what Erving Goffman has famously called the "arts of impression management". (Grehan 2004: 994)

On the other hand, the many possibilities of transgressing this powerful social norm produced violent and dangerous situations:

> The most trifling offenses – a careless word or gesture, an errant glance, the wrong tone of voice – were capable of unleashing dramatic, and sometimes violent, reactions. [...] How might Damascenes actually express their contempt for others? This was a field of much creativity, which ranged from the crudest slurs to the most subtle insinuations and allusions. In fact, words were unnecessary. The body alone could convey a whole range of insults and reproaches through its own vocabulary of gestures, motions, and postures – or just as effectively, through their timely omission. [...] In this armory of snubs and insults, spoken words were perhaps the most cutting weapons. But unlike the mute outrages committed by the body, which come to us relatively uncensored in the local literature, it is harder to detect offensive words. (Grehan 2004: 998–1001)

In the light of the scream having been rationalized as a curse, I find Grehan's observations on Ottoman linguistic thought extremely interesting. The body as a means of swearing and cursing might not have been as potent in deforming or destroying a person as words, but almost.[2] And, this is crucial, offensive language

---

[2] Grehan (2004: 1007–1008) provides striking examples of what might happen upon uttering a curse: "If words were capable of much good, they held an equal and opposite potential for harm. Formulaic curses and imprecations, often sealed with the name of God, were widely feared for their long reach and sure aim. Citing a long line of Islamic scholarship, al-Nabulsi admonished the faithful not to swear at people or animals, and took the injunction so seriously that he

that was expressed through the body and not words could become part of a narrative, could be turned into story and text, whereas offensive language in its verbal form could not. Indeed, telling about an offensive gesture is different from repeating a swear word or curse when narrating one's experiences. Screams, yells and gestures as swearing and cursing acquire a strange ambiguity: more easily managed in narrative reproduction than words, which would mostly account for taboo language, they seem less harmful in metapragmatic representations of hostile encounters. But the encounter itself has the potential to unleash that which I assume we prefer to have safely stowed away in what we deem the unconscious. The scream and the offensively moving body, isn't this also language-out-of-control, communication beyond properly pronounced words and managed self? Because a scream could always be more than just a voice, in the sense of a magical double entendre, the sound of a person as well as of the supernatural, it is that which, in spite of its narratability, has the potential to haunt us and come back to us in certain moments, more than the cutting words that we also experience.

5.3 Now

But what does that mean: the yell of a witch? The unsettling yell as a signifier of blasphemy was also a common trope in early modern European representations of female excessive communicative practices, portraying women who used offensive language or spoke in loud voices as potentially dangerous to the social order. I cannot imagine these screams and yells of the distant past without also considering the material culture that must have surrounded them: cobblestone streets, a wooden yard gate, cast iron tools, chickens, heavy shoes. Perhaps it is childhood memories of swashbuckler movies, the things I have read and the storytelling that I have enjoyed, that all script what resonates in me. In Laura Wright's analysis of *Sunnyside* (2016), the historical sociolinguistic

---

extended it to inanimate objects such as rocks. His contemporaries had no doubt that malicious words could wound, debilitate, even kill. Solemn curses were unnecessary. Among the jottings for his private journal in October 1715, Ibn Kannan reported that a local merchant, famed for stinginess, had thrown a celebration for his children. Disappointed with the festivities, or perhaps still resentful at his history of parsimony, some of the people from his neighborhood cursed him as they left the home. They did not have to wait long for an answer; on the very next day, news came that he had died. [...] The speaker's intentions did not always matter. The most innocent or careless speech could bring about totally unforeseen results. In a treatise on the causes of forgetfulness, a distinguished scholar like al-Nabulsi could gravely warn his readers against excessive laughter, listening to gibberish, or telling a lie."

analysis of a toponym involved the description of shop signs hanging from the fronts of early modern English urban houses and the sound that must have been there when a storm had them beating against one another, or when a facade collapsed under the weight of all the signs and things put on it. Acoustic order and excess must have been hard to keep apart in those places; I wonder if they are now. The yell of the transgressive woman sits in an entangled fabric of social history, memory making, material culture, and place. And therefore, in my imagination, voices fluctuate in animate environments in which all sound makes sense. Yelling is not there without the clangor of bottles, resonances of music that is played too loud, a kickstarted moped.

The materiality of the transgressive yelling and screaming that surfaces in my associative ways of dealing with them does not merely reveal complexity; it also makes it obvious that these sonic phenomena form part of cultural practices that are closely connected to the organization of context, just as literacy is. They are moored to the real world, that which remains after sound has vanished, and that which can be shown and told to others. Literacy, linguist Christiane Bongartz (pers. comm.) says, therefore has the potential for violence: this materiality makes our attempts to explain the world – its sounds – absolute. And as the *Tyranny of Writing* (Weth and Juffermans 2017) shapes the ways in which the world is made into stories, materiality becomes focal. The material proof for the story that is told is what it is: bottles, heavy shoes, a moped. Whatever I experienced, then, in the guinea corn field, and in a poorly lit back street, is removed from the context of my sensations and experiences and translated into another person's emotional repertoire and moored to what there is – guinea corn, street, village, photograph. An absolute script emerges that, because of its mooring to a specific social sphere and specific objects, lacks the openness of the actual experience and provides patterns and stereotyped figures instead. Bongartz observes that we are conditioned into realizing ourselves through this script.

Hölderlin, in a famous fragment, has said that language is the most dangerous of all goods, because it lets us create what we are (1951: 325). Language turns voice into an absolute testimony of our existence. Heidegger, in an equally famous interpretation of Hölderlin's thinking (1981: 55–56), says that the testimony itself is the basis of any expression of being human. Thinking about Hölderlin and silence and the role of translated language – as in literacy – Anne Carson, in her essay 'Variations on the right to remain silent' (2016: n.p.) wonders about the possibilities of madness and transgression:

Maybe Hölderlin was pretending to be mad the whole time, I don't know. What fascinates me is to see his catastrophe, at whatever level of consciousness he chose it, as a method extracted from translation, a method organized by the rage against cliché. After all, what else is one's own language but a gigantic cacophonous cliché? Nothing has not been said before. The templates are set. Adam long ago named all the creatures. Reality is captured.

How tempting to think of a linguistics of the cacophonous cliché. A linguistics that captures the transformation of sound into language-as-voice, that transgresses linguistic phenomena by integrating sounds made by all kinds of things (animals, musical instruments, the built environment, machines etc.).

I wonder what the clichés of my own memories of the yell and its mooring in literacy are based on. Is there a basis after all? How is the yell in a dirty back lane part of the cliché of the unruly woman and her transgressive language? What exactly does my translation make sense of? Harmony, Sarah F. Williams (2011) writes about early modern English music, was considered as being part of masculine practice and behavior. In contrast, "acoustic disorder and excess – that is, musical 'spillage' outside the bounds of masculine, ordered harmony – is characteristically dangerous and categorically feminine", she observes (Williams 2011: 311). In baroque broadside ballads, popular music of past centuries, aural excess, cacophony and discord were common style elements that signified the motif of the witch. And with the figure of the witch and the noise that brings her to life, inverse order manifests itself. Alongside desired conduct and order, there are always also excess and terror that cannot be controlled:

> Witchcraft was conceived as the inverse of the natural world, and the rituals of this demonic craft were often construed in terms of what they were not – for example, the anti-mass or witches' Sabbath, perverse baptisms, and backwards flight. The early modern representational arts, both in England and on the continent, often depicted these inversions and perversions of the natural world through babbling and blasphemous speech, inappropriate outbursts, and disorganized and chaotic gestures. (Williams 2011: 333)

While moderate speech was imposed on Western women as a societal norm, the contrary obviously could be expected: women's voices had in them the quality of transgression and the potential lack of detachment – voices that gossiped, embarrassed and threatened (Williams 2011: 317). Anne Carson, in her text on the gender of sound (1995: 119), describes Hellenic as well as early modern and industrial European ideologies of the voice as ideologies of misogyny. Language out of a man's mouth was different from words spoken by a woman, and the more high-pitched the voice, the worse its implications.

I find it exciting to think of such concepts of the voice, the yell and social order as a basis of the cliché that emerges out of my own translations of a scream and of communicative transgressions. In (academic) linguistics, such connotations of gender are not so much in the focus (Aikhenvald 2016). And while, in Ottoman linguistic thought, as well as in early modern European metalinguistics, the voice itself, as part of the body and its motions, was an integral and agentive part of language – offensive language – the voice has been removed from linguistic theory to a large extent in modernist linguistics. But ancient and early modern representations of language practice saliently focus on the quality of the voice, and sources such as broadside ballads are texts that shed light on language ideologies and linguistic thinking of the past, and on their resonances in the present. Perhaps the voice has been removed from linguistic thought simply because its loudest representation was the excessive acoustic theatre of the horrible voice, which was usually thought to be the voice of a woman, the shrill sound of an ancient goddess calling for a sacrifice, and of the witch? The erasure of the voice enabled linguists throughout the nineteenth and twentieth centuries to consider language as a regular structure of great logical beauty, *un systeme au tout se tient* (Saussure 1916; Koerner 1996/97). Perhaps linguistics owes its modernity to the absence of the disharmonious acoustics of the witch; perhaps the exclusion of the unsaid, the yell and the scream, the horrible theater of the curse (which all, then, had to be taken care of by other disciplines: philosophy, law, psychology, anthropology, literature), results in a linguistics that does not take the power of the voice itself very seriously. For the body, at the very moment that it produces linguistic sound, is so deeply embedded in context, so arbitrary in its visibility and audibility, that any fixed structure is put into question.

The horrible play of the voice of course tells a different story – one where nothing might hold, of language as substance, agency; potentially changing reality. The mere sound of the yell as a curse, and the possibility of speaking without uttering a word and yet making powerful and dangerous oaths, however, were considered important aspects of language elsewhere and at other times. Language was inseparable from its materiality, but also from the body, health, the social context and its norms and boundaries:

> Early modern audiences made cultural agreements as to the types of musical, acoustic, physical, and poetic gestures that would represent excess and its sympathies with the dark arts, social and physical disorder, and uncontrolled femininity. (Williams 2011: 310)

Like linguistic thought in eighteenth-century Baghdad, the conceptualization of communicative practice in early modern England transcends language. And because, like any form of communication, obscene and offensive language was always more than "language", it was important to consider the entire aspects of communication – context, place, body, and so forth. The screams of an old woman in a guinea corn field in Nigeria, the yell of a woman in a seedy corner, the disharmony of the witch, the careless greeting that reveals hostility – these are all instances of swearing and cursing without really using any "bad words". These come later, in the formation of literacy, storytelling, metalinguistic discourse.

One outlet for the cliché that is not new (as Carson observes), that is part of all that has been already said, is song. Near the seedy corner where wide eyes stared at me for a brief moment, with horror and with irony, and where a shrill yell cursed a man whose exposed body could be seen imprinted on a door the next morning, there is a bar and discotheque where they play the party hits of the summer. Then, it was fashionable to cynically celebrate in song those who have no access to the bar: the West African migrants who wait outside, selling drugs, plastic sunglasses or themselves (Nassenstein and Storch in press). Being sold, being made to sell, what do I know? The artist Jürgen Kadel, who performs under his *nom de guerre* Honk!, sings about women who have already received considerable attention by the media coverage of the annual summer party splash on the island of Mallorca, and all the recurring transgressions and scandals (Andrews 2014). Offering blow jobs and other sexual services cheaply in those seedy back lanes through which we have already passed, these women have been portrayed, for years now, as dangerous predators who will ruin any man who comes near them. The slur that goes along with the cliché, that makes it almost tangible, is *Klauhure*, 'snitching whore' (Traber 2019). The *Klauhure* is the bad woman who is controlled by some terrible, dark power (an evil Nigerian Madame who has access to *juju*, 'magic'), and represents the absolute Other of the uncontrolled White female, who might transgress social order as well, but only to harm herself and not men who have sex with her. The predatory *Klauhure* is as elusive as the witch of former times, but she, too, has her physical features that betray her: *Vorsicht vor den Frauen in den flachen Schuhen* 'Beware of the women wearing low-heeled shoes', the German tabloid *Die Welt* warned male tourists in an article on the Nigerian women who are "on the hunt for men" at the Mallorcan party zone.[3] The evil is recognized by looking at the feet: the devil's clubfoot, the sneakers of the witch.

The image of the bad woman and the witch is circulated in a form that resembles that which was established in European early modern literacy, storytelling and performance. And even though we might claim that we, the inhabitants of the metropole, have abandoned all superstition and no longer believe in witchcraft (but in a linguistics of language-as-structure), the song that was played in the club that night, between 04:53 and 04:56, elicited, like the newspaper reports, the cliché of the witch, the transgressive woman who does not speak but yells, whose use of language in any case is different from that of good women, who are yelled at. In the song she says nothing, like the

---

[3] https://www.welt.de/vermischtes/article117196779/Nigerianische-Prostituierte-auf-Jagd-am-Ballermann.html

other women, who wait in silence, gazes directed at elsewhere, waiting to be interrupted and to be asked into that dark and smelly lane. And as a children's tune is played, the voice of an entertainer in the camouflage of a fool sings:

Letztens kam mein Kumpel Klaus
Recently my pal Nick

aus dem Megapark heraus.
left the Megapark.

An die Playa wankte er,
He staggered to the beach,

ja, ihm fiel das Laufen schwer.
well, he was walking with difficulty.

Voll besoffen wie er war
As pissed as he was

eine schöne Frau ihn sah.
a pretty woman saw him.

Da kam sie auch schon angerannt
And as she came running

und der Klaus war abgebrannt:
Nick was already broke:

Kohle, Handy, alles weg – Alter, wasn Dreck.
Money, cell phone, everything gone – boy, what a shit.

Und wir singen
And we sing

Auf der Mauer, auf der Lauer
On the wall, on the lookout

Sitzt ne kleine Klau
Sits a little snitching

HURE
WHORE

The artist's voice first mimics the innocent tunes of a children's song. But then, when the person on whom the blame is put is named, in the chorus that is repeated again and again during these three minutes, a whole group of male voices yell the word 'whore'. A noisy revenge, a shout against evil, the exposure of the witch: WHORE. The song is accompanied by a video clip, a film in which many 'stars' of the island's German party zone appear. Celebs for the summer – what should they have to fear, in this apotropaic play? They perform their mimetic interpretations of the figures of that place, funny representations of the tourists and the tourism industry staff they all play for, and of the Other whom they want to shoo away. We are shown Honk! sitting on the little wall that divides the beach from the paseo, with an actor who does a blackfaced performance of an African sexually transgressive woman (Figure 5.2). A dark fatsuit, a shimmering golden bikini, a black curly wig, rolling eyes, tongue licking over painted lips. Everything we see is a semiotically rich and complex representation of transgression: the nightly beach is where the drunken German party tourists go in order to have sex or to ease themselves (or both), the wall is where tourists sit and get drunk and watch others getting drunk, and the blackfaced performer is a carnivalesque figure that would hardly be acceptable in carnivalesque settings back home. The racist portrayal of the witch takes place, we are told through such images, in the non-place, a neverland where it does no harm; this is a built environment reserved for transgression.

Figure 5.2: Still from Honk!'s *Klauhurensong*.

As the video goes on, the non-place is represented as a mimetic copy of reality. Apotropaic magic needs a representation of the real object in order to disempower it. We therefore see Honk! and the blackfaced performer, the beach and everything else in combination with a teletext that, in an imitation of breaking news, informs us about what is really happening (Figure 5.3). The whore has taken everything from Honk! and triumphs, as evil triumphs over good.

Figure 5.3: Still from Honk!'s *Klauhurensong*.

But this, we know, of course, is only a play, an apotropaic performance. The real evil happens at the bottom of the image, where the teletext is.

:::::::::: BREAKING NEWS :::::::::: TRICKDIEBSTAHL AUF MALLORCA: Wiederholte Diebstähle an der Playa – Kohle, Handy, alles weg – Klauhuren überrumpeln Touristen mit Antanz Trick – Überwachungsbilder der Playa werden derzeit ausgewertet – mutmaßlich vornehmlich volltrunkene Männer betroffen ::::::::::

:::::::::: BREAKING NEWS :::::::::: LARCENY BY TRICK ON MALLORCA: Repeated theft at the beach – money, cell phone, everything gone – snitching whores blindside tourists with pickpocket dancing – security cameras at the beach are being analyzed – alleged mostly drunken men concerned ::::::::::

The text is repeated over and over throughout these three minutes. It does something other than the lyrics that are yelled at us and the performances we see. The teletext imitation links the Nigerian women at the beach with their male counterparts in another party zone – the square between the cathedral and the railway station in Cologne, where infamous sexual assaults took place on New Year's Eve 2015/16, which were much publicized in the German and international press and media. Many of the perpetrators were male immigrants from North

African countries. They were named *Nafri* (***Nordafrikaner***, 'North Africans') by German politicians and media after the incident. In its capacity to affirm a stereotype, *Nafri* quickly turned into a racist slur, serving as a term that portrayed immigrants as rapists (Zavaree 2019). The revealing part of the teletext is *Antanz Trick* [...] *vornehmlich volltrunkene Männer betroffen*: because besides being sexually uncontrollable, young men from Morocco were reported to be thieves who specialize in robbing drunken men – stranded party people who make easy prey. Many Germans only learned of this particular practice of pickpocketing – *Antanz-Trick*– when they learned of the *Nafri*. Public discourse focused on both aspects of this Other – violent sexuality and theft, whereby not only tropes of colonial orientalism were elicited, but also motifs of an early modern male Other, namely the wizard. In the teletext, clichés fuse – that of the witch and the wizard, of the Black female migrant and the Arab male migrant, and of the sexually available African woman and the sexually uncontrollable Oriental man. Interestingly, neither has anything to say, not in the teletext imitation, nor in the song, nor in the media. All we get to hear are voices that yell and scream. Hölderlin, we remember, has said in a famous fragment that language is the most dangerous of all goods, because it makes us create what we are.

References

Aikhenvald, Alexandra Y. 2016. *How Gender Shapes the World*. Oxford: Oxford University Press.
Andrews, Hazel (ed.). 2014. *Tourism and Violence*. London: Routledge.
Austin, John L. 1962. *How to Do Things with Words*. Cambridge: Harvard University Press.
Carson, Anne. 1995. The Gender of Sound. In *Glass, Irony and God*, 119–142. New York: New Directions.
Carson, Anne. 2016. *Float*. London: Jonathan Cape.
Grehan, James. 2004. The mysterious power of words: Language, law, and culture in Ottoman Damascus. *Journal of Social History* 37: 991–1015.
Heidegger, Martin. 1981. *Gesamtausgabe*, vol. 4. Frankfurt am Main: Vittorio Klostermann.
Hölderlin, Friedrich. 1951 [1800 (?)]. In Walde F. Beissner (ed.), *Grosse Stuttgarter Ausgabe – Sämtliche Werke*, vol. 2, 1: Gedichte nach 1800, p. 325. Stuttgart: Kohlhammer.
Jay, Timothy B. and Kristin Janschewitz. 2008. The pragmatics of swearing. *Journal of Politeness Research: Language, Behavior, Culture* 4: 267–288.
Kadel, Jürgen (Honk!). 2018. *Klauhurensong*. Kuppenheim: Summerfield.
Koerner, E.F. Konrad. 1996/97. Notes on the history of the concept of language as a system 'où tout se tient'. *Linguistica Atlantica* 18–19:1–20.
Madadzhe, R.N. 2012. Linguistic taboos in Tshivenda: Communicating across epochs. *South African Journal of African Languages* 30 (2): 180–191.

Nassenstein, Nico and Anne Storch. In press. Balamane. Variations on a noisy ground. In Ingo H. Warnke & Elise Erbe (eds.), *Macht im Widerspruch*. Heidelberg: Springer.
Saussure, Ferdinand de. 1916. *Cours de linguistique générale*. Edited by Charles Bally and Albert Sechehaye. Lausanne & Paris: Payot.
Traber, Janine. 2017. Der Verkauf von Verkehr. *The Mouth* 2: 60–76.
Taussig, Michael. 1999. *Defacement*. Stanford: Stanford University Press.
Taussig, Michael. 2015. *The Corn Wolf*. Chicago: University of Chicago Press.
Weth, Constanze and Kasper Juffermans (eds.). 2017. *The Tyranny of Writing. Ideologies of the Written Word*. London: Bloomsbury.
Williams, Sarah F. 2011. "A Swearing and Blaspheming Wretch": Representations of Witchcraft and Excess in Early Modern English Broadside Balladry and Popular Song. *Journal of Musicological Research* 30 (4): 309–356.
Wright, Laura. 2016. Sunnyside. Keynote presented at the 21st Sociolinguistics Symposium, Murcia.
Zavaree, Sara. 2019. GE|ER|M|ÄCHT|IG|UNG. *The Mouth* 4: 205–218.

Felix K. Ameka
6 "I sh.t in your mouth": Areal invectives in the Lower Volta Basin (West Africa)

Abstract: Languages in the Lower Volta Basin belong to different subgroups of the Kwa family: Gbe, Ga-Dangme, Ghana-Togo Mountain, and Tano, which includes Akanic and Guang languages. These languages share several features, but it is not always easy to detect which features are inherited and which are diffused from one language to the other (Ameka 2006a; Ellis 1984). Taking a cue from earlier studies (e.g. Ameka 1994), where some widespread interactional routines are either inherited, such as *agoo* 'attention getter', or diffused from one language, such as *ayikoo* 'well done, continue' which seems to have spread to the other languages from Ga, I investigate some shared maledicta and taboo expressions in the area. I focus on the performance, perlocutionary effect and uptake as well as the cultural scripts that govern the use of two invective multi-modal embodied utterances in the area. One is an emblematic gesture involving a pointed thumb and its accompanying verbal representations. A common expression that accompanies it comes from Ga "obscene insults" *sɔ́ɔ̀mi!* 'inside female genitalia', *onyɛ sɔ́ɔ̀ mli* 'inside your mother's genitalia' whose equivalents are also used in the other languages. The Ewe-based accompanying verbal expression is literally: 'I defecate in your mouth'. A second form is the one commonly called "suck teeth", which is spread beyond the Lower Volta Basin to the Trans-Atlantic Sprachbund (Muysken and Smith 2015, van den Berg et al. 2015). Drawing on the representation and categorisation of how the enactment of these linguistic practices are reported, I demonstrate that they are viewed as insults or ways of "swearing at" other people because of something bad they may have done to the speaker. I call into question the universality of "swearing" and argue that crosslinguistic studies of "swearing", "cursing" or "cussing" and such phenomena should extricate themselves from the English language labels and attend to the "insider" and indigenous ways of understanding acts of saying bad words to another (cf. Wierzbicka 2014a; Haugh 2016).

Contrary to the norms in the West, swearing is not universal. (Hughes 2006: xxi)

6.1 Introduction

Despite admonitions of the kind given by Hughes in the epigraph of this chapter, much of the work on swearing in the literature assumes the complex Anglo[1] concept of swearing as the analytical category. In a majority of cases, the concept is left undefined, and assumed to be universal. Ljung (2011) opens his chapter on defining swearing with the following sentence, admitting that it is an English term and yet that it will do for a crosslinguistic concept:

> Although *swearing* is an English term denoting a particular type of linguistic behaviour, it is often used in studies of other languages to denote a linguistic resource whose functions and realisations across languages are remarkably similar and seem to emanate from a common pool of emotive utterance types. (Ljung 2011:1, italics in original)

In many cases, swearing is equated with "bad language" or "taboo language". As McGarrity (2017: e372) notes in a review of Bergen (2016), the book is about taboo language "alternatively called swearing, profanity, cursing, obscenity in the literature". It should be clear to the casual reader that these English terms mean different things and are not alternatives. Moreover, these terms are neither transparent nor do they have obvious equivalents across languages. Besides, the terms in English have various relations with one another; for instance, cursing is sometimes presented as being included in swearing or as a synonym of it. Yet some researchers boldly state that "[S]wearing, a linguistic universal, is used to express intense emotions (fear, joy, anger, excitement)" (Finn 2017: 18). This universalist perspective is further reinforced by claims that speakers of languages have an idea that certain words can evoke in others a feeling or an attitude, and that those words can evoke bad feelings because they are profane or are thought of as dirty or offensive. And since "swear words" have this function, swearing is universal. The picture is further complicated by the fact that swearing in some contexts is viewed as "rude" or "impolite". In the literature on impoliteness, there is a debate as to whether there is a distinction between rudeness and impoliteness or not. Culpeper (2011), for instance, distinguishes them in terms of style, while Terkourafi (2008: 61–62) differentiates between them in terms of whether the linguistic act is considered an intentional face-threat, for rudeness, or if it is unintentional, for impoliteness (see Watters 2012 for a discussion of "rudeness"

---

[1] The term Anglo is meant to represent the languages and cultures associated with the traditional bases of English which Kachru (e.g. 2006) describes as the inner circle of Englishes, i.e. British, American, Canadian, Australian and New Zealand.

in Australian English as a key ethno-descriptor in the domain of English impoliteness). Like swearing, these terms are based on the English concepts and do not easily translate cross-linguistically (see Haugh 2016 and also Wierzbicka 2014a on the problem of using English as a default scientific metalanguage). As Jay and Janschewitz (2008: 269) have identified: "A common problem for impoliteness, rudeness and swearing research is that all three phenomena are impossible to define universally because all are culturally and personally determined". This observation is in part reflected in a Facebook post by Christopher Collins of New York University.[2] In the post, Collins reported a dinner conversation he had with James Essegbey, an Ewe native speaker linguist, and other Ghanaians, including some native speakers of Ewe. To get a flavour of the complicated nature of thinking about swearing across languages and cultures, I reproduce part of the post from June 23, 2018 below:

> One of our many topics of conversation was whether there are swear words in Ewe. As usual, James [Essegbey] and I took opposite positions. But it really made me think about what a swear word is. And it was also surprising to see how cross-linguistics comparison (English/Ewe) even in this domain is complicated and interesting. I brought up the possibility that "sucking teeth" is a kind of swear word (tséɖuɖu) in Ewe. One issue that came up is the domain of use of swear words. In English, a person talking to himself can use one to express frustration (e.g., after hitting his finger with a hammer): "S---", or "F---". But we can also use them in other contexts, as when insulting somebody or expressing anger ("F___ you"). What do other speakers of African languages think? Does your language have swear words?[3]

It is true that one can suck one's teeth (ɖu tsé 'bite inside one's cheek' in Ewe) out of frustration at oneself, and do the same to express contempt of another person (cf. Thompson 2019). But does this make sucking teeth a form of swearing? What understanding of swear words is being employed here, given that even across dialects of English there are slightly different understandings of "swear words" (see Goddard 2015; Watters 2012)? In my response to Collins I pointed out that swearing is a complicated notion in English and we need to deconstruct it before we can answer the question of whether there are swear words in African languages.

Hughes (2006) provides a helpful starting point. He distinguishes two types of swearing, formal vs. informal swearing, according to context (cf. Stapleton 2010):

---

2 Christopher Collins is a linguist who is a fluent speaker of Ewe, having conducted fieldwork on one of its dialects, and who continues to carry out linguistic research on the language (see e.g. Collins 1993).
3 https://www.facebook.com/search/top/?q=chris%20collins%20swearing%20in%20ewe&epa=SEARCH_BOX

> Formal swearing is a ritual of social compliance and obligation: in marriage, in court, for high office, and as allegiance to the state. On the other hand, informal swearing constitutes a transgression of social codes ranging from the merely impolite to the criminal.
>
> (Hughes 2006: xv)

This distinction is sometimes referred to in terms of "oath-taking" and "profane swearing". This corresponds to the two senses of the verb *swear* in English. English is in the minority even among European languages in colexifying these two senses in the same word. As Ljung (2011: 1) reports, it is only French and Swedish in his corpus that have comparable words. Thus, if we pose the question, "Are there swear words in your language?", we need to say in what sense we are using the word *swear*.

The two senses of the English word have syntactic correlates, as Hughes further pointed out:

> In terms of mode, *we swear by* some higher force or somebody; *we swear that* something is so; *we swear to* do something; *we swear at* something or somebody; and *we swear* simply *out of* anger, disappointment, or frustration. (Hughes 2006: xxi, emphasis added)

Thus, the syntactic patterns of *swear by* ..., *swear that* ..., and *swear to* relate to one meaning and those of *swear at someone/something* and just *swear* relate to the other (see Wierzbicka 1987: 210, 252–253 for paraphrases of the illocutionary semantics of the two senses). Table 6.1 shows how even the two senses in English itself are carved out by other more specific terms, and when compared to other languages such as Ewe, even particular readings from an English point of view have specific linguistic expressions. This is one of the reasons why the question of whether a language like Ewe has swearing is difficult, even though it feels like "despite its negative connotations swearing remains an intrinsic part of languages and cultures worldwide" (Stapleton 2010: 290).

When one looks at Table 6.1, it is clear that Ewe does not have a linguistic label for cathartic swearing, although there are several terms for other types of swearing. It appears that languages differ in terms of which type or readings of Anglo swearing they elaborate. Floor (2015), for instance, identifies as many as five distinct categories, each with its label, of foul language in the cursing domain in Persian. What is striking, from an Ewe point of view, is if one sucks one's teeth, for example, either in frustration at oneself or towards someone else, it is not reported with the verb *dzu* 'insult, verbally abuse'. This suggests that this linguistic act is not classified with other insults or expressions of abuse. It is hard therefore to think of it as a type of swearing. It is more of an expressive or emotive word-like interjection whose manifestation can be described as a vocal gesture. Thompson (2019) treats its Akan equivalent *tweeaa* as an "interjection of 'contempt'" (see further discussion in Sections 6.2 and 6.3).

6 "I sh.t in your mouth": Areal invectives in the Lower Volta Basin (West Africa) — 125

Table 6.1: The multiple readings of *swear* and their equivalents across languages.

	English	Dutch	German	Ewe
Swear profane (religious)	blaspheme[a]	ketteren	fluchen	yɔ́ X ŋkɔ́ dzódzrŏ call X [=supernatural being]'s name in vain
Swear (profane) invoke supernatural being on someone	curse	iemand vervloeken	jemanden verfluchen	yɔ́ nú dó ame invoke a being on someone sa gbe dó ame cast a spell (with words) on someone
Swear, out of frustration etc. (profane)	curse, cuss	vloeken	fluchen	??
Swear (oath-taking)	take/swear an oath, affirm, vow, pledge	zweren, een eed afleggen	einen Eid schwören	ká atáḿ 'SAY oath' ká X ƒé afɔ 'SAY X POSS foot' ta nú 'put.around thing' fia adzɔgbe 'speak. code destiny'
Swear at someone/ something	insult, abuse	schelden	schelten beschimpfen	dzu 'insult', 'abuse verbally'

[a] Rongier (2015) suggests that *gblɔ busúnya* 'say an abominable word' is the equivalent of *blaspheme*. However, the Ewe expression covers a much wider space and is less likely to be used to talk about blasphemy in the religious sense.

In the rest of this chapter, I examine the interactional meaning and use of two multi-modally packaged emblems that are widely used in two linguistic areas: the Lower Volta Basin (West Africa) and the Trans-Atlantic Sprachbund. The former includes the Lower Volta speech and cultural area as well as the Circum-Carribbean creoles, like the creoles of Suriname and Jamaica. The languages in the Lower Volta Basin belong to different subgroups of the Kwa family: Gbe, Ga-Dangme, Ghana-Togo Mountain, and Tano, which includes Akanic and Guang languages (Ameka 2006a, b). In Section 3 I discuss *tséɖuɖu* 'suck teeth', which has been characterised as a rude sound (Figuero 2005). Perhaps it is the rudeness that links it to swearing. This vocal gesture is used in the Volta Basin and beyond, in other parts of Africa as well as in the Trans-Atlantic linguistic area by peoples of African descent. Its semantics reveals that it is an expressive, emotive interjection. In Section 4, I present a rude physical gesture, a thumb point which can be used to insult someone by itself, or which can be accompanied by verbal expressions that contain words from the scatological domain, or make reference to the mother's genitalia (depending on the language). This emblematic embodied multimodal utterance is widely used in the Lower Volta Basin. It does not seem to have spread to the Trans-Atlantic Sprachbund. To what extent can the performance of these rude pragmatic acts be considered instances of swearing, even if only in one of its readings? Before presenting these forms, I describe the meaning of the Ewe word *dzu* 'insult, verbally abuse' to give a background to what kinds of activities are culturally recognised as verbal abuse in the language. Similar conceptualisations of verbal abuse occur in other Lower Volta Basin languages.[4]

In accounting for the use and meaning of the signs, I use the reductive paraphrase method of the Natural Semantic Metalanguage (NSM) and the meanings and the cultural scripts that describe the cultural norms associated with signs are represented in Minimal English, which "provides informed guidelines and guidance, based on linguistic research, about how to say important things in a clear and translatable way" (Goddard and Wierzbicka 2018: 7).

6.2 The linguistic acts of insult and abuse in Ewe

Ewe has a hyperlexeme *dzu* 'insult, abuse', which has a verbal as well as a nominal form. Westermann (1973 [1928]) has the following entry, with the illustrative example involving a nominal form:

(1) *dzu* to scold, abuse, chide, revile, insult, blame.
 dzu   vé-ná   wú   hẽ   tsɔ́-tsɔ́   si   ame
 insult pain-HAB exceed knife RED-take   cut   person
 'An insult is more painful than being cut with a knife.'
 (interlinearisation and glosses added)

Westerman's example points to the pain one feels when one is on the receiving end of verbal abuse. Example (2) is another saying about *dzu*, which indicates that even though it may be painful it is ephemeral. No matter how much of it is heaped on you, it does not leave a permanent mark (it does not develop into visible spots on your body):

---

[4] The Ga verb *jɛ* [dʒɛ] and the Akan verb *yaw* (Akwapim) or *yeya* (Asante) translate as 'insult', verbally abuse'.

(2) dzu   mé-tó-á   kɔ́   o
     insult NEG-grow-HAB lumps   NEG
     'An insult does not leave scars/marks.'

As a verb, *dzu* obligatorily takes a complement and participates in various argument structure constructions, as shown in (3). (3a) is an agentive two place construction. In (3b) the topic of the abuse is spelled out and has an object function. The addressee of the insult is coded as a dative oblique object. In (3c) the topic of the insult is coded in a complement clause.

(3) a. é-dzu=m   vé-vé-ḍé
       3SG-insult=1SG   RED-pain-ADVZER
       'She insulted me painfully.'
    b. é-dzu   ko   ná=m
       3SG-insult poverty DAT=1SG
       'She insulted poverty for me'
    c. é-dzu   nyɔ́nu=a   bé é-nyé   gbolowɔlá
       3SG-insult woman=DEF QT 3SG-COP prostitute
       'She insulted the woman that she was a prostitute.'

Consider also the following excerpt from a written Ewe play. Amenyo, a middle aged man, is asking for the hand of a young girl (Yawa), whom he had earlier on insulted in public. The girl rejects the proposal, saying she will not marry an old man who is a bachelor. The man reacts by saying that Yawa has insulted him, reporting it with the verb *dzu*.

(4) Yawa: ... adzum le ame dome vɔ ava ḍema? Nyemele ame tsitsi xoxo si nye
           tre tsu la ḍe ge o
           ă-dzu-m   le   ame   dome   vɔ
           2SG:POT-insultPREP   people amidst PFV
           á-vá-ḍe=m=a?
           POT-VENT-marry=1SG=Q
           'You have insulted me in front of people and you now want to marry me.'
    Amenyo: èdzum be menye tre tsitsi xoxo
           è-dzu=m   bé   me-nyétre tsi.tsi   xóxó
           2SG-insult=1SG QT   1SG-COP   bachelor aged old
           'You have insulted me that I am an old aged bachelor.'
           (Setsoafia 1982: 15)

As the examples show, different kinds of expressions are used and categorised as *dzu*. There are insults that relate to the physical characteristics of the target, such as *mo globui* [face hollowed.DIM:IDEO] 'Your narrow pointed face' or *ta gâ̌ wò* [head big 2SG] 'Your big head'. Others involve name-calling based on perceived or assumed behavioural patterns, including habits such as *gbolowɔlá* 'prostitute', as in (3c) above, *fiafitɔ́* 'thief', *dzi-ma-kplá* [born-PRIV-train] 'uncouthe, untrained person' or *yakamĕ* 'useless person'. Some of the insults are animal terms where the addressee is likened to animals. For instance, a common *dzugbe* 'abusive language' that one hears is the term *avŭ* 'dog'. Others are *kesé* 'monkey' and *gbe-me-lã* [bush-inside-animal] 'undomesticated animal' or just *lã* 'animal'. Some insults involve the attribution of low mental capacity or the lack of good thinking abilities to their target. Expressions with such a meaning include *aso* 'a fool', *alĕ* 'a stupid person', *azúi* 'stupid' and *kɔsiaa* 'a foolish person'.

These different categories of abusive language also occur in other languages of the Lower Volta basin. For instance, a common insult in Akan is *aboa* 'animal', and the Ga use a common insult *dzyubɔ* 'thief'. In fact, the term *kɔsiaa* 'a foolish person' is an areal and pan-Ghanaian expression adapted into the other languages, probably from Akan *kwasiaa* 'a fool', and used even in Ghanaian English.[5]

As should be evident from the discussion so far, insulting words or abusive language in the languages of the Volta Basin need not be vulgar, obscene or dirty, as seems to be the case in 'profane swearing' noted in the literature (see Samarin 1969 and Irvine 1993 respectively on Gbeya and Wolof insults for a similar claim). Nevertheless, some acts of insulting can involve the use of vulgar words, as is the case reported in example (5).

(5) Context: two women were having an argument and they were trading insults with one another. One of them used the following simile with reference to the male genitalia to return some of the other person's insults:
[What have I done to you this morning before ...
è-lî̃   *nu*   *abé*   *flɔ̃́-dome-va* ...
2SG-become.erect mouth SEMBL dawn-penis
'What have I done to you before you projected your mouth (in a straight line) like an erect penis at dawn [and insulting me].'

---

[5] Some of the terms I have listed here either as Ewe or as Akan have spread throughout the Volta Basin and are used in English in Ghana. Daku (2003) has the following entries for four of the terms I have used as examples: *kwasia* taboo 'fool' (Akan); *aboa/abua* N. 'animal' (Akan); *dzimakpla* N. 'dirt, bastard, uncouth, wayward person' (Ewe); and *dzulo* N. 'thief' (Ga). It is interesting that Daku classifies *kwasia* as a taboo word and all the rest as just nouns.

Abusive language can thus be vulgar or obscene. And this may be the relationship between profane swearing and the cultural activity of *amedzudzu* 'insulting/abusing people' in Ewe and other languages of the Volta Basin. An English "swear word" based abusive formula is also categorised as *amedzudzu* in (6).

(6) Grandpa and Grandma have an argument and one of the "bad words" that Grandpa always uses is: *damn fool* [dam fuul]. On this occasion, Grandma decides to respond using the same words. Grandpa then invites the grandson, Matthew, to explain to his Grandma, who does not have English in her repertoire, that the expression is an insult.[6] The Ewe variety used here is Anfoegbe, the language of Anfoega.

(6) Grandpa: ... *dám fuul*
damn fool
Grandma: *gbe-síáá-gbe dám fuul! dám fuul!*
day-INT-day damn fool damn fool
dam fuul né weɛ tsyɛ́
damn fool DAT 2SG too
'Everyday, damn fool, damn fool, damn fool to you too'
Grandpa: *Matéo ɖe me né mamá=wò*
Matthew remove inside DAT grandma-2SG
bá-xéé dam fuul yi, ame-dzu-dzu yé
COMP-REL damn fool TP person-RED-insult FOC
'Matthew, explain to your grandma that damn fool is an insult.'

From the discussion so far, utterances that are categorised as *amedzudzu* 'insulting someone' in Ewe are perceived as offensive, contemptuous or rude. From this perspective they are related to profane swearing. As Stapleton (2010: 300, my emphasis) suggests, "The linguistic practice of swearing" has the "capacity to shock, alienate, *insult, abuse* and generally *cause offence*". Similarly, Allan and Burridge (2006: 79) state that "[T]o insult someone verbally is to abuse them with contemptuous, perhaps insolent language that may include an element of bragging. It is often directly addressed". Thus insult and abuse are intertwined and connected with swearing. What is less obvious is whether one can identify some words as "swear words", as is the case in Anglo lingua-cultures. Be that as it may, one can suggest the following paraphrase for the illocutionary meaning of the verb *dzu* 'insult, verbally abuse'.

---

6 There is a subtext here. Grandma, the wife of Grandpa, is not supposed to use abusive language towards her spouse. Grandpa assumes that if Grandma knew that the expression *dam fuul* was an insult she would not use it towards him, as that goes against the cultural norms.

(7) The meaning of the Ewe verb *dzu*
   a. I know something bad about you.
   b. I think something bad about you now because of it.
   c. I feel something bad towards you because of it.
   d. I want to say something bad to you because of it.
   e. I cannot not do it.
   f. I say: I know something bad about you.
   g. Because of this I feel something bad towards you now.
   h. I say it like this because I want many people to hear it.
   i. I say it because I want you to feel something (very) bad.

The assumption is that as a speech act verb, the illocutionary meaning of *dzu* is made up of bundles of features including a dictum, introduced by the 'I say' frame as in component (7f), and an illocutionary point as represented in component (7i) (see e.g. Ameka 2006b). Other components spell out the trigger, that is the insult or abuse, which comes about because the speaker has come to know something that the addressee did which caused them to have a bad feeling. Component (7e) captures the idea that typically the insult is an immediate reaction that cannot be resisted. The speaker expects the target to feel something bad because of what they say.

Having clarified how insult or abuse activities are understood, we now turn to the emblematic areal invectives beginning with suck teeth. The term is understood to be an insulting or abusive word, expression or utterance.

6.3 Suck teeth or kiss teeth – a rude sound in the Trans-Atlantic Sprachbund

As noted above, a rude sound called suck teeth or kiss teeth is very widespread in Africa and in the circum-Caribbean Creoles, which have African language substrates (see Rickford and Rickford 1976 for an initial description). Figuero (2005) has described in detail the pragmatics and variation in the Caribbean on this form. What is common to all uses of the element is that it is a vocal gesture used to express bad feelings of contempt, frustration or disdain towards one's interactants. It is also used cathartically to express one's feelings about oneself or about a situation one finds oneself in. It can thus be used without a targeted addressee. This is the sign that Collins suggests could be considered a form of swearing in Ewe. The only thing it shares with profane swearing, in my view, is rudeness.[7]

Thompson and Agyekum (2016), in discussing what they call the Ghanaian standpoint on impoliteness, propose a continuum with respect to the degree of offence felt or perceived to be caused by different categories of "impolite acts" (see Figure 6.1). On that scale, they put invectives, that is, insults and abusive language, as the most unpardonable interpersonal offence one can commit. They note that sucking one's teeth at someone else is also one of those invectives that are unpardonable.

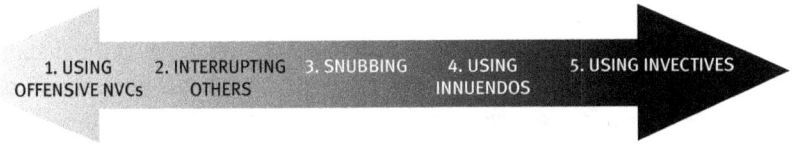

LESS OFFENSIVE/MORE PARDONABLE   MORE OFFENSIVE/LESS PARDONABLE

Figure 6.1: Offensive behaviour (Thompson and Agyekum 2016).

The Ghanaian writer Ama Ata Aidoo gives a vivid description of how this emotive interjection is used in interpersonal relationships in her fictional love story *Changes*. She describes a scene where the behaviour of a husband offends his spouse very much and she expresses her complex emotions of frustration, contempt and disgust by sucking her teeth.

(8) Ama Ata Aidoo's description of Esi's (the wife's) reaction to an extremely unpleasant incident involving her husband:

> Esi's anger rose to an exploding pitch . . . . What really finished her was her eyes catching sight of the cloth trailing behind Oko who looked like some arrogant king, as he opened the door to get to the bathroom before her. *She sucked her teeth, or made the noise which is normally described, inadequately, in English as a sucking of the teeth. It was thin, but loud, and very long.* In a contest with any of the fishwives about ten kilometers down the road from the Hotel Twentieth Century, she would have won. (Aidoo 1991: 10, my emphasis)

---

7 Christopher Collins (p.c.) commenting on an earlier version of this paper suggests that even though *tsédudu* 'sucking teeth' may not be a swear word as it is quasi verbal, there are parallels between the act and swearing: (a) it is conventional; (b) it is linguistic; (c) it is offensive; (d) it is intentional; (e) it is directed; (f) it is taboo/prohibited. It will become apparent that I agree with some of these parallels. I would propose a slight revision of parallels (d) and (e) as follows: (d') it can be intentional or unintentionally uttered and (e') it can be directed; it can also be used carthartically.

As Ama Ata Aidoo's depiction of Esi's suck teeth performance suggests, the emotive interjection is produced by pursing one's lips, creating a hollow in the oral cavity and drawing air in by suction. One's tongue touches the sides of the mouth while the tip and blade of the tongue are in contact with the alveolar ridge. The result is a click sound. As indicated by Ama Ata Aidoo's description above, the vocal gesture can be modulated and manipulated in different ways to express nuances of feelings. Thus, it can be lengthened, as Esi did, to emphasise the degree of contempt. The stricture can also be modified to intensify the contempt expressed.[8]

The embodied click sound produced by sucking one's teeth has been conventionalised in the languages of the Lower Volta Basin. As noted above, it is represented as *ɖu tsé* [bite the inside of cheek] 'suck teeth', with the nominalised form *tséɖuɖu* 'sucking the teeth'. The act of producing the click sound of suck teeth is described in Akan with the verb *twe* 'to suck teeth'. The sound is verbalised as an interjection and represented in Ewe as *Tsuiã!* and in Ga as *Tsyuuu!*, while in Akan it is *Tweaa!* The stand-alone interjectional use of this is delocutivised as *ka tweaa* 'say tweaa' in Akan and as *dó tsuiã* 'say *tsuiã*' in Ewe. As the interjection is quotable and accountable, one often hears in interaction a question aimed at establishing the identity of the target of the rude sound. Thus one can ascertain whether the interlocutor is sucking their teeth towards oneself by posing one of the questions in (9) in Ewe:

(9) a. *nye è-ɖu tsé ná=a*
   1SG 2SG-bite cheek.inside give=QP
   'Are you sucking your teeth at me?'
   b. *nye è-ɖu tsé dó-e=a*
   1SG 2SG-bite cheek.inside put-3SG=QP
   'Are you sucking your teeth at me?'

The Akan interjectional form *Tweaa!* has entered pan-Ghanaian political discourse with a life of its own.[9] Thompson (2019) shows how online commentators used this expression to vent their contempt and disapproval of the two leading Presidential candidates, John Mahama and Nana Akufo Addo, during the 2016 election campaign. The use of the Akan version of the interjection

---

[8] See some of the variations that are possible in the production of suck teeth: https://www.youtube.com/watch?v=JSBMqGCdw84
[9] In 2019 the word tweaa has been adopted into the Oxford English dictionary as an English word from Ghana, see https://awakenewsroom.com/ghanaian-word-tweaa-captured-oxford-dictionary/

increased even in Parliament during 2014. It began when the then District Chief Executive (DCE) for Ahafo Ano South, Mr Gabriel Barima, got very angry when a member of the audience he was addressing at an end of year function (December 2013) in Mankraso Hospital sucked his or her teeth at a comment he made. The DCE was infuriated, stopped his speech at once and was eager to find the one who made the utterance. No one owned up and so he abandoned his speech and stormed out of the event. A video of the scene went viral on both social and mass media outlets in the country. The *Daily Graphic* reported part of what could be heard and seen on the video on January 20, 2014 as follows:

> He exclaimed in Twi [Akan] interspersed with English; "who made that 'tweaa' sound? Am I your size? ... I have been given the platform to talk. You were not given the platform to talk. And so, what you are saying, nobody is listening except mine.
> Am I your colleague? Do you think you're my colleague? ... You sit somewhere and behave like you're talking to your co-equal. Am I your co-equal? If you're a hospital worker, who are you? Why do you have to behave in that manner? I've ended my speech. I'm not talking again. If you don't respect people ... I'm not talking again. Take your programme."[10]

From the excerpt, we infer two things relevant for the semantics of the emotive interjection: first, its use is a sign of gross disrespect, especially if used in an asymmetrical communication. Note that question: "Am I your co-equal?" Second, the use of the utterance causes great anger and fury in the targeted addressee. The DCE's reaction shows how unpardonable this non-verbal offence is and its perlocutionary effect.

The use of *tweaa* gained currency in the ensuing weeks on the floor of Parliament, where some Members of Parliament used the word against their colleagues during debates and discussions in the House. With a clear allusion to the episode involving the DCE, the use of the word usually led to laughter and took attention away from the issues being discussed. This led the Speaker of the House to ban the use of the word in the House. Here is part of the report that appears in the *Daily Graphic* of February 19, 2014:

> **Parliament bans use of 'tweaa' in House**
> The Speaker of Parliament, Mr Edward Doe Adjaho, has banned the use of the Akan word '*tweaa*' in Parliament. He said the use of the Akan word *tweaa* was un-parliamentary and should not be part of the "Parliamentary lexicon."

---

[10] https://www.graphic.com.gh/news/politics/government-investigate-who-said-tweaa-dce.html

Mr Adjaho banned the word after the member for Subin, Mr Isaac Osei (NPP), had drawn his attention to the fact that the word had gained currency in the House lately and sought to find out if that word could be used.

Tweaa is an Akan interjection used mainly to express contempt for a statement made.[11]

The ban on the use of the interjection in Parliament suggests that even among equals, assuming MPs are equals, its use is censured. Thompson (2019: 4), based on a corpus of uses in online commentary on Ghanaweb, proposes the following explication for the Akan interjection *tweaa*:

(10) *Tweaa* [tɕɥɪaa]
  (a) I think like this now: "I know something very bad about this someone; people can know this something
  I feel something very bad towards this someone because of it
  I can't not feel like this"
  (b) I want other people to know this

This explication is linked to the kind of data that Thompson analysed. In particular, it only accounts for the use of the interjection as directed at someone and does not necessarily account for the cathartic uses which involve the use of the interjection out of frustration or anger at oneself. I propose a slightly different explication as in Table 6.2, based on the semantic template for (secondary) interjections as outlined in Goddard (2015). The semantic structure of such signs involves a Cognitive Trigger, i.e. a situation that engenders a thought or realisation in the language user; a Reaction, which signals the feeling and how intensely it is felt; an Expressive Impulsive component, which depicts the strong and immediate urge to say or do something; and then the Utterance component, which may be a word or a noise. As it is a pragmatic act, I would argue that there is an illocutionary point and/or a manner component. Then there is a metalexical awareness component, which Goddard sets apart from the rest of the explication, but which, I would argue, is part and parcel of the significance and the shared understanding of the sign. With all these considerations, I propose the following representation to account for the use and meaning of the embodied sign of suck teeth in the Volta Basin:

This explication in Table 6.2 applies to both the self-directed and the other-directed uses of the interjection. Contextual information will interact with this meaning to yield on-line interpretations for both the speaker and the hearers and other participants. We now turn to the second areal invective, the

---

11 https://www.graphic.com.gh/news/politics/parliament-bans-use-of-tweaa-in-house.html

Table 6.2: The semantics of [tɕʏɪaa] 'suck teeth' in the Volta Basin {tsuiã/tweeaa/tsyuu}.

I know this now: something bad is happening here I don't want it	Cognitive Trigger
I feel something bad because of it	Reaction
I want to do something bad because of it I cannot not do it	Expressive Impulsive
I do this: [tɕʏɪaa]	Performative utterance
I do this like this because I want other people to know how I feel	Illocutionary Point
I know many people think like this It is bad if one does something like this when they feel something bad	Metalexical Awareness

multimodal packaged utterance comprising a non-verbal gesture – a thumb point, and a verbal component that includes themes that are usually used in swearing: scatological in Ewe and the mother theme in Ga.

6.4 "I sh.t in your mouth"

While suck teeth is a noise-like word, an interjection, a vocalisation, as we have seen, the emblematic thumb point physical gesture is a gestural part of a composite signal. It is a quotable gesture, an emblem. It is made up of a thumb point directed at the addressee. The thumb moves from a higher position and rests flat on the other folded fingers. At the same time as one moves the thumb to come to rest on the folded fingers, one can say the accompanying words; see Figure 6.2. This utterance is closer to profane swearing than suck teeth. The accompanying verbal expressions in the different languages make use of words referring to scatological, sex and mother themes (cf. e.g. Ljung 2011 on themes deployed in swearing). The alternative Ewe expressions are given in (11)[12], and those of Ga which have spread in the Volta Basin are given in (12).

---

[12] While the expressions in (11) are used by speakers from Ewe communities in Ghana, Togo and Benin, it is only Ghanaian Ewe users who accompany the expression with a thumb point. In fact the thumb point gesture is not known by Ewe language uses from Togo and Benin. This provides strong evidence for the gesture to be a feature of the Lower Volta Basin in Ghana.

Figure 6.2: Thumb point gesture.

(11) a. *Me-nye   mí   ḍé   nu=wò   me*   Ewe
     1SG-swing faeces ALL mouth=2SG inside
     'I defecate/sh.t in your mouth'
   b. *Me-nye   mí   ná-a*   Ewe
     1SG-swing faeces DAT-2SG
     'I defecate/sh.t onto you'

(12) a. *sɔ́ɔ̀mi!*   Ga
     'inside vagina'
   b. *onyɛ   sɔ́ɔ̀   mli*   Ga
     mother vagina inside
     'inside your mother's vagina'
   c. *onyáe   gbèmí*   Ga
     mother vagina
     'your mother's vagina'

This multi-modal composite utterance is perceived as more rude than the sucking of teeth. Unlike the suck teeth, it carries social censure. In fact, if this thumb pointing, with or without an accompanying verbal expression, is used in asymmetrrical communication by a participant lower in status in terms of variables like gender, age and social status, the user may be summoned for arbitration. Thus it is accountable.

The enactment of this pragmatic act in Ewe can be responded to with a rebuttal from the targetted addressee with expressions that show that despite the formulaicity of the expressions, language users are aware of and deploy the literal meanings. Consider the following occurrences:

(13) Context: An older girl (C) asks a younger one (D) to bring her a napkin from the washing line outside. The younger girl (D) takes a long time and comes and throws the towel from a distance to her (C). The older one (C) insults the younger one (D) with the words and the gesture:
 a. *Me-nye   mí   ɖé nu=wò   me*   Ewe
    1SG-swing faeces all mouth=2SG inside
    'I defecate/sh.t in your mouth'
 The younger one (D) retorts with these words and the gesture back:
 b. *Me-fɛ   kpé   ná-a*
    1SG-knead.3SG feed.fluid DAT-2SG
    'I mash it and feed it to you.'

The message here is that the addressee does not want the thing that the speaker has put in her mouth to be in her mouth, let alone does she want to consume it. The rebuttal therefore just says I take whatever you have put in my mouth and I make it into something that I can feed to you. The interesting thing is that Ewe has two verbs for feeding people: one is *kpé*, which means to feed fluids to someone through the mouth. The sense of the verb is to bring the fluid food to the mouth of the person. (The verb also translates as 'meet'.) It is as if one is saying 'I retaliate'.

A similar rebuttal is used in the occurrence reported in (14). This happened on January 27th, 2019 in Have near the Police Barrier in the Volta Region of Ghana.

(14) Context: The major road that runs through the Have township has potholes, and drivers tend to drive around them by moving from one lane to the other. Two drivers were passing each other at one of these pothole ridden points. One driver (Driver A) was using the right lane going towards Accra and the other (Driver B) was using the left lane going in the opposite direction. Driver B has a huge pothole in his lane so tries to dodge by using the lane of Driver A. One would have expected that, given that

Driver A was moving in his lane, Driver B would have stopped for Driver A to pass. No, he used the narrow edge of the pothole and veered into Driver A's lane, even though he saw that he was moving. When they came abreast, Driver A insulted him with the Ewe expression *Me-nye mí ɖé nu=wò me* 'I sh.t in your mouth', whereupon Driver B retorts as follows:

me-lɔ=e   dó   ná-a
1SG-collect =3SG put   DAT-2SG
'I gather it and feed it (solid) to you.'

In (13b) the retort uses the verb expressing the feeding of fluids. In (14), the retort again suggests that the speaker does not want whatever is being put in his mouth to be in his body, so he gathers it and rather feeds it to the one who put it there. The rebuttals are a clear rejection of whatever the user of the insult is trying to place on the addressee.

As noted earlier, one difference between the suck teeth and this composite utterance is that its performance can be reported by the verb *dzu* 'insult, verbally abuse'. This suggests that it is an illocutionary act. I suggest the following explication to account for its use:

The explication proposed in Table 6.3 accounts for the use and meaning of the utterance in the Lower Volta Basin area. As indicated, the verbal expressions that accompany the physical gesture have different foci, and for a full account of the meaning as used in a particular language such as Ewe, we need a

Table 6.3: The semantics of the composite utterance: thumb point and verbal expression.

I think something very bad about you now Because you have done something bad towards me	Cognitive Trigger
I want to do something very bad to you because of it I know this: people can think something bad about me if I do it I cannot not do it	Reaction
I feel something very bad because of it I want something bad to happen to you because of it	Expressive Impulse

I say it with these bad words:
  [I shit in your mouth]/
  [your mother's vagina]
At the same I do this bad thing:
  [thumb point]
	Utterance Words Actions

I do these things because I want you to feel something very bad	Illocutionary Point

metalexical awareness segment to be added to what is in Table 6.3. For the Ewe expression, I propose the knowledge structure in (15) to account for it. I have framed it in the terms "If I have to say it in words ..."

(15) Metalexical awareness of the Ewe expressions accompanying thumb point
   a. If I want to say what I want in words
   b. I say it like this: sometimes people don't want bad things in their body
      When it is like this: People do something because of this
      After this the bad things move from their body to another place
      People do not want the bad things to touch their bodies
      People do not want to be in the same place as the bad things
   c. I want these bad things to be in your mouth
   d. I want you to feel very bad
      like people feel when these bad things touch their mouth

The rebuttal expressions discussed above suggest that people do not want the things that are said to be deposited in people's mouths to be there. This is part of what is captured in the components in (16b). These are the components that link the expression to notions of vulgarity and obscenity. From this follows a perception that the utterance is rude or impolite. But this aspect is linked to the socio-cultural norms associated with language use. In the ethnopragmatic approach adopted in this study such norms are captured in cultural scripts. In the next section (Section 6.5) the norms and values that govern the use of the invectives are outlined in a cultural script.

6.5 Attitudes towards the two multi-modal embodied utterances

In the discussion so far, it has been noted that people disapprove of others sucking their teeth towards other people, especially if they are not co-equals. Recall the issue of the DCE reported in Section 6.3. The use of dysphemisms in the scatological and sex domains accompanied by a rude thumb point gesture is also disapproved of in the Lower Volta Basin area. Children are trained not to use these utterances. When people use such utterances to people who are thought of as above them, they can be punished. When someone uses the Ewe vulgar expression 'I defecate in your mouth' and they are brought to arbitration, at the end of the process the judgement is usually phrased in terms of 'cleaning the anus' of the speaker, like what one does when one has eased oneself. The speaker may be further asked to provide drinks so that the mouth of the recipient of the insult can be cleaned. Moreover, in Ewe one can use a euphemism instead of the expression that contains the offending words, with or without the thumb point. The expression is given in (17).

(17) me-bíá nya áɖé wò
     1SG-ask word INDEF 2SG
     'I ask you something'

This suggests that people are aware that the expressions involving the dysphemistic expressions are not to be used in polite company. I propose in Table 6.4 a representation of these attitudes, values and norms about the use of these linguistic acts in the Lower Volta Basin using cultural scripts, the instrument used in the Natural Semantic Metalanguage framework for the meta-representation of how people think that many people in their communities of practice think (see e.g. Ameka 2006b; Goddard 2006, 2015; Wierzbicka 2014b).

Table 6.4: Cultural script about the expressive emblems suck teeth and thumb point.

Many people think like this about these words: They are bad words It is (very) bad if someone says these bad words to someone else It is bad if someone does (says) these bad things to someone else because they want them to feel something bad People can think of people of this kind like this: they are bad people People can say bad things about people of this kind	Thinking
Many people think like this: Sometimes, people say these words because they feel something (very) bad It is very bad if people say these words to some people It is very bad if this person is someone people think about like this: This person is someone above many people	Attitude/ Value

The main features captured are that people think of and know that these words are "bad words", and that people should not use these bad words nor perform the physical gesture associated with them. People also know that people can think or say bad things about those who use these words, especially when they use them to people who are above them in any of the socio-cultural variables, especially age and status. This is the way that the use of this form of swearing relates to respect. People also know that it is bad to use them and that it is not good to use them to cause offence.

6.6 Conclusion

I have explored the meaning and use of two emblematic signs that have spread in these linguistic areas. The study confirms the idea that linguistic signs, including gestures, can diffuse across language and culture boundaries. As a backdrop to the discussion, I investigated the semantics of the verb *dzu* 'insult, verbally abuse' in Ewe, which has equivalents in other languages in the area, to show how speakers conceptualise the use of words to cause offence to the other. The question was posed whether the semantics of this verb and similar words is related to swearing. It was suggested that there is a slight family resemblance to swearing, especially profane swearing, when it comes to name-calling and denigrating the physical characteristics of addressees. Nevertheless, the verb covers only a small part of the phenomena labelled in English as swearing. Other forms of swearing, such as invoking supernatural beings to do something to someone, or blasphemy, are not covered by the term *dzu*.

The core of the discussion concerned two multi-modal utterances. It was argued that the enactment of one of them, suck teeth, is not reported by the insult and verbal abuse verb in Ewe (and the other languages). It is rather represented by a descriptor of the action that is performed in the mouth to produce the sound. I suggested, along with Thompson (2019), that the utterance be considered an emotive interjection used to express contempt and frustration at someone else or at oneself. I proposed a semantic explication for it using the semantic template for an illocutionary act. I discussed the possibility noted by Chris Collins in his Facebook post of June 23, 2018, that the suck teeth act might be an instance of swearing in Ewe. I noted that to the extent that the expression is evaluated as being impolite, it bears some relation to profane swearing; however, it does not deploy dysphemisms, as is characteristic especially of profane swearing.

A better candidate for swearing, both from the point of view of its language and its evaluation as a very rude utterance, is the thumb point and its accompanying verbal expressions, which contain scatological and sex references as well as the mother theme. These are the features that Ljung (2011), for example, identifies for profane swearing. What is more, the enactment of this composite utterance is categorised as an insult (unlike suck teeth) as it is reported with the Ewe verb *dzu* and its equivalents. In addition, its effect is that it causes offence to the targeted addressee, and it is socio-culturally disapproved of, as I have tried to capture in the cultural script. Is this composite utterance a manifestation of profane swearing in Ewe and the other languages of the Volta Basin? Probably.

This brings me to the question of whether swearing is a universal. It depends on what is meant by swearing. I think formal swearing in terms of oath-taking might be universal. What about profane swearing? The features or acts that can be characterised as such are so varied that I doubt that it constitutes a universal domain. Perhaps the question should rather be framed in terms of: (i) "How does one express bad feelings towards someone else who has done something bad?" and (ii) "How does one express bad feelings towards oneself when one realises one has done something bad?" in a community of practice. More research is needed to formulate answers to such questions. In the current study I have suggested answers from the perspective of language users in the Volta Basin of West Africa and beyond. Similar utterances should be investigated in order to answer these questions.

Acknowledgements: I am very grateful to Christopher Collins for his comments on an earlier version of this chapter and for our stimulating discussions on various aspects of language and of Ewe in particular. My thanks also go to James Essegbey, Judith Glover, Mercy Bobuafor, Dorothy Agyepong and Rachel Thompson for their insights on the languages of the Volta Basin. Above all, I am greatly indebted to the editors of the volume for their careful editorial work and guidance as well as for their patience. The ideas expressed here were first presented at a Workshop on Swearing at the University of Cologne, organised by the editors. I thank them for the invitation, and I thank the participants for their helpful comments.

Abbreviations

1	first person
2	second person
3	third person
ADVZER	adverbialiser
COP	copula
DAT	dative
DEF	definite determiner
DIM	diminutive
HAB	habitual
IDEO	ideophone
NEG	negative
PFV	perfective
POT	potential

PREP	preposition
PRIV	privative
QT	quotative
QP	question particle
RED	reduplicative
SG	singular

References

Aidoo, Ama. A. 1991. *Changes: A love story*. London: Women's Press.
Alan, Keith, and Kate Burridge. 2006. *Forbidden Words: Taboo and the Censoring of Languages*. Cambridge: Cambridge University Press.
Ameka, Felix K. 1994. Areal conversational routines and cross-cultural communication in a multilingual society. In Heiner Pürschel (ed.), *Intercultural communication: Proceedings of the 17th International LAUD symposium, Duisburg 23–27 March 1992*, 441–469. Bern: Peter Lang.
Ameka, Felix K. 2006a. Grammars in contact in the Volta Basin (West Africa): On contact induced grammatical change in Likpe. In A.Y. Aikhenvald and R.M.W. Dixon (eds.), *Grammars in contact: a cross-linguistic typology*, 114–142. Oxford: Oxford University Press.
Ameka, Felix K. 2006b. 'When I die don't cry'; The ethnopragmatics of gratitude expressions in West African languages. In Cliff Goddard (ed.), *Ethnopragmatics*, 231–266. Berlin: Mouton de Gruyter.
Berg van den, Margot, Pieter Muysken and Norval Smith. 2015. Introduction: Creole studies and contact linguistics. In Muysken and Smith (eds.), 1–14. Berlin: Walter de Gruyter.
Bergen, Benjamin K. 2016. *What the F: What swearing reveals about our language, our brains, and ourselves*. New York: Basic Books.
Collins, Christopher. 1993. Topics in Ewe syntax. PhD dissertation, MIT. *MIT Working Papers in Linguistics*. Cambridge MA: Department of Linguistics, MIT.
Culpeper, Jonathan. 2011. *Impoliteness: Using language to cause offence*. Cambridge: Cambridge University Press.
Daku, Kari. 2003. *Ghanaianisms: a glossary*. Accra: Ghana Universities Press.
Ellis, Jeffery. 1984. Some speculations on language contact in a wider setting. In Robin Fawcett (ed.), *The semiotics of culture and language*. Vol. 1: Language as a semiotic system, 81–104. London: Pinter.
Figueroa, Esther. 2005. Rude sounds: Kiss Teeth and negotiation of the public sphere. In Susana Mühleisen and Bettina Migge (eds.), *Politeness and Face in Caribbean Creoles*, 73–100. Amsterdam: John Benjamins.
Finn, Eileen. 2017. Swearing: The Good, the Bad and the Ugly. *ORTESOL Journal* 34: 17–26.
Floor, Willem. 2015. The practice of cursing and bad language in Iran. *Zeitschrift der Deutschen Morgenländischen Gesellschaft* 165 (1): 155–184.
Goddard, Cliff. 2006. Ethnopragmatics: a new paradigm. In Cliff Goddard (ed.), *Ethnopragmatics*, 1–30. Berlin: Mouton de Gruyter.
Goddard, Cliff. 2015. "Swear words" and "curse words" in Australian (and American) English. At the crossroads of pragmatics, semantics and sociolinguistics. *Intercultural Pragmatics* 12 (2): 189–218.

Goddard, Cliff and Anna Wierzbicka. 2018. Minimal English and how it can add to Global English. In Goddard, Cliff (ed.) Minimal English for a Global World: Improved Communication Using Fewer Words, 5–28. Chams: Palgrave Macmillan.

Haugh, Michael. 2016. The role of English as a scientific metalanguage for research in pragmatics: reflections on the metapragmatics of "politeness" in Japanese. *East Asian Pragmatics* 1 (1): 39–71.

Hughes, Geoffrey. 2006. *An encyclopedia of swearing: The social history of oaths, profanity, foul language, and ethnic slurs in the English-speaking world*. London: Routledge.

Irvine, Judith T. 1993. Insult and responsibility: Verbal abuse in a Wolof village. In Jane H. Hill and Judith T. Irvine (eds.), *Responsibility and evidence in oral discourse*, 105–134. Cambridge: Cambridge University Press

Jay, Timothy and Kristin Janschewitz. 2008. The pragmatics of swearing. *Journal of Politeness Research* 4 (2): 267–288.

Kachru, Braj B. 2006. The English language in the outer circle. In Bolton, Kingsley & Braj B. Kachru (eds.), *World Englishes. Critical concepts in linguistics* Vol. 3, 241–255. London: Routledge.

Ljung, Magnus. 2011. *Swearing: A cross-cultural linguistic study*. London: Palgrave MacMillan UK.

McGarrity, Laura W. 2017. Review of What the F: What swearing reveals about our language, our brains, and ourselves by Benjamin K. Bergen. *Language* 93 (4): 372–374.

Muysken, Pieter C. and Norval Smith (eds.). 2015. *Surviving the Middle Passage: The West Africa-Surinam Sprachbund*. Berlin: Walter de Gruyter.

Rickford, John R. and Angela E. Rickford. 1976. Cut-eye and suck-teeth: African words and gestures in New World guise. *The Journal of American Folklore* 89 (353): 294–309.

Rongier, Jacques. 2015. *Dictionnaire ewe-français*. Paris: L'harmattan.

Samarin, William J. 1969. The art of Gbeya insults. *International Journal of American Linguistics* 35 (4): 323–329.

Stapleton, Karyn. 2010. Swearing. In Miriam A. Locher and Sage L. Graham (eds.), *Interpersonal pragmatics*, 289–306. Berlin: Walter de Gruyter.

Setsoafia, Biɖi 1982. *Fia tsatsala* [The wondering chief]. Accra: Bureau of Ghana Languages.

Terkourafi, Marina. 2008. Toward a unified theory of politeness, impoliteness, and rudeness. In Derek Bousfield and Miriam A. Locher (eds.), *Impoliteness in Language: Studies on its Interplay with Power in Theory and Practice*, 45–74. Berlin: Mouton de Gruyter.

Thompson, Rachel. Tweaa! – A Ghanaian interjection of "contempt" in online political comments. *Ampersand* (2019): https://doi.org/10.1016/j.amper.2019.100047

Thompson, Rachel and Kofi Agyekum. 2016. Impoliteness: The Ghanaian Standpoint. *International Journal of Society, Culture & Language* 4 (1) (Special Issue on African Cultures & Languages): 20–33.

Waters, Sophia. 2012. "It's rude to VP": The cultural semantics of rudeness. *Journal of Pragmatics* 44 (9): 1051–1062.

Westermann, Dietrich H. 1973[1928]. *Ewefiala: Ewe-English dictionary*. Berlin/Nendeln: Dietrich Riemer/Kraus Reprint.

Wierzbicka, Anna. 1987. *English speech act verbs: a semantic dictionary*. Sydney: Academic Press.

Wierzbicka, Anna. 2014a. *Imprisoned in English*. Oxford: Oxford University Press.

Wierzbicka, Anna. 2014b. Language and cultural scripts. In Farzad Sharifian (ed.), *The Routledge Handbook of Language and Culture*, 339–356. Oxford: Routledge.

Part II: **Cultural mobility as context of transgression**

Joseph T. Farquharson, Clive Forrester and Andrea Hollington

7 The linguistics of Jamaican swearing: Forms, background and adaptations

Abstract: Jamaican swear words are popular far beyond the borders of the Caribbean island. Swearing practices in Jamaican are interesting due to their linguistic set-up based on historical language contact and their socio-cultural contexts, their adaptations in music and material culture and their usage among various groups of people around the world. Moreover, the legal situation of swearing in Jamaica provides insights into controversies between law and practices that goes back to colonial times. Despite those various aspects, Jamaican swearing practices have not yet attracted attention in linguistic scholarship. Hence, this paper provides first insights into the linguistics of swearing in Jamaica and discusses not only etymological, semantic and syntactic aspects of swearing, but also reflects on the sociolinguistic background and the usage of swear words outside Jamaica as well as in music. A discussion of the legal background of using swear words sheds light on the colonial history of linguistic censoring and its effects on today's society. This paper starts with some theoretical preliminaries that place linguistic swearing practices in its sociocultural context before examining Jamaican swearing expressions, discussing some aspects of their historical background and etymology, analyzing linguistic constructions and sociolinguistic implications as well as reflecting on social and legal regulation and adaptations in and outside Jamaica. This chapter provides an original and innovative account of swearing in Jamaican and thus contributes to a better understanding of swearing in a cross-cultural perspective.

7.1 Theoretical background: Approaches to swearing practices

A number of disciplines have looked at practices of swearing and cursing in various contexts. However, swearing and cursing did not constitute a major topic of study in linguistics for a long time due to its taboo nature and social stigmatization. As Jay (2000: 10) states:

> Like the topic of human sexuality, the topic of taboo speech is so taboo that it has not been regarded as a legitimate topic for scholarly examination. Cursing is a powerful taboo in this culture and has been too taboo for linguistic scholarship.

In recent years however, linguists have developed a deeper interest in the language of swearing and cursing, which also involves interdisciplinary work with fields such as cultural studies and psychology to investigate the nature, functions, and meanings of swearing and cursing (cf. Jay 2000; Jay and Janschewitz 2008; Vingerhoets, Bylsma and de Vlam 2013). Looking at the various existing accounts on swearing, we realize that they often focus on swearing in Western cultures and languages. This focus and the way in which transgressive practices of swearing are treated in these societies have impacted the academic approaches to the thematic, for instance, with regard to categories and attitudes. On the other hand, the literature usually claims that swearing is culture-specific and connected to cultural conceptualizations of taboo which can be different across societies. This is often exemplified with swear words and swearing categories in different languages (see Vingerhoets, Bylsma and de Vlam 2013). Despite this supposed cross-cultural or cross-linguistic perspective, the categories and concepts used to analyze swear words in non-Western languages are sometimes still based on a Western perspective and not understood within their respective cultural, social and historical contexts. This already starts with the use of English as metalanguage and our reliance on English terms, categories and concepts. Furthermore, the frequent focus on the lexical domain of swearing practices (collecting and categorizing swear words for cross-cultural comparison) has led to a one-sided approach to the complex theme given that other important aspects in the contexts of swearing practices have hardly been studied more deeply. As Storch and Nassenstein illustrate in the introduction to this volume, a more holistic approach to swearing practices includes issues such as linguistic creativity, speaker agency, the performativity of swearing practices and metalinguistic discourses. Moreover, communicative practices such as silence, laughter, gestures, and facial expressions, as well as body posture and movements can be important parts of swearing. As the introduction to this volume also emphasizes, the transgressive nature of swearing and cursing practices is often linked to liminality and power with regard to the destruction and re-establishing of order. Through violating and transgressing social norms, the use of "bad language" in this regard can be a powerful tool pushing boundaries, or constituting in themselves social and linguistic acts of border-crossing. This is also connected to the taboo-nature of swearing practices. Here, specific cultural aspects can be of importance as taboo is a cultural matter and hence, the perception of what is regarded as transgressive or "bad language" varies cross-culturally or even intra-culturally. In this respect, the violation or breaking of taboos when swearing, can also trigger different social reactions and sanctions. Taboo is usually considered as "a proscription of behavior that affects everyday life" (Allen and Burridge 2006: 1). Taboos are considered culture-specific as they "arise out of social constraints on the individual's behavior where it can cause discomfort, harm or injury" (Allen and Burridge 2006: 1). The relation between taboo and swearing is captured by the over-representation of certain lexico-semantic domains in the language of swearing including, among others, bodies and their effluvia; the organs and acts of sex; micturition and defecation; diseases, death and killing; naming, addressing, touching and viewing persons and sacred beings, objects and places; food gathering, preparation and consumption (Allen and Burridge 2006: 1). The relationship between taboo and swearing is more complex when it comes to linguistic expressions: the degree to which swear words are taboo varies and changes over time as expressions develop additional connotations and metaphoric extensions, and as they become socially acceptable. On the other hand, not all words or expressions that are taboo can be used as swear words. With regard to Jamaican, this can be observed with certain taboo words for female body parts which are not generally used as swear words (see discussion below).

In the academic literature, swearing or cursing is defined as "a form of linguistic activity utilizing taboo words to convey the expression of strong emotions" (Vingerhoets, Bylsma and de Vlam 2013: 287) as "offensive speech" or as "the utterance of emotionally powerful, offensive *words* [...] or emotionally harmful *expressions* [...] that are understood as insults" (Jay 2000: 9). These definitions show that swearing and cursing practices are closely tied to the concept of emotion and the expression or release of strong feelings. In this context, the psychological functions of the linguistic acts become apparent, for instance, in the form of catharsis. Moreover, scholars have argued that swearing is closely connected to a range of other aspects and domains. This results in a quite broad perspective on swearing which "include[s] categories such as: swearing, obscenity, profanity, blasphemy, name calling, insulting, verbal aggression, taboo speech, ethnic-racial slurs, vulgarity, slang, and scatology" (Jay 2000: 9). This range also highlights the aforementioned point that swearing practices need to be seen in their respective cultural, social, interpersonal but also in interdisciplinary contexts in order to fully make sense. However, these categories and related domains largely express – although they often include cross-cultural comparisons – approaches to swearing practices as they were formed in Western academic discourse. This hegemony in theory-building has been criticized as a major problem in the social sciences (Connell 2007). Therefore, in this chapter, we aim at presenting a fresh look at Jamaican swearing practices without taking the established domains for granted, but by discussing Jamaican practices within their local and cultural contexts.

Apart from the transgressive and violent nature of swearing, there are other functions and contexts of usage that play a role in the discussion of this chapter. While swearing and cursing are often described as harmful linguistic practices, they are not necessarily considered impolite and actually swear words occur very frequently in daily linguistic practices without being insulting. Jay and Janschewitz (2008: 269) argue "that swearing can be polite, impolite, or neither and it may be used with any emotional state." The particular context and communicative situation play important roles with regard to the appropriateness of swear words. In this regard, the de-tabooization of swear words, especially in informal contexts and when they are used commonly, also impacts the pragmatics of the respective expression. For instance, such swear words are more likely to become used as affirmative expressions or expressions of surprise with a positive meaning, as in *this was fucking awesome* or *what the fuck*? This phenomenon can also be observed in Jamaica, where swear words such as *bomboklaat, bloodklaat* or *pussyklaat* can not only be used as insults but also as expressions of surprise or amusement; a point also discussed in this chapter.

7.2 Some notes on the historical and etymological background of Jamaican swear words

The popular perception in Jamaica is that swear words are mainly (if not only) associated with the Africa-derived elements of Jamaican heritage, and were created by enslaved Africans and their descendants during slavery as a linguistic means of rebellion against their colonial masters. This much is explicit in the editorial question inserted by journalist Karyl Walker (2012) into her reporting of a news story about a pregnant woman who was fatally shot by a policeman for using "indecent language"[1]:

> Is it that the law was implemented to curtail the use of certain slang words *used by people of African descent*, which were not fully understood by the former slave owners?
>
> (Walker 2012, our emphasis)

---

[1] In Jamaica, a law proscribes the public use of swear words. Despite the law, people in Jamaica do use swear words in public spaces. Given the historical context of swear words, the question remains whether it is that the law was implemented to curtail the use of certain words used by people of African descent, which were not fully understood by the former slave owners?

This perception of an African origin for Jamaican swear words has been echoed by academic and public intellectual Carolyn Cooper (2013) who states: "Jamaican bad words have a quite respectable pedigree. They usually refer to perfectly good female body parts and functions. But the language of these bad words *is often of African origin*" [our emphasis]. However, a closer look at the lexicon of Jamaican swearing reveals that while the most popular swear word *bomboklaat* contains an African component, the majority of the others appear to have "English" provenance. Moreover, not all expressions that are classified as indecent language (i.e. taboo) are swear words in the technical sense. For example, one word for the female genitalia, *puni* can be used in the expression *mi puni!* (literally, 'my vagina!') to express excitement and surprise. Like most terms for the female genitalia, *puni* is taboo, but as far as we are aware, it is not used as a swear word.

Jamaican contains a sizeable swear word lexicon which includes words and expressions derived from the English language such as *dyam* (< English *damn*), *fok* (< English *fuck*), *hel* (< English *hell*), *pusi* (< English *pussy*), *(go) sok yu mada!* (< English *(go) suck your mother*), *kis mi aas* (< English *kiss my arse*). However, there is a small set of swear words that are evaluated by native speakers of Jamaican Creole to be more authentically Jamaican than those already mentioned. In terms of their structure, they are compound forms created by concatenating a body part with *klaat* (< English *cloth*): *bomboklaat, blodklaat, pusiklaat, raasklaat*. The first in the series has as its initial element the Africa-derived word *bombo* which in several Atlantic-Congo languages (cf. Temne, Kikongo, Kimbundu, Zulu) means 'vagina, vulva' and is polysemous between vagina and anus in the Bantu languages Bembe and Nyanga (cf. Farquharson 2012: 246).

Etymologically, *bomboklaat* refers to a sanitary towel used by menstruating women (cf. the dictionary entry in Cassidy and Le Page 2002: 79, s.v. bumbo cloth). Cassidy and Le Page (2002: 52, s.v. blood-cloth), provide the same meaning for *blodklaat* as they do for *bomboklaat*, but make no mention of the use of these words as swearwords. Although we assume that *blodklaat* was created on the analogy of *bomboklaat*, it departs from it by switching the thematic focus point from body-part to body fluid. When considered together, the swear words *pusiklaat* and *raasklaat* show an interesting development in the history of this set of words. We infer that both of them were created using *bomboklaat* as a template; but each exploits a different aspect of the polysemous Jamaican word *bombo*, i.e. *pusiklaat* places focus on the vagina, whereas *raasklaat* places the buttocks in focus.

Together, these expressions form a small class of swear words made up of body part compounds. We have no reason to believe that the pattern of concatenating a body-part or body fluid term with the word *klaat* is not an innovation local to Jamaica. In addition, only one out of the four compound swear words contains a word that is of African origin. These conclusions run counter to popular and scholarly perceptions that "the language of these bad words is often of African origin" (Cooper 2013). If Africa-derived lexical items are so poorly represented in swearing registers of Jamaican Creole, why are swear words thought to be African in origin?

Although we strongly suspect that *bomboklaat* 'sanitary towel' stretches back to the period of slavery, we have encountered no attestations of the word in the pre-twentieth century literature, either in that sense or its use as a swear word. The other three swear words that end with *klaat* are also absent from the known literature of the same period. The earliest record we have found of a swear word being used is from a late eighteenth-century account written by a visiting Englishman. The account includes his observation of a white family (women and children) enjoying a repast. When the visitor hands a crab to a boy, around seven years old, the boy protests: "*Him no hab egg, him blue maugre to hell, me no wantee man crab, me wantee woman crab*" (Anonymous 1791: 411, our emphasis) 'It doesn't have any eggs. It's small as hell/damn puny! I don't want the male crab. I want the female crab.' The visitor was appalled that such strong language would be used by a child, "but his mother called him to her, kissed him a dozen times, and picked him out the best *woman crab*" (Anonymous 1791: 411, original italics). The expression *tu hel* 'to hell', is still used as a mild swear word and intensifier in modern Jamaica; however, in polite company, it would be considered too strong for a child that age.[2]

Our second eighteenth-century example, *buss my rassa* 'kiss my arse', comes from the same decade in which *tu hel* was first attested. It was recorded in a song whose protagonist is a young African-descended enslaved woman who is talking about the love affair between her and her married master, and the consequences. When the enslaved woman gives birth to a light-skinned mixed-race child, she is confronted and beaten by her master's wife who claims that the child is her husband's. The husband calls his wife a lying bitch and tells her to kiss his arse: *My massa curse her, "lying bitch!" / And tell her, "buss my rassa."* (Moreton 1793: 154). This provides evidence not only for the vintage of the swear word *buss my rassa*, but also for its social use. On the evidence provided by the song, we can extrapolate that the expression was used among

---

[2] Although we have separated *tu hel* because it stretches across the centuries, it appears that the entire swear expression was *blue maugre to hell* since the string also appears in an early nineteenth-century document (Williams 1826: 283).

whites (master of a plantation to his wife), and that it could be embedded in a song, a text intended for public performance.

This brief historical overview above has revealed two interesting findings. The first is that, despite common perceptions in modern Jamaican society, that Jamaican swear words are chiefly of African provenance, the overwhelming majority neither has an African etymology nor requires an explanation involving Africa. The second finding is that in early colonial Jamaica, swear words appeared to have been common among whites (including children). There is an absence of direct evidence – actual quoted usage – for swear word use among people of African descent. Therefore, the current state of affairs, where "bad words" are believed to be mostly African in origin and their use more typical of people of African descent begs for an explanation.

The current situation may be attributed to the criminalisation of indecent language since the second quarter of the nineteenth century with the passing of the Towns and Communities Act (1843) which proposes a penalty for persons who "use any profane, indecent or obscene language publicly". It is generally believed that the law was made to police the speech of Blacks, but since the regulations do not list words that were considered profane, indecent, or obscene, it is not possible at this time to verify this perception. This does not preclude that the law might have been implemented in a racist way, punishing Blacks disproportionately. The racist application of the law would have also extended to include language, in that, the most offensive swear words (*bomboklaat, bloodklaat, raasklaat, pussyklaat*) have no clear English model and are associated with conservative lects of Jamaican Creole. Conservative varieties of the Jamaican language are perceived as having more African elements, and those elements that cannot be readily attributed to English are generally assigned a default African origin by non-linguists.

7.3 Some notes on Jamaican swearing and legislation

The set of swear words, referred to in Jamaica as "choice Jamaican words", "fabric" or *klaat* (i.e., *bomboklaat, bloodklaat, raasklaat, pussyklaat*), comprise what most Jamaicans would consider to be the most offensive curse words locally. So offensive are these words that their use often attracts fines in the Resident Magistrates courts of Jamaica. The Towns and Communities Act (1843) 3(m) states:

> Every person who shall sell or distribute, or offer for sale or distribution, or shall mark on any fence, wall or any building, any obscene figure, drawing, painting, or representation, or sing any profane, indecent or obscene song or ballad, or write or draw any indecent or obscene word, figure, or representation, or use any profane, indecent or obscene language; shall be guilty of an offence and shall be liable to a penalty not exceeding one thousand dollars.

No specific reference is made about what type of language is considered indecent. As is common in statutes of this sort, it is assumed that a *reasonable* person would be able to determine what kind of language falls within its purview. The clause does however stipulate the different media in which the prohibition holds, namely in painting, "representation" (which could include sculptures), and/or song. The Towns and Communities Act continues in section 4:

> It shall be lawful for any constable to take into custody, without warrant, any person who shall commit any of the offences hereinbefore mentioned within view of any such constable; and in like manner, when the offender is unknown, without warrant to take into custody any such offender who shall be charged by any other credible person with recently committing any of the said offences, though not committed within view of such constable, but within view of the person making such charge.

This second clause makes it possible for any police constable to remand into custody any person who violates the prohibition against indecent language in view of the police officer, but also when the offender is not in view of the constable provided that a "credible" person has witnessed the act. Note that all of this can be done *without* the need for a warrant. It is legally possible for a police to detain an individual because they were accused of swearing.[3]

Many Jamaicans would possibly be surprised that such a prohibition is still on the law books given the wanton abandon with which "bad words" can be heard on any given day in the public space. Admittedly, the law is rarely ever applied, and certainly not on any consistent basis, but it does not mean it lacks teeth. This was made apparent in the incident (mentioned in Section 7.2), involving the woman who was shot dead by the police officer while he attempted to detain her for swearing in his presence (but not *at* him). It is alleged that the

---

3 An exceptional context in this regard is likely Dancehall themed stage shows. However, on several occasions, Dancehall artists have been fined for using expletives during their performance, and in some cases the show has been interrupted or shut down by the police. In an attempt to present a "cleaner", more corporate-friendly Dancehall show, the producers of Sumfest 2017 (a large annual festival in Jamaica) included a "no profanity clause" for performers on the show. Such a proscription serves a dual process in the context of a Dancehall show; it signals to corporate sponsors that the event is taking a *professional* direction while simultaneously flying below the radar of the police.

woman was using the *bomboklaat* swear word in earshot of the police officer who attempted to bring her into the station to be charged. Five years later, the officer was cleared of all charges (murder, and wounding with intent).

7.4 The linguistics and sociolinguistics of Jamaican swearing

Based on the languages surveyed, Ljung (2011: 35) identifies five major taboo themes: the religious/supernatural theme; the scatological theme; the sex organ theme; the sexual activities theme; and the mother (family) theme. Jamaica swearing covers all the themes identified by Ljung:

(1) The religious/supernatural theme
 a. *O Gad!/Mi Gad!* 'Oh God!/My God'
 b. *Almaiti tu di kraas* 'Almighty to the cross!'
 c. *Gad Almaiti* 'God Almighty'

(2) The scatological theme
 a. *Shit!*
 b. *Blodklaat, bomboklaat, pusiklaat, raasklaat* (see above)

(3) The sex organ theme
 a. *bombo-uol* 'vagina/anus', *pusi-uol* 'vagina', *raas-uol* 'anus'
 b. *Mi pusi!*

(4) The sexual activities theme
 a. *Go sok yuself* 'Go and suck yourself.'
 b. *Fok aaf* 'Fuck off'

(5) The mother (family) theme
 a. *(Go) sok yu mada* '(Go) suck your mother'
 b. *Yu mada* 'Your mother!'
 c. *Kis mi grani* 'Kiss my grandmother!'

The swear words considered to be the most offensive by Jamaicans fall within the scatological theme (2), and the sex organ theme (3). The two categories are related seeing that items in the latter category are built up from those in the former via a process of concatenation. The "klaat" terms belong to the scatological theme because they make indirect reference to menstruation – *bomboklaat* being a sanitary towel used by menstruating women. Traditional Jamaican society had a wide range of taboos associated with menstruation. One such taboo prohibited a woman from washing a man's clothes with hers in the same washtub, or even from hanging them close together on the same line to dry. These beliefs suggest that men found menstrual blood and things associated with it to be disgusting. This presents a very logical semantic path from an item of disgust to a deprecatory term.

Notwithstanding their frequent use and international popularity, in Jamaica, swear words are treated as socially inappropriate in public spaces. In crowded areas such as markets and shopping centers, or public transportation, it still remains a social taboo for persons, in particular children, to use swear words. Adults who are found in violation of this social rule are sometimes cautioned about public decency by over-hearers, and children who violate the rule may be sternly reprimanded, sometimes by any adult in earshot.

Despite the potential high stakes involved in using "indecent" language in Jamaica, the practice is so ubiquitous that it signifies Jamaicanness beyond the borders of the country. Jamaican swear words can be used to express emotions and psychological states such as shock, disgust, admiration, disbelief, frustration, and relief. Below are some examples of how the set of swear words collectively referred to as "klaat" by Jamaicans is used. The examples show general usages as well as forms that are unattested and so are deemed impossible.[4]

Expression of shock/surprise (both positive and negative)

(1) *bomboklaat/ blodklaat/ raasklaat/ pusiklaat*

(2) *mi bombo(klaat)!*

(3) **bomboklaat mi!*

Expression of angered bewilderment

(4) Wa   di   bombo-klaat   a   gwaan   ya so?
     what   DET   vagina/anus-cloth   PROG   go.on   here so
     'What the hell is going on here?'

---

4 All examples with * are considered ungrammatical.

Accusations

(5) Yu   tuu bombo-klaat   lai!
     2SG too vagina/anus-cloth   lie
     'You are a damn liar!'

(6) *Yu   tuu lai bombo-klaat!
     2SG   too lie vagina/anus-cloth

(7) Yu   a   wan bombo-klaat   tiif
     2SG COP one vagina/anus-cloth   thief
     'You are a damn thief.''

(8) *Yu   a   wan tiif   bombo-klaat
     2SG   COP one thief vagina/anus-cloth

Frustration

(9) cho   bombo-blod-klaat/   bombo-raas-klaat
     bombo-pusi-raas-klaat   bombo-pusi-blod-klaat
     bombo-pusi-klaat

(10) cho *blod-bombo-klaat *raas-bombo-klaat *pusi-bombo-klaat

These examples show on the one hand, how the same set of swear words can be used to express different meanings or sentiments based on their context of use and their formal composition. Prosodic features also play an important role here, as the meaning can be influenced by intonation, especially to distinguish surprise (examples 1–3) from anger in the use of these swear words. On the other hand, these examples also illustrate syntactic features of the swear words in their linguistic contexts and show that the swear words are promiscuous in terms of their lexical categories (examples 2–8). Moreover, example (9) shows how the swear words can be strung together in order to express strong emotions, in particular frustration, preceded by exclamation introducers such as *wa di* ... ! 'what the ... !', *tu* ... ! 'to ... ', or the ideophone *cho*, which expresses frustration or disapproval (cf. Hollington 2017).

These comprise the standard usage for Jamaican swear words, running the gamut of emotions though still relegated to the taboo-vulgar continuum which researchers have documented existing in polite company in European societies, or, as in the case of Jamaica, post-colonial societies. Indeed, the attitudes towards Jamaican swear words, like the language itself, is a remnant of the island's colonial past. And in the same way that use of Jamaican Creole acts as subversion of and resistance to hegemonic post-colonial morals, so too do the curse words serve to challenge oppressive ways of thinking. Nowhere is this idea of the swear word as resistance more obvious than in Jamaican popular music. Reggae artiste Peter Tosh immortalized *bomboklaat* (and to a lesser extent, *raasklaat*) in his controversial hit song "Oh Bombo Klaat" on the *Wanted Dread & Alive* album (1981). In the song, the swear words are used as a cathartic response to a corrupt and oppressive system. Given that the song is important to highlight the subversive role of swearing in Jamaica, the lyrics are presented below in full:

Peter Tosh – Oh Bumbo Klaat

Oh bumboklaat, oh raasklaat
Oh bumboklaat, oh raasklaat

I said I came upon this land
To guide and teach my fellow man
But one thing I can't overstand
Is why them don't love this brother man

Oh bumboklaat, oh raasklaat
Oh bumboklaat, oh raasklaat

Sometimes I sit and look around
And listen to the daily sound
But when I check, there's so much lies
And that's the reason why the children cry.

Oh bumboklaat, oh raasklaat
Oh bumboklaat, oh raasklaat

It's been so long
We need a change
So the shitstem we got to rearrange.
And if there's obstacles in the road, we got to throw them overboard

Oh bumboklaat, oh raasklaat
Oh bumboklaat, oh raasklaat

One night, an evil spirit held me down
I could not make one single sound
Till Jah told me, 'Son, use the word'
And now I'm as free as a bird

Oh bumboklaat, oh raasklaat
Oh bumboklaat, oh raasklaat
Rept x 6

The entire song is a lengthy lament in the characteristic Tosh style of social commentary. The protagonist laments that despite his coming to teach and guide humanity, he is unable to discern any truth or unity among people. He continues that the *shitstem* 'corrupt system' (< blend of *shit* + *system*) needs to be rearranged and whatever obstacles exist on the journey to doing so should be overthrown. This is a direct reference to the Rastafari concept of "Babylon" – a system of thought and governance originating in Europe meant to oppress and control the lives of members of the Global South, especially racialized peoples, and definitely the Rastafari. Relief comes at last at the end of the song when Tosh reveals that he was held captive by an evil spirit, unable to speak, but then Jah told him to "use the word". The most egregious of Jamaican swear words, frowned upon in polite company, and criminalized by the *shitstem*, ultimately proves to be the protagonist's source of freedom and escape. The evil spirit is exorcised by his chanting the swear words *bomboklaat* and *raasklaat*.

This anti-establishment use of swearing, meant to overthrow a system of oppression, is not given much attention in the literature, though a few authors have noted this dynamic. Hughes (2015: xvi) states:

> At base, swearing is governed by 'sacral' notions of word magic; that is to say the belief that words have the power to change the world. These beliefs tend to be very powerful at primitive stages of society, manifesting themselves in charms, spells, invocations, and curses, so that taboos or prohibitions have grown up around dangerous or offensive usages.

Hughes (2015) observes that laws restricting the use of swear words developed alongside the mysticism surrounding said words; as soon as it became obvious of the power within these words, laws sprang up which regulated their usage in public. Quite different from the usual rationale that such laws are meant to preserve public order and decency, the same laws could be seen as an attempt to curtail the expressive power of those who use these words.

The relationship between curse words and regular language is a complex one. Bergen (2016: 8) comments:

> Bad language deserves inspection on its own merits. But it's also important for a second, perhaps slightly less obvious reason. Profanity is powerful, so it behaves differently from other types of language. It gets encoded differently in the brain. It's learned differently. It's articulated differently. It changes differently over time. And as a result, bad language has the unique potential to reveal facts about our language and ourselves that we'd otherwise never imagine.

There is in fact evidence from studies in neurolinguistics and speech pathology to suggest that cursing might be localized in a different portion of the brain from regular language. This makes it possible for patients suffering from a brain damage which has a global effect on their ability to use language, still possessing the ability to swear, and even do so uncontrollably (Jay 2000: 4). Swear words might have the appearance of regular lexical items, and conform to many of the grammatical rules which exist for a given language, but the fact that swearing can persist when regular language is impaired, lends a whole new perspective to Hughes' (2015) idea of "word magic".

7.5 From Jamaica to the world: The use of Jamaican swear words by non-Jamaicans

In January of 2014, Toronto's former mayor Rob Ford, already infamous for admitting to drug use while in office, attracted another firestorm of media attention when he was caught on camera using the Jamaican swear word *bomboklaat*. Ford, who at the time was chatting with friends in a Toronto fast food restaurant, was secretly recorded in his usual bombastic and animated style explaining to a group of friends an incident between himself and a Jamaican man which caused him a great deal of frustration. Apparently, Ford was accosted by this Jamaican man for not being quick to acquiesce when asked for financial assistance. Ford's speech is slurred throughout the minute-long recording, indicating that he might have been intoxicated during his rant, as he attempts to mimic the speech of the Jamaican who chastised him, and demonstrate to his friends that he could respond with Jamaican swear words in like fashion. Essentially, Ford used the curse words as a feature of storytelling – both as direct quoted speech as well as commentary about the character in the story. His audience was receptive as well as accommodating. Given this non-confrontational context, what caused the swift disapproval from so many who saw the video?

7 The linguistics of Jamaican swearing: Forms, background and adaptations — 161

For one, there is a sizeable Jamaican population in the Greater Toronto Area (GTA), which means that Jamaican language is not only widely heard in and around GTA communities, but it is also understood and incorporated into Afro- and other Canadian vernaculars. It is not unusual then that Jamaican swear words could come to be used by a white Canadian who, while not being Jamaican by birth or parentage, had enough association with Jamaicans to decipher the socio-grammatical contexts in which said swear words were acceptable. Global News Toronto, reporting on the incident, readily identified the words as expletives, but pointed out that Mayor Ford's usage was "never in direct reference to a clear subject" (McQuigge, The Canadian Press, 2014). Bob Authors, then president of the Jamaican Canadian Association in Alberta, when interviewed by Global News, commented that the words were akin to "hurling a vehement f-bomb". Essentially, the Mayor of Toronto was seen on video, in a drunken and disheveled state, using expletives in a foreign language roughly translatable to "fuck". It was poor judgement on his part, and the media did not hesitate to point this out.

Secondly, Mayor Ford had already been embroiled in several other similar backlashes from using explicit language in inappropriate contexts, including cases in which that language was directed at the media. Councilor Michael Thompson, a city councilor in Toronto, claimed that the incident was simply another in a series of events detailing the "unraveling of Rob Ford". Other city councilors also expressed doubt about Mayor Ford's claim of sobriety in light of the video. Ford, when questioned about the video simply responded, "It's how I speak with some of my friends". Ford, an outsider to Jamaican culture and a technocrat employed to the *shitstem* was unable to wield the "word magic" in the same manner that Tosh did, as it embroiled him in yet another media firestorm resulting in further lack of confidence from his fellow city councilors.

As mentioned earlier, Jamaican swear words belong to a part of the lexicon that features prominently in borrowing processes in various parts of the world. In Jamaican Dancehall music, deejays make regular use of a wide range of Jamaican swear words. Through the high profile of Jamaican popular music, these words have become popular in international Dancehall contexts and have been adapted and incorporated into music by various artistes. Especially in English-official African countries where Jamaican music is extremely popular, Jamaican swear words feature in the lyrics of many songs. The word *bomboklaat*, which has been discussed extensively above, stands out in this regard. In fact, it seems to be the most famous and most widely used Jamaican swear word. The Zimbabwean Zimdancehall artiste Bepstar released a song with the title "Bomboclat" on the Chabata Riddim in July 2017. While the lyrics of the song are sung in chiShona, the most widespread African Bantu language in the country, the chorus prominently features the word *bomboklaat*.

Canada and Zimbabwe present just two different examples of how Jamaican swear words are used outside Jamaica. There are numerous other examples in various parts of the world, mostly through the influence of Dancehall music and culture and facilitated through the internet and social media, as websites such as jamaicanpatwah.com, which mainly features swear words, testify.[5] It is interesting to note that the social restrictions and taboo nature of the swear words in Jamaica did not migrate with the lexemes, and thus non-Jamaicans in various parts of the world use Jamaica-derived swear words such as the much-discussed *bomboklaat* much more freely.

7.6 Conclusion

This paper has summarized some preliminary discussions of Jamaican swear words as an attempt to start filling the research gap and opening up the investigation of Jamaican swearing from a linguistic perspective. We have looked at the history and development of some terms, discussed the legal context of swearing in Jamaica and its effects on today's society as well as shed light on the linguistic usage and sociolinguistic implications of Jamaican swearing. Finally, a section has been dedicated to the use of Jamaican swear words in other parts of the world, with examples from Canada and Zimbabwe.

There is much more left to explore and we hope that this contribution will serve as a starting point to further investigate Jamaican swearing, for example with regard to social perceptions and reactions, or in connection to poetic aspects in Dancehall music, or in terms of generational shifts and changes over time, to name just a few of the many remaining aspects.

References

Allan, Keith and Kate Burridge. 2006. *Forbidden words: Taboo and the censoring of language*. Cambridge: Cambridge University Press.
Anonymous. 1791. *A short journey in the West Indies*. London: Murray Forbes.
Bergen, Benjamin K. 2016. *What the f: what swearing reveals about our language, our brains, and ourselves*. New York: Basic Books.

---

[5] http://jamaicanpatwah.com (accessed January 2019).

Cassidy, F. G. and R. B. Le Page (eds.). 1980. *Dictionary of Jamaican English*. Kingston: The University of the West Indies Press.

Connell, Raewyn. 2007. *Southern Theory. Social Science and the Global Dynamics of knowledge*. Cambridge: Polity Press.

Cooper, Carolyn. 2013. Divine Jamaican bad words. *Jamaica Gleaner*. http://jamaica-gleaner.com/gleaner/20130908/cleisure/cleisure3.html (accessed 17 November 2018).

Farquharson, Joseph T. 2012. The African lexis in Jamaican: Its linguistic and sociohistorical significance. Unpublished Ph.D. Dissertation. The University of the West Indies, Mona.

Hollington, Andrea. 2017. Emotions in Jamaican: African conceptualizations, emblematicity and multimodality in discourse and public spaces. In Anne Storch (ed.), *Consensus and Dissent: Negotiating Emotion in the Public Space*, 81–104. Amsterdam/Philadelphia: John Benjamins.

Hughes, Geoffrey. 2015. *Encyclopedia of Swearing: The Social History of Oaths, Profanity, Foul Language, and Ethnic Slurs in the English-speaking World*. Armonk: Taylor and Francis.

Jay, Timothy. 2000. *Why We Curse. A Neuro-psycho-social Theory of Speech*. Amsterdam: Benjamins.

Jay, Timothy and Kristin Janschewitz. 2008. The pragmatics of swearing. *Journal of Politeness Research* 4: 267–288.

Ljung, Magnus. 2011. *Swearing: A Cross-cultural Linguistic Study*. New York: Palgrave Macmillan.

Moreton, J. B. 1793. *West India Customs and Manners*. London: Parsons.

Tosh, Peter. 1981. Oh Bumbo Klaat. *Wanted Dread & Alive*. Netherlands: Rolling Stones Records. LP.

Towns and Communities Act, The. 1843. Retrieved from http://nepa.gov.jm/new/legal_matters/laws/Planning_Laws/Towns_and_Communities_Act_1843.pdf

Vingerhoets, Ad J.J.M., Lauren M. Bylsma and Cornelis de Vlam 2013. Swearing: a biopsychosocial perspective. *Psychological Topics* 22 (2): 287–304.

Walker, Karyl. 2012. That damn badword law. *Jamaica Observer*, 3 September. Retrieved from http://www.jamaicaobserver.com/news/That-damn-badword-law

Williams, Cynric R. 1826. *A Tour through the Island of Jamaica ... in the Year 1823*. London: Hunt and Clarke. Online references http://jamaicanpatwah.com (accessed January 2019)

Muhammad Muhsin Ibrahim and Aliyu Yakubu Yusuf
8 'Don't say it in public': Contestations and negotiations in northern Nigerian Muslim cyberspace

Abstract: Censorship is an age-old practice around the world. Many countries regulate what their citizens watch on television and in films, and sometimes what they read in books. Following the introduction of Sharia law across the Muslim states of northern Nigeria, the government in Kano, the epicentre of a struggling film industry called Kannywood, established a sturdy censorship board. The Board debates, negotiates and even clashes with filmmakers, artists and writers over what is permissible and what is not. However, the emergence of the internet and the subsequent exponential popularity of social media has made the Board a proverbial toothless barking dog, with no mechanism for controlling what the citizenry watches in their private spaces, on their mobile electronic devices. Viewing uncensored, free, and "explicit" content has become more accessible and commonplace. Based on a survey we carried out, we discovered that these highly mobile contents include some hitherto tabooed topics such as sex and intimacy. This article studies this controversy using the cultural reader-response theory, to understand the functions of swearing words and bad language in Hausa culture, among Muslim-Hausa audience.

8.1 Introduction

The tension between religion and art is as old as art itself. The tension between Islam and film is also very old and is marked by much more suspicion than has ever been the case with other religions. This is due to Islam's rigid stand against many things readily accessible in films, such as role-play, male-female interaction and manners of dressing, and particularly against ladies acting in "unruly" female roles, among other things. Lyden (2015: 83) notes that "Movies made in predominantly Muslim countries [...] have to deal with state censors". While the debate on what the content of films should be continued in those places, including in Hausa-Muslim majority northern Nigeria, the people's craving for entertainment grows. Kannywood, a rising Hausa film industry, survives amidst this hurricane. Its stakeholders are trying hard to set up a niche within this "Islamicate" (Adamu 2014: 27) and conservative society that "had resisted western education and missionary influence" (Osofisan 1999: 12).

It is necessary to attempt a definition of "Hausa", in order to situate the argument of this paper. The word "Hausa" refers to both a people and a language, projected to have more than 60 million speakers[1] across West Africa, with northern Nigeria as its heartland. Several jigsaws related to the linguistic diversity of the country, particularly the northern region, make it a tough task to establish what might be called "Hausaness" (see Furniss 1996; Lange 2008; Sutton 2010), and the precise definition of who is Hausa, a contentious issue (Ahmad 2004: 143). Today, as Haour and Rossi (2010: 24) conclude, "'Hausaness' involved considerable negotiated and situational aspects". However, for this study, being Hausa is defined as a person who was born of Hausa parents, raised in the Hausa community and speaks the language fluently, and possibly practises Islam. Religion is significant in the definition of a Hausa person's identity. Haour and Rossi (2010: 14), among others, note that "Islam has certainly been influential in all spheres of social and political life in some of the major Hausa centres since at least the fifteenth century".

In Nigeria, censorship has a colonial (read: Christian) beginning. The practice of censoring predates the independence of the country which took place on October 1, 1960. According to Adamu (2010: 28), the first ordinance (The 1933 Cinematograph Ordinance No. 20), that gave birth to censorship board, became effective on April 1, 1934. This law governed "the exhibition or showing of pictures or related optical effects produced using cinematography equipment and film designated for use with cinematograph equipment". Amended many times both before and after the independence of the country, this law finally led to the establishment of the National Film and Video Censorship Board (NFVCB) in 1993. The NFVCB was set up "to examine, assess, evaluate, classify and register films produced in Nigeria" (Barau 2008: 12). With the law firmly in place, films deemed to cover controversial issues around crime, sex, religion and race are subject to censorship. Thus, even though censorship can be traced back to Euro-Christian tradition, it takes care of issues that are regarded as anti-Islamic and anti-Hausa culture. Little wonder that Muslim *Ulama*[2] had no qualms when censorship was institutionalised in the country. Subsequently,

---

[1] *Ethnologue: Languages of the World*: https://www.ethnologue.com/language/hau (accessed on 28 May 2019).
[2] '*Ulama* (sing. '*alim*) is an Arabic word for someone knowledgeable, mainly in Islamic religious matters. In Hausa, *Malam* (m.), *Malama* (f.) and *Malamai* (plural) are more common and used in both secular (as Mr and Mrs) and religious contexts.

this led to the creation of censorship bureaus in many states across the federation. One of these is the Kano State Censorship Board.

There was a wave of Sharia implementation across the Muslim majority states of northern Nigeria between 2000 and 2001. Following this development, Kano, the major city in northern Nigeria, established a censorship board in March 2001. The state was and still is home to many artistic works, including Hausa romantic novels, songs and films ("Kannywood"). Thus, with the board now operating in a didactic, Sharia-compliant state, all creative constructions produced must be submitted for inspection before they are released for public consumption. This is done to ensure the "suitability" of their contents with Islamic and Hausa sociocultural values. It is in the context of this state-enforced censorship that the internet has emerged, giving people easy access to upload, download or watch whatever they like (deemed illicit or otherwise) on their computers and cell phones, without any form of encumbrance.

8.2 A brief history of the media in northern Nigeria

Given the fact that "any study of the twenty-first-century media scene in Africa must take into account the history of media technologies in Africa and the recent proliferation of new media" (Hackett and Soares 2015: 2), we sketch this history here. Before the colonisation of the northern part of Nigeria by Great Britain, no mass media existed in the region (Adamu 2006). It was in 1932 that the first newspaper (*Northern Province News*) about colonial policies and administration was published. This was followed by several newspaper outlets being established in many northern parts of the country. Yahaya (1988), as cited in Adamu (2006), notes that apart from the newspapers published in Hausa and English, there were a few others, like *Suda* and *Yar Gaskiya*, that were written in *Ajami* script, for those who could not read Roman texts. Thus, it can be argued that it was this epoch that led to the production of the earlier Hausa classics, such as *Ruwan Bagaja, Turmin Danya, Gandoki, Nagari* and *Nakowa,* as well as the latter mostly romantic works of the late twentieth and early twenty-first centuries. These books do not only serve entertainment purposes for readers, but they are also used as recommended texts in school syllabuses.

Broadcast media, on the other hand, is believed to have begun operating in Nigeria as far back as 1924 (Kolade 1979, in Adamu, 2006). Alongside television, radio has been the most popular source of news for most northern Nigerians. According to Vagg and Clifford (2010), its popularity can be attributed to the fact that, unlike newspapers, radio and television do not require literacy on the part of the audience for their contents to be fully grasped. Although the Nigerian Broadcasting Corporation was established in 1957, it was after the independence of the country in 1960 that several radio stations were opened by the then state governments (Adamu 2006: 6). Thus, broadcast media has continued to flourish in northern Nigeria. This led to the establishment of the National Broadcast Commission in 1992, which is "responsible for issuing a license for the establishment of all broadcast outfits in the country". It can, therefore, be understood that with the broadcasting and censorship boards in place, the government has complete control of popular culture and its transmission in the media. As we discuss later on, the government deregulated broadcasting years later.

The coming and subsequent proliferation of mobile phones with their attendant internet facilities have provided perhaps the most robust source of information to the public. With its immediate and unencumbered flow of information, the internet seems to have put a severe dent in the works of censorship boards and broadcasting corporations. While, in the past, the government-owned censorship boards had total control of the flow of popular culture, the internet has now made this an impossibility. Indeed, there is arguably no area that is more influenced by the booming of the internet than film consumption. Through strict censoring, the government used to have absolute control over the production and consumption of film as a form of popular culture. Ibrahim (2018: 55) remarks that

> Kano state government has already established a censorship board and saddled it with the responsibility to monitor the relationship between films, imported or indigenous and society in Kano. The Board was [...] empowered to approve or disapprove the release of any film by the Kannywood, and to ban any movie released without its consent or in case of any foreign film found obscene or harmful in the market.

The restrictions and prohibitions are meant to determine what should be consumed by the people. In other words, censorship is imposed to "preserve" the socio-cultural and religious values of the people, so that the culture of the people does not get contaminated with foreign influences, the government claims. With the emergence of the new media, however, people's consumption of popular culture takes an entirely new dimension. Likewise, the contestations and negotiations with Kannywood actors take a new turn. Hitherto, they were mandated, even compelled, to shun the controversies that censorship proscribed. Now, with followers on social media going over a million, some of them now feel free to share their thoughts and pictures.

8.3 Kannywood and the parable of an "illegitimate" child

The former Director General of the Kano State Censorship Board, Rabo Abdulkareem, once declared that "there was a confusion, or rather mix-up of cultural values which was largely attributed to foreign influence and the weird culture of blind copycatting of foreign cultures by most of the Hausa filmmakers which result to public outcry in the 1999–2000 of then Kano" (Koki 2009). Therefore, supported by the hegemonic religious establishment in the state, he led a fierce battle against Kannywood. The film industry was thrown into crisis. Ibrahim (2013) adds that "The arrests and prosecutions of several filmmakers and actors [that followed] and later a complete ban of the activities of the film industry have further deteriorated the government-filmmakers relationship". The crisis has significantly reduced what the government, as well as the religious establishment, considers unwanted. Filmmakers are often compelled to cut or retake whatever members of Censorship Board deem unfit for the public.

It is amidst this huge challenge that some Kannywood actors willingly engage in scandalous activities that are almost unanimously considered aberrations of the religious ethical and cultural codes. We are aware of the fact that actors enjoy scandals, as they make them more popular. Popularity is often an ingredient for a celebrity's success. However, not every sort of scandal is good, especially in Kannywood, which we advisedly call an "illegitimate" child. In many parts of societies like ours (in northern Nigeria), the child's mother cannot help loving it while also hating it due to the stigma attached to the way the child was born. In any case, she cannot throw it away. That is how Kannywood films are: loved and hated while they continue to exist. Globally, some scandals consume actors and ruin their careers. The recent case of Jussie Smollet, the acclaimed African-American *Empire* actor, is a typical example.[3]

The name of Maryam Usman, popularly called Hiyana, is synonymous with scandal and controversy in Kannywood. In 2007, Hiyana, a brilliant actress in her prime, was entangled in a sex scandal that led to the total shut down of the film industry. She and her boyfriend, who interestingly bears her father's name,

---

[3] 'Jussie Smollet Haunted by Scandal as Ex-Judge Targets Fallen Empire Star' from https://www.ccn.com/jussie-smollett-haunted-by-scandal-as-ex-judge-targets-fallen-empire-star (accessed on 2 June 2019).

Usman, were seen in an explicit sex clip. Although the clip was not from any film, it changed the history and the fate of Kannywood forever. People were already angry with the filmmakers. Thus, many jumped to the conclusion that Hiyana's phone's porno typifies what the film industry does and promotes.

Ten years later, in this era of informational Balkanization,[4] a leading actress, Rahama Sadau, confessed on her Instagram page that she was not a virgin (Ikeji 2017). Another actress, Fati Shu'uma, admitted "Pay me and I will play any role for you. The money you are paying me does not include sex, and if I am to be engaged in sex scandal it will not be with a Director or Producer, but with a first-class actor, that I will not regret if I zip down" (*Blueprint* 2017).[5] Many people we surveyed believed that such utterances are "wanton", "unwary" and "uncalled-for". As our subjects (on Facebook) reacted to our questions, another actress, Amina Amal posted a picture of herself in an outfit considered "un-Islamic" and "too Western", even by her counterparts. She wears a blue floral crop top and blue jeans, baring her midriff. She holds an expensive-looking phone, laughing in a sassy pose. She captions it thus: "I was not born to impress anyone. I don't care what you think about me. #Happygurl". This single picture sank the industry into an even more bottomless pit of a quagmire. In Kannywood, a woman is not allowed "[to] put on tight clothes that reveal [her] figure", an executive director told an American researcher, McCain (2014: 282) in 2006. One can only imagine the gravity of Amal's "crime".

The Nigerian government had deregulated broadcasting in the country in 1992. After that, private and independent ownership of media houses has been allowed, and there are many all over the country already, but, as mentioned above, the state regulates what goes into the public domain. However, the internet, especially its social media platforms, are practically beyond the state's control. Today, several scandals involving Kannywood actors have emanated from their social media space. This fact infuriates many people, including about 99 per cent of our respondents.

---

[4] Fake news spreads like wildfire today. Often, stories are concocted, doctored or taken out of context and use for sinister purposes. In short, information is fragmented, Balkanized into mutually hostile contents.

[5] The newspaper removed the story after the actress protested on her social media pages that she did not say such things. However, we cannot be sure whether or not that is true. For reference purposes, we saved the page before they took that action.

8.4 Prudish culture vs popular culture?

In any human society, there are specific established systems of norms and values which every member of the community is expected to adhere to strictly. When such codes of conducts are violated, the culprit is often regarded as a social zombie, an outlaw whose manners are potentially damaging to the culture of the society. Trudgill (2000: 18) defines taboo as "a behaviour which is believed to be supernaturally prohibited or regarded as immoral or improper". Taboo cuts across all aspects of human life, including the use of language. Thus, in all languages of the world, some concepts are regarded as tabooed and are, therefore, not talked about in public. This is so because when such concepts are talked about openly, they often provoke anger, anxiety and shame. Wardhaugh (2010: 239), supporting this claim, says that "[t]aboo is the prohibition or avoidance in any society of behaviours believed to be harmful to its members in that it would cause them anxiety, embarrassment, or shame". To this end, tabooed topics cover a wide range of areas, including "sex, death, excretion, bodily functions, religious matters and politics" (Wardhaugh 2010: 249).

Linguistic taboos also exist in form of profanities, obscenities or vulgar language, slurs, blasphemy or swear words. In the Hausa language, swearing exists in two primary ways. Hausa people a.k.a Hausawa often invoke the name of God in an angry tone to indicate an act of swearing. For example, *Wallahi sai ka biya ni kudi na* "I swear by Allah you must pay me back my money". Alternatively, Hausawa may swear by using an obscene language. For example, if one says *Sai na ci durin uwarka* "I will fuck your mother's cunt", it will be regarded as the dirtiest form of taboo. It is important to note that while the act of invoking God as a form of swearing rarely raises an eyebrow, swearing through the use of obscenities is generally frowned against. This is so because the obscene language in Hausa is always characterised by the mention of the most sensitive parts of the body, such as cunt, penis, vagina, waist, buttock, breast etc. As Allan and Burridge (2006) argue, tabooed topics centre on the organs and acts of sex, micturition and defecation. Often, a mere mention of these body parts in public is certain to instil anxiety and embarrassment among most people in northern Nigeria, where Hausa is either a native language or a Lingua Franca. Because of this, Hausawa do not use obscene language in public. The coming of social media, however, has allowed people to use most of these tabooed expressions in public. This is perhaps because unlike a face-to-face interaction, social media discussion is done online, devoid of any physical contact. Often, interlocutors on social media do not even know the identities of one another.

Like every society around the world, the Hausa society of northern Nigeria has certain linguistic concepts that are decidedly tabooed. Without a doubt, the most embarrassing tabooed subjects among Hausawa are body parts, sex and sex organs. In this part of the world, one cannot talk about *nonuwa* 'breasts', *gindi/bura* 'penis' or *haila* 'menstruation' in the open. If these topics must be discussed, euphemisms are generally used. Euphemisms here are referred to in the sense of words or phrases "used to substitute words and phrases which were considered impolite and embarrassing since people need to speak indirectly and politely" (Ghounane 2013: 33). In the same vein, Wardhaugh (2010: 249) notes that people normally talk about taboo subjects "in very roundabout ways" or "through deliberate circumlocution".

Furthermore, Allan and Burridge (2006: 29) differentiate between the three interrelated concepts of euphemism, dysphemism and orthophemism. Specifically, they describe euphemism as "sweet-talking", dysphemism as "speaking offensively" and orthophesim as "straight talking". In this sense, one can deduce that while euphemism involves an attempt to hide the offensive undertone associated with taboo, dysphemism involves deliberately being offensive in using a language. Orthophemism, on the other hand, is a term coined by the authors "to account for direct or neutral expressions that are neither sweet-sounding, evasive or overly polite (euphemistic), nor harsh, blunt or offensive (dysphemistic)". Allan and Burridge (2006) further elucidate the aforesaid three concepts by arguing that the words "poo", "shit" and "faeces" are cross-varietal synonymy that denote the same thing but have different connotations. In other words, while the former two are perceived to be euphemism and dysphemism respectively, the latter can be regarded as orthophemism.

Euphemisms are meant to disguise the harmful effects of tabooed expressions so that people can talk about them freely and without embarrassing or provoking the sensibilities of other people or breaking any traditional social and religious mores. However, the spread of popular culture in Hausa-Muslim northern Nigeria seems to have tacitly encouraged the youth to break linguistic taboos, to the disappointment of the social and religious establishments and constituted authorities. In fact, most societies have stipulated punishments for breaking taboo. Indeed, Allan and Burridge (2006: 6) remark that most people believe that "any violation of taboo, however innocently committed, risks condemnation". They add that depending on the infractions, the punishment varies in gravity from severe penalties like illness or death to the lesser ones such as incarceration, corporal punishment, social ostracism and mere disapproval.

Since tabooed behaviour is believed to be forbidden, topics that are deemed to be bordering on taboos are usually subjected to censoring. Allan and Burridge (2006: 238) distinguish between individual censoring of language and institutional public censorship of language. The society enforces the former through political correctness. It compels people to speak and act in a manner deemed acceptable in the society or "run the risk of being lumped together with true bigots with malevolent motives". The latter, on the other hand, is exercised by the government "as a means of regulating the moral and political life of their people, controlling the media and communications between citizens against language deemed to be subversive of the common good". That is why governments in various places set up censorship boards to control the flow of media information so that what is regarded to have violated the moral and religious etiquette of the society is censored. However, the proliferation of popular culture seems to put a serious dent on the work of censorship boards.

As popular culture is mass commercial culture, it leads to the production of TV companies, film and other entertainment corporations that are commercially oriented and aimed at making a profit. From this standpoint, the idea behind popular culture is, first and foremost, to entertain and generate profit. That is to say, popular culture is not meant to teach the moral values of the society to the younger generation. However, the conventional notion of culture can sometimes be quite slippery. As cultures differ from one community to another, what constitutes an acceptable way of life in one part of the world may be rejected as tabooed in another part. Ibrahim (2015) gives an example of a BBC news report that highlights how, in 2009, a popular Hollywood actor, Richard Gere, created an outrage in India by kissing a popular Bollywood film actress, Shilpa Shetty, before the camera. The uproar was the result of a clash of cultures. In the West, kissing is perceived as a sign of affection, while in some parts of the world, it is seen as an embarrassing gesture that borders on blasphemy.

Hausa Muslims make up the majority of Northern Nigerian population. As such, Islam, to a large extent, influences the culture of the people. More often than not, the people can be quite prudish, and usually, classify any action (or inaction) as either right or wrong. This is so because of the centrality of *kunya* "bashfulness" in the life of the people. In other words, shameless people are dismissed mainly as socio-moral outcasts. That is why the emergence of popular culture has thrown the region into a serious moral panic (Furniss 2003). Social institutions and the religious establishments have become increasingly worried that the "sacred" and "prestigious" culture of the people will be ruined, if people are allowed to consume uncensored popular culture freely. Barau (2008: 8) underlines this fear when he claims that "In spite of the relevance of our creative artworks conflict is presently rising between our values and the popular culture". And as Ibrahim (2015) notes, the outrage about popular culture has been manifested in several attacks on symbols of northern popular culture. Ahmad (2015) also recalls that in November 2015, the Kano State Censorship Board closed down 100 games clubs and 50 dance houses for allegedly exposing underage girls to prostitution and encouraging truancy among pupils and students. Additionally, the then Executive Secretary of the Board (Rabo) has vowed that the government must take a harsh position to ensure that the state is free of vices that corrupt the morals of the society.

The aversion to Hausa films as a source of popular culture has been active in many quarters in northern Nigeria. The filmmakers have, several times, found themselves at loggerheads with the authorities. On two separate occasions between 2000 and 2003, filmmaking was banned in Kano (McCain 2012). Likewise, some actors and actresses were suspended or banned from featuring in films. The situation reached a nadir in 2008 when the Kano State Censorship Board jailed a famous actor, Adam A. Zango, for six months, for producing and releasing an uncensored music video album titled *Bahaushiya* ("A Hausa Woman") that allegedly portrayed nudity – an act that "contravenes" the teaching of Islam and Hausa culture. And this is exactly the bone of contention. As Ibrahim (2016: 139) aptly puts it, "the relationship between cinema and the orthodox religious institutions is often marked by uneasiness if not outright hostility". Filmmakers are accused of portraying things that are in stark contrast with Islamic injunctions. These include, but are not limited to, songs and dance sequences, foul language and bedroom encounters.

The compatibility or otherwise of films and Islam is discussed extensively by Ibrahim (2013: 169). He contends that most people accuse filmmakers of misrepresenting and attacking the sociocultural value systems of the very Hausa people they claim to represent. That is why most of the films are seen as "uncultural and against the norms and values of a typical Hausa man". Indeed, this assertion appears to represent the concern of orthodox *Ulama* in northern Nigeria. Adamu (2010: 37) also notes that "when Hausa filmmaking started exploring various globalised configurations of behaviour that have what was seen as direct diluting influences on core Muslim Hausa mindsets, alarm bells started ringing about the possible influence of new media technologies and behavioural modification". Ahmad (2004) further reveals the responses of some *Ulama* to Hausa films, which stress the belief that the movies are corrupting Hausa culture, encouraging blind imitation of foreign cultures, time wasting, divorce, and the intermingling of the sexes, and promoting violence, foul language and promiscuity, etc.

Furthermore, Ibrahim (2018: 132) discovers that the main concerns of *Ulama* with regards to filmmaking revolve around the *tarbiyya* ('moral upbringing') of the younger generation of Muslims. One of the responsibilities of parents and *Ulama* is to ensure that the life of a Muslim is developed socially, physically, morally and spiritually, in line with the teachings of Islam. However, with the spread of films and their influences on the behaviours of youths, primarily via social media and other internet spaces, it becomes difficult for society to control the moral conduct of the people. Ultimately, most *Ulamas* accuse the contemporary filmmakers of spoiling the *tarbiyya* of the people. In other words, "they criticise Kannywood filmmakers on issues related to morality, decency, and decorum within the region's Islamic culture in which they are [a] normative authority" (Ibrahim 2018: 132).

However, the dilemma facing the *Ulamas* and other cultural establishments is that the people for whom popular culture is censored seem to covet unadulterated access to that culture. That is why "despite being described as the path to the hellfire, popular culture thrived tremendously in the north" (Ibrahim 2015: 686). Indeed, because popular culture is aimed at entertainment and making profit, both the filmmakers and most of the audience care very little about the transmission of religious morality or mainstream local culture. Some filmmakers have complained that films whose thematic preoccupations are around cultural and religious moral teaching sell very little in the markets. Adamu (2010: 39–40) cites an example of an interview in which an ace actor, Ali Nuhu, was reported to have said:

> I am a filmmaker because I want to entertain. You often hear viewers claiming they want a video that shows (Hausa) culture, and yet when you do such video, they just leave you with it (and don't buy it). This year a video was released that showed pure Hausa culture, but it was not commercially successful. In fact, a viewer had the cheek to write to a magazine to complain about the video; would that be an encouragement for the producer? (*Ni Don Nishadantarwa Na Ke Yi* ('I am in it for entertainment only'), Interview with Ali Nuhu, *Annashuwa*, December 2002: 31.)

This situation clearly suggests that while the government and other moral crusaders appear hell-bent on "sanitising" the film industry, the stakeholders from within (the filmmakers and consumers) would rather have the status quo maintained. That is why Ibrahim (2015: 685) argues that while taboos are put in place – via culture and religion – to ensure moral conduct of people, "in man's subconsciousness, the things designated as taboos are his greatest desires and the objects of his pleasures". And since most societies dismiss popular culture as largely tabooed, there will always be a conflict between man and society. This is because "Man is forced by society to pretend not to like the things, which in his subconsciousness, he likes the most" (Ibrahim 2015: 685). The onus is, therefore, on the authorities to explore this psychological bond to help produce a popular culture of the highest cultural and ethical values.

8.5 The internet and the censorship Cul-de-Sac

The internet café culture started in the predominantly Hausa northern Nigerian region as a particular type of business, often situated in urban areas, the government reserved areas (GRAs), or in ministries and few other places. Initially, only a few people, usually very educated, had access to it. The story is noticeably different today. From highly placed civil servants, university and school teachers to roadside mechanics and cobblers, the internet is everybody's property. The internet café business has mostly ceased. The market has been liberalised and the niche filled by the availability and affordability of internet-enabled mobile phones and free Wi-Fi spots. The service providers sell their data extremely cheaply compared to the prices charged in the nascent days of the internet. This, however, poses a considerable challenge to both the government and to a certain sector of the public.

Filmmaking in Nigeria started as a private enterprise by some Igbo merchants. The film *Living in Bondage* is credited as the inaugurating movie for what later became known as Nollywood (Haynes 2011: 71). At least fifteen other production outfits soon joined the field (Ayorinde and Okafor 1996: 29). Today, as Oh (2014) states, "Nigerian films have a large following in Africa and among African emigrants around the world (over 30 million worldwide and growing)".

Nollywood produces on average 1,500 films per year. This makes it the largest film industry in Africa, while globally it is second only to Bollywood (UNESCO Institute for Statistics 2009). The *WIPO Magazine* of 2nd April 2014 (p. 2) reports that:

> The US hedge fund, Tiger Global Management, had invested US$8 million in iROKOtv, the world's largest online distributor of licensed Nollywood films. This substantial injection of funds to scale-up iROKOtv's video streaming operations was a testimony to the growing international prominence of Nigeria's film industry.

Although iROKOtv, among other competing pay-on-demand online channels, provides a large chunk of Nigerian films watched online, some are also on Netflix, Amazon Prime, and other platforms. Also, there are hundreds of illegal channels on YouTube. There are also many other websites where anyone with access to the internet can watch Nollywood and other Nigerian films. Jedlowski (2010: 5) reports Jora (2007) as saying that:

> Through a number of interviews with Nigerian video sellers in Europe, the impact of internet streaming and satellite televisions has deeply damaged their business, obliging them to cut the number of videos ordered weekly from Nigeria. Sunday Omobude, a Nigerian

businessman who owns a video store in Amsterdam, for example, is reported to have cut his orders from 8000 films a week to 1500, while the internet site onlinenigeria.com, which broadcasts Nigerian films for free, is reported to have up to 700.000 visitors in 45 countries around the world.

Short films are also widely popular in Nigeria today. Unlike feature-length films, most of which are produced by licenced companies, most short films are by individuals with variable knowledge about shooting with cameras and editing. The NFVCB has attempted to regulate these online contents,[6] but this is technically impossible as it has no mechanism for doing so. The Kano State Censorship Board has yet to make such an effort, lacking the necessary know-how and equipment.

Example 1: *Hausa Sexy* (dir. Isah Aisar 2017).
This short film is only 20 seconds long. It shows a young man standing, symbolically holding his manhood as he urinates on a wall. Two ladies, wearing a typical Muslim-Hausa *Atampa* with a veil and headscarf, turn the corner. Shocked, they halt, take a step backwards and exclaim: *"Inna lillahi wainna ilainhi raji'un,"* a Quranic verse to soothe their purportedly afflicted minds, meaning: "From Allah we came and to Him we must go back". The following brief exchange ensues:

Zo ku wuce, na rike kan nan.
Dallah matsa! Mu da muke da abinda zai hadiye shi!
"Come and pass; I have held the head" [implying his penis by the "head"]
Dismissively, one of the ladies shouted: "Get back! We have what can swallow it!" [implying their womanhood]

The brief encounter is then followed by a peal of loud non-diegetic laughter in the background, insinuating that the ladies are far more shameless than the guy.

Example 2: Yasmin Harka (a YouTuber).
Yasmin is a common female Muslim name while Harka is not; it means 'affair' or 'business' in normal Hausa. In youth language here, it connotes a different meaning. In this context in particular, *Harka* stands for a person who engages in "sex work" or possesses knowledge about sex, although not necessarily a prostitute. Yasmin Harka owns a YouTube channel where she posts videos about intimacy, using gross language and tabooed words that are otherwise either not said in public or are entirely euphemised. She also sells sex-enhancing herbs and other aphrodisiacs called *Kayan Mata*. There is a phone number for anyone seeking further information. She currently has followers numbering 11,063 and growing. The following is an excerpt of the selected video and its translation below:

---

[6] "NFVCB moves against online showing of pornography, piracy" from https://www.vanguardngr.com/2016/12/nfvcb-moves-online-showing-pornography-piracy/ (accessed on 2 June 2019).

Y'ar uwa, idan harka ta fara nisa, ma'ana kin gama wasa da mijinki, kin ganma shan non-onshi. Kin shafashi kin shafashi kin sa burarshi a cikin bakinbki kin tsotsa kin tsotseta kin yi mata sucking. Kin yi sucking kin yi suckin kin tsotse shi sosai, sai ki bude mai gindinki. Idan kika bude mai idan ya fara saka burarshi a ciki kina numfashi a hankali kina numfashi a hankali. Kina tsotson kunnenshi kina zira harshenki a hankali a cikin kunnanshi. Kina zira harshenki kina zira harshenki, sai ki dago kirjinshi sai ki manna da naki, kirjin sai ki manna da nashi ki kankameshi sosai. Numfasshinku yana hada na juna. Ki kamashi sosai a jikinki, ki rungemeshi matuka kina yi kina bude kafafun ki, kina kara budewa yana shigarki sosai ki kara bude jikinki sosai. Idan fa zaki yi ki saki jikinki ba wai ki dinga kankame jiki kina matsa nan kina matsa nan ba. Idan kina yin haka mijinki ba zai ji dadin saduwa da ke ba. Amma idan kuna yi ki saki jikinki ki sa a ranki wannan ibada ne bautar kike yi.

Sister, when the business goes far, meaning when you are done playing with your husband and finished sucking his breasts, you should start massaging him thoroughly and sucking his penis. Suck it very well. You suck [the penis] again and again vigorously, and then open your vagina. When you open it for him, and he begins inserting his penis inside, you should start moaning and breathing softly. You lick his earlobes and play with your tongue around them. While you do that over time, pull his chest and put yours onto it and hug him tightly until both your breaths meet. Hold him to your body tightly while widening your legs as he enters inside you all the more. When doing all this, surrender your body and don't withdraw it in any way. If you draw it back, your husband will not be satisfied. But once you are [in sex action], submit your entire body and remember that this is an act of worship [to Allah].

Example 3: Muneerat Abdulsalam (a YouTuber).
Muneerat is another very popular YouTuber. She currently (in April 2019) has 52,423 subscribers and some of her videos have been watched close to one million times. She is unique for being more open, upfront and from a minority ethnic group of northern Nigeria. Furthermore, she uses an accented Hausa language mixed with English. Her usage of Hausa enrages her Hausa-majority audience all the more. She has recently converted to Islam, yet promises to continue her "sex education" videos but in an Islamic "compliant" manner. It is difficult to say whether or not her conversion to Islam is voluntary or forced. This is an excerpt from the selected video:

Yauwa, yau na zo muku da wata sabuwar bayani. Bayanin sucking na bura. Mata da yawa baku iya sucking na buran mazanku ba. Sucking na bura ba wai ance akan cewa saboda kina so ki nuna masa ke kin iya gwaninta kije ki sa masa bruises a jikin buranshi. Ba haka ake suckin ba. Hajiya suckin bai kamata hakorinki ya taba kan buranshi ba. Akwai sucking kala biyu ne. Akwai deep-throating sannan kuma akwai middle edge wanda ake tabawa akan sama kenan. Kin san akwai massage na bura? Akwai yanda zakiyi massaging na bura kiyi masajin dinshi. Sabida wannan muscles din, bansan mene ne muscles da Hausa ba. Muscles din su tattatashi. In kika yi massaging. Bayan kin gama massaging, in kika zo sucking. Kin gani in zaki fara daga edge. Ni da makilin zan gwada. Saboda yanzu idan nasa vibrator sai kuce min 'yar iska. So, in zaki yi sucking na edge, zaki yi haka... (sai ta gwada da robar man wanke hakori), kinga malama ba abinda ya kawo hakorinki in deep throting zaki yi, haka. Kin gani. Harshe ne kawai zuwa makogoro ba a bin daya kawo maganan hakori. Wasunku in suka tashi wai suna sucking ... za a sashi a yi mishi haka hmmm. Hmmm.

Okay, I today come with another new explanation. It's about sucking penis. Many women don't know how to suck their husband's penis. Don't, in your desperate effort to please him, bruise his penis. That's not how it's done. Madam, don't let your teeth touch the tip of his penis. There are two types of sucking. There are "deep throating", and then "middle edge", which involves touching and licking only the edge [of the penis]. Do you know there is also "massage of the penis"? There is a way to massage his penis and his body. For, this "muscle" [veins]... I don't know "muscle" in Hausa. Let the veins rouse. After massaging, then comes sucking. You see; if you are starting from the edge... I will demonstrate it using a toothpaste tube. Should I use a vibrator, you people will call me immoral. So, when you come to suck, the edge type, do like this... [She demonstrates it]. You see, Madam, nothing brings your teeth if you choose "deep throating". You see. It is only from the tongue to the throat; nothing entails the tooth. When some of you come to do such...you, do like this [she mimics it in a hilarious, hyperbolic manner] ... hmmm. Hmmm.

8.6 Discussion

The *Hausa Sexy* (example 1) clip was uploaded on 14.02.2017. So far, it has been viewed more than one hundred and fifteen thousand times. We shared the same video on Facebook on 22.08.2017 and another with similar content on 12.04.2019. The video attracted 133 responses, which we subjected to content analysis. Of all the respondents, only one supported its content. The rest condemned them outright, with three arguing and preaching that we too should not be "complicit" in spreading obscenity.

The one respondent who went against the rest argued that the clip was just a comedy that reflected the reality in today's Hausa communities across northern Nigeria. Some people attacked his opinion, which he further defended. From our personal point of view as both Hausa and Muslim, this opinion is not entirely untrue. The person who expressed this view may have had some experience beyond the borders of Muslim Northern Nigeria. Therefore, he does not necessarily share the same habituated values as the others. However, some others argue that publicising such content goes against the Hausa cultural codes, as examined by Kirk-Green (1947: 8). These, among others, comprise *kunya* 'bashfulness' and *mutunci* 'self-esteem'. The same line of argument is deployed in condemning the other two examples.

We randomly sampled 100 replies each from Muneerat's and Yasmin's YouTube channels. For the latter, her mode of dressing enrages her audience the most. She wears the *niqab* (face veil) and repeatedly mentions Allah in her expression. She further claims that she does the videos for Allah's sake, and to save marriages. There are, though, a few among her audience who support her. They say that this is what Hausa-Muslim societies lack, and that lack of such enlightment is responsible for the high rate of divorces. Muneerat receives more bashing. A Facebook influencer named Datti Assalafiy stands out in his attacks on her business and person. His criticisms on her is so fierce that she proclaims, after she converted to Islam, that if it were up to people like him who insult her, she would not have accepted the religion. She concludes that "He is putting Islam into jeopardy."[7]

It is indisputable that marriages frequently end in divorce in northern Nigeria. An *Al Jazeera English*, report reveals that "divorce rates in northern Nigeria are among the highest in West Africa with one in three marriages said to fail within the first three years".[8] This opens a market for the age-old *kayan mata* ('women things'), referring to several sorts of aphrodisiacs, produced by sellers in the region and beyond who believe that lack of satisfaction in bed is mainly responsible for the divorces. However, most of these sex enhancing concoctions are sold secretly. The YouTubers, Yasmin Harka and Muneerat Abdulsalam, among others, are therefore also seen as crossing cultural boundaries that are the last to be expected from a woman.

Cultural theorists outline how "readers' cultural roles, attitudes, and values, as well as the larger cultural, historical context, shape responses" (Beach 1993: 9). Understanding the "rationale" behind the above reactions to the three cases requires an understanding of the cultural forces that shape a "typical" Hausa man's way of thinking. Michel Foucault (1980), cited in Beach (1993: 127), calls this force "discourse", "discursive formation" or "practice". Beach (1993: 127) further explains that "discourse [...] serves to limit the definition of language to ways legitimate only for that speech community". With Hausa being the dominant language in northern Nigeria, its speakers, directly or indirectly, attempt to compel other communities in the region to accept the legitimacy of their discourse, their categorisation of certain words, phrases and expressions as taboo, vulgar, obscene and so on. Conversely, to borrow from Ibrahim (2018: 300), these YouTubers, like some Kannywood filmmakers, "stimulate the discursive tradition by generating discussions, contestations, and negotiations among the Muslim actors about what is Islam or rather what is orthodox and unorthodox Islamic tradition" and Hausa culture.

---

7 https://www.youtube.com/watch?v=JWJgMBsR7Lo (accessed on 3 April 2019).
8 https://www.aljazeera.com/blogs/africa/2012/07/24886.html (accessed on 3 April 2019).

Nevertheless, unlike in the case of the YouTubers, Kannywood is an established industry and, therefore, the contents of Kannywood films are always subject to scrutiny. There are guidelines which any registered filmmaker has to abide by. Failure to do so attracts either fines or imprisonment or both. As mentioned earlier, some renowned filmmakers, including one of the pioneering members of Kannywood, were arrested, fined and imprisoned over what the censorship board claimed are violations of its codes. Therefore, the debates the filmmakers generate are not as confrontational as those of the YouTubers. While the censorship apparatus is too defective to regulate the YouTubers, they are not immune to people's severe criticism, intimidation and threats. Ms Muneera Abdulsalam, in particular, has been more severely attacked, and it is perhaps this which "motivated" her to convert to Islam, the "state" religion. Another, perhaps more known online "sex therapist" in Muslim-North, Hauwa Muhammad, popularly known as Jaruma, "The Brave", has to go about her daily life with security guards. Therefore, the threats to those who "transgress" are, possibly, real.

8.7 Conclusion

The video film, whether short or feature, has high potentials for mass communication and propaganda. No doubt film critics and scholars such as the legendary Andre Bazin are of the view that art not only reproduces life but explains it. The Hausa-Muslim people of northern Nigeria may claim to be "reserved", "bashful" and have the "self-esteem" not to talk about swearing and cursing in public. Therefore, as a space where people of different backgrounds gather to view videos and make comments on them, YouTube is regarded as a public sphere. It is this value judgement that enrages most of the respondents to the video clips analysed in this study. The YouTubers are believed to have gone astray by sharing the blasphemous video contents to the public. As such, most of the responses focus on praying to God to forgive them (the YouTubers) and bring them to the right path: *Allah ya shiryeki* "May Allah bring you to the right path", while others curse them for desecrating their 'sacred' language and culture. A few other respondents acquiesce them and go further to praise them for "saving" marriages.

It is crucial, however, to note the world is gradually changing and, thus, in this highly globalised and technologised world, the flow and exchange of cultures, values and norms between people know no boundaries. Therefore, the Hausa culture is getting more and more intermingled with other cultures so much so that topics hitherto regarded as tabooed are now subject to contestations and negotiations, especially among youth. Again, the fact that the world has become a global village – thanks to technology – censorship boards have mainly become powerless, especially with regards to online materials. Gone are the days in which censorship boards determine what media contents one consumes. People now upload and download any uncensored online materials on their devices. This further leads to the spread of swearing, cursing and lousy language even in the public domain, to the disappointment of the religious establishments and many others.

References

Adamu, Abdulla Uba. 2010. Social responsibility, cultural diversity and film censorship. In M. Egbon and U. M. Jibril (eds.), *Media studies in Nigeria: A book of readings*, 21–46. Zaria: Ahmadu Bello University Press.

Adamu, Abdulla Uba. 2014. Imperialism from Below: Media Contra-flows and the Emergence of Metrosexual Hausa Visual Culture. Bayero University Kano Inaugural Lecture Series No. 15. Kano: Bayero University Press.

Adamu, Yusuf M. 2006. Print and broadcast media in northern Nigeria. From www.researchgate.net/publication/2337773440 (accessed 5 April 2019).

Ahmad, Muhammad. 2015. Kano shuts down 50 dance clubs, 100 dance centres. From www.premiumtimes.com/news/more-news/1993353-kano-shuts-down-50-dance-clubs-100-game-centres.html (accessed 8 April 2019).

Ahmad, Gausu. 2004. The response of Kano Ulama to the phenomenon of the Hausa home video: Some preliminary observations. In A. U. Adamu, Y. M. Adamu and U. F. Jibril (eds.), *Hausa home videos: Technology, economy and society*, 142–153. Kano: Gidan Dabino Publishers.

Allan, Keith and Kate Burridge. 2006. *Forbidden words: Taboo and the censoring of language*. New York: Cambridge University Press.

Ayorinde, S. and C. Okafor. 1996. Enter, Boys from the East. *Guardian*, 24 February 1996, pp. 29.

Barau, Aliyu Salisu. (ed.). 2008. Mission and Vision of the Kano State Censorship Board. https://www.researchgate.net/publication/268813777_Mission_and_Vision_of_the_Kano_State_Censorship_Board (accessed 19 April 2019).

Beach, Richard. 1992. *A Teacher's Introduction to Reader-Response Theories*. Illinois: National Council of Teachers of English.

Bazin, Andrew. 1967. *What is Cinema?* Trans. Hugh Gray. California: University of California Press.

Foucault, Michel (ed.). 1980. Power/knowledge: Selected Interviews and Other Writings; 1972–1977. Brighton, Sussex: Harvester Press.

Furniss, Graham. 1996. *Poetry, Prose and Popular Culture in Hausa*. London: Edinburgh University Press.

Furniss, Graham. 2003. *Hausa popular literature and video films: The rapid rise of cultural productions in times of economic decline*. Arbeitspapiere No. 27. Mainz: Johannes Gutenberg Universität.

Ghounane, Nadia. 2013. A sociolinguistic view of taboo language and euphemisms in Algerian society: Attitudes and beliefs in Tlemcen speech community. Unpublished M.A. dissertation, University of Tlemcen, Algeria.

Hackett, Rosalind I. J. and Soares, Benjamin F. 2015. *New Media and Religious Transformations in Africa*. Bloomington: Indiana University Press.

Haour, Anne and Rossi, Benedetta. 2010. Hausa Identity, Language and History. In A. Haour and B. Rossi (eds.), *Being and Becoming Hausa: Interdisciplinary Perspectives*, 1–33. Leiden: Brill.

Haynes, Jonathan. 2011. African Cinema and Nollywood: Contradictions. *Situations: Project of the Radical Imagination* 4 (1): 67–90.

Ibrahim, Daniel. 2015. Desire as taboo: Theorising popular culture in contemporary northern Nigeria. *Algaita Journal of Current Research in Hausa Studies* 1 (1): 685–695.

Ibrahim, Muhammad Muhsin. 2016. Trial Makes Perfect: Reading *As-Habul Kahfi* as a Response to the Critics. In M. O. Bhadmus (ed.), *The Nigerian Cinema: Reading Nigerian Motion Pictures*, 137–150. Ibadan: Spectrum Books Limited.

Ibrahim, Muhammad Muhsin. 2013. Hausa film: Compatible or incompatible with Islam? *Performing Islam* 2 (2): 165–179.

Ibrahim, Musa. 2018. Sharia implementation, filmmaking, and Muslim discourses: Analysis of contestations and negotiations between *Ulama* and Kannywood filmmakers in northern Nigeria. Unpublished PhD dissertation, University of Bayreuth.

Jedlowski, Alessandro. 2010. Beyond the video boom: New tendencies in the Nigerian video industry. ASAUK writing workshop in Birmingham (UK), April 16th 2010.

Jora, Fred. 2007. 'The big rip-off. How Nollywood films are shown on net free of charge . . . Europe based stakeholders cry foul.' The Vanguard, 27 October 2007: pp. 20.

Kirk-Green, A. H. M. 1974. *Mutumin Kirii: The Concept of the Good Man in Hausa*. Bloomington: African Studies Program.

Koki, Salisu Ahmad. 2009. Hausa Home Video Industry AND the Rabo Abdulkareem Phenomenon (The Exclusive Interview with Rabo Abdulkareem). http://ibrahim-sheme-blogspot.com.ng/2009/06/interview-rabo-hausa-movie-chief-censor.html?m=1 (accessed 28 September 2016).

Kolade, Chrsitopher. 1979. *History of Nigerian Broadcasting Corporation*. Ibadan: Ibadan University Press.

Lange, Dierk. 2008. Turning the Bayajidda legend into history: early immigration and the late emergence of Hausaness. Paper presented at the meeting *Hausa identity: history and religion* at the Sainsbury Research Unit, University of East Anglia, Norwich, 11 July 2008.

Ikeji, Linda. 2017. Actress, Rahama Sadau reveals her virginity status on Instagram. https://www.lindaikejisblog.com/2017/12/actress-rahama-sadau-reveals-her-virginity-status-on-instagram-2.html (accessed 7 September 2018).

Lyden, John. C. 2015. Film. In John C. Lyden and Eric Michael Mazur (eds.), *The Routledge Companion to Religion and Popular Culture*, 80–99. New York: Routledge.

McCain, Carmen. 2012. Kannywood: The growth of a Nigerian language industry. From https://nigerianstalk.org/2012/10/09/kannywood-the-growth-of-a-nigerian-language-industry-carmen-mccain-2/ (accessed on 15 April 2019).

McCain, Carmen. 2014. The Politics of Exposure: Contested Cosmopolitanisms, Revelation of secrets, and Intermedial Reflexivity in Hausa Popular Expression. Unpublished PhD dissertation, University of Wisconsin-Madison.

Oh, Erick. 2014. Nigeria's Film Industry: Nollywood Looks to Expand Globally. In *United States International Trade Commission (USITC)* 202. https://www.usitc.gov/publications/332/erick_oh_nigerias_film_industry.pdf (accessed July 31. 2019)

Osofisan, Femi (ed.). 1999. *African Theatre in Development*. Oxford: James Currey.

Sutton, John. E. G. 2010. Hausa as a Process in Time and Space. In A. Haour and B. Rossi (eds.), *Being and Becoming Hausa: Interdisciplinary Perspectives*, 279–298. Leiden: Brill.

Trudgill, Peter. 2000. *Sociolinguistics. An introduction to language and society*. London: Oxford University Press.

Vagg, Trevor. and Clifford, Charlotte. 2010. Qualitative research on the BBC Hausa Service. Prepared for the BBC Trust. London: BBC World Services.

Wardhaugh. Ronald. 2010. *An introduction to sociolinguistics*. New Jersey: Wiley-Blackwell.

Yahaya, Ibrahim Yaro. 1988. *Hausa a rubuce*. Zaria: Northern Nigeria Publishing Company.

Online materials

Aisar, Isah. 2017. ("Hausa Sexy") from https://www.youtube.com/watch?v=7wmXr9c9crU (accessed 3 April 2019).

"Yadda ake Shan Bura" (How One Sucks Manhood) from https://www.youtube.com/watch?v=CT_94wyC2wU (accessed 3 April 2019).

"Yadda ake Cin Amarya 'Yar 18" (How to Have Sex with an 18-year-old Bride) from https://www.youtube.com/watch?v=TPVYGzoBep4 (accessed 3 April 2019).

Nico Nassenstein
9 Mock Chinese in Kinshasa: On Lingala speakers' offensive language use and verbal hostility

Abstract: With the arrival of numerous waves of Chinese workers in DR Congo from the early 2000s onwards, the presence of Mandarin and other Chinese languages has steadily increased in Kinshasa's multilingual landscape. Most Chinese construction workers, small-scale entrepreneurs, and traders who have settled in remote villages, have since gradually acquired the basic fundamentals of regional Congolese languages, especially of languages of wider communication such as Lingala. The increasing presence of migrants of Chinese descent in urban and rural spaces throughout the country has heavily influenced popular culture, advertising and especially has had an impact on Kinshasa citizens' metalinguistic exchange about Chinese immigrants' alleged linguistic practices, contributing to the emergence of different forms of "mock language" in humorous narratives. The present paper aims to analyze Mock Chinese, a recurrent ethnophaulism and racial slur based on onomatopoeia, as well as Lingala speakers' mimicry of "broken Lingala" as used by Chinese migrants. Both phenomena are discussed against a background of a more holistic approach to swearing that also includes a broader understanding of hostile language in metalinguistic discourse. This contribution looks at mock language as a racialized, satirical and hostile performance of Otherness in the margins, reflecting the appropriation and permeability of language, unequal power hierarchies and Lingala speakers' language ideologies with regard to changing migration patterns from a linguistic anthropological perspective.

9.1 The role of Lingala, Chinese migration and socioeconomic change in the Congo

The urban landscape of Kinshasa, the third largest metropolis on the African continent, is characterized both by a rural exodus of inhabitants from the surrounding provinces, and by migration from neighboring countries and, increasingly, from China, mainly for socioeconomic reasons. Apart from colonialism, the presence of foreigners in Kinshasa has, from precolonial times onwards, been linked to trade, particularly with regard to large Portuguese and Greek communities, who had established family businesses already prior to and during Belgian colonial times, and were very well-connected (within the country and with oversea trade partners). In the late 1990s, their numbers were exceeded by Lebanese refugees, who opened up small shops, night clubs and fast food restaurants, who have integrated into Congolese society and who are still present in Kinshasa today. From the early 2000s onwards, they were followed by Chinese workers, with major investment and trade agreements having been signed by the Congolese government and several Chinese state-owned companies. On 17 September 2007, for instance, an agreement worth (an estimated) $6.5 billion was concluded, which envisaged the Chinese construction of roads, railways and hospitals, financed by loans from the Chinese EXIM bank (Marysse and Geenen 2009: 371), and secured by joint ventures of extracting various mineral resources from Congolese soil. The construction works were – and are – usually carried out by Chinese workers who have been flown into DR Congo in large numbers in the subsequent years. Official numbers provided by the Chinese Embassy in Kinshasa range around several thousand individuals; these figures are, however, generally questioned.[1] The presence of non-European migrants to Kinshasa, and the DR Congo in general, has not only led to intercultural contacts but also to language contact and to the migrants having an impact on Lingala, the predominant language spoken in the Congolese capital, and on Lingala speakers' online and offline language practices.

Lingala is a Bantu language, spoken by at least 25 million speakers (or more; see Meeuwis 2013), and is widely diffused both in the capital Kinshasa (DR Congo) and in the northwestern parts of the country, neighboring Brazzaville (the capital of the Republic of the Congo) and in northern regions, northern parts of Angola, potentially also in adjacent areas of the Central African Republic and in European cities such as Paris and Brussels. As the most widely used language out of the four national languages of the DR Congo (alongside Kikongo-Kituba, Cilubà and Swahili), Lingala enjoys great prestige in the entertainment business, music, and also internationally as the language of the Congolese diaspora. As the language of the military and police, it is eyed with suspicion and associated with negative prestige, predominantly in more remote areas of the country where other languages are spoken. In terms of its grammar, the language shows numerous contact features that date back to the late 19th century, when it spread as a contact language between several communities along the Congo River, and was

---

[1] Several journalists working on China-Congo relations assume numbers as high as 230,000 Chinese to have migrated to the African continent during the first decade of the 21st century; see for instance https://www.the-american-interest.com/2014/01/10/chinas-congo-plan/ (last accessed 27 May 2019).

then standardized and modified by missionaries in the colonial system. These processes have led to different – at times competing – varieties and registers of Lingala. The variety used in the capital, Kinshasa Lingala, for instance, diverges from the variety used further upstream in Mbandaka, and also from the closely-related language Bangala in northeastern DR Congo. Over the last two decades,[2] with the arrival of more Chinese migrants in DR Congo, Congolese Lingala speakers have increasingly begun to use mock forms that are supposed to imitate Mandarin. These comprise mock labels (used as names when calling out to Asian-looking passersby), coined terms for purchasable everyday items (especially of inferior quality) that are reminiscent of Chinese words, as well as mimetic interpretations of Asians' use of ("broken") Lingala, which seems to be a more recent practice, triggered by online videos (see Section 9.4). Numerous examples of mock speech are used for advertising (even for Chinese products), reoccur in popular culture and are widespread across social media groups and forums.

The occurrence of mock practices of the Chinese language, utterances that "by indirect indexicality, [...] reproduce[s] highly negative racializing stereotypes" (Hill 1998: 680) of "Chineseness", can be understood as racialized performances of Otherness and exclusion that can be traced back to language ideologies about Lingala that are linked to its colonial past. Lingala is often said to be a (contact) language that can easily be learnt due to its reduced noun morphology, compared to other languages in the Bantu area with more rigid morphological agreement patterns. However, speakers' attitudes toward migrants' acquisition of the language are not necessarily characterized by a high degree of "xenoglossophilia" (see for instance Storch 2014 on Luwo speakers' openmindedness with regard to other languages), neither are they characterized by contentment about others' acquisition of Lingala. In online discourse, as well as in face-to-face interaction, European, American or Asian language learners, in particular, are often confronted with the accusation of "language theft", i.e. appropriating Lingala as an authentic Congolese language as a means of undesired cultural immersion, infiltration, or even espionage. These suspicions can be explained with reference to missionaries' recurrent and radical linguistic interventions in the history of Lingala in the

---

[2] In August 2004, when I first arrived in Kinshasa, children and also young adults made recurrent use of these mock labels and mimetic forms of Chinese when addressing passersby in the streets of Kinshasa, especially in remote neighborhoods where no Chinese workers had hitherto been sent for construction works. In subsequent years these mock practices became more frequent and appeared on social media.

colonial system, and the drastic implications that these had for speakers' actual language practices due to their rigid prescriptive nature.

The data is based on participant observation of and within groups of street children during my fieldwork in Kinshasa in 2009 and 2010, as well as on (more recent) qualitative interviews with Lingala speakers from Kinshasa, recorded in 2015. I also used data retrieved from social media, precisely YouTube (comments), Facebook groups and WhatsApp chats among Congolese, consisting of stories, jokes, and discussions. The data that originated from social media was then discussed with mostly adolescent Lingala speakers from Kinshasa in order to gain insights into speakers' prevalent language ideologies and their view on and judgment of these practices.[3]

The paper intends to validate the hypothesis that mock forms of Chinese in DR Congo (often seen as general racist slurs against Asians) are radical and satiric performative acts of Otherness, and can be understood as the daily life "effect of [Chinese] globalization on the sociolinguistics of migration", whereby "China is one of the engines (if not the engine) of globalization" (Kroon, Blommaert and Jie 2013: 277). I claim that migratory patterns of Chinese are reflected in the emergence of Africans' racist/racialized yet creative mimetic forms of "language crossing" (Rampton 1995), and in the narrative integration in urban storytelling and allegedly humorous interaction among Congolese. My paper further claims that forms of Chinese have become part of speakers' broad global(ized) repertoires. While this does not come along with specific swear words that are easily sorted into lists and analyzed, I propose to consider language practices that include racial slurs and mimetic mock forms as part of a more holistic perspective on swearing as speakers' expression and negotiation of power relations through "bad language".[4] This is also suggested in various other contributions found in this volume (see, for instance, Roque on colonial names, Muhsin on censoring, and Mietzner on transgressive language in a tourism context, just to name a few), as well as in the introduction.

---

[3] I am particularly grateful to my interview partners B. K., F. O., P. A., M. I., the late P. M. and various others, whose anonymity I guarantee. I warmly thank the two reviewers for their comments on a draft version of this chapter and I am indebted to Mary Chambers for carefully checking the text and providing numerous valuable ideas. My co-editor Anne Storch is warmly thanked for sharing my interest in swearing and cursing practices and for her insights and our joint discussions. In the case of inaccuracies, all common disclaimers apply.

[4] Potentially, these imitations performed in Kinshasa, as acts of hostility and disparagement, could be a mimetic interpretation of practices from the Global North, where Mock Asian is (more) widespread, for instance in nursery rhymes, jokes and so on. I am grateful to one reviewer for this important comment.

9.2 Approaching "mock language" from a theoretical perspective

The study of mock language, the use of racial and ethnic slurs as a means of Othering and exclusion, has gained steady academic attention after Jane H. Hill's (1995, 1998, 1999, among others) widely acknowledged works on Mock Spanish (see also Rosa 2016). In a larger study, Hill (2008) relates her findings to other forms of mock language and slurs; while the study of Mock Spanish has certainly influenced Chun's work on Mock Asian, there are fundamental differences concerning the target of mock practice:

> A specialized development of bold mispronunciation is parodic imitation of a Spanish accent in English. Such parodies were a staple of comedy routines in the 1940s and 1950s. Today, however, they are more visible as racist than are other forms of Mock Spanish. They have more in common with the intentional mockery that Ronkin & Karn (1999) labeled "Mock Ebonics" and Chun (2004) called "Mock Asian" than does Mock Spanish, which does not explicitly make fun of Spanish. (Hill 2008: 140)

The fact that Mock Asian, as described by Chun (2004, 2009, 2016), is a more racist, and intentionally racialized, practice, fits my observations in Kinshasa, where Mock Chinese often comes together with racist gestures labeled as *miso ya bachinois* 'Chinese eyes', which is a recurrent practice. Hill (1995) moreover differentiates several strategies that are used by those producing mock language, typically employed by "Anglo speakers of English, addressed to other Anglos" (no pagination), which she classifies as (1) "semantic derogation", (2) "euphemisms", (3) "[a]ffixation of grammatical elements", and the aforementioned (4) "hyperanglization/bold mispronunciation". The first strategy refers to the borrowing of a neutral or positive term from Spanish, which receives a humorous or negative meaning when used in Mock Spanish (as with Mandarin greetings when used and recontextualized as racist slurs in Kinshasa), while the second strategy denotes the borrowing of vulgar or negative terms from Spanish that serve as euphemisms for their rude or vulgar English equivalents (which does not occur in Kinshasa, as will be seen in Sections 3–4). Hill's third strategy explains the affixation rules of Spanish morphology for mocking purposes, especially the definite article *el* and the masculine gender suffix *-o* (this can be seen as being in analogy with phonological modifications, or composition with Chinese-sounding syllables; however, the ones employed in Kinshasa have no meaning/function in Mandarin). The fourth strategy, however, denotes "absurd mispronunciation" (Hill 1995) that often allows for vulgar puns, etc. (while hyperanglicization is not recurrent in Mock Asian, bold mispronunciation is; see the relevant analytical sections). Altogether, these strategies symbolize a tendency to mockingly exclude those whose language diverges from an (imagined) homogeneous speech community (see also Galván Torres and Flores Dueñas 2013 on potential implications for the classroom). According to Hill (1995), and then applied by Vessey (2014) to a Canadian context, borrowing processes in mockery function based on a "dual indexicality", whereby "[d]irect indexicality refers to the referential meaning of the borrowed word, whereas indirect indexicality refers to stereotypes regarding the culture and speakers of the language from which a word is borrowed" (Vessey 2014: 177); this can also be applied to the Congolese context of this study.

Chun (2009: 266–267) lists specific features of Mock Asian, as a typological overview extracted from mock language studies in different contexts and which are recurrent in reported practices. Apart from the lexical and syntactic characteristics (not displayed here), it is especially the phonological features mentioned that correspond with Lingala speakers' mock strategies when mimicking the speech of Chinese migrants (see Table 9.1). These will be discussed in more detail in Section 9.3.

Table 9.1: Prototypical phonological features of Mock Asian (Chun 2009: 267).

Description of Mock Asian Feature	Examples and Comments
Phonological Features	
1. Neutralization of the phonemic distinction between /r/ and /w/	[ɹ]→[w] *wrong* pronounced as *wong*, *right* pronounced as *white*
2. Neutralization of the phonemic distinction between /r/ and /l/	[ɹ] → [l] *fried rice* pronounced as *flied lice* [l] → [ɹ] *Eileen* pronounced as *Irene*, *like* pronounced as *rike*, *hello* pronounced *as herro*
3. Alveolarization of voiceless interdental fricative 'th' [θ] to [s]	*thank you* pronounced as *sank you*, *I think so* pronounced as *I sink so*
4. Nonsensical syllables with the onset 'ch' /tʃ/	*ching-chong, chow*
5. Nonsensical syllables with the coda 'ng'/ŋ/	*ching-chong, ting, ping*
6. Alternating high-low intonational contour; one tone for each syllable	H L H L *ching-chong-ching-chong*
7. Epenthetic 'ee' [i] at the end of a closed word	*break-ee, buy-ee, look-ee*
8. Reduplication of word	*pee-pee*; not unique to Mock Asian

Lipski has approached mock forms of language from a language contact perspective, and has labeled patterns of partial acquisition (2002) as "gringo lingo" and their reverse mock images as "tarzanized speech" or "foreigner talk" (Lipski n.d.) – the patterns of language that are mimicked by those addressing apparent foreigners and assuming that they must speak a sort of pidginized or ungrammatical speech. While foreigner talk presents itself as a sort of linguistic accommodation to individuals with less proficiency ("helping" less proficient speakers to get the message), it actually entails ideologies of mimicry, mockery and ostracism (or Orientalism) that overlap and interact. Tarzanized speech as mock language thus incorporates strong (derogatory) ideologies about the conversational partner's language use and comprehension.

Another recurrent mock strategy is ethnophaulisms, i.e. ethnic or racial slurs, and modified names (that have often become widely known as indexical markers) play a salient role in mock practices around the world. Allan and Burridge (2006: 133) mention, for instance, Jewish ethnophaulisms such as *Itzig*, a corrupted form of the Jewish name *Jitzchak*, instrumentalized as a racialized slur by the Nazi regime, whose social images incorporate strong stereotypes, linked to a history of shame, ostracism and exclusion. Specific names such as the latter have therefore developed from random ethnophaulisms to specific racialized slurs for entire groups, and are more widely known than the unbiased self-designations or accepted labels. These are discussed in more detail in Section 9.3.

Reyes and Lo (2009), later followed by Alim et al. (2016) with the establishment of a subdiscipline of linguistics called "Raciolinguistics", focus on the intersection of race, ethnicity and linguistic ascriptions of Otherness. In their volume, Reyes and Lo approach Asian (American) stylized English, among which Mock Asian is also counted, with the overall term "Yellow English", understood as the "all too common stylizations of Asian (American) speech as a type of foreign accent" (Lo and Reyes 2009: 6). Focusing on "racial shifts", Roth-Gordon (2011) analyzes how non-Whites, through a specific linguistic performance, can be "racially improved" in terms of their recognizability, or how "Whiteness" may be lost or may decrease through close interaction with specific groups.

While most of the studies on mock language and mimesis are situated in the Global North and deal with immigrant discourse, Storch (2011) approaches mock language in languages from the Global South from a mimetic perspective, focusing on power that is embodied in anticolonial practices, in inverted relationships, rooted in witchcraft, possession and secrecy, or used playfully. Mimesis, the powerful use and embodiment of an "imperfect" copy by the Other, plays a salient role in her study. In a more recent contribution, Mietzner and Storch (2019) address mock language with a focus on language practices in a Kenyan tourism sector, where speaking, mocking, and speaking back are recurrent practices in a setting of unequal access to power and economic means. Rosa (2016) describes similar strategies of "Inverted Spanglish", where speakers' agency is reflected in the use of the mock forms with which they were formerly excluded or marked.

Mock language also occurs within close-knit communities, for instance among groups of adolescents, where different roles are often playfully negotiated (or addressed) on the basis of mock strategies of intonational features, phonemes, etc. This has been studied by Rampton (1995) in his works on language crossing[5]; Rampton (1999) goes further with a perspective on "styling the Other" by analyzing "the ways in which people use language and dialect in discursive practice to appropriate, explore, reproduce or challenge influential images and stereotypes of groups that they *don't* themselves (straightforwardly) belong to" (Rampton 1999: 421; emphasis in original). The present contribution presents findings on the form, function and meaning of Mock Chinese in the Congolese capital alongside these existing studies.

9.3 Mock Chinese in Kinshasa: Racialized labels and hostile encounters

Making fun of Chinese migrants' language practices and of iconic features of Mandarin, as perceived by inhabitants of Kinshasa, has become a frequent ritualized joking practice, predominantly among young men and women. These racial slurs, which are found in different languages and settings worldwide and associate invented nonsensical language forms with the sounds of Mandarin (or other Asian languages), are mostly used in quick interactions with the Chinese, and other Asians from the Philippines, Indonesia, Korea etc., for instance in traffic, supermarkets, bars, or around construction sites. It can be assumed that these stereotypical and repetitive mock forms serve a phatic function, attracting attention and addressing the target while simultaneously expressing a specific negative stance. Often, especially when using mock labels for the Chinese (see Table 9.1), these are accompanied by racialized mock gestures, such as slit-eyed grimaces. This can be observed in children's language behavior but is most commonly found with youths and young adults, and at times even with old people.

---

[5] These dynamics are also visible in Paris' (2011) inspiring study on heritage Pacific islanders in South Vista on the American West Coast, where mocked Samoans, Mock Ebonics and Mock Asian all interact in mixed youth groups in a high school setting as a reflection of societal stereotypes and stereotypical ways of speaking and their mimetic subversion. Dovchin (2019) also looks at mock language and practices of exclusion against a background of language crossing.

When asked how certain kinds of mock language were coined or creatively formed, one 22-year old speaker stated:

> Exemple, quand je parle, je peux utiliser un terme comme si … hm 'yangó *ba-ching-chong* bazótonga nzelá óyo bizarre boyé', tu vois? J'utilise seulement les mots que eux utilisent trop, les chinois, comme *shing-shang* … moi aussi, j'emploie seulement '*ba-ching-chang* óyo bazótonga nzelá, basílisí yangó nánu té'. Tu vois? Je mets seulement *ba-ching-chang*. Tu peux les appeler au moment quand tu veux en introduisant, seulement comme '*shing*', comme avec le mot que tu veux appeler ça doit contenir le '-*ing*' et le '-*ang*', cela prouve que c'est vraiment eux! Tu vois – c'est comme ça que c'est à Kin, mais il n'y a pas des mots officiels que tout le monde utilise, non. Tu peux utiliser ce que tu veux, et après ça peut peut-être [été] appliqué par d'autres personnes …
>
> [For instance, when I speak, I can use a term like … hm 'this is why the 'ching-chongs' construct this street in a weird way', you see? I use only those words that they use too much, the Chinese, such as 'shing-shang' … I, too, only employ 'these ching-chang are constructing this road, they are not yet done'. You see? I only put 'the-ching-changs'. You can call them any time you want by just inserting 'shing', just that the word that you want to call them with has to include the 'ing' and 'ang', that shows it's really them! You see – this is how it is in Kinshasa, but there are no official words that everyone uses, no. You can use what you want, and afterwards that may be used by other people, maybe …]
>
> (F. O., interview excerpt, 2015; emphasis on mock forms)

The interview excerpt shows that the social function of using creative mock language is not only considered to be a means of racial discrimination, but that racial slurs intend to "call out" to somebody (*appeler*). This form of contact certainly appears odd and hostile; yet, from the young man's perspective it is explained that the Chinese workers were somehow inaccessible as a result of their segregation, in secluded construction areas with heavy construction vehicles, and that one would thus need more creativity and loud unmistakable (iconic?) language in order to greet one or pass a message, or even to attract their attention. Older inhabitants of the capital often complained in interviews that construction works should be carried out by Congolese instead of Chinese, and that the high unemployment rate was being boosted by the large numbers of Chinese construction workers.

The actual features of Mock Chinese are mostly phonological ones, with some morphosyntactic properties, which are discussed in Section 9.4. Relating to Chun's (2009: 267) overview, the following characteristics apply. The most salient features listed by Chun (2009) that also apply to the case of Mock Chinese in DR Congo are characteristics (4), (5), (6) and (8); see Table 9.1. The neutralization of the phonemic distinction between /r/ and /w/ or /r/ and /l/ (as listed by Chun as characteristics 1–2 in Table 9.1) does not feature, due to the fact that the phoneme inventory of Lingala only has /l/ (apart from borrowed lexical items from other languages). Moreover, when replacing /l/ with /r/, the speakers' intention is not to mock speakers of Chinese but Rwandans, as Kinyarwanda and the language practices of Rwandan "intruders" are generally associated with the tap /ɾ/ whenever they attempt to pronounce /l/ (Wilson 2012: 18). Various memes, jokes and elements from comedy therefore use the phoneme for a type of "mock Kinyarwanda" when targeting Congolese or foreign politicians with alleged origins in the eastern parts of the country.[6] In Mock Chinese, in contrast, the use of nonsensical syllables with the onset <tch/tsh/ch> /tʃ/ or /ʃ/ (Chun's feature 4) is more emblematic since the voiceless fricative /ʃ/ is rare in word-initial position in Lingala. The high-low intonational contour (feature 6) occurs at times but may not always correspond with the prosodic system of Lingala and is therefore not emblematic. As becomes evident in the interview excerpt above, reduplication (8) of nonsensical syllables (4–5) is a recurrent feature. This syllabic modification of "ching-chong may seem bereft of meaning, but it can ultimately bear immensely important and complex cultural significance", as stressed by Chun (2016: 95).

Mock language has become a popular topic in everyday conversations among Congolese youth, based on people's apparent antipathy toward Chinese traders (*ba-hiho*), with a range of ethnophaulisms with which Chinese individuals are commonly addressed. While Allan and Burridge (2006: 189) mention that racialized names, also in the case of Mock Asian, often refer to speakers' diet (for Asians *ricer*, *rice-eater*, *rice gobbling bastard*, among others), which is ridiculed or targeted and functions as a general exoticized transporter of Otherness, this is not the case among Lingala speakers. Table 9.2 lists some of the mock labels that are widespread in Kinshasa and could be extracted from speakers' metalinguistic exchanges when referring to Chinese workers, or when passing construction sites where they were shouted out loud. Most of the Chinese individuals would usually not react or only react with puzzled or insignificant looks.

These racist labels and gestures target not only Chinese nationals, but most other Asians in Kinshasa, as well. During my fieldwork, I was well connected to a diverse community of European and Asian workmates; the Filipinos and Indonesians in that community generally complained that they were either not

---

[6] Apart from Mock Chinese and Mock Kinyarwanda, there is or seems also to be a mock form of missionaries' speech style. In humorous narratives from colonial times, Etambala (2006: 103–104) refers to the description of priests' speech as *Lingala ya Basango* (*Lingala van de Paters*; Fathers' Lingala), which reveals an inherent *gekunsteldheid* ('artificial character') and also narrates how European missionaries were unable to reproduce the correct tones when speaking African languages. Inhabitants of Kinshasa tell similar stories. The contemporary comedian *Kizubanata* also mocks the style of Lingala in which religious film material is produced. I am grateful to Michael Meeuwis for bringing the mock form of *Lofafa*, imitating the Lomongo used by European fathers, to my attention.

Table 9.2: Mock labels/racialized ethnophaulisms for Chinese in Kinshasa.

Chinese mock ethnonym	Origin/Etymology
ba-hiho [hihɔ́]ᵃ	Derived from the Mandarin greeting 你好 nǐ hǎo 'hello, good morning'
ba-tchingitawo	Onomatopoiea of Mandarin-sounding phonemes, coined nonsensical mock label
les noich	Metathesis of Fr. *chinois*, manipulative principle of French-based Verlan
les frères de Jet Lee	French 'the brothers of Jet Lee'
bandeko ya Jacki	lit. 'the siblings of Jacky (Chan)'
ba-pirate	lit. 'the pirates', referring to pirate clothes and brands
ba-ching-chong	Onomatopoiea of Mandarin-sounding phonemes, coined nonsensical mock label

ᵃIn Lingala, the subject marker *ba-* is the prefixed plural marker for [+animate] referents. In these examples, rather than using the IPA symbols, the same orthography is used as in the written examples.

taken seriously in their interactions with the Congolese, or that they were constantly mocked as being *chinois*. Responding to this common nuisance in the streets of Kinshasa, they would reportedly then mimetically impersonate the Other and pretend to approach the molester with invented martial arts moves, which would often scare him/her off. The fact that there is often no distinction made concerning a person's actual origin (China or elsewhere) is also reflected in online interactions, for instance in Facebook groups. After sharing a video of a "Chinese musician" singing in Lingala,⁷ several users exchanged ideas, whereby one commented that the singer was Japanese, not Chinese (*il est Japonais et non chinois!!!*). Others then expressed their indifference (*Japonais ou Chinois.. c est quoi le pb*), 'Japanese or Chinese, what is the problem?'. Another female Facebook user then replied *il est Japonais oh* [smiling emoticon] *mais c vieux ca toutle monde connait niwa ... meme indien au congo parle lingala* ('he is Japanese, oh, this is old but everyone knows nǐ hǎo ... even an Indian in the Congo speaks Lingala'), insinuating that the difference does not matter as long as certain labels (or greetings?) are known by all.

The ubiquitous and increasingly general use of this mock label changing from a racialized Chinese-only ethnophaulism to a general symbol of Othering could be

---

7 See https://www.facebook.com/search/top/?q=chinois%20lingala (accessed 30 January 2018).

testified in the accounts of several young Europeans' (who, in their own view, did not bear any physical traits that could encourage passersby to think they were Asians), who narrated incidents in which they were called *chinois-hiho* in various neighborhoods of Kinshasa. When I asked Congolese colleagues why this seemed to be a general trend, they assumed that the speaker simply intended to disturb, cause confusion or remark on the different physical features of the person addressed, regardless of his/her actual origin (B. K., interview 2015).

Especially in seemingly humorous practices among Congolese youths, Chinese-sounding words are coined, most of which refer to items of inferior quality that are said to easily break and not to last. These products, either sold or produced by the Chinese, are mostly seen as valueless and short-lived, and are often labeled *tshwen-pang*, among other terms. Table 9.3 contains the most frequent labels used in the youth register Lingala ya Bayankee/Yanké (lit. 'the Yankees' Lingala'), which is spoken by street children and street gangsters throughout the capital. Apart from terms for products, markets and money, one term is also used to denote a woman's behind.

It is no surprise that racialized labels and mock forms have become recurrent in jokes that mostly address either the low quality of Chinese products (and, implicitly, of their human producers), or the high numbers of Chinese workers in Kinshasa. In both cases, among the various jokes that could be collected in offline and online communication (e.g. on Facebook), the targeted group is often pictured as ignorant, knowing only rudimentary or pidginized French or Lingala, and often portrayed as stubborn, stupid or clumsy. One joke (see Nassenstein and Hollington 2016: 182–183) that was considered as extraordinarily hilarious addressed the situation of a woman who gives birth to a child of a Chinese father. The child passes away after a short time and the woman's brother asks her whether she did not know that Chinese things generally do not last (*oyebaki te ke biloko ya ba chinois ewumelaka te?*). Other common jokes in Kinshasa deal with Chinese names; one narrates a journey by the former Congolese dictator Mobutu to China, where he encounters a minister called *Lee Bolo*, a name that is homophonous with the Lingala word *liboló* 'vagina', which allegedly causes hilarity among the Congolese delegates. Very often, these jokes contain some of the mock labels presented in Table 9.2, point to other fake names that are supposed to sound Chinese and contain an inherent degree of humor or are based on Chinese-sounding nonsensical coinages.

Apart from specific mock names, jokes and references to low-quality items in youth language, Mock Chinese is commonly used in popular culture. There are various references to nonsensical words and repetitions in Congolese rumba songs, also incorporating melodic elements that are supposed to sound Chinese, as well as Chinese characters. As early as 2001, the musician Werrason launched his

Table 9.3: Mock Chinese in Lingala youth language (adapted from Nassenstein and Hollington 2016).

Forms	Gloss	Origin
tshwen-pang [tʃwɛnpaŋ]	'products of inferior quality, produced in China and expected to rip/break soon'	Mock Chinese, nonsensical coinage
ngwanzŭ	see above (synonym)	Onomatopoetic reference to the city of *Guangzhou*, which has a considerable Congolese diaspora community and serves as many Congolese vendors' main destination for wholesale purchases
shishó	see above (synonym)	Mandarin 市场 *shìchǎng* 'market', toponymic synecdoche
kató	see above (synonym)	Mock Chinese, nonsensical coinage including prosodic LT-HT
mondele ya kató	lit. 'fake White', designation for foreigners who, based on arbitrary factors such as skin and hair color, are not considered to be "American/European"	Lingala *mondele* 'White, European', *ya* CONN; see above
zanzízu	'market'	Mock Chinese, nonsensical coinage?
shan-shi, shai-shi	'money'	Mock Chinese, nonsensical coinage?
zin-zung-yung	'work'	Mock Chinese, nonsensical coinage?
elle a du san-sin-sung ya súka	lit. 'she has the ultimate san-sin-sung'; designation for a girl's impressive behind	can be contextually understood, concealment of taboo term by using Mock Chinese

album *'Opération Dragon'* (based on Bruce Lee's 1973 movie of the same name), with strong (alleged) reference to Chinese made by showing images of dragons, incorporating karate kicks into dance choreographies and other emblematic elements. The decontextualized use of Chinese characters is also a recurrent practice worldwide and is often prone to linguistic creativity. Li Wei and Zhua Hua (2019) label the "emerging phenomenon of creating scripts that defy the writing conventions of Chinese by incorporating elements that are deemed 'foreign' or by manipulating the structural norms of Chinese written characters" as *tranßcripting*. These scripts transcend language boundaries and reveal playful subversion of norms. Most cases in the Western world where Chinese characters are used in order to exoticize songs, movies, for lifestyle items such as clothes, or for tattoos, are different and arbitrary Chinese signs are used that often startle speakers of Mandarin; the same occurs with random English prints in the textile industry in China, for instance.

Due to the import of Chinese goods and the high degree of mobility of Chinese traders who also began to penetrate the interior of the African continent after the first agreements between governments and Chinese companies, the Congolese advertising industry began to oppose the allegedly low quality of Chinese goods by incorporating humorous interactions between Congolese and Chinese into their commercials. One clip features the local comedian Esobe, who advertises the use of Chinese motorcycles; according to the commercial these are the only ones strong enough to deal with the Congolese female heavyweight 'Ya Mado', who was the eponymous star of a party hit in Kinshasa in 2015; see Figure 9.1.[8]

After breaking the first motorcycle, a Chinese woman advises the comedian to use a bike of the Chinese brand Keweseki, which carries Ya Mado easily. Esobe then uses Mock Chinese, probably intending to thank the Chinese woman (0′45″), here also with a specific sequence of high and low tones as an intonational contour (LT-LT-HT, LT-HT; see Table 9.1) before driving off:

(1) *Mamá chinoise, chìnà-chìnà-chów, chòw-chá!*
    Chinese.woman [nonsensical.syllables][9]

I inquired why many Congolese felt strong resentment against the Chinese in Kinshasa, a resentment on which the different forms of mock language were grounded. One young man (M. I., interview excerpt, 2015) expressed his anger in Lingala, again by inserting mock forms in his explanation and addressing the Chinese migrants in Kinshasa directly in replying to my question:

> Bachinois, vraiment, ba-*yang-shi*, ba-*shi-sha-wa*, tolémbí bínó, ba-*yang-shi*, bokómí ebelé! Na moto ayákí na bínó, tozóyéba té! Náni ayákí na bínó vraiment? Ba-*shi-sha-wa*! Tolémbí na moto óyo ayákí na bínó ... tozóyéba pé moto yangó té, sókí azá náni? Heh? Bokómí vraiment partout-partout, bokómí kotéka ba-mikate, ba-mápa, eh, ba-*yang-shi*, ba-*shi-sha-wa*,

---

8 See https://www.youtube.com/watch?v=y82sTP5CWAI (accessed 27 May 2019).
9 The designation of the syllables as "nonsensical" – despite their clear indexicality as derogatory strategy – follows Chun's (2009) characteristics.

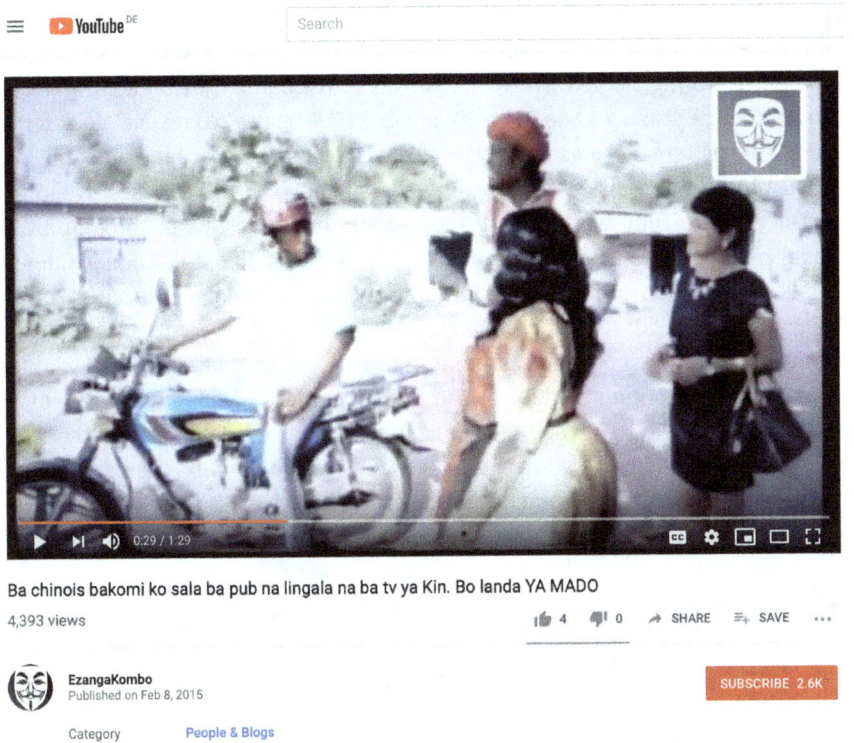

Figure 9.1: 'Chinese began to advertise in Lingala in Kinshasa's TV stations. Follow Ya Mado'.

ba-*ko-fu-shan*! Té, boyé té, tolémbí bínó, Congolais vraiment, tolémbí bínó! Botékaka na magasin, bilóko móko boyé ya 50 francs, ba-100 francs. Boyé té! Bobébiselá bísó nde mbóka.

[Chinese people, really, the yang-shis, the shi-sha-was, we are tired of you, yang-shis, you have become so many! And the one who came with you/brought you, we don't even know [him]! Who really came with you/brought you? Shi-sha-was! We are tired of the person who came with you/brought you ... we don't know that person either, who may that be? Hm? You have really reached everywhere, you started to sell *beignets*, bread, yang-shis, shi-sha-was, ko-fu-shans! No, not like this, we are tired of you, Congolese really, we are tired! You sell in shops, some things for 50 francs, 100 francs. Not like that! You have thus ruined our country.] (M. I., interview excerpt, 2015, emphasis on mock forms)

This example shows that the anger and hostility is linked to socioeconomic fears and hardships, especially in regard to Chinese migrants who become small-scale entrepreneurs. Moreover, the mock forms used in the interview excerpt are not used to attract anybody's attention, nor can they be directly witnessed or heard by any Chinese (the interview session did not occur in public; only the speaker and

I were present at that moment). The frequent repetition of nonsensical mock syllables as derogatory labels for Chinese migrants rather fulfills the function of intrapersonal swearing, as a valve for anger and frustration with a cathartic effect (Vingerhoets, Bylsma and de Vlam 2013: 292–293). The use of creative mock forms even when no target is present may reduce tension and decrease the probability of actual physical aggression (against Chinese migrants). In other cases, when addressing construction workers with these mock forms directly, or through multimodal performances with racist grimaces, it could be claimed that Mock Chinese fulfills the function of inter-individual swearing (Vingerhoets, Bylsma & and de Vlam 2013: 294–295); see also Section 9.5.

The use of mock forms in popular culture and the media have contributed to an increased popularization of the phenomenon and have turned it into a fashionable recurrent element in discourse. Perceived as hilarious by those who use it and as displayed in the entertainment industry and media, it is generally perceived as hostile practice and offensive by the victims.

9.4 A fistfight gone viral: Attitudes toward simplified forms of Lingala

As also illustrated in the literature available on the topic, mock language does not necessarily consist of nonsensical syllables or onomatopoetic coinages that imitate the sounds of existing languages (as in so-called "Ching-Chong English"; see also Chun 2016), but can also mock and mimic imperfect or "broken" forms of language. Due to the relatively high numbers of Chinese nationals acquiring the basics of Lingala, Congolese metalinguistically address migrants' simplified patterns of Lingala, especially in digital discourses in social media. These metalinguistic exchanges are commonly characterized by speakers' dominant language ideologies of speaking "correct Lingala", mostly as an indexical sign of urban belonging (in the capital Kinshasa), of being fashionable, well-informed and of being authentically *kinois* ('inhabitant of Kinshasa'). Online users thus either compliment foreigners' impressive language skills ("She speaks even better than I do!") or mock their attempts to communicate in rudimentary Lingala ("What kind of Lingala is this?"). This model of knowing and speaking "correct Lingala" has to be understood as a mimesis of colonial and, even more, missionary ideologies.[10]

---

[10] Missionaries involved in corpus and status planning activities often also actively changed the grammar of the languages "under the magnifying glass", and contributed to a complicated

9 Mock Chinese in Kinshasa — 201

Another mock form of imperfect or "broken" Lingala is sometimes labeled *Chingala* ('Chinese Lingala'), or more drastically, *Lingalachien* ('Dog's Lingala'), and is based on a recorded dispute between a Congolese delivery man and a Chinese shop clerk, whose Chinese accent (in his realization of Lingala) went viral and has, as an urban myth, become the topic of recurrent humorous on-line narratives (see Figure 9.2).

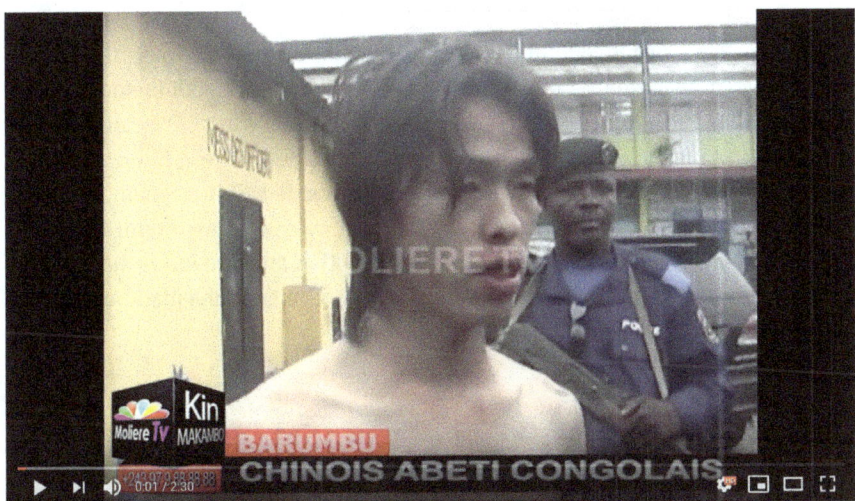

Figure 9.2: A fistfight gone viral.
Note: See https://www.youtube.com/watch?v=MgxkF7WHM4k (accessed 27 May 2019).

In 2014, this video of a fistfight between a Chinese worker, shown with naked torso in the short clip, and a Congolese man went viral, and was frequently shared via WhatsApp, uploaded to YouTube,[11] and also diffused on Instagram. The clip is dubbed as *Chinois abeti Congolais* 'A Chinese beat up a Congolese' and shows a policeman in the background, while the Chinese man is asked (by a reporter or somebody affiliated with the police) whether and why he hit

---

diglossic situation of varieties/registers used for sermons and bible translation vs. those commonly used by the broader population and in all other (informal) contexts. Lingala speakers are therefore aware of a specific language use for liturgical purposes and as employed by priests, which diverges lexically and morphologically from the Lingala commonly used in speakers' everyday interactions.
11 See https://www.youtube.com/watch?v=MgxkF7WHM4k (accessed 27 May 2019).

the Congolese man (*Obétí congolais?*). He replies in a simplified and syntactically non-standard yet understandable idiolect, speaking what would be conceptualized as "broken Lingala".

(2) yé=péta   nga   leki   libosó
     SM3sg=beat OM1sg young.sibling first
     'He beat me first.'

The interviewer's negative attitudes toward the interrogated man become evident at 0′11″, when he addresses the Chinese interlocutor publicly with the mock greeting/label *hiho* [hihɔ̃], whereafter his conversation partner turns his head away. He then adds in Lingala: *Olobaka chinois?* ('Do you speak Chinese?'), followed by *Ozá chinois?* ('Are you Chinese?') at 0′16″. The interrogated Chinese man confirms, whereafter he is asked whether he speaks Lingala, which he also confirms by saying *moké* ('a little'). When asked why he beat the other man, he utters the sentence that later on went viral as a mock formula and became emblematic of Chinese Lingala (0′22″):

   Interviewer:
(3) O-bét-í   papa   óyo   pó na   níni?
     SM2sg-beat-PRS1 man   DEM for   ITRG
     'Why did you beat this man?'

   Chinese interlocutor:
(4) Yé=péta   nga   leki   pua nini?
     SM3sg=beat OM1sg younger.sibling why
     'Why did this younger man beat *me*?'

He then repeats his question (5), which caused online users to repeatedly play with similar-sounding yet to a large extent nonsensical modifications of the Chinese man's statement:

   Chinese:
(5) Na   yé=péta   nga   leki   pua nini?
     and SM3sg=beat OM1sg younger.sibling why
     'So, why did this younger man beat me?'

YouTube commenters, who labeled this realization of Lingala as *Chingala* or *Lingalachien*, seem to address the lack of morphological agreement in the utterance,[12] as well as the syntactic order of the complements. The expected syntactically "correct" reply in Lingala would have been *kási léki abétí nga(i) pó na níni?*, whereas the sentence uttered cliticizes the personal pronoun *yé* to the verb root and shows no tense-aspect marking. Syntactically, the subject *leki* ('younger man') here follows verb and object, which causes confusion for the listener. The interviewer therefore continues to ask whether the Chinese man thought that his Congolese counterpart was actually a madman, or why else he would suddenly start beating him. He further asks how it is possible that a Chinese man could come to Congo to attack Congolese, and if he judged this to be acceptable. The Chinese shop clerk answers (0′54″):

Chinese:
(7) Yó   tála   ngai=zá   mo-to   libóma?
     2sg   look   SM$_{1sg}$=COP   SM$_1$.person   mad
     Ngai=péta   yé   ndéngé   níni?
     SM$_{1sg}$=beat   OM$_{3sg}$ NP$_9$.manner   ITRG
     Yé=péta   ngai   leki   té,   ngai=péta   yé
     SM$_{3sg}$=beat   OM$_{1sg}$ younger.sibling   NEG   SM$_{1sg}$=beat   OM$_{3sg}$
     ndénge   níni?
     NP$_9$.manner   ITRG
     'Look at me, am I a madman? How should I have beaten him? The younger man did not beat me, how/why would I then have beaten him?'

The question of whether he was considered a *libóma* ('fool, madman, idiot'), in particular, triggered hilarity across social media, and he was thereafter associated with this label, which also led to the mock formulas that began to circulate and be performed by Lingala speakers via shared audio recordings on WhatsApp (see below). Among the most common (negative) replies to the video clip that were retrieved from YouTube (between 30 May 2014 and 17 June 2014) were the comments shown in example (6). Both mock formulas *hiho* and the repetition of the man's sentence re-occur, and his Lingala is perceived as "Chinese Lingala".

(8) hahaha hi hao o lobaka chinois?
     '[laughing] nǐ hǎo do you speak Chinese?

---

[12] There is, however, also some variation in the morphological forms. After example (1), he adds with emphasis *yé-só-péta nga leki*, with a progressive prefix derived from *-zó-*.

Lol avc son lingalachien
'[laughing out loud] with his Dog's Lingala'

mdrrr somo trop il a tué la langue de lumumba
'[dead from laughing] terrible, he killed Lumumba's language'

Lingala moko etegama azo loba en dirais aza na rhum
'a Lingala that [?], he speaks as if he had a cold'

franchement il a assassiné la langue lingala mdddr ye betanga leki puanini [...]
'really, he assassinated Lingala language [dead from laughing] *ye betanga leki puanini*'

In the following days and weeks, WhatsApp users would send each other audio recordings in which they began to imitate the Chinese man in different modified voices, with changing intonation, and, interestingly, turning the interview from its original form into a more simplified and often nonsensical copy, consisting of several variations of the same sentence, especially mimicking intonational features of the Chinese man's realization, pronouncing *yé* (3sg) as [jø] or [jə] and inserting numerous interjections in between the (partly) nonsensical repetitions.[13]

(9)   *Yo peta nga leki po na nini, ah, yo peta nga leki! Nga beti leki na gogard te, nabeti ye. Ah, abeta nga leki! Ye peta nga leki, ah! Chinois abeta Congolais! Congolais abeta Chinois! Congolais... Chinois abeta Congolais, Congolais abeta Chinois te. Oh, ye sikoyo abeta nga leki po na nini? Ye peta nga leki ah! Ye peta nga leki po na nini? Ah!*

While this example starts off with a common conversation in which almost no Mock Chinese was used, Lingala speakers turned the Chinese man's voice – as a personification of improper and imperfect language use – through hyperbolic mimicry into the speech of the ultimate Other, who is barely able to utter any understandable sentence, and whose language ridicules itself through nonsensical form and becomes void of any meaning.

---

[13] Example (9) was transcribed from an audio file sent to me by one of my interlocutors (F.O., interview excerpt, 2015).

9.5 Outlook: Mocking as extreme curse?

Different readings of the concept of "swearing" are possible, as already stated in the introduction to this volume, and perhaps even advisable. In order to allow for more global approaches to the concept of offensive, transgressive and taboo language, it has to be acknowledged that swearing does not inevitably have to be represented by specific translatable lexical swear terms (as sometimes conceptualized in more narrow readings of swearing practices). Jay (2002: 160), who also discusses ethnophaulisms and racial slurs in the context of hate speech in his influential monograph on swearing/cursing, stresses the fact that "power differences across ethnic groups are the basis for many ethnic-racial insults", wherever "prestige and income vary along racial and ethnic lines". He further problematizes the essential observation that across ethnic groups, verbal aggressiveness is conceptualized very differently, while most studies that are available are not representative as they focus predominantly on White speakers; this is in clear alignment with the focus of this book.

Language practices and names that "are used to 'put down' outsiders" (Jay 2002: 177), as has been shown in the description of mock labels and metalinguistic mocking of Chinese migrants in Kinshasa, as well as mock practices that target Chinese nationals' allegedly poor realization of Lingala, reflect strict normative language ideologies (in analogy with colonial/missionary linguistic interventions in the history of Lingala). These practices of mimicry and mimesis, resulting in ostracism, exclusion and sometimes also physical violence (see Section 9.4) can be understood as hostile after-effects of unequal interactions, with Congolese who feel exploited (by Chinese supervisors), neglected or abandoned (by the state or lacking social security systems), and project their fears and anger onto Asian migrants. A general hostile attitude towards Chinese immigrants, triggered by multi-billion large-scale trade agreements, in stark contrast to Kinshasa citizens' aggravated economic hardships, transports the potential for conflict from face-to-face interactions onto the metalinguistic platform of online media. In YouTube comments, WhatsApp groups and Facebook posts, the "Chinese Other" and his/her language practices are discursively deconstructed and turned into stammerers, "non-speakers", or into individuals only able to perform "foreigner talk" or tarzanized speech (in Lipski's [n.d.] terms). Mocking here appears as extreme curse, which, unlike interpersonal swearing, leaves the addressee unable to reply, reject or invalidate the mockery, due to the brutal reflection of his/her imperfect, odd, or Othered language use. Acknowledging and conceptualizing this very efficient form of racist/racialized metalinguistic mockery as a form of swearing, or extreme curse, as proposed in this chapter, also means expanding the research horizon to a more focused view on mimetic language use in contexts of hostile encounters, a potentially profitable endeavor for current strands in swearing and cursing research.[14]

While this contribution only constitutes a first and preliminary approach to mock language in the margins, future studies may delve deeper into discourses of inequality in African settings and languages. Methodologically, further studies may profit from utilizing (critical) discourse analysis, or by approaching metalinguistic exchanges in social media within the framework of a digital/virtual ethnography.

Abbreviations

-	morpheme boundary
=	clitic
COP	copula
DEM	demonstrative
DR Congo	Democratic Republic of the Congo
ITRG	interrogative
NEG	negation
NP_1	nominal prefix of class 1
OM	object marker
PRS1	present tense 1
SM_1	subject marker of noun class 1

References

Allan, Keith and Kate Burridge. 2006. *Forbidden Words. Taboo and the Censoring of Language*. Cambridge: Cambridge University Press.
Alim, H. Samy, John R. Rickford and Arnetha F. Ball (eds.) 2016. *Raciolinguistics. How Language Shapes our Ideas about Race*. Oxford: Oxford University Press.
Chun, Elaine W. 2004. Ideologies of legitimate mockery: Margaret Cho's revoicings of Mock Asian. *Pragmatics* 14 (2–3): 263–289.
Chun, Elaine W. 2009. Speaking like Asian immigrants: Intersections of accomodation and mocking at a U.S. high school. *Pragmatics* 19 (1): 17–38.
Chun, Elaine W. 2016. The meaning of Ching-Chong: Language, racism, and response in new media. In Alim, Rickford and Ball (eds.), pp. 81–96. Oxford: Oxford University Press.
Dovchin, Sender. 2019. Language crossing and linguistic racism: Mongolian immigrant women in Australia. *Journal of Multicultural Discourses*. https://www.tandfonline.com/doi/abs/10.1080/17447143.2019.1566345?journalCode=rmmd20 (last accessed 15 June 2019).

---

[14] I am grateful to my co-editor for numerous inspiring conversations on this topic.

Etambala, Zana Aziza. 2006. Lachen met de 'zwartjes'. Humoristische anekdotes uit koloniale reisverhalen (1880–1945). In Marnix Beyen and Johan Verberckmoes (eds.), *Humor met een verleden*, 87–122. Leuven: Universitaire Pers Leuven.

Galván Torres, Adriana Rosalina and Luis Alonso Flores Dueñas. 2013. Mock Spanish: If you're illegal, head south amigo! *Sincronía* 64: 1–18.

Hill, Jane H. 1995. Mock Spanish: A site for the indexical reproduction of racism in American English. Language & Culture Symposium 2. http://language-culture.binghamton.edu/symposia/2/part1/#strategy-1 (accessed 27 May 2019).

Hill, Jane H. 1998. Language, race and white public space. *American Anthropologist* 100 (3): 680–689.

Hill, Jane H. 1999. Styling locally, styling globally: What does it mean? *Journal of Sociolinguistics* 3–4:542–556.

Hill, Jane H. 2008. *The Everyday Language of White Racism*. Malden: Blackwell.

Jay, Timothy. 2002. *Why we Curse: A Neuro-Psycho-Social Theory of Speech*. Amsterdam/Philadelphia: John Benjamins.

Kroon, Sjaak, Jan Blommaert and Dong Jie. 2013. Chinese and globalization. In Joana Duarte and Ingrid Gogolin (eds.), *Linguistic Superdiversity in Urban Areas. Research Approaches*, 275–296. Amsterdam: Benjamins.

Kushner, Jacob. 2014. China's Congo plan. Why the world's poorest nation is embracing Chinese investment over Western aid. *American Interest*, 10 January 2014. https://www.the-american-interest.com/2014/01/10/chinas-congo-plan/ (accessed 27 May 2019).

Li Wei and Zhu Hua. 2019. Tranßcripting: Playful subversion with Chinese characters. *International Journal of Multilingualism* 16 (2): 145–161.

Lipski, John. 2002. Partial Spanish. In C.R. Wiltshire and J. Camps (eds.), *Romance Phonology and Variation: Selected Papers from the 30th Linguistic Symposium on Romance Languages, Gainesville, Florida February 2000*, 117–143. Amsterdam/Philadelphia: John Benjamins.

Lipski, John. n.d. "Me want cookie": Foreigner talk as monster talk. http://www.personal.psu.edu/jml34/monster.pdf (accessed 27 May 2019).

Lo, Adrienne and Angela Reyes. 2009. Introduction: On yellow English and other perilous terms. In Reyes and Lo (eds.), pp. 1–17. Oxford: Oxford University Press.

Marysse, Stefaan and Sara Geenen. 2009. Win-win or unequal exchange? The case of the Sino-Congolese cooperation agreements. *Journal of Modern African Studies* 47 (3): 371–396.

Meeuwis, Michael. 2013. Lingala. In S. Michaelis, P. Maurer, M. Haspelmath and M. Huber (eds.), *Survey of Pidgin and Creole Languages, Vol. III: Pidgins, Creoles and Mixed Languages on Languages from Africa, Asia, Australia and the Americas*, 25–33. Oxford: Oxford University Press.

Mietzner, Angelika and Anne Storch. 2019. This is not about cannibals. *The Mouth* 4: 173–191.

Nassenstein, Nico and Andrea Hollington. 2016. Global repertoires and urban fluidity: Youth languages in Africa. *International Journal of the Sociology of Language* 242: 171–193.

Paris, Django. 2011. *Language across Difference. Ethnicity, Communication and Youth Identities in Changing Urban Schools*. Cambridge: Cambridge University Press.

Rampton, Ben. 1995. *Crossing: Language and Ethnicity among Adolescents*. London: Longman.

Rampton, Ben. 1999. Styling the Other: Introduction. *Journal of Sociolinguistics* 3–4:421–427.

Reyes, Angela and Adrienne Lo (eds.) 2009. *Beyond Yellow English: Toward a Linguistic Anthropology of Asian Pacific America*. Oxford: Oxford University Press.

Ronkin, Maggie and Helen E. Karn. 1999. Mock Ebonics: Linguistic racism in parodies of Ebonics on the Internet. *Journal of Sociolinguistics* 3 (3): 360–380.

Rosa, Jonathan. 2016. From Mock Spanish to Inverted Spanglish: Language ideologies and the racialization of Mexican and Puerto Rican youth in the United States. In Alim, Rickford and Ball (eds.), pp. 65–80. Oxford: Oxford University Press.

Roth-Gordon, Jennifer. 2011. Discipline and disorder in the whiteness of Mock Spanish. *Journal of Linguistic Anthropology* 21 (2): 211–229.

Storch, Anne. 2011. *Secret Manipulations. Language and Context in Africa*. Oxford: Oxford University Press.

Storch, Anne. 2014. *A Grammar of Luwo: An Anthropological Approach*. Amsterdam/Philadelphia: John Benjamins.

Vessey, Rachelle. 2014. Borrowed words, mock language and nationalism in Canada. *Language and Intercultural Communication* 14 (2): 176–190.

Vingerhoets, Ad, Lauren M. Bylsma and Cornelis de Vlam. 2013. Swearing: A biopsychosocial perspective. *Psychological Topics* 22 (2): 287–304.

Wilson, Catherina. 2012. The Congolese Yankee. Language and Identity among Youth in Kisangani. MA thesis, Universiteit Leiden.

All links to social media material are provided in the respective footnotes.

Ricardo Roque
10 The name of the wild man: Colonial *arbiru* in East Timor

Abstract: In this chapter I explore the indigenous incorporation and critique of colonial outsiders through nicknaming. I draw on the history of colonial warfare in Timor-Leste, a former Portuguese colony, in the nineteenth and twentieth centuries, to consider naming practices as a way through which the mimetic excesses of colonial agents could be simultaneously acknowledged, feared, criticized, and even cursed as a form of savagery. For this purpose I follow the cross-cultural history of the term *arbiru*. East Timorese people used this term as a nickname for a Portuguese colonial officer in the 1890s. Portuguese colonial accounts understood this usage as Timorese recognition of European supremacy and supernatural powers. Nevertheless, the colonial viewpoint failed to capture the veiled negative meanings that the Timorese name conveyed. In contrast, this chapter argues, the term *arbiru* entailed hidden indigenous criticism and cursing of the colonizers' excessive, threatening, and transgressive actions. It was a linguistic gesture for naming the wild and wicked nature of colonial mimesis.

10.1 Naming colonial savagery

The relationship between civilization and savagery has been a dramatic and pulsating energy in the history of Euro-American colonialisms. Colonial violence, exploitation, and abuse were accompanied by a proliferation of constructs of barbarism, frequently (though not exclusively) directed towards the Other: a "net of passionful images", as the anthropologist Michael Taussig (1993: xvii) once noted, "spun for several centuries by the colonial trade with wildness that ensure[d] civilization its savagery". This "colonial trade with wildness", powered by notions of alterity, however, was not exclusive to European intruders. It was a reciprocal process. Wildness attributed by Europeans to indigenous peoples could, in reverse, be accompanied by wildness attributed by local communities to colonial outsiders, in their own cultural terms. Over the course of colonial histories, Europeans and indigenous people gave words and names to whom, and to what, they perceived to be wild, to be savage. Trading with wildness as a concept and as a practice offered fertile grounds for linguistic exchange and creativity. Stories and words could be used, re-used, re-signified, or created anew for describing the perceived savagery, for example. Some words in particular, then, may encapsulate the history of this tense and mutual trade. The names indigenous people gave to European colonizers are relevant to understanding experiences and reactions to colonialism (see Likaka 2009). In this chapter, I follow the cross-cultural transits of one such name: the term *arbiru*,[1] once bestowed by East Timorese people as a name on a Portuguese colonial army officer in the 1890s, and still attached to his memory today. This term offers a revealing case study of the role of names and linguistic practices in the broader history of colonialism and its traffic with savagery. In addition, in the context of the present volume, it also makes it possible to discuss, through an ethno-historical (rather than psycho- or socio-linguistics lens), the ways in which transgression, wickedness, and disorder are conveyed and addressed through naming practices in colonial histories. *Arbiru* cannot be taken as a swear word or as taboo language (cf. Jay 2000; Jay and Janschewitz 2008; Ljung 2011). However, the Timorese uses of the word with reference to colonial warfare, as I intend to show, were aimed at signalling the extreme transgressive character of a colonial officer whose daring actions revealed him as a taboo-breaker, perhaps a kind of "swearer" in a non-linguistic sense. Ultimately, then, I argue, the name *arbiru* invoked wild powers and terrible dangers, and it became less a blessing than a curse that the Timorese speakers cast upon the savage mimetic violence of Europeans.

In 1899, during the dramatic siege by colonial forces of a "rebel" mountain village in Atabai – a secluded Timorese kingdom in the Portuguese colony of eastern Timor – the Portuguese commanding officer, *Alferes* (Second Lieutenant) Francisco Duarte was shot dead by his Timorese enemies. Despite his brief time in the colony (1892–99), the life and death of the army officer Duarte, also known by his Timorese nickname *Major Arbiru* or simply *Arbiru*, became legendary in colonial literature throughout the twentieth century. In Portugal and in Timor, he was posthumously celebrated as an imperial hero and became the object of intense colonial mythologizing. Between the 1930s and 1950s, in the atmosphere of the fascist *Estado Novo* regime established in 1933, a wealth of colonial propaganda, memorialistic literature and nationalist-imperialist historiography elevated him to the pantheon of "heroes" of Portuguese late imperial occupation in Africa and Asia. Central to this consecration of Officer Duarte as an imperial hero was his Timorese nickname – *arbiru*. To this word the Portuguese attributed a set of Timorese meanings associated with bravery, invincibility, and sacredness.

---

[1] This word, as we will see, can appear in different orthographies in Portuguese documentation. Unless it is a direct quote, or unless otherwise stated, I use here Tetum orthography according to Costa (2001).

Between 1959 and 1975 (the demise of Portuguese administration in Timor), the colonial government held an annual ceremony (the so-called *Festa do Arbiru*, 'Feast of the Arbiru') at the site of Duarte's death, where a memorial stone still marks the spot where he fell in battle. The Timorese nickname *arbiru* also entered the master Portuguese national narrative of imperial conquest through toponyms. Possibly in the 1960s, a street in Dili in colonial Timor was named after the famous officer – 'Street Second Lieutenant Duarte the arbiru' (*Rua Alferes Duarte o Arbiru*) – and in the 1970s a ship destined for coastal shipping was named *O Arbiru* ('The Arbiru'), as if to embody the aura of invincibility and superiority attached to the colonial reading of the nickname. In 1961, by the decision of the Lisbon City Council, a square in the Portuguese capital received the officer's name on account of his heroism overseas; because, the council proceedings justified it, "he was known in Timor by the nickname of 'Arbiru', a Tetum word that means 'invincible man, man who never rests.'"[2]

According to this lasting Portuguese imaginary, *arbiru* was an original Tetum word first applied to the officer by the Timorese people during the great punitive campaigns of the 1890s. It allegedly signified Timorese acknowledgement of Portuguese colonial invincibility and bravery; it signified the sacredness and supernatural powers with which the Timorese reverently endowed the Portuguese officer. However, this same word carried more complex meanings in Timorese linguistic practices, that colonial constructs overlooked. In Timor, the term *arbiru* evokes the kind of intrepid, daring, and dangerous actions associated with wildness, transgression, and random behaviour. This chapter confronts the colonial mythology with this hidden meaning of the word. In doing so, it ventures an alternative interpretation of the origins and significance of the officer's nickname. I first trace the history of this Timorese nickname as an object of Portuguese colonial anthropologies and mythologies of conquest and mimetic power – what I call the colonial mythopraxis of an indigenous name. I suggest that the name came to stand for colonial fantasies of symbolic power based on mimetic exercise of violence and warfare. Thus, the invention of *arbiru* as imperial hero needs to be placed in relation to a long-term and intimate relationship between the Portuguese colonizers and Timorese ritual violence.

---

[2] The square was – and still is – named *Largo Alferes Francisco Duarte* (see Câmara Municipal de Lisboa, Edital n. 215/1961, http://www.cm-lisboa.pt/index.php?id=8565 (accessed 7 December 2018). It may be indicative of the high symbolic standing of Francisco Duarte as *arbiru* in heroic mythologies of empire that his superior officer, Governor Celestino da Silva, only entered Lisbon toponymy ten years later. In 1971 a "Street General José Celestino da Silva (1848–1911)" was created (Câmara Municipal de Lisboa, Edital nº 80/1971, http://www.cm-lisboa.pt/index.php?id=8565) (accessed 7 December 2018).

The campaigns of the 1890s, in which Officer Duarte was a major protagonist, intensified and amplified this relationship to an important degree. I then contrast the colonial mythopraxis with alternative local meanings, etymologies, and Timorese notions. I argue that, rather than representing subjection and the blessing of a god-like colonial figure, the name constituted an invocation of the powers and dangers associated with the audacious, but also brutal, random, and potentially improper actions of Officer Duarte as war commander. Naming the officer as *arbiru*, I then argue, implied a critique of the colonizers' violent, transgressive, and wicked behaviour. I conclude suggesting the name *arbiru* represented a gesture through which the mimetic excesses of the colonial outsiders were simultaneously acknowledged, feared, criticized, and perhaps even cursed as a form of "savagery" – as a manifestation of wild forces and dangers, powerful and awe-inspiring but also terribly threatening and transgressive.

10.2 Colonial mythopraxis of a nickname

In 1896, the Governor of Timor, Colonel José Celestino da Silva, reported proudly to his superiors in Lisbon on military victories of the armed forces under his command. During the recent punitive campaign against the so-called "rebel" "Western kingdoms" of the colony, he explained: "Our forces marched triumphantly through the kingdom of Cová "destroying and burning everything, killing everyone who offered resistance, and revenging the death of so many of our people who lost their lives in those lands on different occasions, since remote ages" (Silva 1896).[3] The goal of the campaign was to retaliate and punish the people for the "massacre" of a Portuguese military column by Timorese enemy warriors. To achieve these results, the governor used almost exclusively indigenous irregular forces. This was in line with former local practices. For a long time the small and isolated community of Portuguese colonizers in Dili was limited to a handful of soldiers and officers. In the absence of European regulars, governors usually relied on two kinds of Timorese irregulars: the *moradores*, companies of indigenous irregular soldiers who served as volunteers; and the *arraiais*, larger contingents of native warriors provided to the colonial government on occasion of war, as tribute by the vassal Timorese kingdoms.[4] Consequently, colonial wars developed in the image of Timorese warfare, among which existed the practice of

---
[3] Throughout this essay all translations from Portuguese into English are mine.
[4] Here and in the following paragraph, I summarize materials and arguments developed at greater length in Roque (2010).

ritual headhunting. Portuguese governors and their army officers were, by custom, the commanders of these irregular armies of Timorese warriors. They accepted and embraced Timorese warfare; they encouraged the warriors' ritual violence in the service of the government; and, following Timorese dictates, they took upon themselves the role of indigenous war chiefs. This insertion of officers and governors into Timorese ritual life implied active, or passive, compliance with rites of war, including those deemed most "barbaric" by Europeans, such as the headhunting ceremonies of *lorosae* – victorious war chants and dances involving the exhibition and kicking of the severed heads of enemies, often also participated by the Portuguese authorities. The practical advantages of slipping into Timorese headhunting customs tended to prevail over concerns about moral integrity. Ritual violence and the decapitation of enemies were thus justified as a pragmatic expediency in colonial wars, as a means of strengthening Portuguese colonial rule. This approach came to constitute, as I have argued elsewhere, a mimetic and parasitic relationship with Timorese war customs perceived to be barbaric, in the service of colonial governmentality (Roque 2010: 17–38; 2018).

In 1896, the governor resorted to these expedients repeatedly. For, although it had been ordinary practice for a long time, the Portuguese engagement with the perceived "savagery" of Timorese ritual life in warfare was at its most liberal in the 1890s. Celestino da Silva's military campaigns were characterized by extreme violence, the mobilization of vast numbers of Timorese warriors, and by a deliberate engagement with the war customs of the Timorese irregulars. To surrender thus to indigenous "savage" ways could be understood as problematic in the light of the European Christian and "civilizing" ideals of colonization. Contemporary critics of Celestino da Silva's campaigns would denounce his methods as uncivilized. Nevertheless, the governor's strong-handed approach to conquest fitted well with the hard-line militarism that dominated Portuguese imperial policy. Further legitimated by a nationalistic thirst for conquest and revenge, the thirst to gain power from the wild forces of Timorese war customs and beliefs bore almost no limits in the 1890s. Hence, from the outset, the colonizers' fascination with the indigenization of the name *arbiru* can be framed as an event in a history of colonial violence performed as a quasi-dissolution of the colonizer in the savage space of alterity. To borrow again from Michael Taussig (1993: 36, inspired by Caillois 1984 [1935]), this extreme mode of being taken "bodily into alterity" configured a kind of "mimetic excess", a radical "immersion [of the self] in the concreteness of otherness".

In the 1890s, on behalf of fatherland and empire, colonial army officers and governors were eager to plunge openly into Timorese ritual violence. They seemed equally mesmerized by the effects their attraction towards mimetic excess provoked in the minds of the indigenous people themselves. In other words, colonial violence absorbed the perceived savagery of indigenous ritual warfare into its own dynamics of conquest to the point of absorbing – though distortedly, as I will argue below – indigenous words used to name the Portuguese as disruptive agencies of violence. The Portuguese understood the Timorese naming of Officer Duarte as an indigenous proof of colonial imaginaries of power. This understanding, in its turn, would give these imaginaries a new pace. The origins of the Portuguese mythopraxis of the officer's name, therefore, are located in narratives and imaginaries that celebrate colonial conquest as mimetic excess.

10.2.1 "Major Arebéro"

The Ministry of Navy and Overseas published Celestino da Silva's account of the victorious campaigns of 1896 (Silva 1897). Widely diffused, the resulting book would be commemorated as a landmark of imperial conquest and earned this governor a lasting reputation as the creator of "modern colonial occupation" of Timor in nationalist-imperialist readings. I have argued above, however, that this report bears evidence of the Portuguese drive to use, abuse, and even merge with the otherness of Timorese headhunting, as a strategy of colonial power and military conquest. The other reason why I highlight this report here is its foundational significance in the career of the name *arbiru* in colonial imaginaries. Indeed, it was through Celestino's glorifying war account that the colonial legend of Officer Duarte's Timorese name first became visible in the archival record. Celestino da Silva's report was the foundation stone of a pervasive colonial understanding of the officer as the incarnation of a kind of intangible power encapsulated in a word (*arbiru*, or *arebero*) and in an imaginary military rank of alleged indigenous origin: *Major Arebero*.

In 1896, following the governor's commendations, many Portuguese officers and some Timorese irregulars received official praise, military honours, and medals. Yet one man above all the others was considered worthy of the highest military honours: Second Lieutenant Francisco Duarte. For Governor Celestino, this officer stood out in the battlefield; he had excelled as a war commander of the *arraiais*: "[Francisco Duarte] brings together a rare knowledge of fighting in Timor," the governor stated in his report (1897: 44), "a very unusual serenity in the face of danger, a heroic character, bravery that stands as example for the bravest". The sheer force of his presence among the Timorese was moreover sufficient, alone, to sustain Portuguese "prestige" and "authority" in the difficult inland regions. The governor continued (1897: 44) in an extensive eulogy of this officer:

> In the campaign just reported, from Loiciba to Cova, [Second Lieutenant Francisco Duarte] was insurmountably heroic at Passa-Laran and at Sanirihi, and still recovering from such hard works he again called the people under his command to arms and led against Deribate the most tenacious and bloodiest war that has occurred in Timor, always the first to climb the trenches, animating all with his example, and always tireless in providing everything needed for his own people, always on the alert and vigilant. We owe to this officer our prestige and the exercise of our authority across the whole central and western region, that this officer commands with much wisdom, with exemplary diligence and with unassailable honesty.

Celestino da Silva here judged the officer according to the European heroic ethos and military standards of noteworthy behaviour in the war field. He praised his "bravery", his "heroism", his "honourable" character, his leadership based on "example" ("the first to climb the trenches", the governor remarked). This evaluation of the officer in the report of 1896 was followed up by the private praise given by the same governor in Duarte's personal military files for the years 1894–97. In his "private" assessments of the officer, Celestino da Silva indicated the man's warrior reputation among the Timorese: "he is the officer of greatest prestige in this colony;" "he has great prestige among the natives"; he is "truly heroic in every war", the governor observed (Silva, in Duarte 1894–97). The Portuguese authorities in Lisbon recognized the officer's local reputation by awarding him several official honours (*louvores*), all related to outstanding bravery in combat. Additionally, in January 1895, the imperial government granted Duarte the title "Officer of the Ancient and Noble Order of Tower and Sword for Worth, Loyalty and Merit" and, in recognition for his "feats" during the punitive campaigns of 1896, the Supreme Council of Military Justice in Lisbon decided to award him the "Gold Medal of the Class of Military Worth".

Yet the governor's above eulogy of Duarte's valour did not concern merely his adherence to the European military ethos. Importantly for my purposes, it concerned the extent to which the officer's military bravery had been recognised and allegedly sacralized by the Timorese warriors through the media of a nickname. A parallel phenomenon of Timorese cultural incorporation followed the officer's mimesis of indigenous savagery to the benefit of colonial conquest. Second Lieutenant Duarte, the governor implied above, possessed a profound knowledge of the Timorese ways of war that, in the end, translated into a quasi-magical Timorese acknowledgement of his warrior powers. Thus, in the governor's eyes, not only had Duarte been capable of taking possession and exerting command of the wild energies of the Timorese headhunters, but his actions had been indigenized in a most extraordinary manner. A Timorese nickname, *Major Arebero*, Celestino da Silva claimed, encapsulated this mysterious indigenization of the officer as Portuguese power made flesh. This nickname stood for a climax of the colonial mimetic process, as if the officer had achieved an*other* ontological status belonging in the Timorese world by receiving a Timorese name. Yet, more than simply a truthful imitation of the savage ways that made the officer similar to the Timorese Other, he had in fact through mimesis become magically superior to the original. This interpretation is discernible in the governor's concluding lines of his long eulogy on the official report. Celestino da Silva wrote (1897: 44):

> This officer is considered like a supernatural being among the natives, who realized that they should raise his military rank and nickname him very significantly; he is known by everyone as 'major *Arebéro*', a word from the Tetum language that means 'man who never rests, who achieves everything he conceives, *lulic* [sic] (sacred) man, invincible'.

In this early passage, considerations of the significance of the name in the Tetum language are accompanied by extrapolations of the symbolic supremacy achieved by the officer according to indigenous concepts of sacredness and power. For the governor, Francisco Duarte, due to his heroic actions in combat, had become more than an army officer; he had turned into a "sacred" and "supernatural being" through the media of Timorese beliefs. Above all, the governor considered the officer noteworthy through his acquisition of a certain indigenous nickname and a word, *arebero* (Silva's spelling for *arbiru*). For the governor, this term had two main characteristics. First, it was a term of pure Timorese origin ("a word from the Tetum language"). Second, it was a term with one univocal indigenous meaning. It meant "the one who never rests, the *lulik* (sacred) man, the invincible one". Thus, in this description, *arebero* was the name through which the "natives" acknowledged, on their own so-called "superstitious" terms, the superlative bravery of the commanding officer and, through him, also the superiority of the Portuguese colonial authority. In thus emphasising Second Lieutenant Duarte's superior colonial power as the result of indigenous belief in, and "recognition" of, "supernatural" warrior powers, the governor claimed for the Portuguese establishment possession of what Bourdieu termed "symbolic power". That is: "that invisible power which can be exercised only with the complicity of those who do not want to know that they are subject to it or even that they themselves exercise it" (Bourdieu 1991: 164). The name *Major Arebero*, therefore, was the mirror in which the Portuguese saw reflected their colonial fantasies of power as the exercise of a kind of symbolic power based on a kind of mimesis of savagery.

The passage suggests the officer's nickname was an exceptional event and offers straightforward translations of Tetum words. To begin with, however, the governor's assumptions of exceptionality and his translations require a few preliminary remarks. Firstly, the origins and meanings of the Timorese Tetum words at stake were more ambivalent than the governor acknowledged. The governor was referring to the Tetum language form also known as Tetum-Praça or Tetum-Dili (see Thomaz 1994: 613–635). Heavily influenced by the Malay and Portuguese languages since at least the seventeenth century, this form of Tetum became a local *lingua franca* across the complex plurilinguistic territory of East Timor, which comprised more than twenty distinct languages or dialects. Thus, it is unlikely, as argued further below, that this word was purely "indigenous", self-generated by a Tetum linguistic dynamics without external input. Secondly, translation of the Tetum term *lulik* simply as "sacred" overlooks the complex meanings of this term, among which are the ideas of "prohibition" and "danger" surrounding things, people, and landscape that fall into a *lulik* category. Most importantly, the colonial translation overlooks the fact that probably the adjective *lulik* was above all aimed at signalling the presence of the dangerous life-threatening potencies that animated the officer's bodily presence and actions. In Timorese conceptions, anthropologist Judith Bovensiepen recently observed, the complex term *lulik* entails far more than benevolent and life-giving sacredness: "The pure sacred maintains the moral order and the health of the community, while the impure sacred does the opposite: its transgressive tendency generates disorder, disease, and death" (Bovensiepen 2014: 123). Thus applied to people, things, or landscape, *lulik* can refer also to a kind of "transgressive sacred"; to "an active agent", an invisible potency, that can "destroy life"; to a "threatening and awe-inspiring force" that "can inspire horror and dread, as well as awe and fascination" (Bovensiepen 2014: 122–123). Henceforth, I believe, the Timorese conjunction of the notions of *arbiru* and *lulik* fundamentally expressed the officer's emanation of *lulik* as transgressive sacred – a powerful source of harm, destruction, and death. Finally, nicknaming Officer Duarte was not exceptional in Timorese naming practices. Double names were common. Colonial agents, moreover, were favourite objects of Timorese nicknaming.

10.2.2 Nicknaming the Portuguese authorities

During the Portuguese period, East Timorese people with double cultural affiliations to "Christianity" by baptism, on the one hand, and to indigenous cultural traditions by birth and kinship, on the other, could take on at least two personal names: a Christian or foreign name, related to an outsider affiliation;

and an autochthonous Timorese name. In the Portuguese period, foreign names were often taken from the (Portuguese) godfather, or alternatively adopted mimetically from notorious Portuguese officers and governors (see Thomaz 1994: 627; Correia 1935: 73). Furthermore, while at war, Timorese warriors could receive additional war nicknames on account of their warrior actions and persona (see Feijó 2008: 154–56). It was also not uncommon to find Portuguese colonial officers and governors as recipients of Timorese nicknames, bestowed upon the colonizers by their indigenous "subordinates". These nicknames could carry ambivalent meanings of parody, warning and critique. As such, they could in some cases represent a Timorese modality of what James C. Scott (1990: xii) has described as a "hidden transcript", "a critique of power spoken behind the back of the dominant". Governor Celestino da Silva himself, for example, was nicknamed *savarika* ('scorpion') during the terrible wars of the 1890s.[5] The prevalence of Timorese naming practices as a way of incorporating as well as subtly caricaturing or criticizing the Portuguese officers and governors did not pass without notice by the Portuguese. In 1935, for instance, in a widely diffused colonial ethnographic work, *Gentio de Timor*, Captain Armando Pinto Correia referred to the common Timorese practice of nicknaming the Portuguese colonial authorities. "One of the native's favourite hobbies is to occupy himself with authority," wrote Pinto Correia (1935: 95), "and there is no moral aspect or physical detail that they do not observe, that they do not memorize and disseminate in their talks. They enjoy giving nicknames to one another, and not even the whites escape it." And he went on to list a series of famous nicknamed officers and governors of the early twentieth-century (Correia 1935: 95–96) – including the *arbiru*:

> [Governor] Teófilo Duarte [...] – was known by the Timorese as *manu fuic*, in Tetum, wild cock. Governor Raimundo Meira, of friendly attitudes, became the *ema bote amenassa*, the big man who laughs (*ema bote* is the Tetum designation that the natives bestow on the governors, from *ema*, man, and *bote*, big). Lieutenant Manuel Valente, who was of such valour in the war of 1912, was nicknamed as the *bé nacali*, boiling water. Lieutenant Seabra, a good officer worker, who paid excellent services to the development of the colony, but who was severe towards the thieves, became the *catana* [*katana* 'sword']. My predecessor [in the post of Military Commandant of Baucau], Lieutenant Lemos, was the *bobolini*, the one who speaks too much. From *arebiro* [sic], decided, smart, they nicknamed Second Lieutenant Francisco Duarte, hero of Celestino's wars.

---

5 Indeed, Celestino da Silva himself (and/or an army officer named Francisco Xavier) is still known as *savarika* ('scorpion') among the Fataluku people of Lautem, in the eastern regions. It seems that the same term, *savarika*, can also be used in this area as a general name for the "Portuguese colonial government" (cf. Viegas and Feijó 2019: 197; Fitzpatrick, McWilliam and Barnes 2012: 163).

This rich passage suggests the name *arbiru* was one event within a structure of indigenous naming practices concerning the executives of Portuguese judicial-political and military authority (officers and governors). It also suggests that Timorese nicknames were aimed at signalling or caricaturing the officers' excessive, or potentially norm-breaking, actions as executors of power. In fact, significantly, the examples offered by Pinto Correia in the 1930s comprise a set of names that indicate or accentuate behaviour patterns of wildness, excess, abuse, in relation to the exercise of colonial authority in the realms of justice and war: the 'wild cock', the 'boiling water', the *katana*; the officer 'who speaks too much', and, finally, the *arbiru* (a term mistranslated here as simply decided and smart). Back in the 1890s, then, Duarte was the object of common Timorese practices concerned with the generation of second names for the Portuguese authorities in the realms of justice and warfare. These nicknames, as Pinto Correia was aware, were not mere signs of subservience. Instead they were ways through which the Timorese performed a subtle, acceptable kind of mockery and criticism of the colonial outsiders. Through nicknames that could carry hidden or ambivalent meanings, they creatively revealed and criticized the excesses of authority: the angry and wild commander; the over-laughing governor; the severe punisher; the talkative one. Hence it may be in this same vein that Officer Duarte was named the *arbiru*. Nonetheless, the note of criticism remained behind the curtain, as it were. For many decades, it went unnoticed by the Portuguese, who instead developed a distinct colonial mythology of the Timorese name. Celestino da Silva's war report was used as the source of origin for the colonial invention of "Francisco Duarte, the arbiru" as a hero of imperial conquest. The governor's early interpretation of the word would persist, with a few twists, in coming celebratory descriptions of the name. Yet this process of mythic invention did not happen immediately after the publication of Silva's report in 1897.[6] Three decades went past before Officer Duarte, the *arbiru*, took his place in the pantheon of imperial heroes.

10.2.3 The invention of the *arbiru* as imperial hero

Celestino's observations come up in the first heroic eulogy of Duarte in colonial literature and are inscribed in the laudatory biographical entry under the officer's name "Francisco Duarte", prepared for the major Portuguese-language

---

[6] No significant trace of the name of Francisco Duarte (including reference to his death in 1899) appears in the Portuguese written record until circa the 1930s (see Pélissier 1996: 186–88).

encyclopedia, the *Grande Enciclopédia Portuguesa e Brasileira*, published between 1936 and 1960, (see Anonymous 1936–60; Martins 1939). The consecration of the *arbiru* as an imperial hero throughout the twentieth century would reinforce old elements, but also add new ones, to Celestino da Silva's glorifying anthropology of the "native" name in the 1890s. During the twentieth century, the Portuguese colonial mythopraxis of the name revolved around two related themes: first, the idea (discernible already in Celestino da Silva's early note) that the term *arbiru* conveyed magical invincibility and invulnerability in war; and second, the notion (not explicit in Celestino's above description) that *arbiru* meant an outstanding capacity to overcome and dominate the difficulties of wild nature – ultimately by mimicking the wild "native warriors" themselves.

The suggestion that *arbiru* implied indigenous recognition of the officer's superior powers achieved through a skilful mimicry of Timorese "savage" Otherness was, as I will observe below, constitutive of the subsequent Portuguese constructs about the name. However, twentieth-century colonial constructs of the name would tend to erase traces of potential mockery or critique – such as the made up rank of "major" – in favour of a growing mythologizing of the officer as a kind of Timorese "sacred warrior-king". The fake military rank of "major" (*Major Arebero*), however, was perhaps a surreptitious Timorese invocation of the officer's dangerous powers, as commander of a second world, an *Other* world without social norms, where he and his men could take action in war without fear of breaking the rules. Yet, the Portuguese colonial literature after Celestino da Silva simply overlooked this detail. The association between *arbiru* and the imagined rank of "major" (a Timorese word game, I believe, a simulacrum of authority) disappeared. Instead, twentieth century colonial literature and memorabilia expanded and reinforced the governor's early mythologizing of Duarte as a super-human, heroic, "invincible" war chief in Timorese conceptions – and it is to this literature that I now turn.

The influential and rich writings of Captain José Simões Martinho, himself a colonial officer in Timor, stand out in the twentieth century heroic colonial literature about the *arbiru*. Martinho was among the first authors to pick up the theme of the name *arbiru* and to inscribe it in the nationalist historiography of imperial conquest that expanded exponentially under the *Estado Novo* fascist dictatorial regime in the 1930s–40s. In the 1910s, Martinho was appointed to the military command of Maubara, the late Officer Duarte's former district in the 1890s. Back home, after having served as colonial officer, military commander, and district administrator in Timor for twenty-five years, the captain claimed special ethnographic authority over the indigenous meaning of the name *arbiru*. In the late 1930s, he began a literary career as an "expert" on "colonial subjects" in the metropole. Building upon his colonial experience, he wrote on the history of Portuguese Timor, culminating in a widely cited ethnographic and historical monograph, published in 1943 (Martinho 1943).[7]

Martinho's writings about the *arbiru* are worth examining in detail because they contain the key components of the twentieth century colonial mythology of the name. In an early article, Martinho (1938: 208) highlighted the role played by Officer Duarte in the campaigns of 1895–96, in his indigenized avatar of *arbiru*: "He was already known among the Timorese people as *Major Arbiru*, the invincible man, man who achieves everything, 'Lulic' (sacred)." This passage basically reproduced Celestino da Silva's definition of 1897. But Martinho made a significant addition. He complemented it with a Timorese "legend" that had grown in Timor about the officer's violent death a few years later, in July 1899, during a subsequent punitive campaign at Atabai. According to this "legend", the *arbiru* could not be killed by an "ordinary bullet". This reference to a "Timorese legend" about the officer's bodily invulnerability to common bullets in battle added to the colonial construct of the indigenous nickname as an expression of the symbolic supremacy achieved in the magic-driven minds of the "natives" (Martinho 1938: 212).[8] In Martinho's writings, the tropes of invulnerability and invincibility come together with yet another characteristic of the officer's character that his nickname allegedly encapsulated: his skilful management of perceived Timorese "savagery" – both as regards wild nature and wild men. Thus, in his monograph of 1943, Martinho observed that "*Major Arbiru*, as the Timorese called *alferes* Duarte" was in accordance with *the* meaning of the Tetum word *arbiru* (note the fake rank "major" is being excluded from the nickname). This officer gave the following definition (1943: 74, italics in the original): "*Arbiru: person for whom there is no impossible, that conquers anything, that dominates nature itself.*" To this, he added reference to further Tetum phrases (Martinho 1943: 74):

> From that time [1890s] onwards it remains among the Timorese people a phrase that soon will not disappear from tradition: *Dálan Arbíru Nia = Caminhos à Arbíru* [*Arbiru* paths]. Truly, paths did not exist. Second Lieutenant Duarte, the *Arbiru*, crossing and beating rebel kingdoms with his *arraiais* [Timorese warriors], marched through the bush, not worried about the roughness of the land, although he sought the backs of the mountains, of open horizon, avoiding the valleys where ambush and betrayal would be easier and more successful.

---

7 Martinho's views on the *arbiru* resonate in Oliveira (1950: 373); and they continue to echo in more recent revisitations of the colonial mythology (see Gunn 2000: 245).
8 The bullet trope is systematically adapted in Portuguese constructs of the officer's name to emphasize the word's meaning of "invincibility" and the alleged supernatural condition of the military officer. I discuss the bullet trope in detail elsewhere (see Roque 2019).

Captain Martinho here reiterated that *arbiru* was only the name given to a real historical person, Francisco Duarte. It signified recognition of great powers to achieve anything desired and realize extraordinary feats of conquest. The above passage also introduces the idea that the name conveyed a special form of domination over the natural environment, an uncommon ability to overcome the difficulties that most Europeans encountered on the warpath in the mountainous country of Timor, that is: the capacity to find new pathways and overcome the treacherous terrain of the mountains. Dominating the wild nature of Timor, as well as conquering wild men were, then, Duarte's special powers, as revealed (so Martinho claimed) in the Tetum expression *Dálan Arbíru Nia*. In the same vein, later Portuguese mythmakers of Francisco Duarte kept referring to the prevalence of this Tetum phrase as proof of *arbiru* as a conqueror of wild nature that, in some instances, even resembled an animal, "a grasshopper" jumping through the hills, in the words of another colonial writer (Ferreira 1957: 9; see also Thomaz 1970). Martinho's translation of the Tetum phrase seems plausible (although *paths or ways of, or like the/an arbiru* could be other reasonable translations) and it is possible that such an expression was in common use in the mid twentieth century. But Martinho's interpretation is arguably narrow and biased. That phrase contained the ambivalent connotations of the term: both recognition of courage to go beyond established paths, and a word of alert and criticism of impetuosity and disorder. Tetum expressions using the word *arbiru* suggest distinct significations, beyond simply the historical person of the officer. Hence the phrase cited by Martinho (and by subsequent colonial officers) might have reflected general uses of this term as a critique of random behaviour without reference to the concrete historical person of Francisco Duarte.

10.2.4 *Arbiru*, the mimic man

The colonial mythopraxis culminated in a final construct of the word as an index to a kind of colonial mimicry. *Arbiru* meant dominance over men and mountains because, ultimately, the historical person, Duarte, had acted as a skilful imitator, a mimetic master, of Timorese wild violence. In this reading, the name revealed Timorese recognition of the colonial officer's skilful incorporation, and manipulation, of the alterity of Timorese war customs and roles. Hence the Portuguese colonial cult of the name *arbiru* implied the imagination of Duarte as a mimic man – a master of the colonial mimesis of indigenous wild nature, as well as of indigenous savage warfare. In this regard, Martinho's writings are also illuminating. In 1948, in an article published in the small regional newspaper *Diário de Coimbra*, Martinho elaborated further on *arbiru* as a war name attributed to

Duarte by both allied and enemy Timorese warriors. According to Martinho the name implied recognition of Duarte's role as war chief in the image of Timorese warlords. This similitude was of such a nature that the Timorese had elevated the officer to the status of a "war god". Martinho wrote (1948: 3):

> ARBIRU as he was called by his men of war; and, after both friends and enemies had learned about the brave officer's stiffness of spirit and the subtlety, almost oriental, of his tricks of war, this name never stopped being evoked with a mixture of awe and admiration. And so high they placed him, that the older warriors, in their simple-minded beliefs, considered him to be the beloved son of Fúnú, the war God.[9]

The officer was allegedly deified through the force of indigenous "naïve belief". This passage contains yet another aspect worth calling attention to. That is: the idea that the name *arbiru* and its god-like connotations were grounded on the mimetic tactics in which Officer Duarte excelled as a war commander. This officer ruled over the Timorese irregulars, Martinho would suggest, because he revealed a special mimetic capacity to become like Timorese warriors, to yield into the otherness of "their" savage customs, in order to exert power over the *arraiais* under his command and the enemies he confronted. Thus, Martinho referred above to Duarte's ability to enact war tricks in an "almost oriental" manner. "To the domination over the *arraiais* under his command", Martinho also added (1948: 3), "by accepting the processes of war that were tradition among the Timorese peoples, by being severe but human, the ARBIRU added the example of his temerity, tested in tens of assaults to the defences of the rebellious kingdoms." It is thus significant that Martinho's portrayal of the *arbiru* as an invincible warlord is created around the image of Duarte as mimic man, a colonial master of Timorese savagery, who skilfully took the Timorese ways of war as his own – including, implicitly, the barbarity of headhunting rites – to the benefit of the Portuguese victory. In the colonial imaginary of *arbiru*, then, the savagery attributed to Timorese Otherness was mastered and incorporated into the colonial Self, through the officer's skilful mimesis of alterity. Further in the same article, Martinho wrote (1948: 3; see also Oliveira 1950: 374):

> [Duarte] was, principally, a skilful leader of the *arraiais* and irregular troops. And those who followed him were so certain of victory when he was in command, that before an assault to the rebels' strongholds, they came next to him, to ask him, as if he was an old Datu-Lulic ["sacred chief, priest"], and similarly to the gentile ritual [*ritual gentílico*], for their immunity to the enemy's weapons.

---

[9] This presentation of the god-like and mimicking nature of Duarte is reproduced in Luna de Oliveira's widely nationalistic-imperialist history of Timor (Oliveira 1950: 373–75).

In Timorese warfare, including during the colonial campaigns, armed confrontations were understood as a clash of invisible forces and spiritual energies that were expressed through the mediation of warriors and weaponry. Life or death, victory or defeat, could be known in advance through divination rites; through preliminary rites, invisible hostile forces could be invoked. In combat, the energies of a kind of hostility magic interfered in combat through the agency of war costumes and amulets, and especially through *lulik* weapons endowed with extraordinary powers of hostility. Indigenous war cult lords designated as *rai lulik* or *dato lulik* were critical to the management of this war magic, and they usually followed the armies in battle to perform such rites.

Martinho's above passage thus suggest that Officer Duarte came to be seen by Timorese warriors as a kind of ritual war lord that embodied *lulik*. Not only was he perceived to be a *lulik* warlord of some kind, but he moreover performed this role willingly – as if embracing the Timorese warriors' invitation to merge with their own selves. This mutual attraction – apparently felt both by the Timorese warriors and by the Portuguese officers – towards the perceived Otherness of wild powers was a form of mimetic excess, as I mentioned above, characteristic of the 1890s punitive campaigns – an excess in which the actions of Second Lieutenant Duarte were entwined. In 1957, another colonial official, Manuel Ferreira, wrote about the *arbiru* in a similar vein. He imagined Francisco Duarte as a supreme leader of savage warriors. This leadership was achieved by undergoing a true metamorphosis, a transfiguration of his physical body and cultural persona into an entity of a "native" nature: "Picturesque figure," Ferreira wrote (1957: 9), "the *Arbiro* [sic] commanded his groups of Timorese [warriors], shouting and speaking to them in their native language." By embracing native war customs, by "speaking native language", Francisco Duarte became, strategically, a "savage" commander of "savages". Thus, in the emblematic figure of Officer Duarte, the Portuguese mythologists saw the ultimate mimic *condottiere* of wild men; they saw the carnal emanation of a colonial symbolic power of violence that inspired adoration, but also terror and awe, in Timorese spirits. The officer's art of governing the mimetic trade with savagery, in short, was central to the colonial imagination of his indigenization as *arbiru*. This construct, therefore, presumed that the officer's war savagery was acquired through mimesis of the indigenous customs of war. It was not an original part of the colonial self, either of the officer as an individual, or of Portuguese colonialism in general. "Savagery", then, was a quality and a capacity the colonizer had borrowed strategically and temporarily from the alterity of the Timorese world, for the mere sake of colonial domination (see Roque, 2018). In this way, the colonial mythology accepted the officer's mimetic excess, but tried to circumvent the symbolic threat that could come from confusing the virtuous colonial conquest with the alterity of savagery itself.

The nickname *arbiru* thus came to stand for the mesmerized subjection of indigenous people to the control of the colonizers; it came to epitomize colonial fantasies of conquest and power through mimesis. However, these colonial constructs overlooked and concealed alternative local meanings and uses of the word *arbiru*. As Janet Gunter (2004) insightfully observed in a brief note, the word *arbiru* in the Tetum language necessarily carries meanings associated with careless, transgressive, unruly, crazy actions. This suggests a rather more complex reading of the officer's indigenous significance that contrasts with – and even undermines – its celebratory colonial interpretations. Thus, although it seems uncontroversial that Second Lieutenant Francisco Duarte was named *arbiru* and/or *Major arbiru* by the Timorese, significant local meanings of the term were never considered in the Portuguese colonial accounts. In the following section I expand on the alternative and plural connotations and etymologies of the name. I bring forward its associations with the transgressive realm of "swearing and cursing" in which this volume dwells, through its meanings of transgression, wickedness, and disorder. These associations, I believe, help to subvert, or at least destabilize, the colonial fantasies that have long inhabited the term.

10.3 A word for disorder and wickedness

The word *arbiru* does not appear in the first Tetum-Portuguese dictionary, prepared by the Portuguese colonial official Rafael das Dores in the 1870s–90s. First published in 1904, Dores's dictionary is however based on materials collected between 1871 and 1892 – and thus prior to the historical presence of Francisco Duarte in Timor.[10] This absence may suggest the limitations of this first dictionary; it may suggest that the word *arbiru* was either not used or had a rather restricted use in Tetum linguistic practice; or it may even suggest that *arbiru* was *not* seen as an ordinary and authentic word of the Tetum language before the wars of the 1890s. Decades later, however, the word does appear in a new Tetum-Portuguese dictionary prepared by Catholic missionaries in Timor and published in Lisbon in 1935 (although work had began in 1915). This dictionary records an ambivalent meaning. *Arbiru*, this dictionary writes, was first and

---

10 Officer Rafael das Dores, was in Timor in 1871–1873, 1878–1879, 1886 and 1891–1892. His dictionary (dated 1902) was first published in 1904 in the *Bulletin of the Geographical Society of Lisbon* and in 1907 as a book (Dores 1907). On the history and origins of dictionaries and grammars in colonial East Timor, see Cardoso (2017).

foremost used as an adverb, meaning: "At ease, not taking anything into consideration, at your own leisure [*a seu belprazer*], without giving explanations to anyone;" and, secondly, as an adjective: "fearless, hero" (Mendes and Laranjeira 1935: 7). The modern and still referential dictionary of Tetum-Portuguese, prepared in 2001 by the East Timorese scholar and linguist Luís Costa (2001: 40), records the same meanings. Here, if used especially as an adjective and applied to a person, the Tetum term *arbiru* may convey heroic, fearless, and daring actions. If used as an adverb, however, it suggests free, random, egoistical, actions, without attending to rules or norms, "*halo arbiru de'it:* acting without giving explanations to anyone."

The presence of the word in Tetum-Portuguese dictionaries since 1935 (not earlier) suggests that *arbiru* was translated or received in the Portuguese language in the heroic idiom of colonial mythology that had crystallized the *Portuguese* meaning of the word since at least the 1890s. It is also important to observe that the actual Tetum term for designating war bravery or brave warriors is not *arbiru*. During the 1890s–1900s and still today, the Tetum word used for naming and elevating a warrior's standing for his courage in combat is *asuaín*. Hence, the meaning given to *arbiru* in Tetum-Portuguese dictionaries as an adjective that conveys bravery and heroism may not be originally Tetum. It is probably a historical record, already, of the prevalence and impact of the colonial mythology. It is perhaps also in accordance with this hypothesis that the meaning of *arbiru* as a qualifier for "hero" appears only in Tetum-Portuguese language dictionaries. Tetum-English dictionaries do not include this latter meaning of the word in relation to the indigenous Tetum language. Instead, they offer a univocal definition of *arbiru* with reference only to the adverbial content of the word: "*arbiru* adv. arbitrarily, randomly, at random, without good reason" (Williams-van Klinken 2015); similarly, Hull (2001) notes *arbiru* as meaning simply "adv. at random".[11] One can hypothesize, then, that the adjective form of the word, rather than recording an original form of Tetum meaning, is above all an indicator of the colonial history of the term in Portuguese imageries.

This suggests that the adverb form of *arbiru* in Tetum can offer reliable indications of the early indigenous meanings attached to Duarte's nickname. As an adverb, as we have seen, the word evokes, principally, transgression and disorder. In particular, it conveys criticism and caution with regard to random behaviour and to those almost improper and impolite social actions that – like, perhaps, swear words in linguistic practice – constitute potential violations of established norms; or, alternatively, as Gunter has also suggested, the term

---

11 I thank Zuzana Greksáková (p.c.) for this information.

conveys someone who is behaving out of his mind, like the English phrase "running amok" (Gunter 2004). In 2012, in a personal conversation about the complexities of this word in Lisbon, East Timorese linguist Luís Costa emphasized this connection.[12] For Costa, applying the term *arbiru* to people's actions is evocative not simply of random, but especially of dangerous, disrespectful and improper social behaviour, a characteristic, for instance, of someone with no manners who acts almost crazy. Costa thus explained to me that *arbiru* is used in the Tetum language with reference to a kind of fearless behaviour or attitude of someone who is, or acts "*desgarrado* [going astray]"; who is crazy or behaves in a crazy way. It is applied to somebody who "*segue tudo à bruta* [acts so uncouth], without order; who does not follow rules; *à toa* [aimlessly]." The term conveys, then, according to Costa (2012 p.c.) "also violence, but principally *insensatez* [folly, madness]."

Hence, in contrast to the colonial interpretations, it is in accordance with this latter meaning that the word *arbiru* ordinarily appears in a variety of popular Tetum phrases. It is used in everyday language in expressions that convey warning, caution, or criticism concerning random, potentially dangerous, or disrespectful actions, including speech forms. Such characteristic expressions of caution include *Koalia arbiru* ('to speak randomly'); and *La bele halu arbiru deit* ('You cannot do things randomly, with no manners'). Importantly, as Luís Costa highlighted (2012 p.c.), *arbiru* behaviour is epitomized by the image of a person who decides, thoughtlessly and against the rules, to enter one of the most highly regulated zones of Timorese social and ritual life – i.e., a lineage or community's sacred house (*uma lulik*) – without prior permission from the entitled ritual guardians. In such circumstances, the term serves not simply to criticize, but also, it seems, to warn against a potential transgression that may result in a tragic curse coming upon the one who is, or acts, *arbiru*. This web of meanings can be specifically evoked in conversations concerning the memory of Officer Duarte, the *arbiru*. In 2013, Mr Orlando Xavier, an elder from Nuno Mogue, Ainaro, vaguely recalled a certain Portuguese officer under that name. Yet he defined *arbiru* as denoting "without order" and "disrespect towards the law or the will of others". As such, the word *arbiru* was here used as a special sign of warning and caution in connection with rule-breaking

---

12 *Arbiru* constitutes one simple word (rather than a compound term). For this reason the hypothesis – raised by myself in a conversation with Luís Costa – that *arbiru* could result from association with the word *biru* should be rejected. *Biru* is a term commonly used to refer to talismans, namely those used in warfare. However, Costa clarified that *biru* is an Indonesian term that was appropriated by the Timorese. The actual native Tetum word for talisman or amulet is *buissóle*.

actions in ritual contexts where strict obedience to social precepts and respect towards the social standing of others is of the greatest importance.[13]

Thus, against the colonial mythopraxis, the uses and meanings of *arbiru* in the Tetum language invite us to rethink the indigenization of the historical actor. The word carried a double, ambivalent, meaning that the colonizers never considered. Whilst it entailed recognition of an outstanding capacity to act fearless and daringly in war, it also conveyed alarm and criticism concerning the dangers that ill-mannered and transgressive behaviour could unleash. Perceived to be a transgressor, Duarte's commanding powers could be strong and magnetic, but also dangerous and evil. This ambivalence in the term, then, rather than mere subjection to a sacred warrior-king, seems to have signified a veiled critique and a word of caution as regards the great dangers and curses that the officer's terrifying actions in war might bring tragically upon him and upon those who followed his path. Furthermore, and also against the colonial mythology, the Timorese warriors possibly did not bestow upon the wild officer a nickname that originated in "indigenous" linguistic stock. They used a borrowed word. They named the colonial outsider officer using an autochthonous word with outsider origins.

10.3.1 Luso-Asian creolizations

Colonial mythopraxis of the name assumes that *arbiru* was a native word of the Tetum language. In the 1890s, this word had possibly already been incorporated into the plastic repertoire of Tetum-Praça. As mentioned above, this was a variant of Tetum strongly associated with the Portuguese language that developed from centuries of contact between Tetum, Malay, and Portuguese-language speakers. In the course of this history of linguistic contact, the word *arbiru* was possibly appropriated and integrated into Tetum-Praça from foreign origins. Indeed, as Tetum scholar Zuzana Gretsáková (2015 p.c.) explained to me, there is a very high probability that this is an imported word, since "99% of Tetum words starting with the prefix *ar* are borrowings", in this case possibly an archaic borrowing. This borrowing probably occurred in the context of a shared history of linguistic transits between Portuguese and Asian languages. It was one of many expressions of a process of formation of Luso-Asian creoles, as the Portuguese established their maritime and commercial influence across Asia in the late fifteenth century.

---

[13] Orlando Xavier, Interview with Gonçalo Antunes, Nuno Mogue, Ainaro. June 2013. I am grateful to Gonçalo Antunes for sharing his fieldwork data.

Strong similarities between the Tetum meanings of *arbiru* and the meanings of similar terms (*arviru, arviro*) in the Luso-Asian creoles of Macau and Malacca – the two most important Portuguese trading outposts in early modern Asia – support this tentative hypothesis. Maritime connections and circulations of commodities and people between Timor and Macau were especially significant after the Portuguese loss of Malacca in 1641, and for many decades in the nineteenth century, the district of Timor was subordinated to the administrative authority of Macau. In this period, Thomaz hypothesizes (1994: 630), many Portuguese neologisms may have been incorporated into Tetum-Praça through Macau (the very Tetum term *macau* then came to stand for 'foreigner, imported'). *Arbiru* may have been one of these imported words. The words *arviro* and *arvirice* were (and still are) used among speakers of Macanese Patois (a Luso-Asian creole language spoken in the Portuguese colony of Macau) to convey meanings of playful wicked tricks and evil or naughty doings. Ferreira's (1967) first Macanese Patois-Portuguese dictionary records this meaning: "*Arvirice* – Play; wickedness; children's trick; *Arviro* – wicked [*Mauzinho*]; playful; child who enjoys doing naughty tricks". Fernandes and Baxter's more recent English vocabulary of Macanese Patois (2004) also describes this creolized word in terms that are in striking harmony with the Tetum uses of *arbiru*:

> **Arviro** [ar'viru], [ari'viru], **araviro** [ara'viru] *n* (<*M. haru biru*). 1. Trick, prank. 2. Naughty person, somebody who likes to fool around or play pranks.

With similar or related meanings, it seems this word had wider circulation within other Portuguese based creoles of Asia. In contemporary Malaccan Luso-Asian creole (the so-called Kristang), for instance, the word *azbiru* is used to convey 'confusion, fuss'. On this basis, Fernandes and Baxter (2004) suggested that the Kristang word *azbiru* might be etymologically linked to the Malayan expression *haru-biru* (a phrase, however, used in Malayan and Indonesian languages to mean 'commotion' or 'outcry' in a sense rather different from its Luso-Asian creole variants). However, an earlier Portuguese dictionary of this same Malaccan creole, published in 1942 by the Catholic missionary and linguist António da Silva Rêgo, suggests a different (Portuguese rather than Malayan) etymology that seems to resonate more accurately with the Tetum meanings of the term *arbiru*. In Rêgo's dictionary (1942), the word *arbiro* in Malaccan creole means "*transtorno, mudança*" (upset/disorder, change). Yet the author attributes the origins of this word to the Portuguese expression *arreviro*, a term popularly used in the sense of *revirar*, that is, to change or to upset a certain state of things.

In the light of the rather similar uses of *arbiru* in Tetum and in Macanese creole, it is plausible to conjecture that the word was incorporated into Tetum through a Portuguese or Luso-Asian linguistic filter, rather than through a Malayan one. In any case, even if the etymological origins of *arbiru* or *arviro* remain ambivalently located in Malayan and/or Portuguese languages, one fact seems clear. Historically, this word had a strong presence among the Lusophone speakers of Southeast Asia. Across Lusophone Southeast Asia, in the main Portuguese-based languages of the Portuguese Asian colonies, its significance was evocative of wicked behaviour, naughtiness, and social disorder. So it was in the Malaccan Kristang, in the Macanese Patois, and, finally, in the East Timorese Tetum-Praça. In the light of its Luso-Asian sources, therefore, the Timorese naming of Duarte as *arbiru* may have been a recognition of the officer's persona as a radical expression of tumult and disorder; as a special manifestation of wickedness and evil in war; as a force of impoliteness, terror, and danger that interfered with and disrespected proper rules. Colonial *arbiru* was thus articulated in language as a transgressive persona that, as historical events confirmed, could but end his life in tragedy.

10.3.2 The death of the *arbiru*

The name *arbiru* conjured up critique and alarm, rather than surrender and subjection; it pointed to the officer's embodiment of *lulik* potencies of threat and danger, rather than of benign and secure energies. This set of meanings helps explain why the term *arbiru* ultimately served also as a Timorese interpretive device for explaining the causes of the officer's own tragic death in battle, in 1899. The Timorese associations of *arbiru* with bravery, wildness, disrespect, disorder, and the resulting dangers are encapsulated in a rich and complex folk song about the events that led to the death of Francisco Duarte at the site of Hatu Bui Kari, Atabai, in 1899. This song, which still survives in local memory at Atabai, celebrates Timorese victory and resistance against the Portuguese invaders. In the two final verses, it evokes the name of *arbiru*:

> *Arbiru mane sia soi*
> *Mi ligo bali hen no anan*
>
> Arbiru is a brave man
> But he forgot he had wife and children[14]

---

14 My English version is based on Tetum and Portuguese translations of the Kemak original collected at Atabai in July 2012, and kindly arranged by Sr. Alfredo Martins (Atabai) and Dr Vicente Paulino (UNTL Dili). For an analysis of this folk song, see Roque (2019).

This song culminates with what I read as a powerful social critique of the *arbiru*, preceded by an acknowledgement of his bravery. Francisco Duarte was married to a woman in Timor. A "brave man" *arbiru* was indeed, the song ends, but "he forgot he had wife and children". *Arbiru* was neglectful of social ties and disregarded proper norms – he even forgot obligations to his close kin. Hence the song's moral lesson: Duarte was no god after all; he was a social being; he was human, like any other. His death comes as a reminder of what happens to someone who recurrently breaks and disrespects social norms, causes terror and disorder, and ultimately forgets the social bonds of his own humanity. Ultimately, then, it was *Arbiru*'s own excesses – mimetic excesses, perhaps – that caused his tragic death. The nickname was a promise of disaster. It carried in itself the curse of the officer's terrible destiny.

10.4 The curse of the wild man

Cosmology and myths are often regarded as important cultural idioms through which indigenous societies understood and coped with histories of colonial contact. In Timor-Leste, the indigenous inclination to incorporate the Portuguese colonial outsiders through cosmological narratives, as returning ancestors, is well documented (see Traube 1986). In this chapter, however, it was not cosmology and myth that the indigenous idiom of cultural incorporation expressed. I have shifted attention from the grand narratives of indigenous cosmology to more subtle and minute linguistic practices of naming. I have followed a term that allows us to address the issue of the indigenization of colonialism through the lens of the complex transits between civilization and savagery. I have considered indigenous naming as a form of incorporation, control, and critique of the unruly and wild character of European outsiders. Indigenous words and nicknames – such as the term *arbiru* applied to a colonial officer – can be ways of incorporating and manipulating the perceived savagery of European outsiders; they can be ways of managing both the great powers and great dangers associated with their transgressive and disordering behaviours. Mythology, in contrast, appeared in my analysis as a colonial European, rather than an indigenous Southeast Asian, cultural idiom of incorporation in reverse. Heroic myth making, I suggested, was above all a practice of the colonizers, through which the Portuguese incorporated and articulated words and linguistic practices of perceived indigenous origin. Portuguese colonial mythologies of conquest were fed by partial and distorted interpretations of Timorese forms of naming the actions and identities of colonial outsiders as mimic agents of local war customs. These mythologies led to the invention of Duarte, the *arbiru*, as a mimic hero of imperial conquest. In Timorese nicknaming, the colonizers saw reflected their fantasies of power. Duarte the *arbiru* thus emerged as an agent of supernatural forces extracted from his alleged mimetic entanglement with Timorese customs of war. The word *arbiru* was profusely mythologized in Portuguese imaginaries of conquest and mimesis – and yet this word was not mere fantasy. Nicknaming Duarte as *arbiru* was real. As this chapter also demonstrated, the name referred to certain local conceptions and naming practices that carried indigenous cultural significance.

An important trait of the Portuguese colonial construct of the word *arbiru* was the fact that it was fed by the Portuguese fascination with the Timorese alleged fascination with the figure and action of the military officer as a mimic commander imbued with a kind of symbolic war power. The belief that, by naming Duarte as *arbiru*, the Timorese endowed this officer alone with supernatural qualities and sacred-like powers, was a recurrent trope in Portuguese accounts. Yet this colonial mythology was full of occlusions and biases. It first occluded and embellished the mimetic dramas of violence and terror, in which, as I argued above, the officer's war name *arbiru* originally emerged in the 1890s. By evoking the word *arbiru*, colonial accounts saw the officer's mimetic savagery not as an integral constituent of the imperial self, but as an intelligent mastering of Timorese images and conceptions. The officer's "savagery", as it were, was but a temporary mirror image of Timorese otherness. Accordingly, the officer's metamorphosis into *arbiru* through Timorese naming was celebrated as an achievement of imperial conquest. In the colonial eyes, naming him *arbiru* was little more than a reflection of indigenous surrender to the higher powers of the Portuguese in Timor, in the service of a self-glorifying narrative of conquest and supremacy. Therefore, at no point in the colonial heroic literature is there space for considerations that could destabilize or contradict the meaning of the word in relation to this narrative. Yet, as this chapter has revealed, in the Timorese uses of the word *arbiru* in Tetum language, there was much more than met the heroic colonial eye.

Indigenization through naming pointed to the dark side of colonial mimesis. It pointed also to a cultural form of incorporating the colonial officer that implied a gesture of estrangement of the same fearless officer as a wild agent, Other to one's own social and cultural forms of order. In East Timorese cultural notions, transgressors of norms and precepts incur serious dangers that can lead to their own misery and ultimately to death. The officer's mimetic excesses in warfare perhaps read similarly as an outsider's extreme drive to wickedness and transgression. Thus, as I believe the Kemak folk song reveals, calling "Duarte the *arbiru*" also acted as an index of the grave dangers of the officer's careless, evil, and almost mad actions as a military commander. For the Timorese, the colonizer's extreme mimesis of savagery in colonial campaigns was apparently not understood as a way of becoming alike the Timorese. Through the indigenous nickname he received, the officer was marked by the Timorese as Other-within; as an incorporated outsider entity that belonged to a powerful and dangerous kind of ontological alterity. The nickname *arbiru*, I believe, was a Timorese way of simultaneously accepting and othering Officer Duarte as a sort of stranger-savage himself, who could instantiate terrible powers and infernal dangers in the world.

Thus, to carry the name *arbiru* did not merely empower his human bearer, Second Lieutenant Francisco Duarte, to achieve war victories and realize outstanding military actions, beyond order, beyond measure. Being named the *arbiru* was less a blessing than a terrible, and terrifying, symbolic weight. It was also *in potentia* an invocation for harm or injury to come upon the bearer of the name, the wild colonial officer. Hence the name "*Major Arbiru*" did not express indigenous subjugation to and the benediction of colonial outsiders. It was a promise of disaster that would befall upon the unruly colonial venture. It was an invocation of the powers and dangers unleashed by a wild man, whom Timorese warriors could but follow to their own risk. It was also a sign of warning and a mark of savagery. It was – ultimately – a curse.

Acknowledgments: Research for this essay was funded by the Fundação para a Ciência e Tecnologia (FCT), Portugal (grant references HC/0089/2009 and PTDC/HAR- HIS/28577/2017). For generous and fruitful exchanges on the *arbiru*, I am grateful to Gonçalo Antunes, Alan Baxter, Hugo C. Cardoso, Luís Costa, Janet Gunter, Sabina da Fonseca, Zuzana Greksáková, Vicente Paulino, and Lúcio Sousa. Finally, I thank Nico Nassenstein and Anne Storch for insightful comments on an earlier version of this chapter.

References

Anonymous. 1936–60. Francisco Duarte. *Grande Enciclopédia Portuguesa e Brasileira*, vol. IX, p. 319. Lisboa: Editorial Enciclopédia.
Bourdieu, Pierre. 1991. *Language and Symbolic Power*. Cambridge: Polity Press.
Bovensiepen, Judith. 2014. *Lulik*: Taboo, Animism, or Transgressive Sacred? An Exploration of Identity, Morality and Power in Timor-Leste. *Oceania* 84 (2): 121–37.
Caillois, Roger. 1984 [1935]. Mimicry and Legendary Psychastenia. *October* 31: 16–32.
Cardoso, Hugo C. 2017. Descrições Portuguesas das Línguas de Timor-Leste na Transição dos Séculos XIX e XX. *Moderna Sprak* 1: 1–34.
Correia, Armando Pinto. 1935. *Gentio de Timor*. Lisboa: Lucas & Ca.
Costa, Luís. 2001. *Dicionário Tetum Português*. Lisboa: Colibri.
Dores, Rafael das. 1907. *Diccionario Teto-Português*. Lisboa: Imprensa Nacional.

Feijó, Rui G. 2008. Língua, Nome e Identidade numa Situação de Plurilinguismo Concorrencial: o Caso de Timor-Leste. *Etnográfica* 12 (1): 143–72.
Fernandes, Miguel Senna and Alan N. Baxter. 2004. *Maquista Chapado – Vocabulary and Expressions in Macao's Portuguese Creole*. Macau: Instituto Internacional.
Ferreira, José dos Santos. 1967. *Macau sã assi*. Macau: Missão do Padroado.
Ferreira, Manuel. 1957. *Timor. Sua Terra, Sua Gente e Sua História*. s.l., s.ed.
Fitzpatrick, Daniel, Andrew McWilliam and Susanna Barnes. 2012. *Property and Social Resilience in Times of Conflict: Land, Custom and Law in East Timor*. London: Ashgate.
Gunn, Geoffrey. 2000. *New World Hegemony in the Malay World*. Lawrenceville/Asmara: The Red Sea Press.
Gunter, Janet. 2004. Arbiru. http://raiketak.wordpress.com/2011/04/04/arbiru/ (accessed 24 August 2014).
Hull, Geoffrey. 2001. *Standard Tetum-English Dictionary*. London: Allen & Unwin.
Jay, Timothy and Kristin Janschewitz. 2008. The Pragmatics of Swearing. *Journal of Politeness Research* 4: 267–288.
Jay, Timothy. 2000. *Why We Curse: A Neuro-Psycho-Social Theory of Speech*. Philadelphia/Amsterdam: John Benjamins Publishing Company.
Likaka, Osumaka. 2009. *Naming Colonialism: History and Collective Memory in the Congo, 1870–1960*. Madison: University of Wisconsin Press.
Ljung, Magnus. 2011. *Swearing. A Cross-cultural Linguistic Study*. Basingstoke: Palgrave Macmillan.
Martinho, José Simões. 1938. Os Portugueses no Oriente: Elementos para a História da Ocupação de Timor. In *AAVV, Primeiro Congresso da História da Expansão Portuguesa no Mundo*, 189–212. Lisboa: Sociedade Nacional de Tipografia.
Martinho, José Simões. 1943. *Timor: Quatro Séculos de Colonização Portuguesa*. Porto: Livraria Progredior.
Martinho, José Simões. 1948. O Arbiru. *Diário de Coimbra*, 27 January, p. 3.
Martins, Ferreira. 1939. *Glórias e martírios da colonização portuguesa (III)*. Lisboa: Colecção Pelo Império.
Mendes, Manuel Patrício, and Manuel Mendes Laranjeira. 1935. *Dicionário Tétum-Português*. Macau: N.T. Fernandes & Filhos.
Oliveira, Luna de. 1950. *Timor na História de Portugal*. Lisboa: Agência Geral das Colónias.
Pélissier, René. 1996. *Timor en guerre: le crocodile et les portugais (1847–1913)*. Orgeval: Ed. Pélissier.
Rêgo, António da Silva. 1942. *Dialecto Português de Malaca: Apontamentos para o seu Estudo*. Lisboa: Agência Geral das Colónias.
Roque, Ricardo. 2010. *Headhunting and Colonialism: Anthropology and the Circulation of Human Skulls in the Portuguese Empire, 1870–1930*. Basingstoke: Palgrave Macmillan.
Roque, Ricardo. 2018. Dances with Heads: Parasitic Mimesis and the Government of Savagery in Colonial East Timor. *Social Analysis* 62 (2): 28–50.
Roque, Ricardo. 2019. The Death of the *Arbiru*: Mythic Praxis and the Apotheosis of Officer Duarte. In Ricardo Roque and Elizabeth Traube (eds.), *Crossing Histories and Ethnographies: Following Colonial Historicities in Timor-Leste*, 93–130. Oxford: Berghahn.
Scott, James C. 1990. *Domination and the Arts of Resistance: Hidden Transcripts*. New Haven and London: Yale University Press.

Silva, José Celestino da, to Minister of Navy and Overseas Affairs, [x] Oct. 1896. Lisboa, Arquivo Histórico Ultramarino. Macau e Timor. Repartição Militar. ACL_SEMU_DGU_RM_005_Cx 1. 1890–1899.

Silva, José Celestino da. 1894–97. Private Assessments of Second-lieutenant Francisco Duarte, Processo Individual de Francisco Duarte. Lisboa, Arquivo Histórico Militar, Caixa 1052.

Silva, José Celestino da. 1897. *Relatório das Operações de Guerra no Distrito Autónomo de Timor no Anno de 1896 enviado ao Ministro e Secretário dos Negócios da Marinha e Ultramar*. Lisboa: Imprensa Nacional.

Taussig, Michael. 1993. *Mimesis and Alterity: A Particular History of the Senses*. London: Routledge.

Thomaz, Luís Filipe [L. T.]. 1970. O Arbiru. *A Província de Timor*, 27 July.

Thomaz, Luís Filipe. 1994. *De Ceuta a Timor*. Lisboa: Difel.

Traube, Elizabeth. G. 1986. *Cosmology and Social Life: Ritual Exchange among the Mambai of East Timor*. Chicago: University of Chicago Press.

Viegas, Susana Matos, and Rui Graça Feijó. 2019. Funerary Posts and Christian Crosses: Fataluku Cohabitations with Catholic Missionaries After World War II. In Ricardo Roque and Elizabeth Traube (eds.), *Crossing Histories and Ethnographies: Following Colonial Historicities in Timor-Leste*, 177–202. Oxford: Berghahn.

Williams-van Klinken, Catharina. 2015. *Tetun-English Interactive Dictionary*. 2nd edition. http://www.tetundit.tl/Publications.html#Tetun_dictionaries_and_glossaries (accessed 20 February 2019).

Part III: **Disruptive and trashy performance**

Angelika Mietzner
11 Found and lost paradise: Bad language at a beach in Diani, Kenya

Abstract: Diani Beach in Kenya is a space where speakers violate norms through language practices that do not include swear words but tend to challenge the notion of the beach as "paradise", and its rules of politeness, respect and privacy. Language here is used in exchanges where the hosts' presence conflicts with the social expectations of guests, in terms of how they expect to be approached, addressed, and left alone. This results in extreme emotional behaviour as a perlocutionary effect of offence (Culpeper 2011) and presents the beach as a space of transgression.

This article will give an insight into the encounters between Europeans and Kenyan beach boys in a space of bizarre relations and interdependencies of real life and "holiday dreams".

11.1 Introduction

All along the coast of Kenya, tourists encounter Kenyan beach vendors, commonly known as *Beach Boy*s. These tourism workers control an impressive linguistic repertoire, which includes English as well as snippets of German, French, Italian and Czech, mainly depending on which section of beach they work on. They acquire such communicative skills locally, at the *Beach Academy*, as they refer to their informal working environment. This is the public space where they meet other beach boys, where stories are exchanged and new words and phrases are circulated.

This space is contradictory with regard to colonised communicative practices but even more with regard to colonial behaviour mixed with the awareness of White guilt and the intentional reconstruction and inversion of colonial hierarchies. It is a space where tourists are called *mzungu* 'foreigner, European' and tourism workers are called beach boys, ignoring the hierarchical and colonial assumptions inherent in the term *boy*. Calling somebody *boy* does not result from any kind of reflection among the tourists; rather, it seems to be in perfect order, as this is what everybody calls them. Yet it is laden with negative connotations, and thus, none of the tourism workers themselves would refer to themselves as beach boys (see Section 11.3.1).

Numerous tourism studies reflect the concept of postcolonialism and neo-colonialism (e.g. Nash 1977). What is striking in these contexts is the wordlessness of the subjects who fill the touristic places with meaning, namely the locals, whose actions and interactions with tourists contribute to the holiday space. But in Diani Beach, the tourism workers have acquired an impressive repertoire of the guests' languages. They have knowledge of English, German, French, Italian, Czech and even Russian (Nassenstein 2016: 123), and use this repertoire in order to be able to speak back and thus gain an advantage (Chow 2014). Because the beach boys are able to use the language that is forced upon them by tourists, they are able to control the unequal economic situation.

This study intends to illustrate a part of tourism that reflects the agency of the subject in the postcolonial context, as has also been discussed by Heller, Jaworski and Thurlow (2014). As people who are often seen as the Other (Fanon 1952; Said 1978) or the subaltern (Spivak 1988), the *beach boys* use their language abilities to speak back, subvert, and turn existing structures upside down, creating new structures that have an impact on the tourists' behaviour.

In Diani Beach, people and language are on the move (see also Thurlow and Jaworsky 2011). The *beach boys*, who are the ones filling the beach with conversations and emotions, are also the ones who use language as a tool for privacy and business. They are highly flexible with respect to the language that a tourist speaks and to his cultural background.

11.2 Transgressive language

The beach or seaside has been the focus of research mainly in sociological studies (e.g. Shields 1991), social history (e.g. Lenček and Bosker 1998; Walton 2000) and cultural geography (e.g. Preston-Whyte 2004). It has been defined as a liminal space, whereby the liminality mainly concerns restricted concepts of the beach, such as nudist spaces, surfing spaces or spiritual spaces (Preston-Whyte 2004). The beach has been explored from a sociologist perspective, where people of various social backgrounds from the host country and the guest country meet, and it is fondly and tenderly used as the chief scenery in many tales and novels (see e.g. Lenček and Bosker 2000).

Linguistic aspects of general tourism encounters have been under research for a while (Thurlow and Jaworski 2011; Vitorio 2019). As a novelty, language in beach and seaside territories has been investigated and displays completely new facets of language in tourism studies (Nassenstein 2019; Storch 2017, 2018b).

As these beach spaces are "not fixed but are in a constant state of transition as a result of continuous, dialectical struggles of power and resistance among and between a diversity of stakeholder" (Pritchard and Morgan 2006: 764), the language in this space undergoes the very same changes. Finding the right phrase for the tourist is an art, which *beach boys* learn in the "Beach Academy", a metaphor for the whole beach on which language and experiences are exchanged. The continuous acquisition of new German/French/Italian phrases, the exchange of experiences and the knowledge of which phrases can be used to excite and captivate the tourist provide the basic skills that a beach boy needs to start a conversation.

The parties that are found at Diani Beach are all in a constant state of transgression. Social hierarchies for both tourists and beach boys have dissolved at the beach and must be newly established. On this "stage", transgression in the form of crossing cultural, social or spatial barriers almost always happens (Wikström 2005), implying that each section has certain rules. Crossing the borders implies the adaption to the rule which is applied in the specific space: "To move through public space means passing between such territories, adapting one's behaviour according to the current system of rules" (Wikström 2005: 52).

The beach boys have developed their own kind of performance, which involves mainly linguistic strategies in order to play their role in the transgressive space, following the concept of banal globalization (Thurlow and Jaworski 2011). The beach boys' language of transgression is about mixing, performing and subverting, and takes place in various languages, although English, as one of Kenya's two official languages, is found in most conversations between beach boys and tourists along the beach. Often, the beach boys use the language of the tourist as a strategy to attract the tourist and to keep the conversation going, a behaviour that is typical of East African tourism workers (see also Storch 2017, 2018a). As stated above, the beach boys have a broad repertoire of European languages, and even some words of *kiswisi* 'Swiss German' or *deep kijerumani* 'deep German', which refers to Bavarian dialects (Nassenstein 2016: 123). The examples in this article will refer to the German repertoire of the beach boys because the fieldwork was intentionally conducted in German and the examples, data and recordings collected are therefore in German.[1]

---

[1] Alongside the repertoire of the European languages, two other registers are found along the beach, namely *Coasti Slang* (Nassenstein 2016) and *Hakuna Matata Swahili* (Mietzner 2017; Nassenstein 2019; Mietzner and Storch 2019).

11.2.1 Beach boys as a critical construction of people

The beach boys of Kenya as a stereotype are well-known in the world of travellers to East Africa and are commonly regarded as friendly, but also annoying or even dangerous (Fig. 11.1), as can be seen in warnings from other Kenyan citizens (Bergan 2011: 10) and from various travel-blogs:

BEWARE OF THE BEACH BOYS
Bewertung zu **Diani Reef Beach Resort & Spa**
◉◯◯◯◯ Bewertet 23. Februar 2016

robert f
London, Vereinigtes Königreich

⌂62 👍239

This holiday was spoiled by the persistent haranguing and harassment of the huge numbers of highly organised Beach Men who stand in a continual line all along the sands in front of the hotels The minute they see a hapless tourist , moving from the safety of the hotel grounds, towards the beach, they pounce like a pack of hyenas These guys do not take no for an answer !! They surround you at every opportunity and literally force you into purchases of utterly useless goods at extortionate prices Unfortunately, the hotels are unable to do anything about these endless gangs as the Gang Leaders make regular payments to the local Police who simply turn a blind eye This is an appalling situation for Kenya tourism ; we will obviously advise our friends and colleagues to avoid the Diani beaches but to choose Mexico or Dominican or similar , where one is not forced by tough gangs into purchasing unlicensed excursions ; boat trips or badly carved useless wooden ornaments With regards to this hotel , we were very very disappointed We are regular Long Haul travellers to all the world's Tropical countries and always stay in 4 star or 5 star hotels I believe that many years ago, when it was new , this hotel was a 4 star However it is now at best , a 3 star The most endearing quality of this hotel is the friendliness... Mehr

Figure 11.1: Warnings.
Note: See https://www.tripadvisor.de/ShowUserReviews-g775870-d586574-r350240617-Diani_Reef_Beach_Resort_Spa-Diani_Beach_Ukunda_Coast_Province.html (accessed 13 March 2019).

The term "beach boy" is used by tourists for men, mainly from the coast and ranging in age between 20 and 45. The use of the term plays an important role in the whole system of beach tourism in Kenya. The terminology is also extended to other tourism workers, as was found on a website where experiences are exchanged. Here, the term "boy" was given to the *Liegestuhlboy* 'sunbed boy', the *Poolboy* and the *Zimmerboy* 'roomboy'[2]:

---

[2] See https://www.tripadvisor.de/ShowTopic-g775870-i12044-k4357251-Kenia-Diani_Beach_Ukunda_Coast_Province.html (accessed 13 March 2019).

(1) Boy terminology

German: (original orthography)

es ist für mich selbstverständlich, dass ich dem ober nach einem essen ein trinkgeld von 100 kes gebe, das macht man auch in der schweiz, und die angestellten sind auf ein trinkgeld angewieden. es hat mich beschämt festzustellen, wie wenig die gäste ein trinkgeld geben.
es ist für mich selbstverständlich, dass auch der roomboy ein trinkgeld bekommt, oder der gärtner, der liegestuhl boy…die angestellten, an die am wenigsten gedacht wird.
ein freundliches "jambo habari" und die wünsche werden von den augen abgelesen.

English:

For me, it is a matter of course to give a tip of 100 KES to the waiter, that's what one does in Switzerland and the employees are dependent on tips. I was ashamed to see that only a few guests tip. It is a given that the roomboy also gets a tip, or the gardener or the sunbed boy…the employees on whom little attention is put. A friendly "jambo habari" and all your wishes will be fulfilled.

Tourists don't differentiate what kind of specialisation the beach boy has, in contrast to the beach boys themselves, who make a strict distinction between beach operators, beach vendors and sex workers. For these, an exact job description and terms for the respective sectors are used: beach operators have a licence to work along the beach, whereas beach vendors don't. Nevertheless, there is a tendency to refer to others working on the beach as beach boys, according to an internal hierarchy: The beach operators, proud of having a licence, call themselves "beach operators", while they call the others who sell small things at the beach "beach boys". The traders who sell small things without licenses call themselves beach vendors and claim that the sex workers are called "beach boys". The sex workers would never call themselves "beach boys", so that the label is constantly passed on to other groups of lower status.

From years of my own study, there are no *typical* Kenyan tourists. Families, backpackers, sex tourists (male and female) and elderly people are found all over Kenya, especially in the national parks and along the coast. Travel to Kenya is available at an acceptable price so that average-income Germans can afford an exotic holiday. High budget accommodation is not situated in the typical tourist areas like Diani Beach or Malindi but is rather found elsewhere. The tourists of Kenya are often repeat visitors, and the motto *einmal Kenia, immer Kenia* 'once Kenya, always Kenya' is often heard in the conversations of German tourists. Furthermore, expatriates shape the landscape of Diani Beach with their shops and offices (see Berman 2017; Kibicho 2003, 2009).

11.2.2 Ethnophaulisms

Ethnophaulisms,[3] especially those concerning the Europeans who are present at Diani Beach, are found relatively often and mainly at the beginning of conversations between beach boys and tourists. They serve as discursive starters and function in the way that they provoke a reaction from the tourist, e.g. by laughing about the term or wondering where this knowledge comes from.

The names listed in Table 11.1 are not used commonly in everyday German but rather serve the beach boys to indirectly insult tourists of other nationalities behind their backs. There are many more ethnophaulisms for other nationalities in German, but these are not known to the beach boys due to the minor presence of other nationalities along the Kenyan beach.

Table 11.1: Ethnophaulisms used by beach boys of Diani.

Germans	*Kartoffelfresser*	'potato eater'
British	*Inselaffen*	'island monkeys'
Italians	*Spaghettifresser*	'spaghetti eater'

Example (2) presents an excerpt of a dialogue from a recording made during a beach walk along Diani Beach, where various attempts were made by different beach boys to start a conversation with two female German tourists.

(2) Dialogue: Two female tourists (woman 1 (W1), woman 2 (W2)) walk along the beach, followed by three beach boys (BB) who communicate with them either altogether, or separately with each of the women

BB	*Mutter und Tochter?*	'Mother and daughter?'
W1	*Ja, Mutter und Tochter.*	'Yes, mother and daughter.'
BB:	*Aber seht alle nett aus.*	'But you all look friendly.'
W2	*Danke.*	'Thank you!'

---

[3] These are ethnic slurs that are used to refer to members of a group in a derogatory or insulting manner (Roback 1944).

BB	*Denke, kommen Sie aus nette Familie.*	'I think you are from a friendly family.'
W	*Ja. Hoffen wir's.*	'Yes. Let's hope so.'
BB	*Weil die Inselaffen schauen nicht so nett aus.*	'Because the island monkeys don't look that friendly.'
W2	*Wer sind denn Inselaffen?"*	'Who are the island monkeys?'
BB	*Engländer. Oder die Spaghettifresser. Italiener. Hat uns früher Kolonie, die Engländer und er will uns immer unterdrücken. Aber, Gottseidank, alles hat ein Ende nur die Wurst hat zwei.*	'The British. Or the spaghetti eaters. The Italians. The British had us as their colony, and they always want to oppress us. But, thank God, everything has an end, only the sausage has two.'

The women felt demeaned by the offensive way that they were addressed and by the low level of the conversation, which was finally manifested in the last sentence. The German phrase *alles hat ein Ende, nur die Wurst hat zwei* has its origin in a song dated from 1986 by the musician Stefan Remmler. When used in German, this phrase mirrors a superficial indifference towards something or somebody.

What might seem strange but is a well-thought-out strategy of the beach boys is the immediate use of ethnophaulisms; these are part of the derogatory and offending repertoire of the beach boys, and the link to the colonial context. The mentioning of colonial oppression evokes a feeling of guilt in the mind of the Europeans. And even if it was not their country that had once colonised Kenya, Germans are caught by the feeling of collective White guilt as descendants of colonisers of other African countries. The history of one's own ancestors has an impact on one's own feelings, particularly when groups have been mistreated historically (Leach et al 2002: 144; Doosje et al 1998: 872). This history is used at the beach, the liminal space in which new or even reverse social roles are established.

The frequent use of these terms is an uncomfortable aspect of the holiday for the tourist. The beach in a formerly "third-world country" is a touchy space for a European tourist, in which racism and oppression of any kind is to be avoided. The terms given in the example above are never used to address the tourists themselves but rather to make fun of their European neighbours, in order to degrade them and thus to upgrade each tourist's own country and personality. The beach boys use humour to disguise their way of mocking the tourist, as is often seen in TV shows, where mock aggression is part of the participation ritual (Thurlow and Jaworski 2011: 304). The beach boys have understood the way in which mocking works with ethnophaulisms, enabling them to position the tourists as powerless foreigners.

11.2.3 Racist innuendo

Besides references to the colonial context, racialised constructs of difference are used by the beach boys to make tourists incapable of taking action against their unwanted companionship during the beach walk. These strategies again don't insult the tourists, but rather manoeuver them into the position of having to be extremely friendly in order not to be counted among those people who are racists. This in turn reduces the distance between the two parties who meet in these conversations, which the beach boys use in order to establish closer relationships. From a selection of phrases that were heard during the beach walk, the two following examples refer to racial or cannibalistic context.

(3) *Hello. How are you? You don't have to fear me, I will not harm you. I am not a cannibal!*

(4) *You don't have to be scared of my dark skin, I only want to talk.*

These sentences were heard in English, but are also found in German (Storch 2018b; Mietzner and Storch 2019). Both phrases inevitably require a reaction from the tourists. Not answering would bring them into the position of the oppressor. Most of the conversation therefore will continue with the tourists guaranteeing that they are not afraid the beach boys, and particularly not because of their skin colour. Through these phrases the beach boys manage to manipulate the tourists, reversing their decision to ignore or even turn their back on the beach boys. The tourists, who, due to their better economic situation see themselves as the advantaged ones, are made to feel guilty, and again this puts the beach boys in the position of power in the interaction.

11.2.4 Proverbs

Walking along the beach at Diani, one often hears German proverbs, but amazingly, these are not recited by Germans, but by the beach boys.

The acquisition of German proverbs by the beach boys highlights two interesting factors: They are used at the right time, implying that the beach boys have not only learned the German proverb but that they have also understood and applied the semantics appropriately. They are often applied when a transaction is already in action. It seems as if the proverbs serve firstly to remove the seriousness from the deal, and secondly to convey that, whatever criticism is made of the object being traded is a wrong interpretation of the tourist.

It is thus amazing to find German proverbs being used by the beach boys in order to comment upon utterances or actions made by the tourist. The following proverbs were heard during a one-hour beach walk:

(5) German proverbs used at Diani Beach
    a. *Besser den Spatz in der Hand als die Taube auf dem Dach.*
       (lit.: Better the sparrow in the hand than the dove on the roof.)
       'A bird in the hand is worth two in the bush.'
    b. *Es ist noch kein Meister vom Himmel gefallen.*
       (lit: Until now, no master has fallen from the sky.)
       'No one masters anything without hard work.'
       Meaning: implying that someone has made a mistake but still has time to improve.

The first one was the answer of a beach boy in a bargaining situation, where the final price was set for a carving; the second one was the answer to a complaint, that a (different) carving had a defect.

This can be seen as subversion of a special kind, where not only the language of the tourist is used, but where the proverb as a speech genre is so common in the culture of the beach boys that it is transposed to a different language which wouldn't make use of proverbs in these situations. The tourists' reactions often trigger more proverbs.

11.3 Diani Beach: Tourism development and problematic implications

In order to understand the rise and in particular the necessity of the rise of these language repertoires, it is helpful to gain an insight into the history and development of tourism in Diani Beach, and the current situation, as the history of a public space always draws on various dimensions, such as the users' essential needs or their spatial rights (Carr 1992).

Diani Beach is one of the beaches on Kenya's South Coast, with miles of white sand and palm trees; it is a destination for tourists in search of "paradise" and for Kenyan beach vendors in search of work. Kenya is known worldwide for its beaches and its wildlife and was one of the first African countries to experience international tourism. While it was formerly the British settlers who sought recreation along the coast, Germans and Italians increasingly chose independent Kenya as their holiday destination. At that time the country's economic activities were mainly controlled by expatriates and the tourism sector was initiated either by the government or by Europeans (Akama 2004: 145). In the 1970s, tourism increased in the area (see Sindiga 1999: 73) and brought salaried positions in hotels, but neither the state nor other institutions engaged in developing the area. Meanwhile the population grew and so did unemployment and poverty (Berman 2017: 68–74).

In contrast to its careful planning of infrastructure for wildlife tourism, the Kenyan government did not have plans to build a tourism industry on the coast. People living along the coast started small-scale entrepreneurships. Start-up capital was not planned by the government; in consequence, Kenyans were forced into temporary unlicensed kiosks or shops while the Kenyan Indians and Europeans ran the official shops (Sindiga 1999). Even now, it is only between two and five percent of the income from tourism that reaches the local population in the form of working in the tourism industry or through the selling of crafts and food (Akama 2004: 149).

Due to crime within the country, as experienced during the post-election violence in 2008, together with attacks against tourists, as well as international terrorism conducted mostly by Al-Shabaab (e.g. the taking and killing of hostages in the Westgate Shopping Mall in Nairobi in 2013 or the murdering of students at the University of Garissa in 2015), tourism decreased abruptly in 2008, then grew again but stagnated. Additionally, the Ebola epidemic in West Africa in 2014 had an impact on the Kenyan tourism, even if the centre of the epidemic was far away.

Diani Beach, south of Mombasa Island, additionally suffers from being reachable only by using a ferry. The ferries are under constant criticism with regard to safety, the corruption of the staff and the overlong queuing time for cars and buses. Two to three hours are normal, a situation which discourages tourists from the South Coast in favour of the North Coast.

These aspects are all reasons for the declining level of tourism at Diani Beach, which gives immense problems to the Kenyans working in the tourism sector, as an excerpt from an online newspaper explains:

> [...] One of these locals is Francis Marube, manager of the "Leopard Beach Resort" in Ukunda, the village directly adjacent to Diani Beach. With a desperate gaze he points to the sun loungers at the pool, which seems to merge directly into the ocean. With temperatures above 30 degrees one would like to follow his gesture towards the water. But no sun lounger is occupied. "It is like that for six months now. I had to dismiss 180 out of

300 employees," says Marube. At the moment, only Indians and South Africans come to this place. Only a few Britons, US Americans and Germans are seen.   (my translation)[4]

As tourism has an important impact on the place where it happens more than on the tourists themselves (Fisher 2004: 127), this background information makes it obvious that people who have set up a livelihood dependent on tourism now need to change their strategies in order to continue in their profession.

Initially, tourism was a good source of income but as the number of tourists in Diani diminished, an imbalance developed between supply and demand. Those who were unable to find an alternative job remained employed in tourism and had to compete with all the others in the same situation.

11.3.1 Mutual stereotypes

Both of the beach protagonists described above – the tourist and the beach boy – have a clear definition of what they want from each other and how the other is supposed to behave. The focus of this section is the stereotyping of the tourist by the beach boy.

Although the tourists feel individualised in the interaction, which is mainly evoked by statements such as *"Du bist mein erster Kunde heute"* 'you are my first customer today', and also by the Beach Boy remembering them by name, they are one of a mass of potential customers for the beach boys.

Beach boys analyse and categorise groups of tourists with respect to their characteristic behaviour regarding the purchases they might make. This is necessary knowledge for the beach boys in terms of the way the tourists have to be approached. Table 11.2 shows an analysis of tourists' behaviour, which was given by Captain Joseph, a 35-year old local beach operator who sells ship tours along the reef to tourists in Diani Beach.

Captain Joseph admitted that although it is not easy to convince German tourists to buy something, it is very useful to follow them along the beach and

---

4 Original German text reads: "Ein solcher Einheimischer ist Francis Marube, Manager des "Leopard Beach Resort" in Ukunda, dem Ort, der sich direkt an Diani Beach anschließt. Mit verzweifeltem Blick deutet er auf den mit Loungemöbeln bestückten Pool, der direkt ins Meer überzugehen scheint. Bei Temperaturen von über 30 Grad will man seiner Geste in Richtung Wasser gerne folgen. Aber: Keine einzige Liege ist besetzt. "Seit sechs Monaten geht das nun schon so. Ich musste 180 von 300 Arbeitskräften entlassen", sagt Marube. Momentan kämen noch Inder in den Ort, auch Südafrikaner. Briten, US-Amerikaner und Deutsche sähe man nur noch wenige." From http://www.sueddeutsche.de/reise/tourismus-in-kenia-riss-in-der-fototapete-1.2284463-2 (accessed 13 March 2019).

Table 11.2: Analysis of tourists concerning their purchase behaviour.

- Germans
    - need a lot of conversation
    - need to be convinced over days
    - don't buy the same day
    - think it over a lot and get information from other beach boys
- British and Italians
    - seldom book tours at the beach
    - buy small carvings or necklaces to support the beach boys.
- French
    - are good customers
    - buy the same day
- Kenyans
    - are good customers
    - extremely low profit (resident prices)

talk to them continuously, as this often has a positive influence on the business. However, as has been noted before, due to the economic situation of the beach boys, there are usually severeal beach boys accompanying the tourist along the beach. This competition for profit takes place at the expense of the tourist, who did not know that the holiday would be spent on an almost empty beach due to the decreasing number of tourists, and the constant, not decreasing number of beach boys. As a result of this imbalance, the beach boys had to find new strategies of solicitation, which led to the development of their linguistically flamboyant and obtrusive behaviour in order to outplay their rivals (see Section 11.4).

11.4 Borders and transgression

The above described situations, dialogues, and words might not seem aggressive or obtrusive to the reader. They might even appear to be funny or at least normal. But, as asked above, why is it that many tourists of Kenya have the feeling of being harassed by the beach boys or at least unnerved? Online posts in chat rooms or travel platforms show that the behaviour of the beach boys is a problem for tourists and causes unfriendly reactions. The following post was found on Trip Advisor, a website where travellers' questions are answered by other travellers:

(6) Question from a tourist about how to deal with the beach boys[5]

German: (original orthography)

Wie geht ihr mit den Beach Boys um. Natürlich weiss man wie arm die Leute sind, aber ich konnte erst etwas entspannen, nachdem ich unfreundlich geworden bin. Und das war mir unangenehm.

'How do you cope with the beach boys? Of course, I know how poor the people are, but I could only relax after having been unfriendly to them. And that made me feel uncomfortable.'

The whole situation has to do with the very special space of Diani Beach, where borders play an important role, and with the transgression that is happening within this space.

The hotels at the Kenyan beach have obvious borders, demarcating the private from the public space in the form of walls, cordons or other kinds of barrier.

As the schematic sketch and the reality in the photograph in Figure 11.2 show, boundaries, of which the beach is also one, are used to separate European tourists from Kenyan beach vendors. Private hotel beaches have walls erected in order to manifest the border between private and public, silence and noise, rich and poor, decency and obtrusiveness. This is the space where binaries are built, ensouled and kept alive.

The holiday on the private side of the wall is quiet and luxurious, decorated with Bougainville blossoms, whereas on the other side of the wall, the noise waits in form of the beach boys, who reflect the poverty of the country. Figures 11.3 and 11.4 give an impression of the other side, where beach boys wait for the tourists to cross the borders.

The situation of being in the safe enclosure of the hotel reinforces the situation of unequal treatment and the feeling of guilt, but also of interest in the other, a situation of which the beach boys are aware. Meanwhile, the situation on the public space of the beach is not that of a typical shared public space which hosts a variety of "actors" and which has as a precondition that the people in it develop interest in the others (Sennett 1992). The beach boys use the beach as a stage where they have to approach and enthuse their audience in order to achieve the goal with which they went to the beach: to earn money. The tourists are spectators and are involved unwittingly.

---

[5] https://www.tripadvisor.de/ShowTopic-g775870-i12044-k4357251-Kenia-Diani_Beach_Ukunda_Coast_Province.html (accessed 13 March 2019).

Figure 11.2: Beach borders for hosts and guests – scheme and reality.

Figures 11.3 and 11.4: Beach boys waiting on the other side of the wall.

As being harassed by the beach boys is an important issue for tourists and the hotels, a strategy has been developed that guarantees the tourists a walk along the beach without being approached by anybody. As already suggested in the sketch in Figure 11.2, Figure 11.5 shows a so-called beach walk, which is an organised walk of about 90 minutes in which hotel guests can walk in a group, accompanied by a member of the hotel staff and a security officer with a truncheon. By means of the security officer, the tourists create for themselves their own border, within which they are able to move freely without being molested

Figure 11.5: A coconut seller approaching a group of tourists.

by the beach boys, who in their turn have to stay at a safe distance outside this border. However, during the beach walk, the beach boys don't stay away, but constantly orbit the group. As the guarded group is an open and affronting sign of exclusion, the beach boys abandon their routine linguistic strategies and loosen the regulations of hospitality at the beach. Where normally a friendly approach is made, the beach boys react to the compartmentalisation of the tourists with bursts of open hostility and offense. The group we went with was constantly accompanied with shouted words like *Kindergarten, Kindergarten* or *Ziege* 'goat', together with claims such as *Ihr mögt keine Menschen, ihr mögt nur Tiere* 'you don't like people, you only like animals'. As this verbal outburst completely contradicts the codex of hospitality of the Swahili culture, where a polite cooperation is the norm (Yahya-Othman 1994; Nwoye 1992), it makes even more obvious that the exclusion of the beach boys by groups of tourists provokes hostility.

11.5 Beach language and subjective perception

Tourists' perceptions of whether the words of the beach boys are harmful or aggressive depend on subjective aspects and to ask this question surely oversimplifies the complex contextual variables underlying these interactions.

While the dialogue in example (2) would be interpreted in one way by the women who were involved in the conversation, other participants would have received these remarks on the British and the colonial regime differently. Defining language as harmful or aggressive can be complex when no swear word is used and no raised voices can be heard. Typically, aggressive speech contains offensive utterances that fall into categories such as obscenity, indecency, profanity, racial insults, and taboos of scatology (Jay 1992), none of which are found in the verbosity of the beach boys.

Then why do tourists feel harassed? Why do some report that they feel very annoyed or that they fear the aggressive way that the beach boys come close, talk and don't leave? A 38-year old German women (anonymous, p.c.) who stayed for two weeks in Diani felt disappointed that she could not use the beach for pleasure and decided to stay within the hotel compound. She felt completely harassed and besieged by the presence of the beach boys around her. She admitted that she was never harassed physically, and that nobody ever touched her, but she couldn't bear the long speeches from which she couldn't escape. First of all, the behaviour of the beach boys deviates from the tourists' goals; tourists "tend to have high expectations of what they should receive since 'going away' is an event endowed with particular significance. People are looking for the extraordinary and hence will be exceptionally critical of services provided that appear to undermine such a quality" (Urry 1990: 38). Of course, encounters with beach boys and other Kenyan citizens are not included in whatever is purchased when someone books a holiday in Kenya. Nevertheless, the tourist does expect all aspects of the trip to fit in with their holiday expectations. Instead, they report that they avoid going for non-organised walks along the beach due to the harassment and the constant accompaniment of one or more beach boys.

Whether their speech is regarded as offensive is defined by each tourist individually, as it is not possible to set up universal criteria according to which speech is offensive, aggressive or even abusive (Jay and Janschewitz 2008). The repertoires of the beach boys indeed lack offensive words and superficially, in the first few contacts, attempt to develop a sympathetic relation between them and the tourists. The ethnophaulisms and their strategies of addressing and approaching are harmless offensive words which can, when used in a friendly way, rather achieve desirable social effects such as promoting social cohesion and producing harmony (Jay 2009: 89). Friendship is the foundation which is intentionally constructed for this effect by the beach boy within a short time, a strategy is common across the beach environment. They therefore use the German language, as well as their knowledge about Germany and typical German behaviour, reactions, likes and dislikes in order to establish friendship.

11.6 Conclusions

Special places trigger certain patterns of behaviour as they are arenas in which performance, mimesis or transgression play an important role (Augé 2008; Wikström 2005). On beaches, which all around the world are very special places as, whether they belong to peoples' history or heritage or solely to their emotions and pleasure, people act different there from when they are at home. Diani Beach is full of emotions on the part of the tourists, who love to come there in search of romance, or for recovery reasons. This beach strip by the Indian Ocean is an extraordinary and almost unique place where tourists are positioned as powerless foreigners (Said 1978; Fabian 1983; cf. also Thurlow and Jaworsky 2011: 304 for othering in tourism settings) and "Othered" by the beach boys without recognizing it. Their strategically and linguistically complex models of behaviour manipulate the tourist and can be seen as a system of *Othering* (see Jaworski and Coupland 2005) where the beach boys are in total control of the situation and the tourists. They make the tourists join in with their way of speaking *Hakuna Matata Swahili* and with their behaviour, which is atypical of the polite and decent air of the local community to which most of them belong. For the beach boys, it is obvious that language, behaviour and perception are heavily dependent on the space in which they are used and performed. They create their space so that the Other – the tourist – can enter the space across actual and psychological borders and can be trapped on the stage of performance.

Acknowledgements: I am thankful to Anne Storch for the many discussions and inputs on earlier versions of this paper, to Nico Nassenstein for sharing his thoughts and ideas, and to Monika Feinen for designing graphics which help to display the social structure of the beach. The photographs are all mine, as are all remaining mistakes.

References

Akama, John S. 2004. Neocolonialism, dependency and external control of Africa's tourism industry. A case study of wildlife safari tourism in Kenya. In: C. Michael Hall and Hazel Tucker (eds.). *Tourism and Postcolonialism: Contested Discourses, Identities and Representations*, 140–152. London & New York: Routledge.

Augé, Marc. 2008. *Non-places: Introduction to an Anthropology of Supermodernity*. London: Verso.

Bergan, Miriam Eid. 2011. There's no love here. Beach boys in Malindi, Kenya. M.A. thesis, University of Bergen.

Berman, Nina. 2017. *Germans on the Kenyan Coast. Land, Charity, and Romance*. Indiana: Indiana University Press.

Carr, Stephen, Mark Francis, Leanne G. Rivlin and Andrew M. Stone. 1992. *Public Space*. Cambridge: CUP.

Chow, Rey. 2014. *Not like a Native Speaker. On Languaging as a Postcolonial Experience*. New York: Columbia University Press.

Culpeper, Jonathan. 2011. *Impolite language: Using Language to Cause Offence*. Cambridge & New York: Cambridge University Press.

Doosje, Bertjan, Nyla R. Branscombe, Russell Spears and Antony S.R. Manstead. 1998. Guilty by association: When one's group has a negative history. *Journal of Personality and Social Psychology* 75 (4): 872–886.

Fanon, Franz 1952. *Black Skin, White Masks*. France: Éditions du Seuil.

Fabian, Johannes. 1983. *Time and the Other: How Anthropology Makes Its Object*. New York: Columbia University Press. New edition (2002).

Fisher, David. 2004. A colonial town for neo-colonial tourism. In Michael C. Hall and Hazel Tucker (eds.). *Tourism and Postcolonialism: Contested Discourses, Identities and Representations*, 126–139. London & New York: Routledge.

Heller, Monica, Adam Jaworski and Crispin Thurlow. 2014. Introduction: Sociolinguistics and tourism – mobilities, markets, multilingualism. *Journal of Sociolinguistics* 18 (4): 425–458.

Jaworski, Adam and Justine Coupland. 2005. Othering in gossip: "you go out you have a laugh and you can pull yeah okay but like ..." *Language in Society* 34: 667–694.

Jay, Timothy B. 1992. *Cursing in America*. Philadelphia: John Benjamins.

Jay, Timothy B. 2009. Do offensive words harm people? *Psychology, Public Policy and Law* 15 (2): 81–101.

Jay, Timothy and Kristin Janschewitz. 2008. The pragmatics of swearing. *Journal of Politeness Research* 4: 267–288.

Kibicho, Wanjohi. 2009. *Sex Tourism in Africa: Kenya's Booming Industry*. London, New York: Routledge.

Kibicho, Wanjohi. 2003. Community tourism: A lesson from Kenya's coastal region. *Journal of Vacation Marketing* 10 (1): 33–42.

Leach, Colin Wayne, Nastia Snider and Aarti Iyer. 2002. Poisoning the consciences of the fortunate: The experience of relative advantage and support for social equality. In I. Walker and H.J. Smith (eds.). *Specification, Development and Integration*, 136–163. New York: Cambridge University Press.

Lenček, Lena and Gideon Bosker. 1998. *The Beach: The History of Paradise on Earth*. England: Viking Penguin.

Lenček, Lena and Gideon Bosker. 2000. *Beach. Stories by the Sand and Sea*. New York: Marlowe & Company.

Mietzner, Angelika. 2017. The Hakuna Matata tourist. Extreme othering in an extreme setting. Talk presented at the conference *Other's Other*. University of Cologne, 25–26 September 2017.

Mietzner, Angelika and Anne Storch. (2019). Linguistic entanglements, emblematic codes and representation in tourism: Introduction. In Angelika Mietzner and Anne Storch (eds.). *Language and Tourism in Postcolonial Settings*, 1–17. Bristol: Channel View Publications.

Nash, D. 1977. Tourism as a form of imperialism. In V.L. Smith (ed.), *Hosts and Guests: The Anthropology of Tourism*, 33–47. Philadelphia; University of Philadelphia.

Nassenstein, Nico. 2016. Mombasa's Swahili-based 'Coasti Slang' in a super-diverse space: Languages in contact on the beach. *African Study Monographs* 37 (3): 117–143.

Nassenstein, Nico. 2019. The Hakuna Matata Swahili: Linguistic souvenirs from the Kenyan coast. In: Angelika Mietzner and Anne Storch (eds.), *Language and Tourism in Postcolonial Settings*, 130–156. Bristol: Channel View Publications.

Nwoye, Onuigbo G. 1992. Linguistic politeness and socio-cultural variations of the notion of face. *Journal of Pragmatics* 18: 309–328.

Preston-Whyte, Robert. 2004. The beach as a liminal space. In Alan A. Lew, C. Michael Hall and Allan M. Williams (eds.), *The Blackwell's Tourism Companion*, 349–359. Oxford: Blackwell

Pritchard, Annette and Nigel Morgan. 2006. Hotel Babylon? Exploring hotels as liminal sites of transition and transgression. *Tourism Management* 27: 762–772.

Roback, Abraham Aron. 1944. *A Dictionary of International Slurs (Ethnophaulisms). With a Supplementary Essay on Aspects of Ethnic Prejudice*. Cambridge: Sci-Art Publishers.

Sennett, Richard. 1992. *The Uses of Disorder, Personal Identity and City Life*. N.Y.: W. W. Norton and Company.

Said, Edward. 1978. *Orientalism*. New York: Pantheon Books.

Shields, Rob. 1991. *Places on the Margin: Alternative Geographies of Modernity*. London: Routledge.

Sindiga, Isaac. 1999. *Tourism and African Development: Change and Challenge of Tourism in Kenya*. Aldershot: Ashgate Publishing.

Spivak, Gayatri Chakravorty. 1988. Can the Subaltern Speak? In Cary Nelson and Lawrence Grossberg (eds.), *Marxism and the Interpretation of Culture*. Chicago: University of Illinois Press.

Storch, Anne. 2017. Opacity and the other. Talk presented at the conference *Other's Other*. University of Cologne, 25–26 September 2017.

Storch, Anne. 2018a. Linguistic landscapes of tourism – A case study from Zanzibar. In Klaus Beyer, Gertrud Boden, Bernhard Köhler and Ulrike Zoch (eds.), *40 Jahre Afrikanistik*. Cologne: Köppe.

Storch, Anne. 2018b. Hostility / hospitality: language on t-shirts. Talk held at the *20th International Congress of Linguists*, Cape Town, 2–6 July 2018.

Thurlow, Crispin and Adam Jaworski. 2011. Tourism discourse: Language and banal globalization. *Applied Linguistics Review* 2: 285–312.

Urry, Joh. 1990. *The Tourist Gaze*. London: Sage Publications.

Vitorio, Raymund. 2019. Postcolonial performativity in the Philippine heritage tourism industry. In Angelika Mietzner, Angelika and Anne Storch (eds.), *Language and Tourism in Postcolonial Settings*, 106–129. Bristol: Channel View Publications.

Walton, John K. 2000. *The British Seaside Resort*. Manchester: University of Manchester Press.

Wikström, Tomas. 2005. Residual space and transgressive spatial practices – the uses and meanings of un-formed space. *Nordisk Arkitekturforskning* 18 (1): 47–68.

Yahya-Othman, Saida. 1994. Covering one's social back: Politeness among the Swahili. *Text* 14 (1): 141–161

Janine Traber

12 The *sexy banana* – artifacts of gendered language in tourism

Abstract: Mass tourism and its language often come together with souvenirs and special techniques for selling them. On the Spanish island of Mallorca, at the beach of El Arenal, tourists from Western Europe meet with immigrants from mostly West African countries. These encounters often resolve in oversexualized, offensive multilingual constructions of the Other that constitute the basis for ritualized insults. Herein, classical gender roles, racist stereotypes and social class are displayed, as well as being mixed up in unusual ways. The relics of these characterizations are physical souvenirs, but also language phrases that are "taken home" by the tourist and can be found e.g. in music. A rotation between encounters, objects and virtual repetition takes place. According to the participants, the transgressive phrases and souvenirs induce verbal and semiotic games that are characterized by the multilingual actors in the setting. On the one hand, the language and items have become part of a traditional tourism experience and are a necessity for immigrants to survive. On the other hand, they feed the overall generalization of cultures and sexes. Migrants working in direct contact with tourists, especially, are often the target of abusive language. This seems to derive from the easygoing imposition of (sexual) identities practiced on the beach and street that might easily assume male over female dominance. Trying to include as many perspectives as possible, this contribution aims to present different swearing strategies and purposes deriving from sexism and prejudice which appear as a result of extensive on-site multinational tourism.

12.1 Introduction

The island of Mallorca lies in the Mediterranean Sea and is next to Ibiza and Menorca, the biggest of the Balearic Islands. As a prominent holiday destination, it has become famous for its mass and party tourism during the last

---

Note: I would like to express my deep gratitude to the editors of this volume and the proofreaders of this chapter. Their open eyes and ears on the text and their advice and constructive criticism have helped and inspired me to improve it as much as possible.

decades. In 2017, more than ten million visitors, mostly from Germany, Britain, Switzerland and the Netherlands, arrived at the airport in Palma de Mallorca.[1]

In 2016 the University of Cologne started a research project, investigating the language and culture of migrants and tourists in the German-dominated area of El Arenal, located on the West coast of the island. The data presented in this paper have been collected during several field trips between August 2016 and October 2018.

While Mallorca offers quite a range of touristic activities, including hiking, cycling, local winery tours and cultural monuments, El Arenal has specialized in attracting tourists seeking liminal experiences of several kinds. The agenda of most visitors consists of extreme drinking and partying, sunbathing or looking for sex at the beach or in nearby clubs. This phenomenon is also well-established in other parts of the island, e.g. in Magaluf and Palmanova where most of the tourists are from the United Kingdom (see Andrews 2007; Andrews et al. 2011). Within the tourist culture, Magaluf is given the nickname *Shagaluf*, which refers to the idea of sex being available to anyone at any time in this area. Furthermore, the expression *shagging* is loaded with the notion of quick and dirty or even animalistic intercourse, in comparison with other possible terms for having sex. "They don't call it Shagaluf for nothing, you know. Just make sure you have photo documentation to make sure they remember their one night of romance for years to come",[2] wrote the author of an online journal about what to expect in Magaluf. The etymology of El Arenal's nickname *Ballermann* is more complex. Along the promenade, numbered bars named *Balneario* adjoin the beach. The term *Ballermann* usually refers to the area around Balneario 6, where most of the party attractions for Germans are located. Therefore, many tourists believe that their name for El Arenal is a Germanization of the name of the beach bar. However, there is no semantic connection between *balneario* (lit. 'spa') and *Ballermann* (lit. 'a man shooting off guns' or coll. 'gun'), which leads to amusing confusion, so that this phenomenon can be interpreted as a malapropism. Szabo (2011) describes the *Ballermann* furthermore not only as a toponym, but as both a social phenomenon and a brand of party series. He additionally considers the term's roots to have originated in the name of a sausage food truck in southern Germany.

This chapter discusses multilayered verbal practices and their extensions in material culture between tourists and migrants in El Arenal which can be

---

[1] See https://de.statista.com/statistik/daten/studie/746143/umfrage/ankuenfte-flugreisender-auf-mallorca-nach-herkunftsland/ (accessed 12 November 2018).
[2] See https://www.breakingnews.ie/discover/15-things-you-should-really-know-before-you-go-to-magaluf-683284.html (accessed 26 May 2019).

interpreted as swearing and offensive strategies. Some of them include subversive elements that might be interpreted as the opposite, rather as flirting or befriending behavior. By utilizing swearing theory, following Jay (2000, 2008) and Ljung (2011), I aim to deconstruct the diverse social processes that merge in the scenery of migration and tourism and describe a complex system of "appropriate" transgression in this special context.

12.2 On migration from West Africa to Europe

During the last years, as well as the tourists, many migrants from non-European countries have arrived in Mallorca, for reasons such as to support their families back home or to avoid political instabilities in their places of origin. The most prominent group of migrants is from West Africa. To name just a few, there are many Senegalese working as street vendors at the beach or Nigerian men as construction workers, Nigerian women working as lavatory attendants or sex workers and Senegalese women as hair braiders at the beach. Other commonly found nationalities are Indians and Pakistani, often working in t-shirt shops, Romanians, often selling flowers or building elaborate sand castles as art, or Chinese, often either working in beauty salons or offering massages at the beach.[3]

Many (but not all[4]) of the tourism workers from West African countries have arrived undocumented after weeks, months or even years of traveling in extreme circumstances. Some come by plane, others by boat after crossing the Sahara. Kastner (2014) has provided an ethnographic study on women from Nigeria on their way to European countries. Since the European Union began raising political and factual fences for migrants to cross, many of them reach Europe through a well-established system of *madams* and *trolleys / connection men*. These networks set them up with contacts and finances (which would later have to be

---

[3] These data were collected in qualitative semi-structured interviews. It is assumed that not all answers provided by the interlocutors represent the exact place of origin of a person. Someone might claim not to be a migrant at all and not to know any African language, yet later be seen communicating in a Nigerian language with a colleague. Explanations for this behavior might be personal reasons like being afraid of deportation, suggesting that the interviewer does not know where the person's origin is, or simply living up to social role play in tourist culture (as further explained below).
[4] To ask about the residence permit status of interlocutors felt quite risky and introduces a range of ethical problems. Therefore, this was only done in better established relationships. It should be clear that (despite the predominant view among the tourists) a lot of migrants do have legal papers.

repaid) for their way through the desert and across the Mediterranean. Most routes lead through Mali or Niger to Algeria and Morocco. It can be assumed that the routes male migrants travel on do not differ significantly, although for men it is much more common to finance their own travel by working along the way as construction workers or the like. Although such networks appear to be extremely professionalized, there is no security while on the route. Violence, being robbed and suffering from the heat seem to be common experiences.

12.3 El Arenal's tourist culture

As the biggest industry in Mallorca is tourism, many migrants rely on it. As mentioned earlier, tourism in El Arenal is dominated by stag and hen parties, football team members on tour, high-school graduation celebrators and so on.

To amuse the customers and gain the attention of the partying groups, the street vendors present themselves in colorful costumes (see Figure 12.1). Most of the tourist groups consist of 5–20 individuals of the same gender, with no limits regarding age or social status, and tend to dress up in matching group outfits (see Figure 12.2). During the summer months, more younger people, mainly between 18 and 30 years, visit the island. In the off-season, i.e. early spring (April) and late fall (October), more groups of older visitors arrive and populate the party districts. Nonetheless, the overall concept of a typical *Ballermann* holiday does not change throughout the year.

Regarding the strikingly different backgrounds of the actors (migrants and tourists) it is interesting to take a look at the communicative practices between them in this highly transgressive setting of the party zone. Due to the extensive touristification of El Arenal in the last 30 to 40 years, there are extremely few locals still living in the area who have not rented their property to the tourism industry. Most of them are pensioners who try to avoid the inevitable noise and party goings-on, and who usually do not take part in the interaction practices established between the migrants and the visitors.

As a tourist, on the other hand, walking along the promenade is quite impossible without being spoken to. Groups of men try to get in contact with groups of women or the other way around. Heterosexuality is predominant in the outward presentation of this tourist culture. The lyrics of the music that is played in the clubs and on the beach are about romance and sex between men and women, while homosexuality or queerness is only named in the context of insulting someone. There are gay bars only a few kilometers from El Arenal, but they are not prominently advertised. Some homosexual couples who publicly

12 The *sexy banana* – artifacts of gendered language in tourism — 263

Figure 12.1: Dressed up street vendors with plastic tiaras, umbrellas and sunglasses (photo by Angelika Mietzner 2017).

hold hands or kiss do visit the same established drinking halls as heterosexuals, but they do not seem to be part of the main target group. Further research on queer visitors at the Playa de Palma would be needed to better understand how they experience the music played, which is not infrequently homophobic, and the extensive performance of heteronormativity in the party space. The average tourist experiences a feeling of freedom and being on vacation, while the heat and the massive consumption of alcohol lead to the impression of a space without boundaries (see Traber 2017 for a more detailed analysis of the tourists' self-perception) – but with commitments, as one can see in Figure 12.3. Even if

Figure 12.2: Tourist group outfit (photo by Janine Traber 2016).

a tourist is visiting the place for the first time, it is made very clear how the place is constructed to require specific behavior from its guests. This supposed agency of a place, being able to transfer expectations onto the short-time inhabitant, is described by Augé (1995 [1992]). Due to the way a surrounding is constructed architecturally, or an object is created in its shape and design, they effect, provoke and allow for certain things to be done in or with them. The big beer halls of El Arenal, filled with masses of people, foster the visitors to get lost in them. The loud music makes it impossible to understand what individuals might say, therefore it automatically becomes unimportant what a single person might have to communicate. The masses are packed onto one huge floor, not in many smaller rooms. This is how the architecture imposes the feeling of belonging to one equal homogeneous mass on its visitors. Other ways of telling the tourists what to do are the task lists displayed all around the beach and party zone (see Figure 12.3). Completing these tasks will be rewarded with social approval, like reaching a sporting goal such as finishing a triathlon or marathon. Prints like the t-shirt in Figure 12.3 make it clear that the planned trip is not merely a vacation but rather a war-like experience whose survival will create heroes and heroines.[5]

---

[5] During my research, I have seen this t-shirt worn only by men, and unlike other prints this image does not appear on "lady's cut" shirts. Nevertheless, it could be worn by women without my knowledge, and groups of women do display behavior that conforms to this war-like situation as well.

Figure 12.3: Established practices (photo by Angelika Mietzner 2017).

Out of the serious setting of everyday life, one is now freely able to do and say things that would usually fall in the category of disrespectful and transgressive language. "Why so serious?" could well be a motto of El Arenal. Anyone who complains about the permanent display of freedom experienced by the tourists will definitely be named a bore and told to relax. My role as a researcher was continually impossible to uphold, due to several expectations the place seemed to impose on me. Storch, Shepherd and Deumert (forthcoming) discuss in their trialogue the necessity of acknowledging the impact of the researcher's presence, as well as his or her responsibility within the event, as not simply innocent ones. We need not only to gain an emic perspective to better understand what is going on, but sometimes the researcher is not even given a chance to decide whether or what role he or she is going to play. As Mietzner writes about her experiences in El Arenal:

> Even if my first intention, summarized by the three words "to research, to write, to interview", very much resembled those of my research colleagues, I was inhaled by the place and the people, inspired and somehow even exploited and I can only show which maelstrom created a community out of all these people, neither comprehensible nor explainable at first sight [...].[6]
>
> (Mietzner 2017: 36, my translation).

To wear long trousers on a warm day (as I usually do at my working site) created unwanted attention. Soon people were commenting on it, and even trying to explain what I was doing led only to more confusion. No matter what I thought of myself, to everyone else it was clear that a European from the mainland coming to Mallorca (and El Arenal especially) was here for the holiday experience described above. Neglecting it was interpreted as a sign of being a newbie to the local tourists' tradition (summarized in Figure 12.3) or even as being unintelligent. Those who, on the other hand, were capable of embodying even more transgression than was expected by the tourist culture so far, would automatically present themselves as the most experienced tourists and thereby earn respect amongst the others.

Like the t-shirt print above, other objects have become part of the material culture of the Mallorca experience as well (Figures 12.4–12.6), all of them displaying transgression. In any usual context most of these would be considered as being insulting, sexist, racist and/or embarrassing. But being in the party zone, the wearing of and playing with these artifacts appears not to be an expression of the wish to provoke, but rather to be part of the culture and therefore represents the desire to belong to an in-group.

Another example of this specialized material culture is the so-called Sexy Banana (Figure 12.7).

It looks like a banana made from plastic. The peel is removable and inside there is a penis-shaped and colored squirt gun, which can be filled with water.

> Souvenirs [...] are acquired by tourists [...] to act as material reminders of a holiday experience through the crystallization and perpetuation of its memory. Being codified and predefined as "memory-triggers", souvenirs are firstly objects of a nostalgic imagery: they filter, purify and beautify the remembrance of the holiday experience. To sum up, souvenirs attribute a coherent, continuous and positive meaning to the memory of an event, which implies immediate consumption and avoids the necessary distance for critical investigation.
>
> (Francesconi 2005: 382)

---

6 Original: „Und auch wenn meine ursprüngliche Absicht mit den drei Worten „Forschen, Schreiben, Interviewen" der Absicht meiner Forscher-Kolleginnen und -Kollegen doch sehr ähnelte, wurde ich von dem Ort und den Menschen inhaliert, inspiriert und irgendwie auch instrumentalisiert, und ich kann nur zeigen, welch ein für mich zuerst weder verständlicher noch erklärbarer Sog all diese Menschen zu einer Gemeinschaft macht [...]".

12 The *sexy banana* – artifacts of gendered language in tourism — **267**

Figures 12.4–12.6: Material transgression. Hot pant prints: Big ass, no looki looki, look my ass [sic], Timo Werner is an assholes [sic]. Shirt print: Big boobs potato salad (photos by Traber 2016–2017).

Figure 12.7: The *Sexy Banana* (photo by Traber 2018).

According to this definition, the material objects of transgression shown above cannot be categorized as souvenirs. They are not used in the home context once the purchaser has returned from vacation. Additionally, it is highly unlikely for someone returning to the office after a holiday on Mallorca to present gifts like t-shirts with prints like the one shown in Figure 12.6 to their colleagues. Detailed stories about excessive alcohol consumption in the *Bierkönig* would be unlikely to increase one's standing in most professional relationships, nor would anyone place the Sexy Banana on his or her desk as a holiday reminder. Since these items are solely produced for immediate consumption on site and afterwards hidden (until the next trip to El Arenal) or thrown away, I suggest the term "artifact" as a description. They are specially crafted for this very experience and their immediate consumption also hinders any reflection on the concepts of stigmatizations presented. Their purpose is to transfer aggressive catchy slogans that could not be used in everyday life because they violate social norms and political correctness. Thus, the artifacts are used by the tourists to amplify their holiday experience of breaking free from the regulations of their home society, while irony is turned into a tool for the legitimization of the breaking of taboos. Of course, the slogans on the shirts shown above are not only to be read but are also sung in songs, used as conversation openers and as hashtags on social media.

12.4 Migrant – tourist interactions

The sexy banana is not only used by the tourists as a funny way of squirting water at others and maybe starting a chat, but also by the street vendors as a conversation opener to potential female customers: "Hello sexy banana! Look nice watches", is a common phrase they would direct at women. But how deeply can transgression be seated within a touristic setting that the confrontation of a woman with the verbal equivalent of a penis-shaped squirt gun has become a usual opener for sales talk? The sexy banana can be replaced by other vegetables in practice (see Figure 12.8) and language alike: "sexy tomato", "sexy cucumber" and "sexy coconut" are phrases used as well, although the banana remains the most common one. What seems inevitable is the imposition of a sexual identity on almost every female customer.

Although starting a conversation by calling someone *sexy* could be interpreted as complementing the person, the general use of the word without a distinguishable filter of when it would or would not be appropriate to direct it to a woman gives it a strange connotation. No matter if the addressee is sun-bathing at the beach, eating a *XXL Currywurst* or leaving one of the huge club arenas completely drunk at 2 AM, the phrase would still be the same.[7]

Jay (2000: 161) describes how sexual harassment is a marker of speaker power in many occupational settings. Considering that this kind of approach is only used in the context of male street vendors speaking to female tourists, the setting can be defined as one of business. If we suppose that the sexualization of a person and the comparison to a fruit is received as an unwanted comment in a sales situation, it can be assumed that the speaker implies the creation of a hierarchy. By being the one who is able to make such remarks, the street vendor grants himself a higher position in the structure of the scene. This might appear quite surprising, as one would probably expect a more respectful approach towards a potential customer wherein the salesperson would present himself as a supportive person in order to establish a

---

7 This clearly does not mean that there should be situations in which women are told by society that they may not feel confident about themselves. The crucial point here is the sexualization from outside. In any other setting in everyday life, it would clearly be regarded as taboo, or at least rude, to make such a comment while the person is eating or vomiting, for example.

Figure 12.8: Bottle openers (top) and other squirt gun fruit (below) in a tourist shop (photo by Traber 2016).

trustful relationship. To understand why this phrase is nonetheless so widely spread in the context of this tourist culture, it is helpful to take a closer look at the speakers.

In most of the Senegalese cultures, public flirting and displays of affection are inappropriate (Castaldi 2006; Fatou Cisse Kane and Ahmed Cisse p.c. May 2018). This clearly does not mean that sexuality is absent. Kane (2018) has been working on the topic of the intimacy of Senegalese women in Mallorca and states that all of the women she interviewed made it clear that sexuality is something private. Signs of it might be, for example, *bin bins*, which are strings of beads which can be worn around the hips and are usually covered by clothes. Showing someone one's *bin bins* or handing them over is an act of flirting, but these gestures are not usually part of publicly displayed spoken communication.

Therefore, it must be assumed that the phenomenon of the highly sexualized language used by many Senegalese street vendors is specific to the tourist setting. The explanation requires some further comments on this particular context.

12.5 The Helmut phenomenon

During the past years, several games of interaction have evolved between the groups of migrants and tourists. They include and mostly consist of naming and identifying the Other to "[reinitiate] a dialogic circus of calling and being called all over again, day after day, until the touristic high season was over" (Nassenstein 2017: 83).

The most famous word game or tradition is probably *Helmut*. Although there are some theories about how it began, its starting point remains a myth. A typical *Helmut*-based word game can be found in Table 12.1.

Table 12.1: Identifying Helmut.

Tourist	*Hee Helmut!*	Hello Helmut!
Street vendor	*Hallo Helmut! Du Helmut ich Dunkelmut. Looki looki Sonnenbrille!*	Hello Helmut! You Bright-mut me Dark-mut. Looki looki sunglasses!
(Tourist stops and takes a look at the offered products.)		
Street vendor	*Andere Farbe. Heute billig morgen teuer. Hundert Jahre Garantie!*	Different color. Today cheap tomorrow costly. Hundred years of warranty!

There are some variants in which it is unclear whether the street vendor or the tourist is named Helmut. Apparently, this does not really matter. But when Dunkelmut appears in the conversation, the speaker clearly addresses a difference in skin color between the two parties. Sometimes this is even accompanied by gestures towards the limbs.

What is visible here is the initialization of a sales talk with Othering and racialization strategies being treated as language games. No differentiation is made between the individual street vendors and the tourists. For this reason, interactions such as the one described in Table 12.1 can be classified as ritualized.

Coly (2017: 110–112) describes similarly structured word games from Senegal in Wolof. In his examples, Person 1 throws a short phrase to Person 2 to test his or her attention or to confront him or her. Person 2 would then pick up phonemes or parts of them to create an answer, although the literal content might be completely different. The picking up of pieces from the first speaker's approach proves attention, creativity, being smart (turning the word the other has used into an answer) and the willingness to engage in interaction.

In the tourist context of El Arenal's beach, the interaction can be framed with little gifts (small bracelets for example) which might lead to the tourist being willing to reciprocate, and by claiming scarcity and the quality of the product, a relationship is created (Cialdini 2006). This turns out to increase the probability of doing business, embedded in a Wolof-style conversational strategy based on attracting attention and repetition of the other speaker's phonemes the like.

Nonetheless, the Helmut ritual must still be interpreted as a ritualized act of swearing (Ljung 2011: 118) for several reasons. As both parties name each other *Helmut,* it could be assumed that the term serves simply as a common nickname. However, given the fact that the provenance of the name is typically German, the possibility of a Senegalese being truly named Helmut is quite unlikely. Therefore, the act of calling the street vendors *Helmut* can be considered as a bizarre ridiculing signal for a ritualized insult (Ljung 2011: 119). Furthermore, the exclusivity of the use of *Dunkelmut* as a name for the Senegalese street vendors is remarkable. If we assume that the term was used by the tourists first, it must be interpreted as a tool to emphasize that migrants and tourists do not belong to one big group of foreigners in Mallorca.

From the customer's point of view, the *Helmut* performance seems quite entertaining and there is a growing number of videos and photos with hashtags like, for example, *#helmutbestermann* (#helmutbestman) *#heutebilligmorgenteuer* (#todaycheaptomorrowcostly) or *#lookilooki.*

Many tourists post photos and videos of the generalized image of all Senegalese street vendors as *Helmut* on their social media accounts, ridiculing their looks, their language and their voices. The Senegalese are sung about in songs, saying that they are "illegal" and "don't matter" (see Table 12.2).

One of the biggest Mallorca party hits from 2017 presents a Senegalese street vendor as a major interruption in a pick-up situation. This is what Sullivan (2014) describes as a method of desexualization. Someone is presented as alone, untouchable and vulnerable and fails to find closeness in society. By being in contrast to that Other, one tries to appear as the embodiment of heteronormative claims for sexual aggression and masculinity. Judging the Other's (in)capability to attract someone, like in the song, again creates a hierarchical relationship between the singer (emblematic as the tourist) and the street vendor (as the migrant).

What at first might seem like a softening of these harsh relationships are the videos and photographs in which the tourists present themselves with *Helmut* as their new friend. They can be found numerously on *Instagram* under

Table 12.2: Lyrics of *Hallo Helmut (Andere Farbe)*.

Original	Translation
(Verse:) *Ey Jungs, ihr kennt das Ihr habt die hammer Braut klar gemacht (so geil) Wollt mit ihr hoch auf's Zimmer und dann steht ein Helmut vor euch und sagt:*	(Verse:) Yo guys, you know this situation, you just hooked up with some hot chick (so horny) want to go to your hotel room with her, and then a Helmut steps in your way and says:
(Bridge:) *Aber hallo, andere Farbe, hallo Helmut, andere Modell, Heute billig, morgen teuer, lookilooki, neue Kollektion.*	(Bridge:) But hello, different color, hello Helmut, different variant, today cheap, tomorrow costly, lookilooki, new collection
(Chorus:) *Wir singen: Senegal, gal, gal, Illegal, Scheiß egal, gal, gal, Wuppertal, Senegal, gal, gal, Illegal, Scheiß egal, gal, gal, Wuppertal.*	(Chorus:) We sing: Senegal, gal, gal, illegal, Don't matter, atter, atter, Wuppertal, Senegal, gal, gal, illegal, Don't matter, atter, atter, Wuppertal.

Performed by Honk!, published 2017 by Budde Music Publishing GmbH.

the hashtags mentioned earlier. It might appear as if the street vendors were integrated in the tourist culture as an integral part of the party group. But the hierarchical order shown within songs, such as for example by *Honk!*, turns this representation again into a desexualizing situation. The tourist becomes the ultimate caretaker of the Other by spending time with the one who is untouchable and unloved.

Othering is the main strategy of desexualization in this context. In the song, again, the street vendors are reduced to their sales slogans in imperfect language and their constant presence, which is described as being annoying. The tourist, in contrast, is presented as the fulfiller of heteronormative masculinity. Nixon (2009), speaking about a British context, showed that in the past (from the 1970s onwards), service was regarded as women's work and women were much more likely than men to be engaged in work that involves "social" or "people" skills (Nixon 2009: 306).

Street sales is definitely a profession that requires a huge amount of social skills, especially in tourism. Using the profession of the street vendors to underline the tourist's own masculinity, like in the song lyrics cited earlier, leads to the reverse conclusion that the former is being feminized by the tourist, or at least made un-masculine.

Simonton (1998: 237–246) states that in the 20th century, men worked in the low-skilled service sector as well, but were much more likely to be employed in "higher"[8] positions. For example, they might have been involved in the production of the goods offered, or have a greater amount of financial responsibility (accounting). Until today, some areas are stigmatized as typically masculine service niches, for example police or security services, where the expression of emotions or emotional labor is generally kept to a minimum (Nixon 2009: 307).

Willis (1977: 148) states that physical or manual labor was "associated with the social superiority of masculinity, and mental labor with the social inferiority of femininity". This means that, by stressing one's own working class identity in contrast to feminized and racialized sales work, one's own superiority and masculinity is presented.

And again, the concept of increasing one's self-esteem by emphasizing one's belonging to a non-academic or not-upper-class is very present in the whole party scene of El Arenal.

In Table 12.3 you can see the lyrics of one of the most famous *Schlager* stars in El Arenal. Mia Julia sings in her song:

Table 12.3: Lyrics of *Scheiss auf Schickimicki*.

Original	Translation
Scheiss auf Schickimicki, ich will noch 'n Bier, Monaco, St. Tropez, nicht mit mir!	Give a shit about the fancy-schmancy, I want a beer instead, Monaco, St. Tropez, I'm not going there!
Scheiss auf Schickimicki, ich will kein Champagner, wir nehmen jetzt die Hütte so richtig auseinander!	Give a shit about the fancy-schmancy, I don't want champagne, let's do some real party in here now!

Performed by Stefan Stürmer and Mia Julia, published 2015 by DA Records.

It can be seen in these lyrics that the detachment from and opposition to what is considered as the higher social classes is now also common amongst female actors. Jay (2000: 157–159) describes how social class heavily affects the ways in

---

8 These quotation marks highlight the point that being higher in hierarchy historically indicated more social validation as well. From a contemporary perspective, this perception and construction of "better", "clean" or "morally valuable" work is quite problematic (see e.g. Simpson et al. 2012; Anderson 2000).

which speakers swear. Those who are in power are able to curse as they do not fear losing their positions by using bad language. Not being powerful and using swear words is perceived as marker of low social status. "So an effective speaker is one who is able to adapt cursing to appropriate situations" (Jay 2000: 159). By using swear words in the lyrics of the song, the singer presumably identifies herself with the working class. However, the fact that the final "t" of the word *nicht* is pronounced remarkably clearly in the song hints at the speaker actually being at least middle class. German speakers of the working class do not usually pronounce it. This parallels the statements of Fussell (1983), mentioned by Jay (2000: 159), about a bohemian class that would freely use many swear words but distance itself from the working class repertoires by clearly pronouncing the final phoneme /ng/ in *fucking*. Although, in the El Arenal case, this precise pronunciation is not found in a specific swear word but only traceable in a non-taboo word, I argue that this instance shows that neither the artists nor the audience necessarily need to belong to the working class to use their strategies of creating communities by using swear words.

What is still strongly male-dominated is the offensive display of "toughness" or the presented absence of emotion, hiding any feelings in action and language. As in the research cited before, sticking up for yourself and not letting anyone get away with actions one does not like is still perceived as a defining characteristic of the masculine habitus in the El Arenal tourist culture. In Figure 12.9 you can see a t-shirt referring to a German football player who has made himself unpopular due to some mistakes he made during soccer games. It is bought and worn almost exclusively by men and is also a popular slogan to be shouted while strolling the streets in groups.

Therefore, it seems as if the self-representation of women as being in opposition to a higher social class or the opposite gender in general (Traber 2017) is quite strong in comparison with other touristic settings, although explicit swearing and cursing about specific persons is still male-dominated and is even used to construct masculinity.

But violence in language to support the speaker's sexual self-representation is not only targeted at the street vendors, nor at other men in general. Bird (1996) (following Gilligan 1982 and Messner 1992) describes how, alongside emotional detachment,

> [...] competition in the male homosocial group supports an identity that depends not on likeness and cooperation but on separation and distinction [...]. Competition facilitates hierarchy in relationships [...]. Bird (1996: 122)

This competition and hierarchy is visible in the differing presentations of migrant and tourist identities, provided by the latter through the media and

Figure 12.9: 'Timo Werner is a son of a bitch' (photo by Traber 2017).

material culture shown above. The artifacts clearly construct a racialized Other in opposition to the tourist. Such practices of

> [r]acial division [help], as with labour and gender divisions [...] [to provide] an ideological object for feelings about the degeneracy of others and the superiority of the self (thus reinforcing the dominant ideological terms which make the comparison possible).
> (Willis 1977: 152)

Bird (1996: 123) goes on to say that the objectification of women provides a basis on which male superiority is maintained. With this assumption, it is possible to explain the behavior of many male tourists towards the female migrants from West African countries in the streets of El Arenal.

Hair braiders working in the daytime along the beach are often faced with sexual harassment from the male tourists. On a hot day in 2017, a colleague and I were speaking to a group of Senegalese hair braiders who were chatting while waiting for customers at the beach. It was around noon when a drunk tourist from Germany approached them. He told them their bodies were beautiful and smelled of coconuts. Their dark skin was so sexy and he would give them some money if they took good care of him.

The reaction of the women was impressive: they told him to leave and bother somebody else, without showing any anger, and seeming generally rather unimpressed. They went back to talking about everyday business again and ignored him until he had slowly staggered away. This can be interpreted as an adoption of the formerly described strategy of emotional detachment, which is presented in the literature as socially gendered male performance (Nixon 2009). Nonetheless, it is used again in this context to strengthen the self-esteem of the actors and therefore represents a strategy of empowerment.

12.6 Making sense of the banana

To come back to the description of the Sexy Banana and the sexualization of female customers at the beginning of a sales pitch, it can be concluded that the beach and the surrounding areas are places of transgression. Identity and sexuality are permanently expressed and impressed, and the verbal relationship between tourists and migrants presents no exception to this. A well discussed swearing device is the evocation of disgust in reference to a person. Being identified with disgusting or dirty words that usually describe things that "cannot be incorporated into the body without harming the person" (Jay 2000: 199) is clearly insulting. With regard to the "sexy banana" references, I recommend the broadening of this definition of a swearing method. Being named as a fruit that is a sexual reference and can very well be taken into the body of the speaker can either work as a flirting method or repel the recipient. This case shows that such terms can either be understood as transgressive verbal tools in order to mark the hierarchical standing of the two parties, or as ways to express desire and attempts at approximation. The tourist zone is a highly complex semantic field and its multilingual actors play with the possibilities of its liminality.

The street vendors' working space is a field of competing identities, most of them based on masculinity, where the tourists' practices appear to prevail in the public discourse. The latter use racialized and sexualized language against the migrants, constructing them as desexualized subordinates.

Female tourists can adopt strategies of self-representation in the tourist context that were formerly male-dominated, like e.g. the identification with working class attitudes. Thereby, they question traditional sexual identities and strengthen their own position. On the other hand, in doing so, they are no exception to the racializing and discriminating tourist culture.

The use of sexualizing language as a conversation opener by the street vendors can be interpreted as a reestablishment of the role of heteronormative masculinity. As female tourists in El Arenal do not appear to be a marginalized or less-differentiating group, the street vendor's approaches towards them must not necessarily be read as an attack on the female identity by the immediate imposition of a sexual identity. Instead, it can be interpreted as a reaction to the predominant tourists' self-representation as being in opposition to a racialized Other, who is in turn constructed as inferior. Like any person joining a new social environment, a non-native speaker needs to learn the local rules of swearing (Jay and Janschewitz 2008: 269). Migrants in El Arenal are confronted with the broad acceptance of swearing in the verbal and material culture of the tourists. Adjusting to this environment means learning that traditional perceptions of what is defined as politeness and intimate discourse must be rearranged and renegotiated. Public speech practices here include ritual transgressions, like in Figure 12.10, that are necessary for the establishment of a communal experience. Similarly, they are learned and adopted by the migrants as a way of interacting properly with their customers' culture. In this respect, the use of transgressive and sexualizing language by the street vendors is rather (or also) a strategy to mirror and ridicule the hierarchies established by the tourists and their verbal practices, by creating carnivalesque identities and mocking the tourists' language repertoires.

References

Anderson, Bridget. 2000. *Doing the Dirty Work: The Global Politics of Domestic Labour*. London: Zed Books.
Andrews, Hazel. 2011. *The British on Holiday: Charter Tourism, Identity and Consumption*. Bristol: Channel View.
Andrews, Hazel, Les Roberts and Tom Selwyn. 2007. Hospitality and eroticism. *International Journal of Culture, Tourism and Hospitality Research* 1 (3): 247–262.
Augé, Marc. 1995 [1992]. *Non-places. Introduction to an Anthropology of Supermodernity*. London, New York: Verso.
Bird, Sharon. 1996. Welcome to the Men's Club: Homosociality and the Maintenance of Hegemonic Masculinity. *Gender and Society* 19 (2): 120–132.
Castaldi, Francesca. 2006. *Choreographies of African Identities: Négritude, dance, and the National Ballet of Senegal*. Urbana: University of Illinois.
Cialdini, Robert. 2006. *Influence: The Psychology of Persuasion*. New York: Harper Business.

Coly, Jules Jacques. 2017. Emotion, gazes and gestures in Wolof. In Anne Storch (ed.), *Consensus and Dissent. Negotiating Emotion in the Public Space*, 105–122. Amsterdam: John Benjamins.

Francesconi, Sabrina. 2005. The Language of Souvenirs: The Use of Humour in London T-shirts. *Textus* 18: 381–396.

Fussell, Paul. 1983. *Class: A Guide through the American Status System*. New York: Summit.

Gilligan, Carol. 1982. *In a different voice: Psychological theory and women's development*. Cambridge: Harvard University Press.

Jay, Timothy B. 2000. *Why We Curse. A Neuro-Psycho-Social Theory of Speech*. Amsterdam/ Philadelphia: John Benjamins.

Jay, Timothy B. and Kristin Janschewitz. 2008. The pragmatics of swearing. *Journal of Politeness Research: Language, Behavior, Culture* 4: 267–288.

Kane, Fatou Cissé. 2018. Intimacy in the Wolof society. *Third Workshop on Language and Tourism: Workshop on Language and Intimacy*, El Arenal 13–14 October 2018.

Kastner, Kristin. 2014. *Zwischen Suffering und Styling. Die lange Reise nigerianischer Migrantinnen nach Europa*. Berlin: Lit.

Ljung, Magnus. 2011. *Swearing: A Cross-Cultural Linguistic Study*. Basingstoke: Palgrave Macmillan.

Messner, Michael. 1992. Boyhood, organized sports, and the construction of masculinity. *Journal of Contemporary Ethnography* 18 (4): 416–444.

Mietzner, Angelika. 2017. Mein Ballermann – Eine hervorragende Fernbeziehung. *The Mouth* 2: 33–45.

Nassenstein, Nico. 2017. Une promenade linguistique with a Senegalese street vendor: Reflecting multilingual practice and language ideology in El Arenal, Mallorca. *The Mouth* 2: 79–95.

Nixon, Darren. 2009. 'I Can't Put a Smiley Face On': Working-Class Masculinity, Emotional Labour and Service Work in the 'New Economy'. *Gender, Work and Organization* 16 (3): 300–322.

Simonton, Deborah. 1998. *A History of European Women's Work, 1700 to the Present*. New York: Routledge.

Simpson, Ruth, Natasha Slutskaya, Patricia Lewis and Heather Höpfl (eds.). 2012. *Dirty Work. Concepts and Identities*. Hampshire: Palgrave Macmillan.

Storch, Anne, Nick Shepherd, and Ana Deumert. Forthcoming. Trialogue / Tryalogue. *The Mouth* 6.

Stürmer, Stefan and Mia Julia. 2015. *Scheiss auf Schickimicki*. DA Records.

Sullivan, Katie. 2014. With(out) pleasure: Desexualization, gender and sexuality at work. *Organization* 21 (3): 346–364.

Szabo, Sacha. 2011. *Ballermann. Das Buch. Phänomen und Marke. Eine wissenschaftliche Analyse eines außeralltäglichen Erlebnisses*. Marburg: Tectum.

Traber, Janine. 2017. Der Verkauf von Verkehr. *The Mouth* 2: 59–77.

Willis, Paul. 1977. *Learning to Labour: How Working Class Kids Get Working Class Jobs*. Farnborough: Saxon House.

Anna-Brita Stenström
13 English- and Spanish-speaking teenagers' use of rude vocatives

Abstract: So far the description of teenagers' linguistic habits has been restricted to Europe and the United States. This paper broadens the description by comparing the use of rude vocatives by teenage boys and girls in Latin-America (Buenos Aires and Santiago de Chile) and Europe (London and Madrid) on the basis of four corpora of spontaneous conversation. The paper highlights that the teenagers use rude vocatives with no intention to insult but as intimacy-markers signalling social bonding. This is illustrated by extracts from the corpora, which also show that rude vocatives are more often used by the Spanish-speaking than by the English-speaking teenagers, and by the Latin-American teenagers in particular. Chilean *huevón*, for instance, is used so often that it is developing into a pragmatic marker, while the London teenagers use the neutral vocative *tío/a* for the same purpose. The rude vocatives are most often used by boys, above all the Spanish-speaking boys, with two notable exceptions: the girls' *boluda* in Buenos Aires and *gilipollas* in London, which points to the ongoing linguistic levelling between the sexes, when it comes to the use of rude words. To end up, three words that have changed from extremely offensive vocatives to more or less accepted intensifiers are given special attention, notably *motherfucker, cunt* and *coño*.

Cállate gilipollas
'Shut up dickhead'

13.1 Introduction

Expressions that are generally regarded as offensive, such as Spanish *hijo de puta* and English *son of a bitch,* may not have an offensive effect at all. In everyday casual conversation among friends, and among teenagers in particular, they tend to be used as social devices intended to keep an intimate contact. This "friendly" usage is emphasized by Mateo & Yus (2000), who discuss insulting words in terms of "offense-centred", "praise-centred", and "interaction-centred", arguing that the interaction-centred insults are used to reinforce the social bonds between speaker and hearer rather than offend. Others, for instance Rodríguez (2002: 48), refer to similar expressions as *"vocativos cariñosos"* ('affectionate address terms'), a view that is also expressed by Zimmermann (2002), while Jaworski and Galasinski (2000: 35) describe the relationship between speaker and addressee reflected in the use of address terms as follows:

> Terms of address do not only reflect the relative positions of interactants vis-à-vis one another and in society as a whole. The speaker's choice of a particular form of address locates the addressee in social space and defines, or constructs, the social actors' mutual relationship.

As this paper will show, some of the most frequent rude, and potentially insulting, vocatives are used as intimate address terms by English- and Spanish-speaking teenagers alike in their everyday conversational encounters. This is reflected in *The Bergen Corpus of London Teenage Language* (COLT) and its Spanish correspondence *Corpus Oral de Lenguaje Adolescente,* which consists of three subcorpora: COLAm (Madrid), COLAs (Santiago de Chile) and COLAba (Buenos Aires). The corpora are highly comparable, considering that the COLA subcorpora were compiled with COLT as a model. They all consist of everyday conversations, chats, between teenagers aged 13 to 19, which were recorded by voluntary students provided with adequate recording equipment and asked to record as much talk as possible with their friends in various situations, with no instructions whatsoever on what to talk about. Two important differences between the corpora with implication for the result of this study have to be kept in mind, however: time of corpus collection and corpus size. One is that COLT was collected at the beginning of the 1990s, COLAm about ten years later and COLAs and COLAba another couple of years later. The other is that COLAs and COLAba are much smaller than the roughly half-a-million-word-corpora COLAm and COLT.

13.2 The favourite rude vocatives

13.2.1 Presentation

The difference in corpus size, with COLT consisting of 431,528 words, COLAm of 456,340, and COLAs and COLAba consisting of a mere 70,354 and 68,539 words each, had inevitable consequences for the comparison of frequency and use of the most common rude vocatives. To make up for the unbalance, an upper limit of five vocatives per corpus with a frequency of at least 0.1 per thousand words were included in the present comparison. The result is reflected in Table 13.1, which shows that, despite the limitation, no more than four vocatives reached the limit in COLAba:

Table 13.1: The favourite rude vocatives.

COLT	COLAm	COLAs	COLAba
London	Madrid	Santiago de Chile	Buenos Aires
Bastard	Cabrón	Huevón	Boluda
Bitch	Gilipollas	Puta	Boludo
Dick	Hijo(de)puta	Loca	Loca
Cunt	Maricón	Culiado	Loco
Wanker	Puta	Huevona	

13.2.2 Definitions

What is referred to as 'rude' vocatives in this study varies from 'vulgar' and 'derogatory' to 'abusive', 'offensive' and 'insulting' in *Diccionario de la Lengua Española* (2001) and *The New Oxford Dictionary of English* (1998). In Sanmartín Sáez's *Diccionario de argot* (2003) and Green's *Cassells' dictionary of slang* (2000) they are simply referred to as slang words. The encyclopedic information below emanates from *Real Academia Española* online (RAE), *Etymological Dictionary* online and OED online.

SPANISH

Boludo/a	a typically Argentinian word; origin *bolas* ('testicles'); used as an insult meaning stupid.
Cabrón/a	originally a colloquial adjective said about a man whose wife is unfaithful, or a coward, later about somebody who causes trouble, equivalent to *asshole* and *fucker*.
Culiado/a	origin *culo* ('arse'), said about a person with bad intentions.
Gilipollas	a compound of the vulgar adjective *gilí* ('stupid') and the vulgar noun *polla* ('penis') is an insult equivalent to English *asshole*.
Huevón/a	the Chilean counterpart of *boludo*, refers to 'testicles'.
Hijo/a de puta	literally 'son/daughter of a prostitute': the masculine form originally the most frequent insult in Spanish, which has developed into a much less pejorative word than it used to be.

(continued)

Loco/a	from Castilian *loco* has an uncertain origin.
Maricón	used as a vulgar term for an effeminate man, originally homosexual.
Puta	means 'prostitute'.

ENGLISH

Bastard	originally used for an illegitimate child and later for a sexually contemptuous man, or a man who is objectionable; nowadays often said affectionately.
Bitch	originally female dog; later used as a term of contempt applied to a woman, in particular a malicious, unpleasant and selfish woman.
Dick	a euphemism for penis and a pejorative epithet.
Cunt	vagina; is an obscene term for woman.
Wanker	British slang from *wank* 'masturbate', said about a stupid, lazy contemptible person.

13.2.3 Distribution

The inventory of rude words in the present corpora shows that the Latin-American teenagers do not only use them more frequently than the English but also the Madrid teenagers, as demonstrated in Table 13.2, which shows the distribution in relation to corpus size:

Table 13.2: Number of rude words in relation to corpus size.

	COLT	COLAm	COLAs	COLAba
Corpus size	431,528	456,340	70,354	68,579
Number per 1000 words	0.2	0.8	5.0	3.4

The Latin-American figures are amazingly high, considering the very modest size of the corpora. The study shows that the Latin-American teenagers use the rude vocatives in question far more often than the teenagers from Madrid, with the teenagers from Santiago de Chile by far the most frequent users. Going into more detail, Table 13.3 shows the frequency of the rude vocative in relation to the total occurrence of the word:

Table 13.3: Vocative use in relation to the total occurrence of the rude word.

COLT		COLAm		COLAs		COLAba	
	rude/total		rude/total		rude/total		rude/total
bastard	35/118	puta	161/654	huevón	292/786	boluda	174/189
bitch	29/108	cabrón	69/123	puta	29/64	boludo	56/82
cunt	15/55	gilipollas	59/204	huevona	17/29	loca	6/14
wanker	11/34	hijo de puta	51/140	culiado	12/68	loco	4/11
dick	9/98	maricón	15/31	loca	1/19		
Total	99/413		355/1155		351/966		240/296
% rude	.24		.31		.36		.89

Male vocatives dominate in the London and Santiago conversations with *bastard* and *huevón*, respectively, and the female vocatives, represented by *puta* and *boluda* in the Madrid and Buenos Aires conversations. Notice that the Latin-American rude vocatives, except *puta*, do not appear among the most common rude vocatives in the Madrid conversations, and that the only rude vocatives that Santiago de Chile and Buenos Aires have in common is *loca*.

A scrutiny of the texts, reflected in Table 13.4, suggests that the girls are the most frequent users of the top five rude vocatives in Buenos Aires and the

Table 13.4: Boys' and girls' use of rude vocatives.

COLT		COLAm		COLAs		COLAba	
	boys/girls		boys/girls		boys/girls		boys/girls
bastard	90/26	cabrón	43/34	huevón	344/38	boluda	7/174
bitch	56/49	gilipollas	43/125	huevona	13/15	boludo	70/10
dick	72/24	hijo de puta	116/24	puta	51/12	loca	4/10
cunt	35/20	maricón	29/5	loca	16/3	loco	7/3
wanker	26/7	puta	479/175	culiado	66/2		

boys in Santiago de Chile, addressing each other by the abundant vocatives *boluda* and *huevón*, respectively, with only the female vocative *loca* in common. In the London conversations the tendencies are less clearly pronounced, but it is obvious that the boys dominate, and so do the Madrid boys, except when it comes to *gilipollas*, which seems to be a girls' word. Gender follows gender in that the boys and girls address each other with male and female vocatives, with some exceptions. One is illustrated in Example (1) from COLT, where Karen addresses Louise by *wanker*:

(1) Karen: *let's have a bit of your York's*
Louise: *no it's for my lunch tomorrow you see*
Anne: *don't lie [just don' give her any]*
Louise: *[I'm not eating] it tonight, I am, I'm not eating it*
Karen: *oh ya bullshit*
Anne: *yeah bollocks*
Karen: *bollocks you **wanker*** 36501

In this context the word *wanker* has lost much of its "masculinity"; it is likely to indicate no more than intimacy and friendship, regardless of the sex of the addressee in much the same way as *cunt* in utterances such as *sod off you cunt, fuck off you cunt* and *oh shut up you fat ugly motherfucking cunt*, said jokingly by London boys. But the function obviously depends on how the word is pronounced in terms of stress and tone of voice – and in what context. As far as the girls are concerned, the data also shows that they more often address a boy as *hijo de puta* than a girl as *hija de puta*, while vice versa that boys more often address a girl as *hija de puta* than a boy as *hijo de puta*. It also appears that the female form *maricona* is sometimes uttered by a boy addressing another boy.

13.3 The use of rude vocatives illustrated

13.3.1 Preliminaries

With an insult defined as "a disrespectful or scornfully abusive remark" *(The New Oxford Dictionary of English* 1998: 948), the question to consider when judging the effect of the rude vocatives presented above is: What is it that decides that what looks like an abusive remark or insult does not always function as one? This question is discussed in detail by Mateo and Yus (2013: 90), who argue that even if one purpose of an insult may be to offend, utterances cannot be considered insults unless the addressee reacts to them as such. In other words, what counts is not primarily the speaker's intention but more so the addressee's reaction. The function typical of adolescent speech, they say, is to praise or to reinforce social bonding; adolescents "use insults in a phatic, group-membership-fostering strategy" (2013: 95; cf. Stenström and Jørgensen 2008), which is influenced by the addressee's background in terms of sex, age, race, and social status, in addition to the constraints of the speech event. My argument here is that the intention of the teenagers in the extracts illustrated in the following is not to insult but, primarily, to reinforce social bonding (For the role of swearing to achieve in-group solidarity see Beers Fägersten 2012).

In order to place the dialogue in context, each extract below is preceded by a brief comment explaining what is going on. The extract is followed by a concluding comment, which shows how I interpret the use of the vocative in each situation.[1]

Cabrón/a & *asshole*

(2) **Situation:** Anita, Daniel, Clara and Isabel have met for a chat somewhere in town.

Anita: *yo me quedaría aquí chaval no me apetece irme ahora*
'I'd stay here man I don't fancy leaving now'

Daniel: *y ahora nos pellizcamos*
'and now let's take a shot'

Clara: *eh ah **cabrón** me he metido un pellizco en el culo sabes*
'eh ah you dickhead I've taken a rump shot you know'

Anita: *qué drogadictos sois eh*
'what drug addicts you are eh'

Isabel: *vamoosssss* MABPE2
'let's goooo'

Interpretation: The four teenagers in this episode do not seem to agree on whether they should stay where they are or move on. To begin with, Anita is inclined to stay, but seems to change her mind when it turns out that Clara and

---

[1] The labels MABPE2, MASHE3, etc. and 36501, 4205, etc. accompanying the Spanish and English extracts respectively indicate where the extracts are found in the corpora.

Daniel are injecting drugs, judging by her ironical-critical remark (*qué drogadictos sois*). Isabel is apparently keen on leaving, which she shows by the drawn-out pronunciation *vamoosss* for *vamos* ('let's go'). Daniel is apparently not the least upset when addressed as *cabrón*, despite the originally negative meaning of the word, which signifies "Persona que tolera el adultero de su cónyuge" ('person who tolerates husband's or wife's adultery') or "Persona mal intencionada" (a person with bad intentions') according to Sanmartín Sáez (2003: 156–157). It is a very common address term among the boys in COLAm, and has probably become so common that nobody is aware of its origin. The slang vocative *chaval* ('boy'), in comparison, is completely neutral and almost integrated in standard Spanish (Sanmartín Sáez 2003: 215). It corresponds to English *man* with a vocative function.

(3) **Situation:** John, Ben and Matthew are discussing the death penalty system in the US and the American legislation regarding the possession of weapons.

Ben: *Everyone was allowed to carry a gun. That's stupid.*

Matthew: *That is cool.*

John: *Why?*

Matthew: *Freeze* **asshole**

Ben: *He says he says that it's gonna stop crime so much cos if everyone can have a gun.*

John: *Stop that.* 41405

Interpretation: The topic is brought up by Ben, who has just been told that all Americans are allowed to carry a gun, which he thinks is stupid. Matthew, on the other hand, unless he is provoking, seems to think that the American penalty system is cool, and he objects strongly (*Freeze asshole*), when John asks him to clarify his standpoint. He obviously thinks that John's objection (*Why?*) is extremely stupid. But John does not give in; he does not agree to the crime preventing function of American citizens' right to carry a gun and would rather put an end to the dispute (*Stop that*). John is probably not offended by Matthew's rude utterance, since he does not seem to react. *Stop that* is apparently directed to Ben.

Gilipollas and *dickhead*

(4) **Situation:** Mario is explaining why he will record teenage conversations and how it is done.

Adam: *¿qué vais a hacer?*
    'what are you going to do'

Mario: *estamos grabando tronco*
    'we are recording man'

Adam: *¿qué?*
    'what'

    ...

Mario: *que es que para los noruegos* **gilipollas** *quédate*
    'cos it's for the Norwegians blockhead stay'

Juan: *¿que es para qué?*
    'it's for what'

Andrés: *para los noruegos*[2]
    'for the Norwegians'

Gonzalo: *es verdad*
    'that's right'

Adam: *pues si ése es el micrófono ...*
    'well if this is the microphone'

Mario: *sí eso es el micrófono de un minidisc MALCE2*
    'yes this is the microphone of a minidisc'

Interpretation: What precedes this extract is a long "discussion" about recording Spanish teenagers' conversations. At this point, a newcomer, Adam, turns up and wants to know what it is all about, and Mario explains that he is recording conversations *para los noruegos*, and he also tells him what equipment is being used. But why should he address Adam by *gilipollas*? He probably either thinks that Adam ought to be aware of what is going on, that he is stupid, or uses this term as an intimacy signal, which would explain why Adam does not appear to be the least offended, although *gilipollas* is a typical girls' address term (cf. Table 13.4).

(5)   **Situation:** Boys listening to music.

    Michael: *Turn it on.*

    Jonathan: *It is.*

    Michael: *It's on?*

    Terry: *Jonathan's a dancing queen.*

    Jonathan: {laughing} *Yeah, {unclear} you* **dickhead.**

    Michael: *Jonathan's a queen, period.*

---

2 The corpus collection was administered by a Norwegian research team.

Jonathan: *Yeah your mum's a queen.*

Many: {nv} laugh{/nv}[3]{unclear} 38906

Interpretation: When addressing Terry as *dickhead,* Jonathan emphasizes that he does not like to be referred to as *dancing queen*. Terry, on the other hand, does not react to being addressed as *dickhead*, which shows that he takes the potential offense as a friendly term. In other words, this is an amicable exchange, which might easily have turned into a slightly more "serious" word game, or play with words, a so-called "ritual insult", realized as "swearing by mother" (cf. Hasund et al. 2014: 13–15). Notice that Jonathan turns Michael's *Jonathan's a queen* into *your mum's a queen*. Michael could have responded, for instance, with 'your mother is a bitch', whereupon Jonathan could have gone on with 'your mother is a whore', and so on.

Hijo de puta and *son of a bitch*

(6) **Situation:** Manuel and Carlos discuss football and the Madrid club El Leganés in particular.

Manuel: *El Leganés en el primer equipo del segundo debe está* (sic) *jugando el hijo de puta*
   'El Leganés in the first equipment in the second half ought to play the bastard'

Carlos: *sí **hijo de puta** MALCE4*
   'yes son of a bitch'

Interpretation: Despite the fact that El Leganés is a football club and not a football player Manuel calls it *hijo de puta*, which is apparently used for strong emphasis. Manuel is convinced that El Leganés should play, and so is Carlos. But his *hijo de puta,* on the other hand, is apparently just echoing the first occurrence and seems to be slightly ironical rather than insulting.

(7) **Situation:** Sally from Hackney is telling a story with an unexpected end: a man was thrown out of a cab, a bus and a train as soon as he showed a letter he had received from a fortune teller.

Sally: ... sharp intake of breath {/nv} *and he goes* {shouting} *Get out of my fucking cab,* **you dirty son of a bitch***!* {unclear{/} *He gets out of the cab, right. So he gets out of the cab...* 32701

---

3 {nv} indicates nonverbal sound.

Interpretation: This is one of the two examples of *son of a bitch* in COLT, both from this same narrative and said with the same emphasis, reflecting anger and frustration. That there are only two examples altogether in COLT – not even used by the teenagers themselves – seems to indicate that English *son of a bitch* is far less frequent than the Spanish corresponding expression *hijo de puta*. One might speculate why this is so. The fact that *son of a bitch* has American roots might be part of the explanation. On the other hand, the expression dates back to the 17th century, which would have given it ample time to spread to Europe.

Maricón and *wanker*

(8) **Situation:** The students were only instructed to record as much spontaneous speech as possible, with no preferences, but Tonio, Daniel, Sergio and Mike are convinced that the main reason was to collect their use of taboo words, as this extract shows:

Tonio: *se trata de decir insultos no/*[4]
    'the idea is to use insults isn't it'

Daniel: *putas*
    'whores'

Sergio: *putas venga **maricón***
    'whores come on wanker'

Mike: *y si se dice que sí no ja ja ja ja*
    'and if it means yes ha ha ha ha'

Sergio: *se trata de que se aprendan los insultos en español*
    'it's a matter of learning insults in Spanish'. MASHE3

Interpretation: Here, nobody can be offended, since the taboo words are uttered with no particular target. In a different context both *puta* and *maricón* might have been regarded as insults.

(9) **Situation:** Louise does not let Karen and Anne taste the Yorkshire pudding that she is keeping for next day's lunch.

Karen: *let's have a bit of your York's*

Louise: *no it's for my lunch tomorrow you see*

Anne: *don't lie [just don't give her any]*

---

4 / indicates rising tone.

Louise: *[I am I'm not eating]*[5] *it tonight, I am, I'm not eating it*

Karen: *oh ya bullshit*

Anne: *yeah bollocks*

Karen: *bollocks you* **wanker**

Louise: *you're a stirring little woman you are*

Anne: *I know* 36501

Interpretation: Karen objects to Louise's refusal to let Karen taste the pudding that she is saving for next day's lunch. She is supported by Anne (*don't give her any*), although she does not seem to believe that Louise is saving it for the following day. Nor does Karen, who objects (*oh yeah bullshit*). Now Anne appears to have changed her mind and is supporting Karen (*yeah bollocks*), who goes even further addressing Louise directly by what looks like a personal insult (*bollocks you wanker*), but Louise does not appear to be the least insulted. What is interesting is that *wanker*, despite its male reference ('masturbator'), is used by a girl to address another girl. This is not uncommon in the COLT conversations, however. Similarly, the female word *cunt* is sometimes used to address a boy by another boy (*fuck off you cunt*).

Puto/a and *bastard/bitch*

(10) **Situation:** Tonio and Clara are chatting and apparently eating something. And they are revelling in taboo words.

Clara: *dame un cacho*
    'give me a piece'

Tonio: **puta**
    'bitch'

Clara: *zorro*
    'bastard'

Tonio: *maricón que eres que eres que eres que eres maricona hala pero hija de puta*
    'bastard you are you are you are you are a cow damn it but bitch'
pero zorra te llevas aquí medio bollo de golpe hija de la gran puta
    'but bitch you are getting a beating you daughter of the bloody bitch'
me cago en tu puta madre coño joder asquerosa de mierda
    'I shit on your bloody mother damn fuck bloody shit'

Clara: *ja ja ja ja ja ja ja ja ja*

Tonio: *jo jo jo jo jojo* MABPE 2

---

[5] The square brackets indicate simultaneous speech.

Interpretation: Clara and Tonio are thoroughly enjoying using foul language. But notice that, in this context, the word *puta* is not used in order to cause offense; it is only an example of the "bad words" that the speakers are convinced that "the Norwegians" would be interested in.

(11) **Situation:** Ben, Set and John are busy trying to solve a chemistry task in class. John seems to be fairly familiar with the problem. The others are not.

Ben: *So hold on, what's the formula?*

Set: *Oh shit.*

John: *You're supposed to put the lid on, otherwise it won't, switch off.*

Set: *Seriously?*

John: *Yeah.*

Set: *Why not?*

John: *Dunno. Something, don't know what it is.*

Set: *I'll tell you what I'm gonna see how fucking, white this water* ...

John: *V equals point two five, eight, cubed* .... *Oh Gordon Bennet*[6] ....

Set: *You sad* **bastard**.

John: *What did he want?*

Set: *China girls, by David Bowie. 42001*

Interpretation: Neither Ben nor Set knows the formula that is required for the task to be carried out. But it turns out that John knows. Here, Set's reaction (*You sad bastard*) is not at all insulting but ironical, meaning 'you are so clever'. John does not seem to react to the comment but goes on to a matter that has nothing to do with the chemistry lesson. He probably takes Set's comment as a compliment.

(12) **Situation:** Three 17-year old boarding school girls, Lucy, Anne and Kate, are looking forward to the approaching Christmas holidays, and Lucy reveals that she has been promised a car for Christmas:

Lucy: *guess what my dad told me today*

Anne: *[look]*

Kate: *[what]*

---

[6] Gordon Bennet is originally the name of a newpaper magnate, James Gordon Bennet, who lived an extravagant life as a playboy and took over the control of *The New Herald* after his father, the founder, in 1835; the expression is used as a euphemism for *gorblimey*, which is Cockney for *god blind me* and expresses surprise.

Lucy: *he says he said he might er might be able to get me a car for the Christmas holidays*

Kate: *ah!* ***bitch****.*

Lucy: *just for the Christmas holidays* 42304

Interpretation: Kate's *bitch* is said jokingly, with a touch of irony, reflecting that Kate is just envious. Nothing personal. Lucy fully understands her reaction and assures that the car is not a permanent present; it is just a loan for Christmas.

13.3.2 Summing up

Are the rude vocatives offensive?

The effect of the vocatives in all the extracts except (7), which is a narrative, is to intensify, insist, tease, and so on besides signalling intimacy and social bonding. They do not seem to reflect the addresser's intention to insult. Consequently, I agree with (Mateo and Yus 2013: 90) that "[i]nsults have meanings insofar as the context where they are embedded favours an insulting interpretation"; more precisely, that they "have to produce cognitive effects that lead to a reaction". The implication is that rude vocatives do not function as insults if the addressee does not react to them as such, regardless of the addresser's intention. But let's reconsider example (2) above, where Matthew comments on the American legislation allowing everyone to carry a gun. If John's *Why?* is interpreted as a reaction to Matthew's *That's cool*, to which Matthew reacts by *Freeze asshole,* John's final *Stop that*! might indicate that John was offended – despite the otherwise friendly atmosphere. The contextual situation has a crucial role, which includes the "interlocutors' sex, age, race, or social status, as well as situational constraints of the speech event." (Mateo & Yus 2013: 92). Thus, in the right context an utterance such as *You fucking bastard!* could mean 'You are a great guy!', a phenomenon that is "particularly frequent among adolescents, who use insults in a phatic, group-membership fostering strategy" (2013: 92.).

Mateo and Yus (2000: 17) emphasize the role of taboo words as phatic devices, arguing that insults have a social function, "where the meaning is almost irrelevant". Likewise, Stenström and Jørgensen (2008) point out that the function of taboo words is often of a purely social nature: to help the speakers keep a conversation going and create a feeling of rapport, which points to their phatic use, as illustrated, for instance, in examples (8) and (9), where the dialogue goes on simply by means of rude words (cf. Beers Fägersten 2012).

When considering the COLA and COLT teenagers' rich use of rude language, one should not forget that all the speakers, and not only the recruits, were probably fully aware that the recordings would be used for research, and since they believed that the researchers were particularly interested in "bad" language, in terms of slang, taboo and swearwords in particular, it is not too far-fetched to assume that they uttered as many rude words as possible to meet the expectations.

Some notes on form and function

As the extracts above have shown, the way Spanish and English vocatives are structured may differ in terms of form as well as function. For instance, English vocatives are more often than not preceded by the personal pronoun *you,* as in extracts (5) *you dickhead* and (9) *you wanker,* often in combination with a pre-modifying adjective, as in (7) *you dirty son of a bitch* and (11) *you sad bastard.*

In Spanish, vocative constructions do not include a personal pronoun, so combinations such as **tú cabrón* or **tú hijo de puta* do not occur. On the other hand, vocative constructions involving a pre-modifying adjective occur in combination with *cabrón,* so we get *ahuevonado cabrón* ('egg-shaped bastard'), *chulo cabrón* ('stuck-up bastard') and *loco cabrón* ('crazy bastard'), to be compared with the English vocative in (2) above – but without the personal pronoun. Three of the Spanish top five rude vocatives have a nominal as well as an adjectival function: *cabrón, gilipollas* and *puto/a,* as in *un profesor que era más cabrón que todos* ('a teacher who was more unpleasant than all'), *es un poco gilipollas el pobre* ('he is a bit stupid the poor thing'), *con una puta camiseta negra* ('with a bloody black T-shirt'). Among the English top five only *bastard* can have both functions, for instance *you joined the sad bastard queue*. In some cases only the immediate co-text decides whether the adjectival or the nominal function predominates. One ambiguous example is ¡*qué gilipollas!* which can either be an adjective meaning 'how stupid' or a noun meaning 'what a dickhead'. What looks like corresponding examples in COLT are *Reg is a bastard man* and *his dad's a bastard boy,* were it not for the fact that both *man* and *boy* are used as vocatives, which is revealed by the pronunciation with *man* and *boy* preceded by a brief pause.

13.4 Change of function

In addition to the top five rude words discussed so far, three other rude words serving as vocatives merit special attention: *motherfucker*, *coño* and *cunt*, all of which have undergone a process involving a change from extremely offensive nouns to more or less accepted intensifying expressions.

Motherfucker

At the beginning of the 20th century *motherfucker* was looked upon as a supreme insult. Later it was used for anything one dislikes and from the middle of the century to express not only bad but also good feelings (cf. Green 2000: 806). In COLT, there are only two instances of *motherfucker*, one of which is demonstrated in extract (13). The example illustrates a way of insulting (if taken seriously) that is not exemplified in the previous extracts is by means of so-called 'battling', or 'playing the Dozens', which is a kind of verbal game, where the speakers try to overdo each other by exchanging indecent remarks about each other's mothers, or occasionally other family members (cf. Hasund et al. 2014: 36*)*. The game tends to get more and more indecent and goes on until there is no come-back. A short version is illustrated in (13):

(13) Toby: *And you see that truck what just went by*

Roger: *Yeah . your mum's got her fanny stuck up the exhaust of it. Beat that one* **motherfucker***!*

Toby: *Don't be funny.*

Roger: *Your mum's got a kick start on her electric wheelchair* 35808

As regards the role of *motherfucker* in this extract, it might of course be used as an insult, considering the insinuations, but is more plausibly meant as an inoffensive vocative used for fun between two friends.

The kind of verbal game illustrated in (13) is quite common in the London data but occurs only twice in the Madrid data. One occurrence is illustrated in (14), where the Spanish teenager is addressing "an imagined audience in Norway" (cf. Drange et al 2014: 22), knowing that what s/he said would ultimately be listened to by the Norwegian researchers when the corpus had been collected.

(14) Tu madre es una puta, **hijos de puta,** maricones, Noruega, puta
  'Your mother is a whore, sons of a whore, queer, Norway, whore' MALCE2

The very frequent expression *hijo/hija de puta* ('son/daughter of a whore'), which seems to be an obvious candidate in this connection, does not directly refer to the addressee's mother but is a more general term of offence.

(15) Alan: *Hey where you going*

  Bert: ***Motherfucker**! I was supposed to be going home.* 38001

Cunt

Cunt has long been regarded as the most offensive word in the English language (Stenström 2017; Christie 2013). It has been a taboo word since the 15th century but has gradually weakened. In the late 17th century it was said about a woman as a sex object, and in the 19th century about a male or female unpleasant person. Later, like *motherfucker,* it was used so frequently that it has "lost its taboo value and became a neutral synonym for 'person'" (Green 2000: 3000–3001). Nowadays, *cunt* can either be used to address somebody (*you cunt*) or be said about males as well as females (*he/she is a cunt*).

Coño

Coño has undergone a development partly similar to that of *cunt.* The difference is that the grammaticalization of *coño* has gone even further and turned it into an intensifier. Both *coño* and *cunt* originate from Latin *cunnus,* a vulgar term for 'vagina', but only *cunt* is used as a vocative. This means that, despite appearances, *coño* is not used as a term of address in an example such as *¿por qué corres coño?*; it corresponds to English 'why do you run for god's sake?' and not to 'why do you run dickhead?'. In other words, it is used as an interjection and not as a rude vocative. On the other hand, it is sometimes said about somebody, e.g. *el puto coño* ('the bloody bastard') or *¡qué coño!* ('what a bastard'). It is frequently used as an interjection indicating surprise or irritation, but the typical function is as an intensifier, where it either occurs alone (¡*coño!* 'dammit') or in questioning expressions such as *¿quién coño?* ('who the hell') and *¿por qué coño?* ('why the hell') and other expressions beginning with an interrogative (Sanmartín Sáez 2003: 267). It is sometimes used in the same way as *fuck!* or *damn!*, which indicates that it is not as strong as it used to be, and it is sometimes used to express fear, anger, surprise and even joy, e.g. *coño te quiero* ('I love you for god's sake') (cf. https://www.speakinglatino.com/cono-what-a-bad-Spanish-word/).

Boludo/a and *huevón/a*

Boludo/a (Argentina) and *huevón/a* (Chile) have a similar origin. *Boludo/a* derives from the plural form *bolas* 'testicles' and the suffix *-udo/a* and *huevón/a* from the singular form *hueva* 'testicle' and the suffix *-ón*. Literally they are both insults, but the insulting effect vanishes when they are uttered in friendly chats. As pointed out by Ramiro Gelbes and Estrada (2003: 342), being 'bad words' they are even more intimate than other vocatives and used among adolescents in particular, where their absence would be noticed. The present data shows that the male form *huevón* and the female form *boluda* are extremely common among the boys in Santiago de Chile and among the girls in Buenos Aires. *Huevón*, in particular, is so frequent that it resembles a conversational 'filler', helping the speaker to get the conversation going. In other words, its role as a vocative is fading and it is developing into a discourse marker (cf. Rojas 2012: 156).

13.5 Conclusion

This paper has demonstrated that English and Spanish teenagers use rude vocatives with no intention to offend but as a social, and interaction-centered element when talking to friends, a tendency that was found to dominate in the Spanish-speaking teenagers' conversations.

13.5.1 Comparing the use of rude words

All in all, the most frequent rude words turned out to be far more as common in the Spanish as in the English teenagers' conversations (Table 13.2), while the Latin-American teenagers' usage far exceeds that of the teenagers from peninsular Madrid (Table 13.1). With regard to gender and overall frequency, the London boys were found to use the rude vocatives slightly more often than the girls, while there seemed to be no gender difference in this respect among the Madrid boys and girls, which points to the levelling that is going on between sexes when it comes to the use of bad language. That this is not only a teenage phenomenon but an ongoing development in the adult population is witnessed by McEnery (2006), who found that adult males no longer use bad language more than females, when it comes to the frequency of use. As regards word choice on the other hand, he observed that some words are overused by males and some by females, which agrees with the observations in this study. The order of frequency among the Spanish boys and girls was *cabrón, hijo de puta* and *gilipollas* versus *gilipollas, hijo de puta* and *cabrón*, respectively. This shows that the most frequent rude vocatives are generally aimed at boys, with *gilipollas* the only exception, which is used to address boys as well as girls. The order among the English boys is *bastard, bitch* and *cow* and among the girls *bitch, cow* and *bastard*, which shows that, unlike the Spanish teenagers, the boys as well as the girls in COLT direct their most frequent rude vocative, *bastard* and *bitch*, respectively, at their own gender in the first place. (For more information about Spanish and English teenage girls' use of taboo words see Stenström 2006). Unfortunately, the small size of the two Latin-American corpora rules out all comparison in this respect.

Likewise, the role of the teenagers' socioeconomic background can only be partly commented on, since the search program accompanying the corpora only provides figures for COLT and COLAm. Briefly, it shows that the teenagers with a middle class background are the most frequent users of rude vocatives in Madrid – while the low figures in COLT do not permit any conclusions regarding the tendencies among the English teenagers.

13.5.2 Comparing the use of rude and inoffensive vocatives

The comparison involving the use of inoffensive as opposed to rude vocatives pointed to an overwhelming difference between the corpora: It showed that the most frequent inoffensive vocatives in COLAm, *tío* and *tía*, were eleven times more common than the closest English corresponding vocatives in COLT, *man* and *girl*. This, and the fact that the rude vocatives were three times more frequent in COLAm than in COLT does not indicate, of course, that the English teenagers were less intimate or less socially competent than the Spanish, considering the abundant use of phatic devices such as *you know* and *I mean* and tags like *yeah* and *innit* in the COLT data, and the use of the personal pronoun *you* (*you bastard*), which is not matched by a corresponding *tú* in Spanish.

There is no doubt that what is regarded as taboo and rude language changes as time goes by, which is reflected in the more frequent use of originally rude words overall in recent years. Take for instance English *motherfucker* and *cunt* and Spanish *coño,* which have developed from extremely insulting words to (almost) neutral intensifying expressions. The difference in use between rude and inoffensive vocatives is noteworthy, the inoffensive ones being far more frequent than the rude ones in both corpora. In COLT, both rude and inoffensive vocatives are extremely rare. All in all, we can conclude that the use of rude vocatives is an exception rather than the rule, which is heavily accentuated in COLAm. What is particularly noteworthy is the ongoing development of originally rude (*huevón*) as well as neutral vocatives (*tío/a*) into pragmatic markers.

References

Beers Fägersten, Kristy. 2012. *Who's swearing now? The social aspects of conversational swearing.* Cambridge: Cambridge Scholars.
Christie, Christine. 2013. The Relevance of Taboo Language: An Analysis of the Indexical Values of Swearwords. *Journal of Pragmatics* 58: 152–169.
Diccionario de la Lengua Española. 2001. Real Academia Española.
Drange, Eli-Marie, I. Kristine Hasund and Anna-Brita Stenström, 2014. "Your mum!" Teenagers' swearing by mother in English, Spanish and Norwegian. *International Journal of Corpus Linguistics* 19 (1): 29–59.
Green, Jonathon. 2000. *Cassell's dictionary of slang.* London: Cassell & Co.
Hasund, I. Kristine, Eli-Marie Drange and Anna-Brita Stenström. 2014. The pragmatic functions of swearing by mother in English, Spanish and Norwegian teenage talk. In M. Rathje (ed.), *Swearing in the Nordic Countries*, 11–35. Copenhagen: Dansk Sprognaevn.
Jaworski, Adam and Dariusz Galasinski. 2000. Vocative address forms and ideological legitimization in political debates. *Discourse Studies* 2.1: 35–53.
Mateo, José and Francisco Yus. 2000. Insults: a relevance-theoretic taxonomical approach to their translation. *International Journal of Translation* 12(1): 97–130.
Mateo, José and Francisco Yus. 2013. Towards a cross-cultural pragmatic taxonomy of insults. *Journal of Language Aggression and Conflict* 1 (1): 87–114.
McEnery, Anthony. 2006. *Swearing in English.* Routledge: Abingdon-on-Thames.
Ramirez Gelbes, Silvia and Andrea Estrada. 2003. Insultivos y insultativos: acerca del caso de *boludo. Anuario de Estudos Filologicos*. XXVI: 335–253. Universidad de Extremadura.
Rodríguez, Félix. 2012. (ed.). *El lenguaje de los jóvenes.* Barcelona: Ariel.
Sanmartín Sáez, Julia. 2003. *Diccionario de argot.* Madrid: Espasa.
Stenström, Anna-Brita. 2006. Taboo words in teenage talk: London and Madrid girls' conversations compared. *Spanish in Context* 3 (1): 115–138.
Stenström, Anna-Brita. 2017. Swearing in English and Spanish teenage talk. In K. Beers Fägersten and K. Stapleton. (eds.). *Advances in Swearing Research. New languagees and new contexts*, 157–181. Amsterdam. Benjamins.

Stenström, Anna-Brita and Annette Myre Jørgensen. 2008. A matter of politeness? A contrastive study of phatic talk in teenage conversation. *Pragmatics* special issue 18(4): 635–657.
The New Oxford Dictionary of English. 1998. Oxford: Clarendon Press.
Zimmermann, Klaus. 2002. La variación juvenil y la interacción verbal entre jóvenes. In F. Rodríguez (ed.). *El lenguaje de los jóvenes*, 137–161. Barcelona: Ariel.

Online dictionaries

Diccionario de la lengua española
Etymological Dictionary
OED
Real Academia Española

Elisabeth Steinbach-Eicke and Sven Eicke
14 "He shall not be buried in the West" – Cursing in Ancient Egypt

Abstract: This chapter deals with various types of curses that can be found in the textual material of Ancient Egypt. This topic, which has already been worked on extensively, is presented here with a specific focus. Using basic elements of Ancient Egyptian religious anthropology, the study outlines the targets of the curses and the various agents involved. It also explores the question of whether, in addition to the mainly magical-religious cursing, a more profane kind of swearing might be traceable in the written records of Ancient Egypt.

14.1 Introduction: Cursing and swearing – ancient and modern

In modern times, cursing can to a certain degree be understood as the use of "offensive speech" and the term can be used interchangeably with "dirty words", "taboo words", "emotional speech", "obscene speech", "profane speech" or "swearing" (Jay 2000: 9–10). Among other things, cursing sometimes conveys insults (Jay 2000: 9). In this context, it is a verbal instrument applied by human beings to express emotions and to regulate social interactions – as can be seen in many of the contributions in the present volume.

In many ancient societies, the most central aspect of *cursing* was wishing someone or something ill (Helck 1977: 275; Vittmann 1982: 977; Morschauser 1991: xi), a definition that is still present in modern times (cf. Jay 2000: 9: "*cursing* [T.J.] is wishing harm on a person"), but seems to be secondary. Another important element of this kind of cursing was the status of the agent who would execute the harmful action. In ancient sources, we find the invocation of supernatural entities (e.g. gods, demons) or initiated human specialists (e.g. priests, magicians) who performed a ritual for the client. Thus, cursing was a religious or magical action with a distinct, violative but also defensive aim.

A few recent publications on curses in the ancient world illustrate this characterisation: in her book about cursing in cuneiform and Hebrew texts, Kitz (2014: 3) defines curses as "petitions to the divine world to render judgement and execute harm on identified, hostile forces". At the beginning of her overview of Ancient Greek and Roman curses, Eidinow (2013: 1877) describes such curses as speech acts "invoking supernatural powers and reinforced by ritual". In the introduction to his co-edited volume, Sommerstein (2014: 1–2) shows the interconnection in Ancient Greece between an oath, formulated by a "swearer" and witnessed by "a superhuman power or powers", and a conditional curse called down on the swearer by him/herself, "to take effect if the assertion is false or if the promise is violated".

Each of these analyses is based on a large number of ancient sources, which cover long periods of time and many geographical areas. Due to the number and diversity of sources and the lengthy span of their research, the above-mentioned scholars were able to identify the basic elements of ancient curses and to summarise fundamental patterns and categories. The same advantages exist in the case of Ancient Egypt, due to the long tradition of scripture and the generally high volume of religious-magical material in which curses occur frequently. However, the case is different for evidence of *swearing*, in the sense of the use of offensive and obscene speech. In contrast to Ancient Roman texts, for example, which have been studied for their use of swear words by Mohr (2013: 16–54) in her history of swearing, relevant Ancient Egyptian textual material is more limited.

14.2 Ancient Egyptian curses: Sources and structures

Religious and magical texts,[1] written on different objects and collected in several corpuses (by modern scholars) spanning millennia, are the most important textual sources for Ancient Egyptian curses. But curses are also to be found in official endowments and agreements (usually made by a king) as well as in other documents (see Colledge 2015, chapters 2–5). They are written on the walls of tombs, on papyri and on stelae (see Hsieh 2012); they are found in the so-called *Pyramid Texts*, in snake spells and in prayers; and they are attested from the Old Kingdom[2] to the Graeco-Roman period (323 BC–313 AD).

---

1 The classification "religious" was established by modern Egyptologists and does not correspond to any Ancient Egyptian category. Because of the omnipresence of the feature, it is scarcely transcribable and was not separable from everyday life (Assmann 1991: 9–11); for a critical discussion see also Quirke (2015: 1–37). Ancient Egyptian "magic" is also a very complex category that is not easy to define; see Ritner (2008: 1–72).

2 In the following, only the rough dates of so-called "Kingdoms" and "Periods" in Pharaonic Egyptian history are given: Old Kingdom (ca. 2543–2210 BC), First Intermediate Period (ca. 2118–1980 BC), Middle Kingdom (1980–1760 BC), Second Intermediate Period (1759–ca. 1539 BC),

These texts provide a lot of information on the form and content of curses, but not on the Ancient Egyptian terminology. There are a handful of words that can probably be translated as "curse" or "to curse", but their attestations are poor and in many contexts their sense is not very clear. Nordh (1996: 6–8) gives a short list of the best-documented words (cf. Hannig and Vomberg 1999: 804–805), but their semantics is not without controversy (for example, see Quack 1993: 61). For this reason, an analysis of these expressions will not be carried out in this article. Instead, we focus on documents that do not carry the Ancient Egyptian label "curse" but can be classified as curses based on the basic and well-known elements and patterns. However, such an approach may not be generally accepted, as the various positions of individual researchers show.

Morschauser (1991) and Nordh (1996) analysed the structures and patterns of what they call "threat formulae" and "curse formulae". Nordh (1996: 1) prefers "to merge the two concepts and place them in the same box", which she labels "curse formulae, without considering the rank or status of executor". In contrast, Guglielmi (1975: 1146) differentiates between a curse, whose calamity is to strike the wrongdoer with the help of a transcendental power, and a threat, which presupposes fulfilment by one who makes the threat or by another power; other Egyptologists also use further terms (see Morschauser 1991: xii–xiii). In her dictionary entry on curses, Régen (2013: 1) speaks of "curse formulae" that are "based on the performative value of writing". Their function, she says, is to describe and identify "a potential act performed by the recipient of the formula", which is "contrary to the sender's self-interests and the norms of Egyptian society" (i.e. "anti-*maat* acts"; see below), leading "to various consequences for the recipient".

The main points of disagreement are thus the questions of which agent(s) execute(s) the action and of when to speak of threats and when of curses. The different designations and definitions are therefore strongly dependent on the perspective of the individual researcher. All in all, we do not know if the Ancient Egyptians actually considered the following and other examples, which are also discussed in most of the works mentioned, to be curses, threats, or something else, and whether there was such a distinction for them at all. It is therefore for pure practical reasons that we concentrate in this article on well-researched formulae and analyse them under the label "curses".

A formula usually begins with a conditional clause, the so-called *stipulation* (Morschauser 1991: 1) describing potential transgressions, which can be seen as the cause of the subsequent curses. What follows is a punitive clause, a

---

New Kingdom (ca. 1539–1077 BC), Third Intermediate Period (ca. 1076–944 BC), Late Period (ca. 722–655 BC). The chronology is based on Hornung, Krauss and Warburton (2006: 490–495).

so-called *injunction* (Morschauser 1991: 1), a special directive to threaten the potential violator. This apotropaic threat turns immediately into an actual curse if one of the aforementioned transgressions has taken place (Vittmann 1982: 977).

Some examples shall illustrate this model[3]:

Stipulations:
(a) "Every dignity, every official, or every person, who shall remove any stone or any brick from this (my) tomb ..."
(b) "As for the one, who shall remove [my name] in order to place his name ..."
(c) "Moreover, as for them, who shall commit violation against this offering ..."

Injunctions:
(a) "... (my) claim shall be litigated with his by the Great God".[4]
(b) "... (the god) Amun shall cut off his life-time on earth".[5]
(c) "... they shall fall to the knife of (the god) Horus, who is in (the city) Asyut".[6]

As Morschauser (1991: 1–2) has pointed out, there are "generic similarities" with respect to grammatical forms and syntactic structures between the Ancient Egyptian threat formulae and legal statutes, and "their approximate simultaneous appearance or use in Ancient Egyptian documents, suggests a parallel development". Thus, the patterns of legal documents form the syntactic basis for the curses.

For this reason in particular, Colledge (2015: 10–16) criticises the work of Nordh and Morschauser (who, she claims, "secularise cursing and demonstrate that curses are actually legal texts"), because they only consider those documents that correspond to their schema (of stipulation and injunction) and ignore or dismiss other "cursing methods". In contrast, her own study "targets an understanding of the role which cursing played in the lives of ancient Egyptians via monument curses, magic spells, execration figures, *damnatio memoriae* [S.L.C.], reserve heads and corpse mutilation" (Colledge 2015: 20).

---

[3] The aim of this article is to provide a brief overview of an extensively researched topic in Egyptology for a wider readership. For this reason, the cited sources and Ancient Egyptian words were not reproduced in Egyptological transcription. Virtually all documents cited can be assigned to the male elite culture.
[4] Tomb of Nenki (Old Kingdom, at Saqqara); see Morschauser (1991: 49, 75).
[5] Inscription of the High Priest Amenhotep (New Kingdom, at Karnak); see Morschauser (1991: 44, 91).
[6] Offering table with an appeal to tomb visitors (Middle Kingdom, now in the British Museum); see Morschauser (1991: 41, 85).

All of the works mentioned provide excellent philological material and clearly illustrate the structures of the curses dealt with. Therefore, the following examples and additional references in the footnotes are taken from them, especially from the sources listed in Colledge's "Monument Curse List" (Colledge 2015: 217–266) with her designations (A01–A28, B01–B12, C01–C12, D01–D03). Her last three groups (execration figures, *damnatio memoriae*, reserve heads and corpse mutilation) are excluded here, since we intend to focus on textual evidence for the sake of limitation. We also exclude another source in Colledge's appendix, *The Book of Overthrowing Apophis*, even though it provides a vivid example of cursing embedded in a ritual, which is another complex aspect of Ancient Egyptian curses that cannot be dealt within the narrow scope of this contribution. Instead, most of the evidence will come from the funerary context. Furthermore, there will be a focus on religious anthropology (see below). The already-mentioned transcendental powers, which are often supposed to take over the execution of the curses (Guglielmi 1975: 1146; Helck 1977: 275; Vittmann 1982: 978), are given a separate section.

14.3 Ancient Egyptian connections: The physical and the social sphere

A second look at the examples of stipulations above shows that the initiators of the curses seem to have had the following fears: the destruction of their tomb, the erasure of their name and the loss of offerings. All these anxieties are based on the culture-specific concepts of personality and the afterlife, for which Ancient Egyptian religious anthropology (Hasenfratz 1990; Assmann 2009 and Assmann 2010: 80 "constellative theology and anthropology") is fundamental, especially in the tomb context.

As Assmann (2010: 54–88) has shown, Egyptians' essential requirement for life and survival was maintaining connectivity, which extended to their "physical sphere" and their "social sphere", both associated with the elements of the person (overview by Ikram 2015: 23–31; cf. Gee 2009). The physical sphere was grouped around the mortal body, i.e. the corpse, the limbs, the bones, the *ba* (which is mobile, travelling in this world and in the afterworld and reuniting with the body of the deceased) and the shadow – all of which, in the case of the deceased, were usually protected by a tomb. The social sphere was connected with a person's name and his *ka* (which receives offerings and remains in the tomb), and was usually maintained by fellow human beings – in a funerary context by the family members and especially by the son of the deceased (see below). If one of the spheres was destroyed – for example by annihilating the body (physical sphere), or by erasing the memory of a person or harming his reputation (social sphere) – the person became disconnected and thus was not able to exist, either in the world of the living or in the afterlife. The latter was particularly serious, since otherworldly existence was regarded as "a more permanent life in a place that was an enhanced Egypt" (Ikram 2015: 23). There the deceased wanted to become an immortal *akh* (a person transformed from a mortal to an immortal being with divine characteristics by the reunion of *ba* and *ka*), who would lead a glorious otherworldly life after death and resurrection.

The Egyptian image of the Netherworld, as reflected in the written sources (Hornung 1997), changed over time, but the later concepts never really replaced the earlier ones. In contrast, various expectations about otherworldly locations, inhabitants and situations could be combined and were often interchangeable. The basic element at all times was the belief in dying and being resurrected again, or in living on in the beyond after the occasion of death. To achieve this aim, it was necessary to maintain connectivity in the physical and social spheres. Most importantly, the corpse had to be mummified and preserved in order to keep the bodily part of the person intact.

The archetype for the process of death and resurrection was the myth of the god Osiris (Ikram 2015: 32–35; Assmann 2010: 29–34), who ruled as king over Egypt and was killed and dismembered by his brother Seth, until his sister-wife Isis and his sister Nephthys collected his limbs and magically reanimated him again. Osiris became ruler of the Netherworld, while his son Horus, who was begotten posthumously and then born of Isis, became his successor on earth and thereafter took care of the restoration of his father's position among the gods. Accordingly, every person wanted to share Osiris's fate after dying.

The significant aspect of this prototypical legend is that the collection of Osiris's limbs and their junction by Isis effected physical connection, while the son's deeds for his father were crucial for the social connectivity that was also required (Assmann 2010: 59–78). Both were necessary for anyone who wanted to share the fate of Osiris: the physical integrity of the corpse and the devotional care of the descendants beyond death were indispensable. The following examples of curses can best be understood with these culturally rooted concepts of Ancient Egyptian personality and afterlife in mind.

One other important concept has to be considered when talking about cursing: *maat*. *Maat* played a significant role in Ancient Egyptian thinking, culture and religion, as it combined aspects such as justice, order, truth and law and it can be seen as the basis of the created world and the regulation of social life (see Helck 1980; for a detailed study on this all-encompassing concept, see Assmann 2006). The opposite of *maat* was *isfet*, which represented chaos, disorder and wrongdoing, and needed to be expelled to maintain justice. In this context, a curse must be understood as part of *isfet*, because it is meant to ensure that something or someone who does not behave in a *maat*-like way (as mentioned in the stipulations) is made harmless and falls into non-existence.

14.4 "He shall not be buried in the west": Targets of cursing

Morschauser (1991: 38–129) has already analysed the "typological and lexical characteristics of the threat" (i.e. the curse) and has put them in categories. Most of them can be seen as belonging to the physical or the social sphere, be it as part of what the curser seeks to protect (stipulation) or as part of the curse itself, threatening potential abusers (injunction). Many of Morschauser's categories and collected documents will be cited below in the footnotes as further evidence. The passages within the following examples that are particularly relevant to the aspects presented are reproduced in italics.

The tomb

A well-known element in funerary texts is called *Appeal to the Living* (Müller 1975: 293–299). It is a formula written on walls, stelae or statues of private persons, which addresses visitors of the tomb, primarily in order to beg for prayers or offerings, and promises protection and assistance in return (Müller 1975: 293–294; Leprohon 2001: 570–571). Such appeals go back to the Old Kingdom and also mark the beginning of a long tradition of Ancient Egyptian curses, as they also threaten those who disregard the tomb. Among other things, the deceased is especially concerned about preventing the destruction of his grave, his coffin and other goods for the hereafter.

(1) Tomb of Inti (Old Kingdom, at Deshasha):

Indeed, as for *any person who will [do] something evil against this (tomb), who will do anything destructive against this (tomb)*, or who will erase the inscriptions within, there will be judgement with them about it by the Great God, lord of judgement, in the place where judgement is.⁷

This instance and other similar examples (e.g. Colledge 2015: 233, text A23) that mention potential evil acts against the tomb or parts of it show how great the fear was of losing "the House for Eternity" (Ikram 2015: 139).

But it was not just the destruction of the tomb or its contents that could endanger the deceased. Entering his resting place in a state of impurity or after doing abominated things were also a threat for him.

(2) Tomb of Harkhuf (Old Kingdom, at Qubbet el-Hawa):

As for any man *who will enter [this] tomb of mine [in his impurity]*,

[I will wring] him like a bird, he will be judged about it by the Great God.⁸

(3) Tomb of Hesi (Old Kingdom, at Saqqara):

As for anyone who will enter this tomb *after he has eaten abominations which the akh abominates (or) after he has copulated with women*,

I will be judged with him in the council of the Great God.⁹

A document in which the grave owner warns against entering his resting place in a hostile or angry mood also seems to go in that direction (see Colledge 2015: 227, text A16). Because of the sacred character of the tomb (as the house of the blessed dead), which was comparable to a temple (as the house of the gods), certain taboos were established.

In all the examples, the grave owner threatens the potential wrongdoers with a divine judgement. While this may seem relatively inoffensive, the phrase that is often documented[10] implies the consultation of a higher power by and in

---

7 Colledge (2015: 222, text A08; cf. A01, A02, A03, A04, A07, A09, A10, A11, A13, A14, A17, A18, A19, A20, A22, A24, A25, A26, A27). See also Morschauser (1991: 38–42, 47–50) with further evidence of "Damage to Property" and "Theft".
8 Colledge (2015: 220, text A05; cf. A01, A07, A19, A21). See also Morschauser (1991: 67–70) with further evidence of "Sacral Violations".
9 Colledge (2015: 221, text A06; cf. A12). See also texts C04/D01 (Colledge 2015: 255), where the wrongdoer himself is called the abomination of the god: "The abomination of (the) god is one who goes against his people, he never fails to turn away the hand of the destroyer".
10 See texts A01, A04, A07, A09, A11, A14, A16, A17, A18, A19, A22, A23, A26, B06, B07, B10, C04/D01, D03; see also Morschauser (1991: 70–77) with further evidence of "Threats Involving Litigation/Judgement".

favour of the initiator, as is customary for many curses (cf. also the citation from Assmann 1992b: 162 below in this paper).

On the other hand, there are several sources documenting injunctions, which furthermore concern the burial of the miscreants themselves.

(4) Tomb of Tefibi (First Intermediate Period, at Asyut)

As for any chief, a son of any noble man, any august one, any commoner, who will not protect this tomb and what is in it,

his god will not accept his white-bread offering, *he will not be buried in the west*, their bodies will be fire together with criminals, who have been made as non-existent ones.[11]

In this case, the penalty corresponds to the offence: the negligent person, who endangered the otherworldly existence of the deceased by not paying attention, would not himself receive a funeral in the necropolis, mostly located on the west side of the Nile at the place of the sunset (while the settled area was in the east where the sun rises in the morning; see Ikram 2015: 140–141).[12] But there are also other crimes that cause this kind of curse.[13]

All in all, the loss of one's own grave was one of the worst things that could happen to an Ancient Egyptian, as it meant, among other things, the loss of the corpse's protection. The destruction of the corpse (or the body) itself is also addressed several times.

The body

As mentioned above, the preservation of the unity of the body was an important prerequisite for a life in the hereafter and was thus of utmost importance to Ancient Egyptians. Therefore, it was one of the worst scenarios when a corpse was burned. Additionally, of course, it makes for a painful death in the case of living

---

[11] Colledge (2015: 235, text A25).
[12] As in another passage in this tomb (Colledge 2015: 234–235; see texts A13, A21). Text A10 (Colledge 2015: 223) actually emphasises the agreement between wrongdoing and punishment: "[As for you who will act] against this (tomb), the like will be done against your possessions by your successors". Text C04D/01 (Colledge 2015: 253) says: "the end of one who acts likewise happens to him, the monuments of a destroyer are destroyed, the liars achievements do not last".
[13] E.g. texts A28, B08, C05, C10; see also Morschauser (1991: 120–122) with further evidence of "Denial of Ritual Burial". (Sources concerning the destruction of the *ba* will be discussed below.)

subjects. Grave owners (as well as others who wanted to protect their interests during their lifetime) took advantage of this fear and threatened potential enemies with this fate, as can be seen in example (4) above.[14]

In some cases, there is not just the possibility of ordinary fire but also an element of divine punishment, as in the following example.

(5) Donation Stela (Late Period, now in the British Museum)

As for the one who will displace them (i.e. the allocation of land mentioned previously),

he will be for (the goddess) Sekhmet's fire, and for (the goddess) Bastet's heat.[15]

The two goddesses here represent the violent aspect of female deities, who are referred to in many other documents from various eras of Egyptian history as the terrible executors of the Sun God and as almost wiping out humanity (see Stadler 2012: 51–55, 60–68). Thus with them, the curser has extremely powerful agents for enforcing his interests.

Other primarily physical punishments are also mentioned in the curses.

(6) Tomb of Ankhmahor (Old Kingdom, at Saqqara)

[As for] any [man or woman] who will enter into this tomb of mine in their impurity,

[...]

[I will wring] him *like a bird* and fear will be put in him about seeing akhs upon earth, so they will fear an excellent akh. [I will be judged] with him in the august council of the Great God.[16]

This downgrading of the criminal, treated like poultry, is intensified on an additional level, in that the grave owner simultaneously pretends to be an actor able to act beyond the hereafter (probably because of his new status; cf. examples (13) and (14) below).

---

14 Cf. texts A28, C04/D01, C11 (C05 mentions the cooking of the evildoer); see also Morschauser (1991: 96–102) with further evidence of "Terms Referring to 'Physical' Punishment: Fire, Flame".
15 Colledge (2015: 264, text C12); cf. B01: "he is for the fiery eye of (the god) Horus and it shall have power over him". For the intervention of divinities, see below.
16 Colledge (2015: 217, text A01; cf. A05, A17, A26, B08).

Other sources mention the chopping or slaughtering of potential enemies (or parts of them)[17] and several acts of physical punishment and killing.[18]

The name and the image

The name of a person given in inscriptions on walls or objects, as well as his image represented in the sculpture or relief, is also particularly (but not exclusively) important in the context of the grave. The knowing and remembering of a person's name allows his connection to the world of the living, and the image is his representative. For this reason, its erasure would be a great danger and thus again something to fear.

(7) Tomb of Djefayhapy (Middle Kingdom, at Asyut)

As for any person, any scribe, any wise man, any commoner, or any inferior, who will do [something] evil in this tomb, *who will damage its inscriptions, who will destroy its images*,

they will submit to the wrath of (the god) Thoth.[19]

It also provides him with a chance to protect his interests against others.

(8) Tomb of Khety (First Intermediate Period, at Asyut)

But, as for any dissident or any ignorant who will overturn (the tomb endowment) after this which he has heard,

[his] name will not exist, [he will not] be buried in the necropolis, he will be cooked together with criminals, who the god has planted obstacle against, [his] local god rejects him, and his town rejects him.[20]

---

17 E.g. texts A02, B08, C01, C11; see also Morschauser (1991: 102–109) with further evidence of "Terms Referring to Knives; Blades; Cutting".
18 Cf. Morschauser (1991: 88–96, 109–110) for "Terms for Killing/Execution", "Terms Referring to Premature Death", "Reference to Death by Hunger, Thirst, or Disease", "Terms Referring to 'Physical' Punishment: Divine Wrath", "Other Terms for Instruments of Punishment".
19 Colledge (2015: 219, text A03; cf. A08, A25, A27/B09, B03/C01, B04, B05, B11); see also Morschauser (1991: 42–47) with further evidence of "Effacement".
20 Colledge (2015: 256–257, text C05; cf. A25, A28, B04, B07, C10); see also Morschauser (1991: 114–116) with further evidence of the erasure of the name (listed under "Terms Referring to the Legal Status of the Criminal").

Social connectivity, which was already of elementary importance on earth for the individual, had to continue in the hereafter, as otherwise a continued existence was impossible. It was the duty of the family or the successor to keep the deceased's name in mind and to take care of his needs. At the level of kingship, it was the successor who was responsible for this, because the "living pharaoh is always identified with Horus and the deceased king with Osiris" (Ikram 2015: 34).

Offerings and (mortuary) cult

Another important duty for the heirs and successors of a deceased person was the making of different kinds of offerings for his life in the Netherworld. Not only were the dead dependent on such a supply in the afterlife, but the gods also demanded them. One example from the so-called *Pyramid Texts*, a corpus of royal funerary texts dating back to the Old Kingdom, shows that threatening the supplies of gods in the afterlife could also be used by a pharaoh to secure his place among the gods. In this spell, the gods are addressed, in order to take King Pepi I to the sky, where the afterlife was located in this period.

(9) Pyramid of King Pepi I (Old Kingdom, at Saqqara)

Any god who will take this Pepi to the sky, alive and stable – he is the one who will become esteemed, he is the one who will become ba, he is the one who will smell a wafer, he is the one who will go up to the Horus's enclosure (i.e. the goddess Hathor) that belongs to the sky. Any god who will take this Pepi to the sky, alive and stable – bulls will be slaughtered for him, forelegs will be selected for him, and he will go up to the Horus's enclosure that belongs to the sky. Any god who will not take him to the sky

– he will not become esteemed, he will not become ba, he will not smell a wafer, and he will not go up to Horus's enclosure that belongs to the sky [...].[21]

One difference between this and the examples above is that there is a blessing formula right before the cursing formula (see Nordh 1996: 1–8). It can be seen as being in diametrical opposition to the cursing part, and additionally stresses the significance of the need to perform the good deed. By refusing the king's acceptance into the realm of gods and glorified spirits, the offender would risk

---

[21] Allen (2005: 132); for this passage and the threat of the gods by the deceased in general, see Grapow (1911) and Altenmüller (1977) with numerous documents.

his own existence, he would lose her or his divine potency and could not take offerings. Thus, the king turns the tables on potential dissenters and threatens them by cursing, a measure that can be seen even better in the private tombs of all periods, where many more injunctions focus on the malefactor's physical and/or social sphere, in order to avoid disadvantaging the tomb owner.

The threat of withholding one's offering with a curse was an extremely strong sanction[22] and, as mentioned above, one of the most important duties of the families and successors of the deceased was to ensure that something like that did not happen to her or him.

Heritage and family

It seems that the fundamental importance of heritage is why many injunctions relate to the family of the potential transgressor.

(10) Block Statue of Montuemhat (Late Period, at Karnak)

> As for anyone against this tomb in my place: the one who disturbs is a criminal,
>
> his years will be diminished, one whose burial does not exist, *without an heir from his wife* [...].[23]

The fear of losing one's family and especially one's children as heirs can also be seen in stipulations as early as the Old Kingdom (e.g. Morschauser 1991: 18). In other injunctions, the beneficiary does not try to prevent the birth of a child and thus a successor, but to prevent the handover of the criminal's possessions to the already existing children.

(11) Statue of Wersu (New Kingdom, at Koptos)

> As for anyone who will desecrate my corpse in the necropolis, who will remove my statue from my tomb,

---

[22] E.g. texts A25, A27/B09, A28, B02, B08; see also Morschauser (1991: 116–120) with further evidence of "Threats Referring to Exclusion from Religious Life", "Threats Relating to the Mortuary Cult".
[23] Colledge (2015: 225–226, text A13; cf. A02, A16, B01, B02, B04, B06, B08, C03, C10, C11); see also Morschauser (1991: 122–129) with further evidence of "Threats Against the Family of the Transgressor", "Threats of a Sexual Nature" (see below), "Threats to the Legal Status of Offspring".

he will be a hated one to (the god) Re, he will not receive water from the water-jar of (the god) Osiris, *he will not hand over his possessions to his children, ever.*[24]

The loss of (especially) paternal property on the side of the heirs could endanger several generations. It endangered not only the material supply basis for the bereaved family but also the costly provisioning of the deceased and the performing of the funeral and mortuary cult (see Ikram 2015: 95–137, 183–193). In addition, the withdrawal of the inheritance may have meant that the son could not succeed his father in office, which was exceedingly grave for officials and priests, whose offices were usually supposed to be inherited within the family (see Sauneron 2000: 43–45).

14.5 Kings, the dead, divinities and animals: Agents in curses

As can often be observed, Ancient Egyptian curses usually affect at least two entities: a beneficiary, who gains one or more advantages, and a victim, who is harmed by the curse. The beneficiary employs professionals to inscribe one or more objects (e.g. amulet, papyrus, statue, stela, tomb wall) with the cursing spell, and when the potential enemy reads the inscription, the spell becomes effective (see Assmann 1992a: 62–63).

There are some cases in which the initiator himself takes over the execution of the curse. This is especially the case when the initiator is the king, perceived as superhuman, who in this way wishes to prevent the violation of his decrees.

(12) Decree of Demedjibtawy (Old Kingdom, at Koptos)

As for any men of this entire land who will do a destructive, evil thing [...]

my Majesty does not permit that their goods or their father's goods are attached to them, my Majesty does not permit that they join the akhs in the necropolis, and my Majesty does not permit that they are amongst the living upon earth.[25]

---

[24] Colledge (2015: 236–237, text A27/B09).
[25] Colledge (2015: 243–244, text B03/C01).

Although the style of the injunction initially sounds like ordinary royal instructions ("my Majesty does not permit"), the content of the middle passage definitely belongs to the sphere of otherworldly destiny, which has nothing to do with "secular" ordinances of the pharaoh, and rather has the character of a curse threatened by the king as a superhuman entity.

In some cases it is the deceased who, in his new status, also has abilities that living people usually do not have.

(13) Tomb of Nenki (Old Kingdom, at Saqqara)

> As for any dignitary, any magistrate, or any person who will rip out any stone or any brick from this tomb of mine,
>
> I will be judged with him by the Great God, I will wring his neck like a bird, and *I will cause all the living upon earth to be afraid of the akhs in the west*.[26]

The dead person acts as a supernatural entity and "presents himself as a source of terror and violence" (Assmann 1992a: 57).

In other cases, the power of the deceased becomes even more concrete, for example, when he threatens to transform himself into dangerous animals.

(14) Stela of Sarenput (Third Intermediate Period, at Elephantine)

> As for any governor, any wab priest (i.e. a purifying priest), any ka priest, any scribe, or any official who will take it (a meat offering mentioned previously) from my statue, [...]
>
> *I am against him as a crocodile on the water, as a snake on the land and as an enemy in the necropolis.*[27]

The two reptiles were highly feared creatures, on the one hand because of their threatening nature, on the other hand because of the ambivalent roles that they could take on at a mythological level (e.g. as gods or demon-like creatures in the Netherworld). The curser therefore takes advantage of this religious and cultural attitude towards the animals. Through this, and also in principle through his ability to transform, he gives his threat a strong weight.

---

26 Colledge (2015: 228, text A17). For the ability to cause others to be afraid or to put fear in someone, see A26, and see also Eicke (2017: 235–238).
27 Colledge (2015: 248–249, text B08); for crocodile and snake, see example (15) below.

But in many other cases a third party is involved, namely one or more agents, who shall directly implement the action by themselves. As mentioned above and also documented in some of the examples, these agents are often supernatural entities. In particular, gods are often invoked or mentioned in order to fulfil the curse. They could have a special connection to the beneficiary (e.g. Colledge 2015: 233, text A24), to the place where the curse shall take place (e.g. Colledge 2015: 252, text C03), or to the harmful action itself (e.g. Colledge 2015: 239–241, text B01). Sometimes a divine family or dynasty consisting of a father deity, mother deity and a divine child is involved, in order to persecute the opponent together with his wife and children (e.g. Morschauser 1991: 79–80).

What is crucial is that these gods were responsible for keeping up law and order, i.e. *maat*. They were supposed to guarantee that those who violate, destroy or steal become hunted by divine wrath[28] or are otherwise punished by the gods.[29] One reason for this was the on-going robbery of tombs, which is attested from the Old Kingdom onwards and remained a problem until the end of Pharaonic Egypt. The government was not able to prevent the crimes and even kings' tombs were looted, as documents about tomb robberies from the time of the New Kingdom show (Vernus 2003: 1–49; see also Ikram 2015: 194–199). People searched for other protectors and turned towards the gods (Colledge 2015: 230, text A20), realising the powerlessness of the responsible authorities. Assmann (1992b: 162) sums it up as follows: "Curses and laws are parallel in that both establish a link between crime and punishment, the defining difference being that curses are to be enforced by superhuman powers and laws by legal institutions. In Egypt, the vizier acts as the head of legal institutions, whereas the king already belongs to the superhuman sphere."

On the other hand, there are documents that seem to demonstrate the "conscious use" of certain animal agents in order to get hold of the adversaries in any circumstances.

(15) Tomb of Petety (Old Kingdom, at Giza)

> (As for) anyone who will do anything evil against this (tomb), who will enter there destructively,

---

[28] The wrath or hate of divinities is mentioned several times: texts A03, A27/B09, A28, B02, B05, B12, C02.
[29] For example, see texts A12, A24, A28, C03, C11.

> the crocodile is against them in the water, the snake is against them on land, the hippopotamus is against them in the water, the scorpion is against them on land.[30]

Apparently, the knowledge of Ancient Egyptian fauna has flowed into the choice of cursing agents: dangerous water dwellers are supposed to attack the evildoers in the river and lakes while terrible land animals threaten them on the ground, so they cannot escape. But an all-encompassing persecution of the enemies in all accessible areas of the cosmos is not the only reason for the choice of animal punishers. They also embody elements of chaos that the (simple) human being cannot fully control and therefore they threaten the human wrongdoer (especially physically).

This can also be assumed for other animals that appear in curses as agents, including the donkey. As Morschauser (1991: 110–111) and Assmann (1992b: 157) summarise, the donkey can be regarded as the embodiment of the god Seth. However, his mode of action within the texts allows a potentially different (or additional) interpretation, as will be shown in the following.

14.6 Excursus: Religious cursing and profane swearing

As noted above, *cursing* in Ancient Egypt seems to differ from our modern understanding of the phenomenon. It has a special *Sitz im Leben* ("setting in life"), which is that of a religious and magical practice, very often located in a funerary context, frequently with the aim of harming something or somebody physically or socially who does not behave in a *maat*-like way. Thus, it has to be separated from cursing in the sense of *swearing*, i.e. offensive, obscene or profane speech with the aim of insulting someone. It is difficult to identify such a primarily oral phenomenon for Ancient Egypt, because hieroglyphic writing on monuments has its own function and usually does not reflect any spontaneous expression of everyday life. This kind of swearing might of course have existed and could possibly be found in personal letters (barely preserved due to the perishability of the material), graffiti or to a certain degree in the so-called

---

30 Colledge (2015: 231, text A20); cf. A11 and B02 ("he is a hated one of the gods of the sky and the gods of the land, he is a hated one of the reigning king"); see also Morschauser (1991: 110–112) with further evidence of "Animals as Agents of Punishment".

Reden und Rufe (i.e. reported speech; see Erman 1919) in the private tombs of high officials. However, these contexts are very specific and the interpretation of meaning is also debatable (see Grunert 2009a, 2009b; Vonk 2015; Störk 1984. Hannig and Vomberg 1999: 457–458 give a short list of Ancient Egyptian abusive nicknames). Köhler et al. (2010: 50) note that the existence of swear words in the modern sense cannot be proven for Ancient Egypt at this point. Thus there seems to be no clear philological evidence for swearing.

But if we try to trace a mere hypothetical development from magical-religious cursing towards swearing, we could suggest that the "original" cursing received a new meaning over the course of time, which includes some of the aspects mentioned. Some of the very drastic and pictorial injunctions get close to swearing and are even comparable to modern swearing. Therefore, we would like to suggest considering the following examples of curses tentatively as insults:

(16) Smaller Dakhla Stela (Late Period, now in the Ashmolean Museum)

The ass shall (sexually) assault him, the ass shall (sexually) assault his wife and his children![31]

(17) Donation Stela (Third Intermediate Period, at Kom Firin)

[…] he will copulate with a donkey, a donkey will copulate with his wife, and his wife will copulate with his child.[32]

On the level of cursing, the examples can easily be understood in the context of violating the transgressors' physical sphere and – as regards his family – his social sphere. The link with (the beast of) Seth, a donkey, could also address the religious element. On the level of profanity and obscenity, the texts seem on the one hand more intense than other examples. On the other hand, the focus on sexual intercourse (as well as on incest) and sodomy makes them very appropriate for affronting someone, because as Sadek (1987: 243) mentions, the donkey is "known for its powerful virile member", and Assmann (1992b: 156) also aptly calls these curses "'obscene'".

While a key feature of swearing thus exists in this regard, to classify these curses as instances of swearing would ignore the actual *Sitz im Leben* of these texts, if one wanted to understand them as valid evidence. As royal decrees, their main function was not to offend with profane speech. Rather, they were about

---

[31] Morschauser (1991: 112; see also 110–111).
[32] Colledge (2015: 263, text C11); cf. Morschauser (1991: 124–125).

representing the edicts of a king and ensuring their implementation with the threat of curses. However, one can speculate as to whether phrases like these were used in the spoken language of everyday life. In this case, they would have possessed their own *Sitz im Leben* as insults and would be a true instrument of social interactions with no actual relation to religious-magical practice.

On the other hand, we have one famous passage in which an insult that ranks between a religious and a profane "everyday" context seems to be very probable. In the story *The Contendings of Horus and Seth*, the two gods battle for the office of the departed Osiris and a long trial with many other gods takes place. Those gods are separated into two parties, each of them supporting one of the wranglers, and some of them seem to be short-tempered, like the god Baba, who says to the sun-god Re-Harakhty:

(18) The Contendings of Horus and Seth (New Kingdom, Papyrus Chester Beatty I recto, now in the Chester Beatty Library, Dublin)

Your shrine is empty![33]

The exact meaning of this passage is hard to grasp, but most interpreters agree that it is an insult (for example, see Popko 2014), as can probably also be seen from the reaction of the other gods, when they shout loudly at Baba and say to him: "Go away; you have committed a very great crime" (Lichtheim 2006: 216). Most likely, Baba's exclamation indicates that Re-Harakhty is about to make an *ill-considered* and *foolish* decision. In any case, it seems to be the way in which gods offend each other, since the shrine is the earthly living area of the cult image in which an Egyptian deity manifests itself. To imply that it was empty would mean that the god could no longer receive worship. Therefore, this is a serious thing to say.

In addition to this rather small example from the literary text about Horus and Seth, there is plenty of evidence of religiously motivated insults against Seth himself. These can be found in Ancient Egyptian religious sources. For example, in the temples of the Graeco-Roman era, he or the animal representing him (as well as other enemies of the gods) is called "coward" (Erman and Grapow 1971: 80.8–11), and other designations (Meurer 2005: 173–188), instead of his actual name, exist too (see also Kahl 2008, who has studied Egyptian techniques of avoiding the name of Seth in the so-called *Pyramid Texts* and *Coffin Texts*). This measure is to be seen in the context of magical practices. The goal is to banish the power of words and characters, which could be dangerous in the case of a god who is often

---

33 Lichtheim (2006: 216).

viewed negatively (see Velde 1967). In contrast to phrases like those in examples (16) and (17), where the once religious sphere may have been profaned in order to insult, here use is made of the hierarchically degrading effect of the insult (perhaps derived from the profane context) in order to lessen its divine force.

14.7 Conclusion

Ancient Egyptian curses belong to the very broad area of religious-magical practice. They are documented in different contexts, such as funerary ones (graves) and official ones (decrees), and are thus used by various beneficiaries, such as the deceased (who want to protect themselves and their belongings) and the king (who wants to know his written orders will be respected). Those entrusted with the implementation of the curses are also diverse, including, for example, the dead who has become powerful as a result of his transfiguration, the superhuman pharaoh, or beings of the divine sphere.

On the other hand, what is almost always the same is the function of the curse, that is, to show potential troublemakers the consequences of their anti-*maat* acts. These misdeeds are tangible in the so-called stipulations and, in the majority of cases, concern central aspects of religious anthropology. According to Ancient Egyptian understanding, components of a human's personality that were linked to the physical and social sphere needed to be maintained in order to ensure that person's wellbeing in the afterlife. These components could be targeted by wrongdoers and needed protection. The initiators of the curses thus took advantage of the fact that those who could destroy their wellbeing were equally vulnerable in this regard. This is recognisable in the injunctions that contain the curses.

A prerequisite for the success of such curses is a shared belief in their effectiveness. Whether this was really the case cannot be assessed here, but it seems to be contradicted by the innumerable graves already plundered in ancient times. In any case, all of these documents remain religiously-magically motivated, despite their sometimes simple form (which they often share with legal texts). Therefore, it is all the more exciting to imagine the merely hypothetical path from "original" cursing in a sacral sense to possibly "profane" swearing and the application of (potentially) offensive swearing in a magical-religious context for the purpose of reducing higher-ranking and/or supernatural powers.

Acknowledgements: We are grateful to Anne Storch and Nico Nassenstein for their acceptance of this contribution and are also indebted to the reviewers for helpful comments.

References

Allen, James P. 2005. *The Ancient Egyptian Pyramid Texts*. Atlanta, GA: Society of Biblical Literature.
Altenmüller, Hartwig. 1977. Götterbedrohung. In Wolfgang Helck and Wolfhart Westendorf (eds.), *Lexikon der Ägyptologie*, Volume 2, 664–669. Wiesbaden: Harrassowitz.
Assmann, Jan. 1991. *Ägypten – Theologie und Frömmigkeit einer frühen Hochkultur*. 2nd ed. Stuttgart, Berlin and Cologne: Kohlhammer.
Assmann, Jan. 1992a. Inscriptional violence and the art of cursing: a study of performative writing. *Stanford Literature Review* 8: 43–65.
Assmann, Jan. 1992b. When justice fails: jurisdiction and imprecation in Ancient Egypt and the Near East. *The Journal of Egyptian Archaeology* 78: 149–162.
Assmann, Jan. 2006. Ma'at. Gerechtigkeit und Unsterblichkeit im Alten Ägypten. 2nd ed. Munich: C.H. Beck.
Assmann, Jan. 2009. Konstellative Anthropologie. Zum Bild des Menschen im alten Ägypten. In Bernd Jankowski and Kathrin Liess (eds.), *Der Mensch im Alten Israel. Neue Forschungen zur alttestamentlichen Anthropologie*, 95–120. Freiburg: Herder.
Assmann, Jan. 2010. *Tod und Jenseits im Alten Ägypten*. 2nd ed. Munich: C.H. Beck.
Colledge, Sarah L. 2015. *The process of cursing in Ancient Egypt*. PhD dissertation, University of Liverpool. Published online at https://livrepository.liverpool.ac.uk/3000011/1/ColledgeSar_Sep2015.pdf (accessed 14 June 2019).
Eicke, Sven. 2017. Affecting the gods. Fear in Ancient Egyptian religious texts. In Anne Storch (ed.), *Consensus and dissent. Negotiating emotions in the public space*, 229–246. Amsterdam: John Benjamins.
Eidinow, Esther. 2013. Curses, Greece and Rome. In Roger S. Bagnall, Kai Brodersen, Craige B. Champion, Andrew Erskine, Sabine R. Huebner (eds.), *The Encyclopedia of Ancient History*, 1877–1878. Malden, MA: Wiley-Blackwell.
Erman, Adolf. 1919. *Reden, Rufe und Lieder auf Gräberbildern des Alten Reiches*. Berlin: Verlag der Akademie der Wissenschaften.
Erman, Adolf and Hermann Grapow. 1971. *Wörterbuch der aegyptischen Sprache*. Volume 3. Berlin: Akademie-Verlag.
Gee, John. 2009. A new look at the conception of the human being in Ancient Egypt. In Rune Nyord and Annette Kjølby (eds.), *'Being in Ancient Egypt': thoughts on agency, materiality and cognition. Proceedings of the seminar held in Copenhagen, September 29–39, 2006*, 1–14. London: Archaeopress.
Grapow, Hermann. 1911. Bedrohung der Götter durch den Verstorbenen. *Zeitschrift für ägyptische Sprache und Altertumskunde* 49: 48–54.
Grunert, Stefan. 2009a. Das "Arschloch" – kein Esel, nur eine Eselei. *Göttinger Miszellen* 221: 37–39.
Grunert, Stefan. 2009b. Vertrackt, aber nicht "bekackt". *Göttinger Miszellen* 223: 63–68.
Guglielmi, Waltraud. 1975. Drohformeln. In Wolfgang Helck and Eberhard Otto (eds.), *Lexikon der Ägyptologie*, Volume I, 1145–1147. Wiesbaden: Harrassowitz.
Hannig, Rainer and Petra Vomberg. 1999. *Wortschatz der Pharaonen in Sachgruppen: Kulturhandbuch Ägyptens*. Mainz: von Zabern.

Hasenfratz, Hans P. 1990. Zur "Seelenvorstellung" der alten Ägypter. Anmerkungen zur altägyptischen Anthropologie und ihrer geistesgeschichtlichen Bedeutung. *Zeitschrift für Religions- und Geistesgeschichte* 42(3): 193–216.
Helck, Wolfgang. 1977. Fluch. In Wolfgang Helck and Wolfhart Westendorf (eds.), *Lexikon der Ägyptologie*, Volume 2, 275–276. Wiesbaden: Harrassowitz.
Helck, Wolfgang. 1980. Maat. In Wolfgang Helck and Wolfhart Westendorf (eds.), *Lexikon der Ägyptologie*, Volume 3, 1110–1119. Wiesbaden: Harrassowitz.
Hornung, Erik. 1997. *Altägyptische Jenseitsbücher. Ein einführender Überblick*. Darmstadt: WBG.
Hornung, Erik, Rolf Krauss and David A. Warburton (eds.). 2006. *Ancient Egyptian chronology*. Leiden and Boston, MA: Brill.
Hsieh, Julia. 2012. Discussions on the daybook style and the formulae of malediction and benediction stemming from five Middle Kingdom rock-cut stelae from Gebel el-Girgawi. *Zeitschrift für ägyptische Sprache und Altertumskunde* 139: 116–135.
Ikram, Salima. 2015. *Death and burial in Ancient Egypt*. Cairo and New York, NY: AUC Press.
Jay, Timothy. 2000. *Why we curse: a neuro-psycho-social theory of speech*. Philadelphia, PA: John Benjamins.
Kahl, Jochem. 2008. Religiöse Sprachsensibilität in den Pyramidentexten und Sargtexten am Beispiel des Namens des Gottes Seth. In Susanne Bickel and Bernard Mathieu (eds.), *Textes des pyramides & textes des sarcophages: d'un monde à l'autre. Actes de la table ronde internationale « Textes des Pyramides versus Textes des Sarcophages ». Ifao – 24–26 septembre 2001*, 219–246. Cairo: Institut Française d'Archéologie Orientale.
Kitz, Anne M. 2014. *Cursed are you! The phenomenology of cursing in cuneiform and Hebrew texts*. Winona Lake, IN: Eisenbrauns.
Köhler, Ines, Anke I. Blöbaum, Kathrin Butt, Meike Becker, Laura Sanhueza-Pino, Simon Stamer and Benjamin Wortmann. 2010. Vom Schimpfen und Schänden und vom Lügen und Betrügen . . . und vom kleinen Unterschied. *Göttinger Miszellen* 227: 47–60.
Lichtheim, Miriam. 2006. *Ancient Egyptian literature. A book of readings*. Volume 2: The New Kingdom. Berkeley, CA, Los Angeles, CA and London: University of California Press.
Leprohon, Ronald J. 2001. Offering formulas and lists. In Donald B. Redford (ed.), *The Oxford Encyclopedia of Ancient Egypt*, Volume 2, 569–572. New York, NY: Oxford University Press.
Meurer, Georg. 2005. Die Verfemung des Seth und seines Gefolges in den Pyramidentexten und in späterer Zeit. In Heinz Felber (ed.), *Feinde und Aufrührer. Konzepte von Gegnerschaft in ägyptischen Texten besonders des Mittleren Reiches*, 173–188. Stuttgart and Leipzig: Verlag der Sächsischen Akademie der Wissenschaften zu Leipzig and Hirzel.
Mohr, Melissa. 2013. *Holy shit: a brief history of swearing*. Oxford: Oxford University Press.
Morschauser, Scott. 1991. *Threat-formulae in Ancient Egypt. A study of the history, structure and use of threats and curses in Ancient Egypt*. Baltimore, MD: Halgo.
Müller, Christa. 1975. Anruf an Lebende. In Wolfgang Helck and Eberhard Otto (eds.), *Lexikon der Ägyptologie*, Volume 1, 293–299. Wiesbaden: Harrassowitz.
Nordh, Katarina. 1996. *Aspects of Ancient Egyptian curses and blessings. Conceptual background and transmission*. Stockholm: Almqvist and Wiksell.
Popko, Lutz. 2014. In *Thesaurus Linguae Aegyptiae* (last version: 31 October 2014) http://aaew.bbaw.de/tla/index.html (accessed 10 April 2019) in the commentary of the section of the text.
Quack, Joachim F. 1993. Ein altägyptisches Sprachtabu. *Lingua Aegyptia* 3: 59–79.
Quirke, Stephen. 2015. *Exploring religion in Ancient Egypt*. Chichester: Wiley Blackwell.

Régen, Isabelle. 2013. Curses, Egypt. In Roger S. Bagnall, Kai Brodersen, Craige B. Champion, Andrew Erskine and Sabine R. Huebner (eds.), *The Encyclopedia of Ancient History*, 1875–1876. Malden, MA: Wiley-Blackwell.

Ritner, Robert K. 2008. *The mechanics of Ancient Egyptian magical practice*. 4th ed. Chicago, IL: The Oriental Institute.

Sadek, Ashraf I. 1987. *Popular religion in Egypt during the New Kingdom*. Hildesheim: Gerstenberg.

Sauneron, Serge. 2000. *The priests of Ancient Egypt*. Ithaca, NY and London: Cornell University Press.

Sommerstein, Alan H. 2014. What is an oath? In Alan H. Sommerstein and Isabelle C. Torrance (eds.), *Oaths and swearing in Ancient Greece*, 1–5. Berlin: De Gruyter.

Stadler, Martin A. 2012. *Einführung in die ägyptische Religion ptolemäisch-römischer Zeit nach den demotischen religiösen Texten*. Münster: LIT.

Störk, Lothar. 1984. Schimpfwörter. In Wolfgang Helck and Wolfhart Westendorf (eds.), *Lexikon der Ägyptologie*, Volume 4, 634–637. Wiesbaden: Harrassowitz.

Velde, Herman te. 1967. *Seth, god of confusion: a study of his role in Egyptian mythology and religion*. Leiden: Brill.

Vernus, Pascal. 2003. *Affairs and scandals in Ancient Egypt*. Ithaca, NY and London: Cornell University Press.

Vittmann, Günther. 1982. Verfluchung. In Wolfgang Helck and Wolfhart Westendorf (eds.), *Lexikon der Ägyptologie*, Volume 4, 977–981. Wiesbaden: Harrassowitz.

Vonk, Thomas. 2015. Von Betrügern und schimpfenden Hirten. Über den Humor einiger "Reden und Rufe". *Göttinger Miszellen* 245: 79–93.

Neal R. Norrick
Afterword

The most important theme of this volume is use in context: Swearing here is seen as doing things with words, in the sense of speaking as doing, when words obtain the power to change reality, not just illocutionary force but perlocutionary force in the sense of Austin (1962). This perspective on swearing highlights the ways in which transgressive, reality-changing speech is performed: swearing can only be understood against a backdrop of cultural values and assumptions, and viewed within specific contexts involving specific groups of people, where not just the swearer or deliverer but also the recipient must be considered, including how recipients receive and react (Storch, Ameka, Traber, Mietzner): Both the verbal attacker and the victim become participants in transgressive events in which each constructs the other – even the tomb raider reading the threatening inscription must react to it, fearing it or ignoring it.

The conference in Cologne was an eye-opener for me: here young scholars were embracing a whole range of transgressive verbal (and embodied) behaviors and interactions earlier research on swearing and cursing had ignored, addressing forms of constructing the other, different in power, race, gender, ethnicity, and class, not just with sexual and religious epithets, but with aggressive formulas and even unholy, blasphemous screaming, embodied performances and artifacts – just the opposite of quiet, orderly, religious language and rituals. The authors here investigate an impressive array of linguistic practices related to power, race, and hegemony in post-colonial contexts, some at quite a distance from traditional work on swearing and cursing. Nassenstein in his chapter stresses the need for "more global approaches to the concept of offensive, transgressive and taboo language, swearing does not inevitably have to be represented by specific translatable lexical swear terms."

The linguistic practices and embodiments may be more important than the actual words, as Ameka shows. The quasi-linguistic practices may continue to be recognizable as such even when the words themselves are no longer identifiable. Central is the formulaicity and the ritual character of the practices surrounded by cultural beliefs and attitudes: not just regarding words but embodied performances like screaming, crying and spitting (Storch). At the same time, variation by

Neal R. Norrick, Saarland University

https://doi.org/10.1515/9781501511202-015

region and age always occurs: the terms used and effect of swearing by boys versus girls, kids versus their parents and so on, as Jay stresses in his chapter.

From the Egyptian tomb curses described by Steinbach-Eicke and Eicke to the modern-day swearing scenarios treated by Mietzner and Traber, the main common feature consists in performance in a particular context. A list of swear words or even curse formulas can only record language used by certain individuals in certain social cicumstances after the fact. The list is really only useful for someone who knows how the words are used by certain individuals in specific contexts. But also formulaicity especially in written forms is necessary for the magic of the curse: hence also the similarity with legal language where a specified form is required. And consequently, swearing formulas like "fuck you" are not real imperatives in syntactic terms, as discussed by Aikhenvald: invective seems to demand and develop grammatical forms of its own, recognizable as distinct from everyday forms.

Narrative is a recurrent theme in the volume, arising both in the form of swearing in narrative and narrative as transgressive performance. Already in the introduction Nassenstein and Storch cite the phenomenon of a whole narrative as transgressive. Aikhenvald analyzes maledictive imperatives from narratives, stressing the importance of ethnographic immersion to collect real data of this kind. Storch tells stories involving aggressive language and screaming: she relates a story of her own with suggestive body positions and screaming as well. Ameka cites an example of a suck teeth episode from a written narrative. Farquharson et al. discuss a story told by a city mayor offensive to Jamaicans using curse words as a feature of storytelling – both as direct quoted speech and as commentary about the character in the story. His immediate audience was receptive as well as accommodating, but the recording of the event created political problems. They also mention swearing in narrative within a song text, where a husband calls his wife a lying bitch and tells her to kiss his ass: "My massa curse her, 'lying bitch!' / And tell her, 'buss my rassa'." In his chapter, Roque traces the development of an epithet through time in a series of narratives. Nassenstein refers to different forms of "mock language" in humorous narratives, and explores how a Chinese accent has become, as an urban myth, the topic of recurrent humorous online narratives. Steinbach-Eike and Eike cite a famous passage from a traditional narrative in which an insult that ranks between a religious and a profane "everyday" context seems to be very probable. In the passage from the *Contendings of Horus and Seth*, one god mocks another saying, "Your shrine is empty," thus taunting occurs as reported speech in narrative here. Stenström supplies another excellent example, where swearing occurs in dialogue with a narrative context. In the excerpt below Sally from Hackney is telling a story where a man is ejected from a taxi:

Sally: ... sharp intake of breath {/nv} and he goes {shouting} Get out of my fucking cab, **you dirty son of a bitch**! {unclear/} He gets out of the cab, right. So he gets out of the cab. ...

The man does not respond verbally, but he does submit to the driver's demand. Notice that the slur "son of a bitch" follows the phrase "fucking cab," already a formulation within the area of swearing, both phrases delivered in a shouting register, all characteristic of swearing performances. Here again we find the transgressive language within the frame of dialogue.

My own work on conversational narrative indicates that tellers use swearing for a whole range of functions besides dialogue. I find tellers swearing to obtain the floor, to justify telling, to evaluate action, to mark climaxes and closings, in addition to portraying their characters as swearing and insulting each other. These sorts of observations require lots of work on ample real conversational data: they probably will not show up in literary treatments of narratives or even in everyday conversational reports of who said what to whom. As Aikhenvald writes, immersion fieldwork is "the only way of experiencing and documenting the language in its spontaneous use."

Moreover, in conversation, tellers may hear their listeners swearing along with them, not only to support and evaluate, but also to oppose and even complain about their telling performance. A few authors in this volume stress the reactions of recipients of transgressive language and stories, but none of them describe recipients returning the bad language or responding with transgressive stories of their own, yet this certainly occurs. In fact, as I argue in my article on swearing in literary narrative and conversational storytelling (Norrick 2012), swearing tends to elicit swearing, so that exchanges like the one below are typical rather than exceptional. In this excerpt, the teller Alina produces some swearing dialogue as the climax of her story, to represent it as what she said in anger to a salesman.

Alina: and he keeps staring at my chest,
and it's [like],

Lenore: [((laughs))]

Alina: you know,
fuck you,
asshole,
why don't you look at my fa:ce.

Lenore: ((laughing)) **oh shit.**

Alina: (H)but he didn't believe me I was ma:rried.

Here the constructed dialogue begins with swear words, the formulaic curse "fuck you" and the direct address epithet "asshole." The speaker uses no explicit quotative forms, and she does not even mark the dialogue with a shift of voice, apparently trusting that swearing will be sufficient to introduce the dialogue by itself. Notice here also the listener's laughing reaction "oh shit," which counts as a swearing assessment or evaluation. Multiple swear words within a single turn or adjacent turns leading up to, within or in reaction to a narrative performance occur frequently. There seems to be a general tendency for swearing to cluster around activities like storytelling in conversation; swearing apparently engenders more swearing in conversational interaction: indeed, swearing appears to be a contagious behavior like laughing and yawning in group interaction. Thus, too, transgressive language and other practices can over time result in "a complex system of 'appropriate' transgression," as Traber writes in her description of the "multilayered verbal practices and their extensions in material culture between tourists and migrants in El Arenal," where offensive strategies "merge in the scenery of migration and tourism." Dirty talk engenders more dirty talk till it becomes the norm in some contexts, and participants become inured to it, no longer sure whether to be offended, perhaps to be amused, or not. Indeed, tourists vacation in some towns in Mallorca with the express purpose of immersing themselves in behavioral patterns transgressive and intolerable at home: hence the tee-shirt motto "What happens in Mallorca stays in Mallorca," itself modeled on the slogan "What happens in Vegas stays in Vegas," that is to say: Las Vegas, Nevada, known for both high class and sleezy strip joints, sex shows and prostitution, another place tourists visit to engage in behaviors unacceptable if not outright illegal where they live their normal lives.

Is there then an interrelationship between this general transgressive language and individual verbal swearing? Does the public use of transgressive language filter into other forms of expression? Do the tourists find themselves addressing each other less respectfully or even swearing at each other while they are on vacation? And do these transgressive practices infect their everyday speech patterns once they leave for home, just as they take along transgressive souvenirs like banana dildos? The transgressive language habits seem to go along with a generally permissive atmosphere and transgressive behaviors. But do tourists just engage in loose talk about sex or are they really having sex? And with whom? With each other or with sex workers? These last are not linguistic questions as such but they do bear asking in some related research contexts. For linguists it would suffice initially to begin investigating the interpenetration of general public transgressive language and individual private speech styles. Even the more mundane matter of interpenetration between styles of swearing remains to be resolved: the relations between sexual, scatological and blasphemous swearing and insults, and the very possibility of forms like "Jesus motherfucking Christ Almighty" and "you goddamn cocksucker."

In expanding the scope of studies on swearing from sexual and blasphemous interjections and epithets to a wide range of transgressive linguistic and extra-linguistic practices, this volume takes research on swearing to a whole new level and into uncharted domains, at the same time developing a range of new questions and challenges. In opening fresh avenues of research, it simultaneously evinces the need for more and more varied data. Even as it offers new insights, it exposes areas where much additional research must follow, particularly in the various interfaces between swearing and narrative, between public transgressive language and private speech style, and the whole range of transgressive language patterns in intercultural settings along with their relation to power, race, and gender in a shrinking post-colonial world.

References

Austin, John L. 1962. *How to Do Things with Words*. Cambridge: Harvard University Press.

Norrick, Neal R. 2012. Swearing in literary prose fiction and conversational narrative. *Narrative Inquiry* 22: 24–49.

Index

abject 3, 6, 12–14, 16, 21, 22, 29
abusive language 5, 13, 23, 44, 80, 83, 128, 129, 131, 259
agency 3, 4, 8, 29, 32, 103, 109, 114, 148, 192, 224, 240, 264
aggression 25, 149, 200, 245, 272
Ancient Egypt 32, 303–322
audience 5, 7, 22, 23, 29, 42, 114, 133, 160, 165, 168, 175, 178–180, 251, 275, 296, 328
avoidance 4, 59, 67, 68, 86, 171

bad language 3, 4, 6, 22–28, 30–32, 79, 80, 122, 148, 160, 165, 188, 239–256, 275, 295, 299, 329
body 4–6, 12, 14, 25, 28, 31, 37, 38, 59, 64, 90, 96, 110, 111, 113–115, 126, 138, 139, 148, 149, 151, 152, 171, 172, 178, 179, 224, 277, 307, 308, 311, 328

cannibalism 9, 11, 14–16, 246
censoring 31, 147, 166, 168, 172, 188
censorship 4, 31, 165–169, 172–174, 176–179, 181, 182
colloquial 11
coloniality 6, 8
commands 7, 53–74, 98, 210, 212–216, 218–220, 223, 224, 228, 232
communication 4, 13, 18, 23, 28, 32, 40, 42, 46, 49, 111, 114, 133, 137, 173, 181, 185, 196, 270
conflict 19, 27, 89, 103, 173, 175, 205, 239
corpse 12, 16, 306–308, 311, 315
curse 11, 22, 23, 28, 53–55, 59, 67, 70, 72, 73, 80, 90, 97, 106, 110, 114, 152, 153, 158, 160, 181, 205–206, 210, 227, 231–233, 275, 304–307, 309, 311, 315–318, 322
cursing 3–5, 22–24, 26, 28, 29, 31–33, 46, 67–69, 73, 74, 109–111, 114, 121, 122, 124, 147–150, 160, 181, 188, 205, 206, 209, 225, 275, 303–322

danger 11, 58, 210, 212, 214, 217, 228, 230–233, 313
death 3, 5, 23, 27, 45, 65, 149, 171, 172, 210, 211, 212, 217, 219, 221, 224, 230–232, 288, 308, 311
derogatory term 15
dirt 128
dirty words 277, 303
discourse 5, 6, 9, 11, 15, 29, 31, 48, 54, 55, 86, 103, 114, 119, 132, 148, 149, 180, 185, 187, 191, 200, 206, 277, 278, 298
disease 5, 20, 23, 54, 67, 149, 217
DR Congo 9, 19, 24, 26, 31, 185–188, 193

emotion 7, 20, 30, 39, 40, 41, 46, 48, 50, 67, 74, 88, 97, 103, 122, 131, 149, 156, 157, 240, 256, 274, 275, 303
excess 5, 9, 18, 21, 32, 112–114, 213, 214, 219, 224
exclusion 31, 114, 187, 189, 191, 192, 205, 254, 315

face 5, 16, 19, 30, 37, 64, 67, 73, 104, 109, 122, 128, 171, 179, 187, 205, 214
funniness 17, 19, 22

gender 29, 32, 38, 43, 44, 60, 86, 87, 113, 137, 189, 259, 262, 275, 276, 286, 298, 299, 327, 331
gesture 4, 6, 22, 23, 28, 30, 107, 110, 111, 113, 114, 121, 124, 125, 130, 132, 135–141, 148, 173, 189, 192, 194, 209, 212, 232, 248, 270, 271
Ghana 121, 125, 128, 132, 135
Global South 6, 9, 31, 159, 191

hostility 105, 114, 174, 185–206, 224, 254
humor 8, 16–18, 20–22, 29, 39, 40, 196

https://doi.org/10.1515/9781501511202-016

identity 6, 8, 91, 96, 132, 166, 269, 274, 275, 277, 278
ideology 88, 113, 114, 185, 187, 188, 191, 200, 205, 276
imperative 7, 30, 53–74, 328
impolite 122, 124, 131, 139, 141, 150, 172, 226
impoliteness 5, 122, 123, 131, 230
impure 12, 217
inequality 8, 13, 21, 206
inter-individual swearing 5, 22, 28, 200
intra-individual swearing 23
invectives 30, 121–142, 328
irony 15, 21, 22, 29, 115, 268, 294

Jamaica 31, 125, 147, 150, 152–156, 158, 160–162
Jamaican 31, 147–162
Java 29

Kenya 239–256
Kinshasa 10, 11, 16, 185–206
kinship 30, 79–98, 217
kissteeth 130–135

laughter, bitter 14, 16–22, 32
Lingala 10, 11, 31, 185–206
linguistic anthropology 30

Mallorca 105, 107, 115, 118, 259–262, 266, 268, 270, 272, 330
membership 6, 92, 96, 287, 294
metapragmatic 80, 81, 87, 90, 92, 111
mimesis 3–33, 191, 200, 205, 209, 215, 216, 222–225, 232, 256
mimicry 31, 185, 191, 204, 205, 220, 222
mock language 31, 185, 189–194, 198, 200, 206, 328

name 8–10, 15, 16, 25, 26, 38, 44, 81, 84, 86–91, 96, 110, 128, 141, 149, 162, 169, 171, 177, 188, 191, 196, 209–233, 249, 260, 261, 272, 293, 306, 307, 313, 314, 321

naming 3, 5, 7, 12, 15, 16, 32, 89, 149, 209, 210, 212, 214, 217–219, 226, 230–232, 271
Nigeria 9, 14, 26, 107, 108, 114, 165–169, 171, 171, 174, 176–181, 261
noise 6, 110, 113, 131, 134, 135, 251, 262
nonverbal communication 4, 111, 114, 133, 137, 196

obscene 8, 46, 114, 121, 128, 129, 153, 154, 168, 171, 180, 303, 304, 319, 320
offence 79, 83, 84, 129, 131, 133, 141, 154, 239, 297, 311
Other 3, 7–16, 19, 32, 33, 57, 65, 74, 83, 115, 117, 119, 130, 141, 161, 191, 192, 195, 196, 204, 205, 209, 216, 220, 232, 233, 240, 256, 259, 261, 264, 271–273, 276, 278, 312–313
Othering 6, 8, 9, 14, 28, 29, 189, 195, 256, 271, 273

pejorative label 8, 16
performance 4, 5, 9, 11, 13, 15, 16, 18, 22, 23, 28, 28–33, 43, 88, 103, 104, 115, 117, 118, 121, 126, 132, 138, 153, 154, 185, 187, 191, 200, 241, 256, 263, 272, 277, 327–330
phallus 21, 32
play 6, 9, 16, 20, 30, 84, 103–119, 127, 150, 157, 165, 170, 178, 191, 202, 229, 241, 251, 256, 261, 265, 277, 290
politeness 54, 239, 278
postcolonial situation 32, 240
power 3, 5, 8, 9–12, 15–17, 22–24, 26, 28, 29, 43, 45, 103, 107–110, 114, 115, 148, 159, 185, 188, 191, 192, 205, 211, 213, 214, 216, 218, 219, 223–225, 232, 241, 246, 269, 275, 304, 305, 310, 312, 317, 321, 327, 331
pragmatics 29, 30, 38–40, 43, 82, 126, 130, 134, 137, 150, 213, 281, 300
purity 12, 32, 103, 109, 175, 216, 217, 294, 305

racial slur 149, 185, 188, 191–193, 205
racism 15, 245

religion 49, 98, 165, 166, 175, 180, 181, 308
response cries 7
ritual 5, 7, 11, 21, 23–25, 29, 32, 43, 56, 79, 87–96, 98, 103, 113, 124, 192, 211, 213, 214, 223, 224, 227, 228, 240, 245, 259, 271, 272, 278, 290, 303, 304, 307, 311, 327
rudeness 5, 122, 123, 125, 131

secrecy 6, 7, 29, 88, 191
Self 3, 12, 15, 19, 21, 223
self-reflexivity 9–12, 14, 16
sex 5, 26, 27, 31, 37, 45, 47, 79, 86, 150, 107, 115, 117, 135, 139, 141, 149, 155, 165, 166, 169–172, 177, 178, 180, 181, 243, 260–262, 286, 287, 294, 297, 330
slang 37, 38, 45, 149, 150, 241, 283, 284, 288, 295
sociolinguistics 4, 6, 41, 95–96, 111, 147, 155–160, 162, 188
sociopragmatics 40
Southern Theory 6
Spanish 32, 59, 97, 98, 107, 189, 259, 281–300
spell 27, 109, 125, 130, 314, 316
spirit possession 4
spitting 24–26, 30, 103, 327
substance 3, 22, 23, 26–28, 33, 107, 109, 114
swearing 3–33, 37, 39–44, 46–51, 54, 59, 74, 79–98, 103–119, 121–126, 128, 129, 131, 135, 140–142, 147–162, 165, 171, 181, 182, 185, 188, 200, 205, 206, 225, 259, 261, 272, 277, 278, 287, 290, 303–304, 319–322, 327–331

taboo 5, 16, 24–26, 30, 31, 37–51, 56, 65, 70, 74, 80–82, 87, 98, 111, 121, 122, 128, 131, 147–151, 155–157, 159, 162, 165, 171–173, 175, 180, 205, 210, 255, 268, 269, 275, 291, 292, 294, 295, 297, 299, 300, 303, 310, 327
Tanzania 79–99
threat 17, 67, 122, 224, 230, 305, 306, 309, 310, 314, 315, 317, 321
Timor 32, 209–233
tourism 32, 103, 107, 117, 188, 191, 239–242, 247–249, 256, 259–278, 330
transgression 5, 7, 16, 19, 21, 29, 31–33, 103, 105, 107, 112, 113, 115, 117, 124, 210, 211, 225–227, 232, 239, 241, 250–254, 256, 261, 266, 268, 269, 277, 278, 305, 306, 330

Uganda 19, 27

vocatives 32, 88, 227, 230, 281–300
vulgar 32, 38, 54, 128, 129, 139, 149, 157, 171, 180, 189, 283, 297

witchcraft 9–11, 23, 24, 26, 27, 29, 103, 109, 113, 115, 191

Youth 9, 28, 29, 33, 88, 89, 172, 174, 177, 181, 192, 194, 196

www.ingramcontent.com/pod-product-compliance
Lightning Source LLC
Chambersburg PA
CBHW061931220426
43662CB00012B/1873